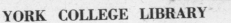

AMERICAN
HISTORICAL ASSOCIATION

INVESTIGATION OF THE
SOCIAL STUDIES IN THE SCHOOLS

∴

STAFF

A. C. KREY
Chairman, Director of the Investigation

G. S. COUNTS
Research Director

W. G. KIMMEL
Executive Secretary

T. L. KELLEY
Psychologist, Advisor on Tests

COMMISSION ON DIRECTION

FRANK W. BALLOU, Superintendent of Schools, Washington, D. C.

CHARLES A. BEARD, formerly Professor of Politics, Columbia University; author of many books in the fields of history and politics.

ISAIAH BOWMAN, Director, American Geographical Society of New York; President of the International Geographical Union.

ADA COMSTOCK, President of Radcliffe College.

GEORGE S. COUNTS, Professor of Education, Teachers College, Columbia University.

AVERY O. CRAVEN, Professor of History, University of Chicago.

EDMUND E. DAY, formerly Dean of School of Business Administration, University of Michigan; now Director of Social Sciences, Rockefeller Foundation.

GUY STANTON FORD, Professor of History, Dean of the Graduate School, University of Minnesota.

CARLTON J. H. HAYES, Professor of History, Columbia University.

ERNEST HORN, Professor of Education, University of Iowa.

HENRY JOHNSON, Professor of History, Teachers College, Columbia University.

A. C. KREY, Professor of History, University of Minnesota.

LEON C. MARSHALL, Institute for the Study of Law, Johns Hopkins University.

CHARLES E. MERRIAM, Professor of Political Science, University of Chicago.

JESSE H. NEWLON, Professor of Education, Teachers College, Columbia University; Director of Lincoln Experimental School.

JESSE F. STEINER, Professor of Sociology, University of Washington.

THE SOCIAL FOUNDATIONS
OF EDUCATION

REPORT OF THE COMMISSION
ON THE SOCIAL STUDIES
PART IX

THE SOCIAL FOUNDATIONS
OF EDUCATION

BY

GEORGE S. COUNTS

Professor of Education, Teachers College, Columbia University

AND OTHERS

32863

CHARLES SCRIBNER'S SONS

NEW YORK   CHICAGO   BOSTON   ATLANTA
SAN FRANCISCO   DALLAS

PREFACE

This is the ninth volume of the Report of the American Historical Association Commission on the Social Studies in the Schools. As the title indicates, it deals with the social background of American education from the beginnings of national organization and activity.

The author has long been interested in American education and has become one of the recognized leaders in this field of study. He has concerned himself primarily with the relations of school and society, not only the actual operation of those relations as studied in educational sociology, but also the underlying thought and ideas involved in those relations as dealt with in educational philosophy. The Commission, of which he has been a member since its formation, has profited greatly from his knowledge and interest in both of these fields.

Recognizing the school as an instrument of society, perhaps its most important instrument for the perpetuation of its culture, his association with the work of the Commission led him to develop the collateral interest which this volume presents. He came to feel that contemporary activity and thought about education were insufficient to explain or even reveal the full purpose and function of the public school. Tradition, accepted ideals and ideas, social habit as well were playing a larger rôle in the operation of education than was apparent from any strictly contemporary survey or appraisal of its developments. He undertook, therefore, to examine the development of American society from the time of its definite organization to the present.

He had gradually become convinced of the necessity of making this study and was planning to work upon this task when the Commission asked him to assume a large part of the active direction of its work as Director of Research in 1931. The systematic and intensive study of American society in its historical development was alone sufficient to engross his whole energy and attention even with such assistance as the Commission might render. Nevertheless he complied with the wishes of the Commission and undertook both tasks.

The plan for the present work was submitted to the executive committee of the Commission for criticism and suggestions. It was then approved by the Commission. The detailed account of assistance received appears in the author's foreword. An early draft was submitted for criticism to those members of the Commission most directly concerned with the problem involved. In light of the criticism and suggestions he undertook the preparation of a second draft. This draft, when completed, was submitted to all the members of the Commission as well as to several professors of American history not on the Commission. The suggestions and criticisms thus received served as the basis for the final revision.

Though profiting greatly from the suggestions and criticism of his colleagues on the Commission which he has generously acknowledged, the achievement is essentially his own. There was no convenient work in American history to furnish him the broad complex of society which lay behind present education. Nor was there any work on recent American education which recognized adequately the bearing of these social forces upon education. He had therefore to ransack a vast literature in both history and education, much of it original source material, to find the solution of his problem. It is in the effective linking of these two elements that the distinctive contribution of this volume lies. It is at the same time, therefore, a contribution to the literature of American education and American history. A. C. KREY, *Chairman.*

ACKNOWLEDGMENTS

In the preparation of the present volume I became deeply
indebted to many persons. In fact I have served primarily as
an instrument of the Commission for bringing to bear upon
the problem at hand the knowledge and thought of numerous
scholars. In seven of the seventeen chapters of the book the
analysis and discussion are based upon and derived from manu-
scripts submitted to me by selected individuals. Such contributions were made to the chapter on natural endowment
by Mr. William Hewitt, a special investigator; to the chapter
on family by Mrs. Carl B. Swisher, a special investigator; to
the chapter on economy by Dr. George S. Mitchell, instructor in economics in Columbia College; to the chapter on communication by Dr. Carl B. Swisher, instructor in government in Columbia College; to the chapter on health by Dr.
Nels Anderson, instructor in sociology in Seth Low Junior
College of Columbia University; to the chapter on recreation
by Dr. LeRoy E. Bowman, director of extension activities for
the summer play schools of the Child Study Association of
America; and to the chapter on art by Dr. Houston Peterson,
instructor in philosophy in Columbia College. Whatever of
merit these chapters may have is due primarily to the work
of these scholars. For much of the historical material in the
volume I am indebted to Dr. Donald L. McMurry, formerly
professor of history at LaFayette College. Drs. McMurry,
Mitchell, and Peterson also read the entire manuscript and
gave me many valuable suggestions.

Others, beside members of the Commission, who read the
manuscript and gave me the benefit of their criticisms are
Dr. Merle E. Curti, professor of American history in Smith
College, Dr. Dixon Ryan Fox, professor of history in Columbia

University, Dr. Sidney Hook, assistant professor of philosophy in New York University, and Dr. Lester B. Shippee, professor of American history in the University of Minnesota. I would also mention three members of the Commission to whom I am greatly indebted—Dr. Charles A. Beard who helped me plan the book, furnished some actual manuscript for the chapters on technology and government, and left his imprint through criticism and suggestion on every page of the volume; Dr. A. C. Krey who read the manuscript with great care and discussed with me at length its underlying philosophy, making innumerable suggestions which have improved both the plan and the substance of the argument; and Dr. Jesse H. Newlon who gave uncounted hours to the discussion of every phase of the work.

Finally I wish to make acknowledgments of debt to the following authors and publishing companies for permitting me to quote from the books indicated:

American Public Health Association, *The City That Was,* by Stephen Smith.

D. Appleton-Century Co., *Democracy in America,* by Alexis de Tocqueville; *Practice of Municipal Administration,* by Lent D. Upson; and *Women in Industry,* by Edith Abbott.

Carnegie Foundation, *Justice and the Poor,* by Reginald Smith.

Carnegie Institution of Washington, *History of Agriculture in the Northern U. S. 1620–1860,* by Percy Wells Bidwell and John I. Falconer.

Cleveland Foundation, *Criminal Justice in Cleveland,* by Roscoe Pound and Felix Frankfurter.

Covici, Friede, Inc., *The Power Age,* by Walter N. Polakov.

John Day Co., *Debt and Production,* by Bassett Jones; and *The Farmer is Doomed,* by Louis M. Hacker.

Doubleday, Doran and Co., *Cimarron,* by Edna Ferber.

E. P. Dutton & Co., *Confessions of the Power Trust,* by Carl D. Thompson.

Ginn & Co., *Folkways,* by William Graham Sumner.

Gotham House, *The Mooney-Billings Report,* suppressed by the Wickersham Commission.

Harcourt-Brace & Co., *North America*, by J. Russell Smith; *America As Americans See It*, edited by Fred Ringel; *Freedom of Speech*, by Zechariah Chafee; and *The History of British Civilization*, by Esme C. Wingfield-Stratford.

Harper & Brothers, *Industrial Hygiene*, by Carey P. McCord.

Henry Holt & Co., *The Frontier in American History*, by Frederick J. Turner; *American Social History as Recorded by British Travellers*, by Allan Nevins; *A History of Modern Culture*, by Preserved Smith; *Criminal Justice in America*, by Roscoe Pound; *American City Government*, by William Anderson; and *State Government*, by Finla Goff Crawford.

Herbert Hungerford, *Forest Bankruptcy in America*, by Colonel George A. Ahern.

Johns Hopkins Press, *Justice in Colonial Virginia*, by Oliver Perry Chitwood.

Benjamin S. Kirsh, *The National Industrial Recovery Act*, by Benjamin S. Kirsh.

J. B. Lippincott Co., *Practical Book of Early American Arts and Crafts*, by Harold Donaldson Eberlein and Abbot McClure.

Little, Brown & Co., *The Case of Sacco and Vanzetti*, by Felix Frankfurter.

Liveright Publishing Corporation, *Our America*, by Waldo Frank.

Ray Long and Richard R. Smith, Inc., *The Written Constitution and the Unwritten Attitude*, by Charles E. Merriam.

Longmans, Green & Co., *On Understanding Women*, by Mary Beard; and *Toward Civilization*, by Charles A. Beard.

McGraw-Hill Book Co., Inc., *Recent Social Trends in the United States*, report of the President's Research Committee on Social Trends; and *Problems of Education in the United States*, by Charles H. Judd.

Macmillan Co., *The Framework of an Ordered Society*, by Sir Arthur Salter; *The Modern Corporation and Private Property*, by Adolf A. Berle and Gardiner C. Means; *A Planned Society*, by George Soule; *The American Leviathan*, by Charles A. and William Beard.

National American Woman Suffrage Association, *History of Woman Suffrage*.

National Popular Government League, *Report Upon the Illegal Practices of the United States Department of Justice*.

W. W. Norton, Inc., *Art in America*, by Suzanne LaFollette.

G. P. Putnam's Sons, *The Works of Alexander Hamilton*, edited by Henry Cabot Lodge.

University of Chicago Press, *The Negro in Chicago*, by the Chicago Commission on Race Relations; *Medical Care for the American People*, by the Committee on the Costs of Medical Care; and *The Family*, by Ernest R. Mowrer.

University of North Carolina Press, *Aspects of the Social History of America*, by Theodore Sizer.

Viking Press, Inc., *Dynamite*, by Louis Adamic.

Yale University Press, *The American Spirit in Architecture*, by T. F. Hamlin; and *Our Social Heritage*, by Graham Wallas.

GEORGE S. COUNTS.

CONTENTS

PART THREE: PHILOSOPHY AND PROGRAM

THE SOCIAL FOUNDATIONS
OF EDUCATION

INTRODUCTION

EDUCATION AS STATESMANSHIP

The historical record shows that education is always a function of time, place, and circumstance. In its basic philosophy, its social objective, and its program of instruction, it inevitably reflects in varying proportion the experiences, the condition, and the hopes, fears, and aspirations of a particular people or cultural group at a particular point in history. In actuality it is never organized and conducted with sole reference to absolute and universal terms. While the biological inheritance of the race presumably remains practically unchanged from age to age and thus gives a certain stability to the learning process, education as a whole is always relative, at least in fundamental parts, to some concrete and evolving social situation. It possesses no inner logic or empirical structure of its own that dictates either its method or its content. In both its theoretical and practical aspects it expresses the ideals of some given society at some given period in time, either consciously with clear design or half-consciously with hidden and confused purpose. There can be no all-embracing educational philosophy, policy, or program suited to all cultures and all ages.

Hence the problem of education assumes one form in ancient Athens in the time of Pericles, another in China during the Tang dynasty, another in Mediæval Saxony, another in modern Japan, still another in Russia under the Communists, and yet another in twentieth-century America. It is clear therefore that any group, charged with the task of shaping educational theory or practice for any people, should begin with an examination of the society to be served—its natural surroundings, its major trends and tensions, its controlling ideals, values, and interests. And when that group is composed of social scientists, such a procedure is peculiarly imperative, since the contribution of the social sciences to education is by no means confined to providing valuable materials of instruction. A far more fundamental contribution is the discharge of the responsibility here suggested. Along with the psychological disciplines they provide the primary data out of which educational philosophies, policies, and programs should be fashioned.

In the United States periodic recurrence to fundamental study and analysis is especially necessary because of the highly dynamic character of American life and institutions in the age of industrialism. In a comparatively static society an educational program, if once adjusted to definite and acknowledged conceptions of social need, may remain unchanged for generations and even for centuries, and yet perform its functions effectively. As long as the balance of ideas and interests, which such a program reflects, remains essentially undisturbed, it is likely at least to be deemed satisfactory and adequate. But by common consent, confirmed by the comprehensive survey just completed by President Hoover's Research Committee on Social Trends and by countless other inquiries, American society has been and is changing rapidly in its basic institutions and relationships. The nature and extent of many of these changes have been expressed in some measure in indisputable mathematical terms.

The impression should not be given, however, that the task of formulating educational policies and programs is merely a matter of gathering social data. Facts must be selected, interpreted, and woven into patterns of utility and purpose. Also this task should not be confused with scientific neutrality, on the one hand, or with unfettered speculation, on the other. Always and everywhere genuine education is a form of practical endeavor—a form of social action. This means that the educator fails in his line of duty if he refuses to step out of academic cloisters, even leave the research laboratory, reject the rôle of disinterested spectator, take an active part in shaping events, make selections among social values, and adopt, however tentatively and broadly, some conception of social welfare and policy. No inquiry into American society, profound and comprehensive though it may be, can remove from his shoulders the responsibility of embodying in his theories and programs some interpretation of history in the making, some general outlook upon the world, some frame of reference with respect to society, some conception of things deemed necessary, of things deemed possible, of things deemed desirable in the proximate future. This responsibility he may discharge openly, deliberately, and intelligently, or furtively, impulsively, and ignorantly; but discharge it he must. He may rightly inquire what choices of purpose and direction are practicable and feasible; but being compelled to act he inevitably makes such choices, even though he may conceal his decisions from himself as well as from others.

The limitations of the social sciences in the sphere of action, when divorced from all value-judgments, have been fully demonstrated.[1] These disciplines provide neither the American people nor American statesmen with positive and definitive guidance in the realm of practical affairs. They give no direction; they make no ethical or æsthetic choices. In the presence of the perpetual battle of conflicting interests and values, they cultivate neutrality, striving to report the social situation in terms of objective truth. The task of making use of these findings is left to men of action, although the two functions of discovery and of application may occasionally be combined in the same individual. The fact should be observed, however, that when viewed in appropriate perspective the development of the social sciences in their entirety or in their special divisions must itself rest upon choices and judgments of value and express some broad social policy.

Among men of action the educators of the country occupy an important position. Consequently, in the light of the data provided by the social sciences and within the limits imposed by

[1] Charles A. Beard, *The Nature of the Social Sciences, passim.*

necessity, as revealed by the data, educational leaders are obliged to make an interpretation of contemporary history and with full recognition of all the hazards involved, submit their interpretation in educational program to the judgment of time. Since, being denied the privilege of neutrality, they must act, no other rational course is open to them. But it should never be forgotten that in acting they, in proportion to the power of organized education, mold the minds of the coming generation and thus share in shaping the future of the nation and even of world society.

This problem may be illuminated through a consideration of the relation of social science to statecraft. While the social scientist, pursuing the tested methods of research, cannot determine the destination and chart the course of the ship of state, he can place his findings at the disposal of the statesman. The latter, as distinguished from the politician, will take these findings and thus make his action informed and intelligent. In the light of the dominant and emergent ethical and æsthetic values of the age and on the basis of the potentialities of the natural endowment, the technological resources, the cultural heritage, and the great social trends of the time, he must make his choices and frame his policies. Also, sensing and defining the problems occasioned by tensions arising in the never-ending movement of ideas and interests, he must decide on positive lines of action. His greatness depends on his success in gauging necessity and possibility, in divining the coming event, and in achieving the ideal in the long-time judgment of mankind. That this task is hazardous in the extreme cannot be denied. Yet it is a task that must be discharged in every society.

Education is one of the highest forms of statesmanship. The educator working in the public schools is a servant of the state. As distinguished from the educational jobholder, he is under obligation to foster the most complete development of the capacities of the citizens, upon whose powers the state depends for its existence, its security, and the fulfillment of its ideals. And since the American state, at least in theory, is not the government or some independent authority standing above the masses of the people, but rather the whole body of citizens functioning in their collective capacity, the educator, besides discharging mandatory obligations, is required to provide educational leadership for the nation and to assume general responsibility for the formulation of educational philosophies, policies, and programs. In the performance of these heavy duties he must, like the statesman, make the fullest use of the empirical findings of the social sciences. In the light of the dominant and emergent ethical and æsthetic values of the age and on the basis of the potentialities of the natural endowment, the technological resources, the cultural heritage, and the great social trends of the time, he must define problems, make choices, and decide upon courses of action. This is the supreme task which the educational profession faces today in America.

That the educator should conceive his task in terms of broadest statesmanship is peculiarly imperative in the present epoch. During the past century life has become extremely complex. Not only does the burden of education in general increase with the growth in complexity of society, but the rôle of organized education in particular advances *pari passu*. In America in recent generations therefore the school has expanded with unprecedented rapidity, assumed the form of a major social institution, been saddled with correspondingly heavy responsibilities, and become a significant factor in shaping the future of the nation. Moreover, it is a matter of common knowledge that both American and world society are passing through a critical period in history. Consequently, the educational leader, entrusted with the function of shaping the policies of the public school, must prepare himself for enlightened action and must take his place in the front rank of statesmanship. The primary object of the present volume is to bring the findings of social science to bear upon this difficult problem.

In an effort to chart the way for education in contemporary

society, the volume is organized into three parts. In Part One attention is directed to three basic forces or factors which strongly condition the development of American civilization, giving direction to the evolutionary process and providing the instrumentalities of achievement—the democratic ideal, the natural endowment, and the methods and products of science. In Part Two are set down the great social trends and tensions of the age and the major movements of ideas and interests in the several departments of life since the founding of the nation— family, economy, communication, health, education, recreation, research, art, justice, government, and world relations. Thereafter, in Part Three, these findings are related to the task of formulating an educational philosophy suited to the needs of industrial America.

It is perhaps needless to point out that no new data are presented here. On the contrary, the intention has been to utilize, in establishing points of reference and in framing broad educational policies, facts that were already at hand. Indeed much of what appears in Parts One and Two is the common knowledge of the informed citizen, or even of the intelligent high school pupil, while all of it is the stock in trade of the student of the social sciences. The materials employed, however, are selected, organized, and integrated in the light of a definitely conceived purpose. Everything has been subordinated to the single practical aim of illuminating the educational problem in its larger social relationships. For refusing to prosecute new investigations no apology is offered. The need everywhere today, as former Justice Oliver Wendell Holmes once remarked, is "less inquiry into the abstruse and more thought about the obvious." Certainly in the field of education this is the counsel of wisdom. The shelves of the libraries are groaning under the weight of volumes of undigested and meaningless data. The time for the utilization of this vast store of knowledge in the formulation of social policies and programs is over-ripe.

PART ONE

BASIC FORCES

DEMOCRATIC TRADITION

The highest and most characteristic ethical expression of the genius of the American people is the ideal of democracy. Throughout the major part of their history as a nation they cherished the conviction that they were marching in the vanguard of the age-long struggle against tyranny, that they were the foremost champions of human liberty, that they were engaged in a bold experiment in social relationships conceived in terms of the interests of ordinary men and destined to have meaning for the whole of mankind. "The preservation of the sacred fire of liberty," said Washington in his first inaugural address, "and the destiny of the republican model of government, are justly considered as *deeply,* perhaps as *finally,* staked on the experiment intrusted to the hands of the American people."[1] More than two generations later, when the nation was torn by civil strife, this thought was expressed again by Abraham Lincoln in language never to be forgotten.

Possessing a land of unsurpassed natural riches, separated by the waters of the Atlantic from the stratified societies of Europe, composed for the most part of representatives of the oppressed classes of the old world, and forced to fashion institutions and purposes for life under new conditions, the American people began their national existence during one of the great revolutionary and creative epochs of history. To a peculiar degree therefore they became the heirs of the

[1] *The Writings of George Washington,* edited by W. C. Ford (New York, 1891), XI, 385.

thought, the hope, the enthusiasm of that age—an age immortalized in the oft-quoted lines of Wordsworth:

"Bliss was it in that dawn to be alive,
But to be young was very Heaven! Oh times,
When Reason seemed the most to assert her rights,
A prime enchantress—to assist the work,
Which then was going forward in her name!
Not favored spots alone, but the whole earth,
The Beauty wore of promise—that which sets
The budding rose above the rose full blown.
What temper at the prospect did not wake
To happiness unthought of?"

Generation after generation the American people proclaimed to themselves and to the world their devotion to democracy— to the ideal of a land unmarked by class divisions and dedicated to the realization of the highest dreams of mankind—to a land of social equality and justice where no man would be debased or exalted by the accidents of birth, but where all would be provided with opportunities for the fullest and richest development of their powers. That this faith was not wholly without substance is fully attested to by the fact that it was shared in no small measure by the poor, the underprivileged, the downtrodden of other nations. To multitudes throughout the earth, laboring under the disabilities imposed by centuries of class or despotic rule, America was a land of hope, freedom, and opportunity to which they were drawn as by a magnet. During the single century from 1820 to 1920 approximately 35,000,000 persons migrated to the United States from foreign countries. To say that they were lured by the material riches of the new continent is to direct attention to a single aspect of a complex situation. They were lured also by the promise of escape from a state of society in which the masses of men were bound to poverty of body and spirit by the forces of law and custom.

The point of course is at once conceded that the history of the United States has been marked by many contrary influences and tendencies. The legions of democracy, not infrequently battered and leaderless, have always had to fight for their existence; and the ideal has often been confused with the reality.[2] Yet the very fact that no one aspiring to political leadership dares even today to challenge openly the democratic faith and the further fact that even men of great wealth frequently cloak themselves with its mantle, reveal its strength in the popular mind. Though often repudiated in practice by both the individual and the mass and though but vaguely defined and understood by the average citizen, democracy remains today a vital and powerful force in American life—one of the major necessities to be reckoned with in every venture in statecraft or education. Here is the basic ethical reality in the history of the nation.

ORIGIN OF THE DEMOCRATIC IDEAL

The democratic ideal is not to be identified with any particular set of institutions. Rather is it to be regarded as a conception of human worth, a belief in the essential dignity of the ordinary man, produced by ages of travail and struggle. It is the modern expression of that rich heritage of thought and aspiration bequeathed to the race by a great line of seers and prophets reaching back through the centuries to Jesus and Plato and doubtless to a myriad of names not recorded on the pages of history. "The good of man," said Aristotle almost twenty-three hundred years ago, "must be the end of the science of politics. . . . To secure the good of one person

[2] See such works as Charles A. Beard, *Economic Interpretation of the Constitution* (New York, 1913); Dixon Ryan Fox, *Decline of Aristocracy in the Politics of New York* (New York, 1919); Matthew Josephson, *The Robber Barons* (New York, 1934); Harry W. Laidler, *Concentration in American Industry* (New York, 1931); Arthur Meier Schlesinger, "The Decline of Aristocracy in America," Chapter IV in *New Viewpoints in American History* (New York, 1928); Lillian Symes and Travers Clement, *Rebel America* (New York, 1934).

only is better than nothing; but to secure the good of a nation or a state is a nobler and more divine achievement." The spirit of this ancient conception has animated countless battles for human freedom—the abolition of serfdom and chattel slavery, the overthrow of despotism and tyranny, the war against cruel and inhuman social practices, the spread of popular education and enlightenment, the rise of the common man to political power, the emancipation of woman from masculine rule, and the advance of the organized workers of the world.

Millions of men and women coming to America during the past three centuries shared in this ethical heritage of the human race and more especially of the western peoples. Moreover, as already pointed out, many of them fled from economic oppression, political despotism, or religious persecution in the old world and were thus selected to a degree because of their democratic sympathies and hopes. Then on reaching the new continent, at least from the days of the earliest settlements along the Atlantic seaboard down to the closing of the western frontier, and particularly after passing the barriers of the Appalachians, they were subjected to powerful influences that fostered the development of the democratic ideal and the moulding of that ideal according to a distinctively American pattern.

As soon as the first European settlers touched foot in North America these new forces made themselves felt. Everywhere houses had to be built, forests subdued, fields cultivated, and the physical foundations of civilization laid. Since there was no native labor that could be exploited successfully, this meant that the great majority of the colonists, if they were to survive, had to work with their hands. A reappraisal of the accepted values of European society was the inevitable result. Thus, Captain John Smith, the soldier of fortune who was accused by a social superior of having once begged in Ireland, proved himself a far more useful citizen than those men of rank who accompanied the first expedition to Virginia. And in the early days of the Massachusetts Bay Colony the necessity of labor was so great that "so soone as Mr. Winthrop was landed, perceiving what misery was like to ensewe through theire Idleness, he presently fell to worke with his owne hands, & thereby soe encouradged the rest that there was not an Idle person then to be found in the whole Plantation."[3] In view of the fact that these settlers came from the stratified society of England and were very conscious of differences in social position, this action on the part of Winthrop was literally pregnant with meaning for the future. It revealed at the very beginning of the life in America the levelling tendency of the frontier.

As the frontier swept westward and the old world receded farther and farther into the background, the influence of the new environment waxed ever more powerful. In the pioneer settlement a general condition of comparative economic equality prevailed and social distinctions were relatively feeble and unstable. At least, the knowledge of the existence of unoccupied land to the west greatly weakened the coercive power of any inequalities that might exist. On arriving at the frontier the individual was forced in very considerable measure to leave his past behind him and to seek favor largely on the basis of his own worth as a man, as measured by the comparatively crude standards of a pioneering community. Neither pride of ancestry nor cultural possession, unsuited to life in the wilderness, was of value to him. In a very genuine sense the heritage from older societies founded on the class principle was cast aside and social life was forced to develop anew from the beginning. In the eighteen-thirties De Tocqueville, comparing America with Europe, recognized this relative equality of condition as the outstanding feature of life in the United States:

"Amongst the novel objects that attracted my attention during my stay in the United States, nothing struck me more

[3] J. H. Twitchell, *John Winthrop* (New York, 1892), 70.

forcibly than the general equality of condition among the people. I readily discovered the prodigious influence which this
primary fact exercises on the whole course of society; it gives
a peculiar direction to public opinion, and a peculiar tenor
to the laws; it imparts new maxims to the governing authorities, and peculiar habits to the governed.

"I soon perceived that the influence of this fact extends far
beyond the political character and the laws of the country, and
that it has no less empire over civil society than over the government; it creates opinions, gives birth to new sentiments,
founds novel customs, and modifies whatever it does not produce. The more I advanced in the study of American society,
the more I perceived that this equality of condition is the
fundamental fact from which all others seem to be derived,
and the central point at which all my observations constantly
terminated."[4]

The influence of the economics of the frontier on politics
is well illustrated by the remarks of a representative from western Virginia in the debates of the Virginia convention in
1830:

"But, sir, it is not the increase of population in the West
which this gentleman ought to fear. It is the energy which the
mountain breeze and western habits impart to those emigrants.
They are regenerated, politically I mean, sir. They soon become *working politicians;* and the difference, sir, between a
talking and a *working* politician is immense. The Old Dominion has long been celebrated for producing great orators; the
ablest metaphysicians in policy; men that can split hairs in all
abstruse questions of political economy. But at home, or when
they return from Congress, they have negroes to fan them
asleep. But a Pennsylvania, a New York, an Ohio, or a western
Virginia statesman, though far inferior in logic, metaphysics,
and rhetoric to an old Virginia statesman, has this advantage,

[4] Alexis de Tocqueville, *Democracy in America* (New York, 1898), I, 1.

that when he returns home he takes off his coat and takes hold of the plow. This gives him bone and muscle, sir, and preserves his republican principles pure and uncontaminated."[5]

The comparative equality of economic condition of course was a product, not of laws or conventions, but of the abundance of land and natural resources. As long as the west was open, which meant until almost the close of the nineteenth century, no enterprising individual need submit to exploitation by another more fortunately situated, unless inordinately handicapped or bound by poverty or social obligation. He could move to the frontier and there among comparative equals participate in building a new community. The basic significance of this economic factor was clearly sensed by a textile manufacturer of Glasgow who made several trips through the United States in the years from 1806 to 1811. Note his comparison, exaggerated though it doubtless was, of the condition of the poor American with that of the poor Briton of his time:

"Farmers and mechanics are best adapted to the country, and, if they are industrious they are sure to succeed. A farmer can get a quarter section of land, 160 acres, for 560 dollars, with eight years to pay it. If he is industrious, he may have the whole cleared and cultivated like a garden by the end of that time; when, in consequence of the rise on property, by the encrease of population, and the cultivation by his individual industry, his land may be worth 50 dollars per acre, or 8,000 dollars; besides his stock of cattle, etc., which may be worth half as much more. Mechanics are well paid for their labour; carpenters have 1 dollar per day and their board; if they board themselves, 1 dollar 25 cents. Other trades have in proportion, and living is cheap. Flour is about 5 dollars per barrel; beef 4 cents per lb.; fowls 12½ cents each; fish are plenty and cheap. A mechanic can thus earn as much in two days as will main-

[5] Quoted in Frederick J. Turner, *The Frontier in American History* (New York, 1920), 31.

tain a family for a week, and by investing the surplus in houses and lots, in a judicious manner, he may accumulate money as fast as the farmer, and both may be independent and happy. Indeed, these two classes cannot too highly prize the blessings they enjoy in this country, nor be sufficiently grateful to the Almighty Disposer of all events, for casting their lot in a land where they have advantages so far transcending what the same classes have in any other. I know there are many who hold a different opinion, but I must take the liberty to dissent from it, and the reader who has travelled with me thus far, will allow that my opinion is not founded either on a partial or prejudiced view of the subject; it is deduced from plain, unvarnished facts, which no reasoning can set aside, nor sophistry invalidate. What would the farmers, and mechanics, and manufacturers in Britain give to be in the same situation? There (I speak particularly of Scotland), there a farmer pays from 7 to 28 dollars per acre, yearly, for the *use* of his farm, besides the taxes and public burdens. He gets, in many instances, a lease of 19 years, and is bound to cultivate the ground in a certain way, prescribed by the tenure of his lease. If he improve the farm, the improvements are for another, not for him; and, at the end of the lease, if another is willing to give one shilling more than him, or if the proprietor has a favourite, or wishes to turn two or more farms into one, or has taken umbrage at his politics, or his religion, or any thing else regarding him or his family, he will not get a renewal of the lease. Many a family have I known, who have been ruined in this way. Being turned out of the farm, they retire to a town or city, where their substance is soon spent, and they pine away in poverty, and at last find a happy relief in the cold grave. Nor is there any remedy; the lands are nearly all *entailed* on the great families, and the lords of the soil are the lords of the laws; they can bind the poor farmer *in all cases whatsoever*.

"Compare this with the situation of the American farmer.

He cultivates his own soil, or if he has none, he can procure it in sufficient quantity for 200 or 300 dollars. If he has no money, he can get credit, and all that is necessary to redeem his credit, is to put forth his hand and be industrious. He can stand erect on the middle of his farm, and say, 'This ground is mine; from the highest canopy of heaven, down to the lowest depths, I can claim all that I can get possession of within these bounds; fowls of the air, fish of the seas, and all that pass through the same.' And, having a full share of consequence in the political scale, his equal rights are guaranteed to him. . . . None dare encroach upon him; he can sit under his own vine, and under his own fig tree, and none to make him afraid.

"Look at the mechanic and manufacturer; in America they can earn from 6 to 9 dollars per week, and have provisions so reasonable, that they have their wheat-bread and roast-beef, or roast-pork, or fowl every day, and accumulate property for old age and their offspring. In Britain they can earn from a dollar and a half to three dollars per week, and pay at the rate of 14 or 15 dollars for a barrel of flour, and from 16 to 22 cents per lb. for beef. But, why do I talk of flour and beef? Small, indeed, is the portion of these that fall to their lot. No; they are doomed to drag out a miserable existence on potatoes and oat-meal, with this farther curse entailed upon them, that, by the mandate of the powers that be, they are bound to the soil; they *cannot,* they DARE NOT leave their country, except by stealth!"[6]

These basic conditions of life, re-enforced by the War of Independence, the rise of the middle classes throughout the western world, and the spread of the egalitarian doctrines of the French philosophers of the age, tended to obliterate or at least to moderate the inherited differences in social rank. The

[6] John Melish, "Travels in the United States of America in the Years 1806 and 1807, and 1809, 1810, and 1811." Quoted by Allan Nevins, *American Social History as Recorded by British Travellers* (New York, 1931), 74–76.

situation in the young Republic toward the end of the eighteenth century is thus described by the Crèvecœur impersonating an enlightened Englishman arriving in America:

"He is arrived on a new continent; a modern society offers itself to his contemplation, different from what he had hitherto seen. It is not composed, as in Europe, of great lords who possess every thing, and of a herd of people who have nothing. Here are no aristocratical families, no courts, no kings, no bishops, no ecclesiastical dominion, no invisible power giving to a few a very visible one; no great manufacturers employing thousands, no great refinements of luxury. The rich and the poor are not so far removed from each other as they are in Europe."[7]

EXPRESSION OF THE DEMOCRATIC IDEAL

The American democratic ideal, compounded from the general experience of men in many lands and ages and from the special circumstances of life in North America during the past three centuries, has been given expression in state papers, in the thought of great popular leaders from Thomas Jefferson to Woodrow Wilson, in the writings of poets and philosophers, in political and educational institutions, and in the ordinary social relationships which prevail widely in the United States. A brief illustration of each of these forms of expression will reveal the nature of the democratic conception and show how deeply it has become rooted in American culture.

The most powerful formulation of the democratic ideal contained in American state papers appears in the Declaration of Independence. The preamble of this document, says A. M. Schlesinger, "is the most eloquent and succinct defense of the rights of the masses and of popular rule that can be found anywhere in the English language."[8] Though couched in the

[7] J. Hector St. John de Crèvecœur, *Letters from an American Farmer* (Philadelphia, 1904), 49.

[8] A. M. Schlesinger, *op. cit.*, 77.

phrases of the new political philosophies of the time, which expressed the aspirations of the rising middle classes, this document strikes a universal note and speaks to all ages. In language that can never be misconstrued or outmoded it proclaims the moral equality of individual men and places human rights above the rights of property, the privileges of every special class, and the institutions of government. These ideas, set forth in the opening paragraph of the Declaration, are known, if not understood and practised, by every citizen of the Republic:

"We hold these truths to be self-evident, that all men are created equal, that they are endowed by their Creator with certain inalienable rights, that among these are Life, Liberty and the pursuit of Happiness.—That to secure these rights, Governments are instituted among Men, deriving their just powers from the consent of the governed.—That whenever any Form of Government becomes destructive of these ends, it is the right of the People to alter or to abolish it, and to institute new Government, laying its foundation on such principles, and organizing its powers in such form, as to them shall seem most likely to effect their Safety and Happiness."

At the time of the founding of the nation Thomas Jefferson was perhaps the ablest and most forceful exponent of the democratic ideal. The Declaration of Independence was largely the work of his hand. It was he that introduced into this document the concept of "pursuit of happiness" in place of that of "property" and thus gave to it a timeless quality which enables it to speak to the twentieth no less than to the eighteenth century. His writings, moreover, are replete with expressions of faith in the common man of his time, scorn of the badges and pretensions of aristocracy, and hatred of the exactions of privilege and wealth. In a letter to John Adams, written from Paris in February, 1787, he even championed the popular right of rebellion: "The spirit of resistance to government is so valuable on certain occasions, that I wish it to be always kept alive. It will often be exercised when wrong but better so than not to be exercised at all. I like a little rebellion now & then. It is like a storm in the atmosphere."[9] In November of the same year he observed in a letter to John Jay that "The tree of liberty must be refreshed from time to time with the blood of patriots & tyrants. It is it's natural manure."[10] In 1800 he announced: "I have sworn upon the altar of God eternal hostility to every form of tyranny over the mind of man." In a letter written to Roger C. Weightman on June 24, 1826, just ten days before his death at the age of eighty-three, he reaffirmed his life-long faith in democracy: "All eyes," he wrote, "are opened, or opening, to the rights of man. The general spread of the light of science has already laid open to every view the palpable truth, that the mass of mankind has not been born with saddles on their backs, nor a favored few booted and spurred, ready to ride them legitimately, by the grace of God."[11] And the following epitaph, written by himself and engraved on his tomb at Monticello, gives a clear picture of the man and of the ruling passion of his life: "Here was buried Thomas Jefferson, author of the Declaration of American Independence, of the statute of Virginia for religious freedom, and father of the University of Virginia." This man had twice been elected president of the United States.

Since the days of the founders the democratic ideal has been re-stated and reformulated by the great popular leaders of every generation. In 1828 Andrew Jackson carried the victorious banners of the crude but vigorous frontier democracy to Washington. Thirty-two years later Abraham Lincoln, himself a product of that democracy, assumed the burden of preserving the union and of ridding the nation of the institution of human slavery. In his Gettysburg Address, delivered on November

9 *The Writings of Thomas Jefferson,* edited by Paul Leicester Ford (New York, 1894), IV, 370.
10 *Ibid.,* 467.   11 *Ibid.,* X, 391–392.

19, 1863, he put in imperishable form the deepest political loyalties and convictions of the American people:

"Fourscore and seven years ago our fathers brought forth upon this continent a new nation, conceived in liberty, and dedicated to the proposition that all men are created equal.

"Now we are engaged in a great civil war, testing whether that nation, or any nation so conceived and so dedicated, can long endure. We are met on a great battlefield of that war. We are met to dedicate a portion of that field as the final resting-place for those who here gave their lives that that nation might live. It is altogether fitting and proper that we should do this.

"But, in a larger sense, we cannot dedicate—we cannot consecrate—we cannot hallow—this ground. The brave men, living and dead, who struggled here, have consecrated it far above our poor power to add or detract. The world will little note nor long remember what we say here, but it can never forget what they did here. It is for us, the living, rather, to be dedicated here to the unfinished work which they who fought here have thus far so nobly advanced. It is rather for us to be here dedicated to the great task remaining before us—that from these honored dead we take increased devotion to that cause for which they gave the last full measure of devotion; that we here highly resolve that these dead shall not have died in vain; that this nation, under God, shall have a new birth of freedom; and that government of the people, by the people, for the people, shall not perish from the earth."

Since the opening of the twentieth century the democratic ideal has been expounded vigorously, though not always relevantly, in certain of its aspects by two presidents who succeeded in capturing the imagination of the masses—Theodore Roosevelt and Woodrow Wilson. While neither of these men was able to relate the ideal to the realities of industrial civilization, they both spoke the language of the democratic tradition and thus succeeded in gaining wide popular support.

In an address delivered before the Ohio Constitutional Convention in February, 1912, Theodore Roosevelt reaffirmed in militant mood and phrase the devotion of the American people to the supremacy of human rights and gave the substance of his fiery attack on "malefactors of great wealth":

"We Progressives believe that the people have the right, the power, and the duty to protect themselves and their own welfare; that human rights are supreme over all other rights; that wealth should be the servant, not the master, of the people. We believe that unless representative government does absolutely represent the people it is not representative government at all. We test the worth of all men and all measures by asking how they contribute to the welfare of the men, women, and children of whom this Nation is composed. We are engaged in one of the great battles of the age-long contest waged against privilege on behalf of the common welfare. We hold it a prime duty of the people to free our Government from the control of money in politics. For this purpose we advocate, not as ends in themselves, but as weapons in the hands of the people, all governmental devices which will make the representatives of the people more easily and certainly responsible to the people's will."[12]

Woodrow Wilson, champion of "the new freedom" and founder of the League of Nations, struck a more universal note. Again and again in his public papers he returns to the theme that the ideal of democracy is not to be identified with a narrow nationalism. "The United States," he said, in addressing the Grand Army of the Republic in 1915, "were founded, not to provide free homes, but to assert human rights."[13] The following year in Omaha he told an assemblage of citizens that "the States of America were set up to

[12] Theodore Roosevelt, "A Charter of Democracy," *The Outlook* (February 24, 1912), Vol. 100, 390.

[13] *The Public Papers of Woodrow Wilson,* edited by Ray Stannard Baker and William E. Dodd (New York, 1926), III, 371.

vindicate the rights of man and not the rights of property or the rights of self-aggrandizement and aggression."[14] In speaking before the graduating class of the United States Naval Academy in 1914 he called for the humane use of national power. "Other nations," he declared, "have been strong, other nations have piled wealth as high as the sky, but they have come into disgrace because they used their force and their wealth for the oppression of mankind and their own aggrandizement; and America will not bring glory to herself, but disgrace, by following the beaten paths of history."[15] He championed the tradition, then becoming weakened, that America was an asylum for the oppressed from other lands. "This is a home," he told a body of business men in Detroit in 1916, "the doors of which have been opened from the first to mankind, to everybody who loved liberty, to everybody whose ideal was equality of opportunity, to everybody whose heart was moved by the fundamental instincts and sympathies of humanity."[16] Finally, in an interpretation of the Declaration of Independence given on July 4, 1914, at Independence Hall, Philadelphia, he asserted that "America will come into the full light of the day when all shall know that she puts human rights above all other rights and that her flag is the flag not only of America but of humanity."[17]

The meaning of the democratic ideal and of the whole American experiment has been developed by many native philosophers and poets. Ralph Waldo Emerson was at the same time a most ardent exponent of the ideal and a most severe critic of the practice. In 1834, as a young man of thirty-one, he declared that "Democracy, Freedom, has its root in the sacred truth that every man hath in him the divine Reason, or that, though few men since the creation of the world live according to the dictates of Reason, yet all men are created capable of so doing."[18] In referring to the masses and com-

[14] *Ibid.*, IV, 347.   [15] *Ibid.*, III, 130.
[16] *Ibid.*, IV, 243-244.   [17] *Ibid.*, III, 147.
[18] *Journals of Ralph Waldo Emerson 1820-1872* (Boston, 1910), III, 390.

mon men he observed that "there are no common men," that "all men are at last of a size." And apparently he was deeply convinced of the historical significance of the new social order taking form in the United States. "At every moment," he said in 1878 near the end of his life, "some one country more than any other represents the sentiment and the future of mankind. None will doubt that America occupies this place in the opinion of nations, as is proved by the fact of the vast immigration into this country from all the nations of Western and Central Europe."[19] In this same address he pointed out that the American people had finally disposed of the institutions and practices of feudalism: "America was opened after the feudal mischief was spent, and so the people made a good start. We began well. No inquisition here, no kings, no nobles, no dominant church. Here heresy has lost its terrors."[20] The United States, he observed with pride, was the home of the laboring classes:

"Ours is the country of poor men. Here is practical democracy; here is the human race poured out over the continent to do itself justice; all mankind in its shirtsleeves; not grimacing like poor rich men in cities, pretending to be rich, but unmistakably taking off its coat to hard work, when labor is sure to pay. This through all the country. For really, though you see wealth in the capitals, it is only a sprinkling of rich men in the cities and at sparse points; the bulk of the population is poor. In Maine, nearly every man is a lumberer. In Massachusetts, every twelfth man is a shoemaker, and the rest, millers, farmers, sailors, fishermen."[21]

Emerson, however, did not view his country or his times with complacency. He looked with apprehension upon the disintegration of the simple agrarian democracy before the ad-

---

[19] Ralph Waldo Emerson, "The Fortune of the Republic," in *Miscellanies*, Volume XI of *Emerson's Complete Works*, edited by J. E. Cabot (Boston, 1878), 399.
[20] *Ibid.*, 410–411.   [21] *Ibid.*, 408–409.

vance of industrial capitalism and anticipated the struggle for
the adjustment of the democratic ideal to the changed conditions. "A question which well deserves examination now," he
wrote at the age of thirty-nine, "is the Dangers of Commerce.
This invasion of Nature by Trade with its Money, its Credit,
its Steam, its Railroad, threatens to upset the balance of man,
and establish a new, universal Monarchy more tyrannical than
Babylon or Rome. Very faint and few are the poets or men of
God. Those who remain are so antagonistic to the tyranny that
they appear mad or morbid, and are treated as such. Sensible
of this extreme unfitness they suspect themselves. And all of
us apologize when we ought not, and congratulate ourselves
when we ought not."[22] And with the following words he
closed his essay on Napoleon: "As long as our civilization is
essentially one of property, of fences, of exclusiveness, it will
be mocked by delusions. Our riches will leave us sick; there
will be bitterness in our laughter, and our wine will burn
our mouth. Only that good profits, which we can taste with all
doors open, and which serves all men."[23]

In Walt Whitman the American democracy produced its
greatest and most authentic poet, even though it failed to appreciate him during his lifetime. "America," he wrote, "is not
for special types, for the castes, but for the great mass of people
—the vast, surging, hopeful army of workers." To him, however, the full realization of the democratic ideal was to be
found, not in the present nor in the past, but in the future.
"Here," he told the readers of the Brooklyn *Daily Eagle* in
1846, "we have planted the standard of freedom, and here we
will test the capacities of men for self-government. . . . Doctrines that even now are scarcely breathed—innovations which
the most fearless hardly dare propose openly—systems of policy
that men would speak of at the present day in the low tones

[22] *Journals of Ralph Waldo Emerson 1820–1872* (Boston, 1911), V, 285–286.
[23] Ralph Waldo Emerson, "Napoleon; or the Man of the World," in *Essays and Poems of Emerson,* edited by Stuart P. Sherman (New York, 1921), 401.

of fear, for very danger lest they might be scouted as worse than Robespierrian revolutionists . . . will, in course of time, see the light here, and meet the sanction of popular favor and go into practical play."[24] And in the following words he sang of the rise of the average man to power, of the upward rush of common humanity, of the aspiration toward a universal brotherhood of races and peoples:

"Never was average man, his soul, more energetic, more like a God,
Lo, how he urges and urges, leaving the masses no rest!
Are all nations communing? is there going to be but one heart to the globe?
Is humanity forming en-masse?"

In "Democratic Vistas" he, like Emerson, sensed the passing of the frontier and the coming of industrial society and wrestled boldly with the problem of adjusting the democratic conception to the changing conditions of life. In the following prophetic passage he voices his distrust of that narrow individualism in economy which was to dominate American business for more than a generation after his death:

"And, topping democracy, this most alluring record, that it alone can bind, and ever seeks to bind, all nations, all men, of however various and distant lands, into a brotherhood, a family. It is the old, yet ever-modern dream of earth, out of her eldest and her youngest, her fond philosophers and poets. Not that half only, individualism, which isolates. There is another half, which is adhesiveness or love, that fuses, ties and aggregates, making the races comrades, and fraternizing all."[25]

The democratic ideal has found vigorous expression in American political institutions. Although the colonists clung tenaciously for generations to many undemocratic practices

24 Walt Whitman, *The Gathering of the Forces* (New York, 1920), I, 11.
25 Walt Whitman, "Democratic Vistas," in his *Prose Works* (Boston, 1898), 213.

brought from beyond the Atlantic, although the federal Constitution with its system of checks and balances represents a deep distrust of popular rule and a triumph of the propertied classes, although the founding fathers strove to establish a republic rather than a democracy, although in the early years of the nation's existence property qualifications were frequently attached to the suffrage, and although the rise of modern industrial society has greatly complicated the problems of popular government, the American people since the days of Andrew Jackson have firmly believed in the democratic character of their political institutions. The nineteenth century witnessed the establishment of universal manhood suffrage for the whites and the abolition of chattel slavery for the negroes. The twentieth century has seen the extension of political rights to women and the adoption of numerous devices, such as the initiative, the referendum, and the recall, intended to make government more responsive to the popular will. Whatever may be the actual facts in the case, there is a widespread belief in the United States that the masses of the population do and should rule. And an enormous amount of effort has been devoted to the fulfillment of this faith. If it is not fulfilled, the fault does not lie in the lack of conviction on the part of the American people.

In the organization of educational institutions the democratic ideal has also been expressed. The principle of the taxation of property for the extension of elementary educational privileges to all was established in certain regions even in colonial times. Then after the founding of the nation the American people, recognizing the importance of education in the equalization of opportunity, rejected in principle and in practice the dual educational system of Europe, which was based upon and designed to perpetuate class divisions, and fashioned a single educational system embracing elementary school, secondary school, college, and university. The creation of the free public high school, as an upward extension of the edu-

cational opportunities of the masses, and the consequent building of an educational ladder reaching to the most preferred
occupations and positions in society, constitute one of the most
striking manifestations of American democracy. Although, for
various reasons, the ideal of equality of educational opportunity is by no means attained, the achievement in this direction has been stupendous. Until very recently there were more
young men and women enrolled in the secondary schools, colleges and universities of America than in the corresponding
institutions of all other countries of the world combined.

Finally, the democratic ideal has found expression in the
ordinary social relationships of men. The power of the middle classes in early American history and the levelling tendency
of the frontier combined to create a deep hatred of the marks
and emblems of class distinction and of monarchical rule. This
particular prejudice was even recorded in the federal Constitution. "No title of nobility," declares the fundamental law of
the land, "shall be granted by the United States. And no person holding any office of profit or trust under them shall,
without the consent of the Congress, accept of any present,
emolument, office, or title, of any kind whatever, from any
king, prince, or foreign potentate."

In spite of the rise of industrial society, with its complicated
hierarchy of economic functions and its extremes of poverty
and wealth, much of the camaraderie of the frontier and the
simple agrarian life of the early nineteenth century continues
to prevail. In comparison with the older societies of Europe
birth and social position count for relatively little. The individual is still judged in considerable measure by his own
worth and attainments, warped of course by the actual differences in opportunity which flow from inequalities in parental
wealth and cultural heritage and generally from the operation
of capitalist economy. Even in marriage the somewhat hazy
and shifting lines of social class are often disregarded. And
for anyone to affect the airs and manners of a superior human

breed is regarded as bad form and is likely to call forth social disapproval. The code requires that, even though one may be a member of some privileged group, the fact should not be too clearly revealed in outward behavior or too openly paraded before the public. While the result is frequently gross incongruity and hypocrisy, the fact offers unimpeachable testimony to the strength of the democratic ideal, as understood and interpreted, in the thought and habits of the American people.

AUTHENTICITY OF THE DEMOCRATIC IDEAL

In this exposition of the foundations of the democratic ideal, there is of course no desire or intention of concealing the contrary tendencies in American history or of glossing over "the stark and bitter realities of the (present) social situation."[26] It is unquestionably true that even on the frontier injustice and inequality abounded; that many leaders, statesmen, philosophers, and poets have despised the people; that the forms of democracy have often been employed to destroy its substance; that the ideal has commonly been identified with a rugged and ruthless individualism in economy; that the Indian, the Negro, and other social and cultural minorities have usually been the victims of severe discrimination; that little of genuine democracy can be found in the organization and conduct of modern business and industrial enterprise; and that the ideal, if it is to survive, requires reformulation and re-interpretation in terms of the facts of industrial civilization.

These discords and contradictions will be brought out clearly, even though briefly, in the present volume. Yet their existence does not destroy the central thesis here advanced. The United States *has* been the scene of a great and bold experiment in the democratization of social relationships; the American people *have* developed and cherished a genuine faith in democracy. This truth cannot be questioned. Although the more sophisti-

[26] The President's Research Committee on Social Trends, *Recent Social Trends in the United States* (New York, 1933), I, lxxiv.

cated members of a disillusioned and cynical generation may
find satisfaction in denying both the authenticity and the per-
tinence of the democratic ideal, the facts of history remain unchanged. Democracy provides the dominant spiritual note in
the development of the nation and may be expected to guide
both statesmen and educators in the definition of the goals of
their practical endeavors. That it is not to be identified with
any special set of institutions—economic, political, or social—
is one of its merits. Rather is it to be regarded as a point
of reference in the creation and reconstruction of all social
forms and arrangements—a great ethical principle to be con-
sulted in the formulation of all policies and programs touching
the welfare of the American people.

CHAPTER II

NATURAL ENDOWMENT

The American people have received from the past—from the
peoples of the Western World and more particularly from
their immediate ancestors on the North American continent—
a vision of a society in which ordinary men and women may
have opportunities for full and rich development. But the realization of this vision is not merely a matter of human aspiration and will; it must depend in some measure on the natural
endowment of the country in which the drama is being played.
Although men have learned to surmount innumerable physical obstacles and to tame one-time hostile forces, they have
nowhere become independent of the resources supplied by
nature. In spite of the advances of technology there are still
many regions of the earth where life must remain harsh and
barren for the great majority of the population—where the
fulfillment of the democratic ideal would be forced to follow
narrow and niggardly patterns.

EXTENT OF RESOURCES

In its natural endowment the United States stands unrivalled
among the nations of the world. That both the extent and the
utility of this endowment change with the advance of culture
and technology is of course fully realized. A resource that is
utterly worthless at one level may be extremely valuable at
another. Also a resource that is necessary for the survival of a
primitive tribe may be of little value to a highly developed
society. "The dark and forbidding mountains of one epoch,"
says Isaiah Bowman, "become the playground and inspiration

of another epoch. . . . The geographical elements of the environment are fixed only in the narrow and special sense of the word. *The moment we give them human associations they are as changeful as humanity itself.*"[1] Yet up to the present time man has not succeeded in freeing himself from reliance on certain resources that are strictly limited in quantity and very unevenly distributed over the face of the earth. In the possession of these resources America is exceptionally fortunate, whether for the building of a hunting, an agrarian, or an industrial civilization. A brief review of the climate, the soil, the flora, the fauna, the minerals, the energy resources, and the natural beauties of the country will demonstrate the truth of this statement.

Climate. Of all the natural conditions affecting the growth of a civilization climate is probably the most potent. Representing, as it does, the combined action and effect of varying degrees and seasonal combinations of heat, cold, moisture, and atmospheric pressure, it strongly conditions the development of every form of life and sets bounds to the diffusion of those varieties of plants and animals which man has domesticated and upon which his welfare so largely depends. Wheat, maize, rice, and cotton, as well as the ox, the horse, the camel, and the reindeer, thrive only in certain climates, although through breeding and selection the geographic range of many varieties and species has been greatly extended. As a consequence, the movement of civilized man from one part of the earth to another has always been influenced by the ability of his stock of plants and animals to survive and multiply in the new land.

Also man himself seems to be greatly affected by these same forces. While he has shown himself to be extremely adaptable and capable of sustaining life in almost every climate, from the scorching sun of Java to the icy winds of Greenland and from the steaming jungles of the Congo to the dry wastes of Mon-

[1] Isaiah Bowman, *Geography in Relation to the Social Sciences* (New York, 1934), 34, 37.

golia, he nevertheless prospers best only within a narrow range of conditions. After extended investigation Ellsworth Huntington concludes that "a mean temperature of 64 degrees (Fahrenheit), a mean humidity of about 80 per cent, and frequent changes of temperature are the most desirable conditions for purely physical health."[2] For mental work he found that humidity and variability should be about the same, but that "the mean temperature should be much lower, perhaps 40." If these conclusions are to be trusted for members of the white races, then these peoples at least can be expected to reach their highest level of achievement in only a few regions of the earth. Elsewhere, until practicable methods for the more complete control of the climatic factor are devised, they cannot expect to make the maximum use of their talents and energies.

One of the largest, if not the largest, of the favorable regions is to be found in the United States. On the basis of his inquiry into the climatic conditions affecting the release of human energy, Mr. Huntington divided the land surface of the earth into five zones. In the highest zone, which embraced only those areas where the factors of temperature, humidity, and variability are most conducive to mental and physical vigor, he placed but two regions of any magnitude. The first embraces practically the whole of western and northwestern Europe, including the British Isles; the second lies in North America and is bounded by a line that starts on the northern bank of the mouth of the St. Lawrence, follows this river to the region of the Great Lakes, moves westward and a trifle northerly to the Rocky Mountains, turns back to the southeast and then south into Colorado, bends sharply eastward through Kansas, Missouri, and Illinois, and finally cuts the Atlantic on the Virginia coast. Although a small part of this region falls within the borders of Canada, all but a fraction is in the United

[2] Ellsworth Huntington, *World-Power and Evolution* (New Haven, 1919), 98. Also see his *Civilization and Climate* (New Haven, 1915), *passim*.

States. Moreover, except for a narrow strip in the extreme south extending from coast to coast, the rest of the country lies in Huntington's second zone. According to this theoretical analysis therefore, the climate of the United States is exceptionally congenial to the white races.

The history of the settlement of the New World during the past four centuries lends support to this conclusion. Despite the fact that Europeans first visited Greenland and Labrador and the shores of the Caribbean, their numbers in these regions have increased but little during the centuries. The one-time flourishing British settlements in the West Indies have gradually melted away. On the other hand, in that middle region of temperate climate, lying between the 26th and 55th parallels, the population has grown to more than 130,000,000 and European civilization has taken deep and permanent root. While numerous cultural factors have played their several roles, this unprecedented development would have been impossible under an unfavorable climate.

The range of climate to be found within the borders of the United States is in itself a valuable resource. The fact that the country contains large areas peculiarly suited to human habitation does not mean uniformity of conditions. On the contrary, as Mr. Huntington has pointed out, variability of temperature and atmosphere is a crucial factor in promoting physical and mental vigor. One of the most striking features of American climate is its changeableness. But aside from its beneficent effect on health and vitality, this factor of variability possesses other merits. It means that, within certain broad limits, climate is of the moment and the locality. As a consequence, the country never has experienced and probably never will experience a famine of the type that periodically for centuries has swept over parts of Europe and Asia and exacted its toll of millions of human lives. The United States has its droughts and floods, to be sure, but such catastrophes are never widespread or long-sustained. As an eminent geog-

rapher has said, "while New Jersey burns, Virginia is sometimes too wet, and the plenty of one locality can supply the
shortage of the other. Further than this, the drought east of
the 100th meridian rarely if ever covers a whole season. Thus
April and May may be dry, injuring the hay, but June and July
may be wet, injuring the wheat but making good corn and
pasture."[3]

The range of climate from region to region is also very wide.
In a country of three million square miles with its eastern
and western shores lapped by the waves of two great oceans,
with its exposure on the north to the unbroken sweep of arctic
winds and its penetration on the south by the warm waters of
a subtropical gulf, with its low-lying Appalachian range in the
east and its snow-capped Cordilleras in the west, with its great
rivers and lakes and forests and prairies and plains and plateaus—in such a country great diversity of climate is inevitable.
Of the six temperature provinces defined by C. W. Thornthwaite[4]—tropical, meso-thermal, micro-thermal, taiga, tundra,
and frost—the first four are all found in the United States.
Also, although the land is comparatively well-watered, the
average annual precipitation being twenty inches or more for
the entire eastern half of the country, the figure may range
from two or three inches in Death Valley to 120 inches in the
Olympic Mountains. Much of the eastern United States enjoys
a yearly rainfall of over 50 inches, while precipitation is generally deficient from central Kansas to the region of the Pacific coast. Snow falls throughout the country, with the possible exception of certain districts in the extreme south. Wide
variations likewise occur in the degree of humidity, the prevalence of fog, and the frequency and intensity of atmospheric
changes such as winds, clouds, storms, cyclones, tornadoes,
cold snaps, hot waves, and blizzards. To America nature has
given climates in great variety.

[3] J. Russell Smith, *North America* (New York, 1925), 17–18.
[4] C. W. Thornthwaite, "The Climates of North America According to a New
Classification," *The Geographical Review* (October, 1931), 645.

Soil. When combined with favorable climate the soil is the most important natural resource. In the last analysis practically all forms of terrestrial life, grasses and shrubs and trees, birds and beasts and domestic animals, man himself with his armies, his cities, his art and science and philosophy, are derived from this thin film of disintegrated rock and organic matter which in varying thickness, content, and pattern enshrouds the earth. In its absence, however congenial the climate, the land surface of the globe would be but barren unyielding stone, capable of supporting only the most primitive of organisms. With it and its natural products, given appropriate conditions of temperature, moisture and atmosphere, all civilizations, except the most advanced, are possible. The riches of soil of a country constitute a basic resource.

Fertile soil, accompanied by favorable climate, is found in abundance in the United States. Vast areas are consequently peculiarly fit for human life and at the same time exceptionally suited to agriculture and animal breeding. So rich is the soil and so varied is the climate that few indeed are the products of garden, field, orchard, and pasture, useful or pleasing to man, that cannot be grown somewhere in the country. Although for various reasons only two-fifths of the total area are adapted to farming, the American nation possesses more than its proportionate share of the soil resources of the world. Five-sixths of the land surface of the globe cannot be cultivated at the present level of technology; and almost one-fourth of the arable land lying within the temperate zones is in the United States. Probably no other single country possesses on a similar scale such a happy union of climate and soil; and the region bounded by the Great Lakes, the Gulf of Mexico, the Atlantic Ocean, and the Rocky Mountains has been called "the choicest large block of homeland in all the world, with the possible exception of western Europe."

Dominating this huge block of land is the basin of the Mississippi. Lying between the eastern and western mountains, embracing an area larger than the whole of British India, and prepared through the ages to become one of the great granaries of the world, this wide expanse of fertile soil, drained by the Father of Waters, is truly one of the picked spots of the earth for the habitation of man. Located within its broad domain are the gently rolling prairies of Ohio, Indiana, Illinois, Wisconsin, Minnesota, Iowa, and Missouri; the great treeless plains of Texas, Oklahoma, Kansas, Nebraska, Colorado, Wyoming, Montana, and the Dakotas; the valleys of the Ohio, the Missouri, the Arkansas and the other tributaries of the Mississippi; as well as the valley of the Great River itself which extends from the Gulf of Mexico to Minnesota. Although the entire basin, with the exception of the semi-arid region along the western border, is unusually well-suited to agriculture, its northern reaches are of unsurpassed fertility. Here may be found loessal deposits of great depth and of almost inexhaustible productivity. "The valley of the Mississippi," said De Tocqueville, "is, upon the whole, the most magnificent dwelling-place prepared by God for man's abode."[5] In this region is grown the major part of the wheat, the corn, the cotton, and the livestock of the country.

The Mississippi basin, however, is not the only important block of arable land in the United States. Mention should be made of the Atlantic Coastal Plain that starts at Cape Cod, runs southward along the Atlantic, expands to a breadth of 120 miles in Georgia, and envelops the whole of Florida; of the Gulf Coastal Plain that carries the Atlantic plain westward, wraps around the southern ridges of the Appalachians, bears westward along the Gulf in a strip 150 miles wide, sweeps northward up the Mississippi for 500 miles, narrows to 250 miles in southwestern Louisiana, and after a further contraction loses itself in the broad coastal plain of Texas; of the renowned Appalachian Valley that reaches from Alabama to the Gulf of St. Lawrence and includes in its course the fertile lands

[5] Alexis de Tocqueville, *Democracy in America* (New York, 1898), I, 22.

of the Potomac, the Shenandoah, the Delaware, and the Hudson; of the Central Valley of California that lies between the coast range on the west and the Sierra Nevada on the east, maintains a breadth of 30 to 70 miles for a distance of 400 miles, and forms a basin for the Sacramento and San Joaquin rivers; of the valleys of the Connecticut, the Rio Grande, the Red, the Columbia, the Willamette, and Puget Sound; and of the numerous other valleys, basins, plains, and plateaus that literally dot the intermontane regions and add variety and wealth to the soil resources of the nation.

Flora. The fertility of this land is fully reflected in the abundance of its flora and fauna. The indigenous plants have been estimated at 5000 species; wild fruits, nuts, and edible roots grow in great profusion; and nutrient grasses cover the forest glades everywhere, the prairies of the Mississippi basin, the High Plains of the Rocky Mountain region, and occasional open districts both east and west. Also, before the coming of the European, the Indian had brought under cultivation a number of plants that have added billions to the wealth of the world. Maize as a food for man and beast is unsurpassed; the potato has become the mainstay of the poor in many lands; and the leaf of the tobacco has brought pleasure to uncounted millions throughout the earth.

But it was the seemingly boundless forests that impressed so many early visitors to America. No less than 120 native species of timber trees grow in the United States in sufficient quantities to be of commercial importance. In their primeval state these forests were the finest to be found anywhere in the world and covered an area of 850,000,000 acres. Although the country was by no means one vast woodland, few large areas east of central Kansas and Nebraska were wholly treeless. Even on the High Plains and the drier regions beyond the Mississippi cottonwoods and willows grew along the streams and rivers.

The original forests, which were composed almost equally of hard and soft woods, have commonly been divided into five great timber regions. The first was the Northern Forest which comprised New York, New England, the district of the Great Lakes and the higher elevations of the Southern Appalachians, and consisted mostly of conifers with a liberal sprinkling of hardwood trees. This forest was particularly noted for its white pines. The second was the Southern Forest and included New Jersey, the South Atlantic and Gulf States, Arkansas, and Oklahoma. Here the dominant species were pine (particularly the yellow pine), cypress, and certain hardwoods. The third and most extensive of all, the great Central Forest, covered the greater portion of the valleys of the Ohio and the Mississippi and was perhaps the finest hardwood forest that human eyes ever gazed upon. It included twenty distinct species of valuable timber—walnuts, oaks, elms, hickories, birches, maples, poplars, and others—and seemed inexhaustible in its wealth of logs and lumber. The fourth was the Rocky Mountain Forest and embraced the loftier ridges and slopes of the arid southwest and the progressively lower elevations of the northern plateaus and ranges. Although dotted with occasional stands of poplar and birch, it was composed almost entirely of conifers. The fifth and last of the great forest regions of the United States was the Pacific Coast Forest. It occupied the eastern slopes down to the dry timber line, the lower crests, and the western slopes of the Sierra Nevada, Coast, Cascade and allied ranges and consisted almost altogether of pine, fir, hemlock, spruce, and cedar. In places this forest boasted the largest trees and the densest growth of timber per acre known anywhere in the world. Though smallest in extent, it originally contained as many feet of merchantable lumber as any of the other forests.

Fauna. At the time of the settlement the waters and forests and grasslands of the continent teemed with animal life. The rich variety of fish and beast and bird made it the paradise of the angler, the huntsman, the trapper, and the naturalist. Songbirds in both bright and sombre plumage cast a peaceful mantle over "nature red in tooth and claw" and brought color and music to wood and thicket and tuft of grass. Squirrels and rabbits, muskrat and beaver, quail and grouse, ducks and geese in appropriate season were to be found wherever conditions were suitable. The wild turkey ranged from Mexico to Canada and from the Atlantic to the Pacific; the white heron in great flocks fed in the shallow and sheltered waters of Florida and the Gulf Coast; and the passenger pigeon darkened the sun in its migratory flights and roosted by the million in the hardwood forests of the Mississippi basin. The deer and the elk were widely distributed, the moose inhabited the northeastern forests, the pronghorn fed on the grasses of the western plains, the mountain sheep made its home in the high Cordilleras, and, most majestic of all, the American bison in countless herds roamed over plain and prairie and grassland and with his sharp hoofs cut deep trails through forest and mountain pass. Then there were the birds and beasts of prey—hawks, eagles, weasels, minks, martens, coyotes, catamounts, wolves, panthers, and grizzly bears. Here were food and clothing and sport in abundance for men. Also history records that the lure of the peltries could be matched only by the lure of silver and gold.

And the streams and rivers and lakes and seas of this land were full of fish. In the cold waters of the New England coast haddock, cod, and mackerel abounded; and in this same region during the spring of the year herring, shad, and salmon came in from the sea to spawn in bay and stream. Also in these waters lobsters and crabs made their home; and to the south in Long Island Sound, Delaware Bay, and the mouth of the Chesapeake, oysters were more plentiful than anywhere else in the world. On the other side of the country, off the coast of Oregon and Washington, were fishing waters of unrivalled richness. Here tuna, halibut, and sardines moved through the seas in vast schools; and the salmon, as in New England but in far greater numbers, swam up the rivers in springtime to lay their eggs. In the fresh waters of the Great Lakes white fish, lake trout, blue pike, lake herring, sturgeon, and other species of excellent fish multiplied their kind. And in the smaller lakes and streams and rivers catfish, pickerel, pike, bass, shad, and trout awaited the rod and the net of the fisherman.

Minerals. Before the rise of industrial civilization the account of natural resources which has already been given would have seemed practically complete. In that day most men would have been satisfied, as indeed they were, to know that the country was endowed with a favorable climate, fertile soil, magnificent forests, rich pastures, and an abundance of game, fish, and fur-bearing animals. The minerals, except for the precious metals, would either have been disregarded or taken for granted. That the small quantities of these materials required could be found in any land would have been confidently assumed. Apart from their thirst for gold and silver, the early settlers in North America consequently knew little and cared less about the mineral resources of the new continent. But in the meantime a great change has come over the world. A civilization, whose appetite for coal and iron and other minerals seems insatiable, has rapidly taken form. Private companies employ every conceivable device to gain property rights in the mineral deposits of the earth; and great nations through both war and diplomacy struggle for the possession of these things. Since the opening of the present century more minerals have been mined than in all preceding history. The might of a modern nation is measured, not in man power, but in terms of coal and iron and oil and copper.

What then are the mineral resources of this land that seems so favored in other respects? Are they in keeping with its endowment of climate and soil and forest? Since for the most part minerals lie concealed beneath the surface of the earth, this question cannot be answered with complete precision. For generations following the first settlements along the Atlantic seaboard almost nothing was known regarding the nature and extent of these riches. And today knowledge is far from perfect. Only through costly methods of exploration can mineral reserves be calculated; and the application of such methods is practically confined to the first one-thousand feet. Yet sufficient is known to make possible a rough estimate of the relative position of the United States among the nations of the world. While deposits of consequence may be found at any time, the chances grow increasingly slender with every passing year. Except for petroleum and natural gas, no major source of minerals has been discovered in Europe since 1850 or in the United States since 1907.

A survey of the mineral resources of this middle portion of North America shows it to be the most favored spot of all the earth for the building of an ·industrial civilization. In this sphere its position is even more pre-eminent than in the realm of climate or soil or timber. According to C. K. Leith,[6] approximately 40 per cent of the mineral reserves of the earth are found in the United States.[7] "It is the only country in the world," he says, "possessing adequate quantities of nearly all the principal industrial minerals." He also states that nowhere else, regardless of national boundaries, are these minerals grouped so favorably for human use.

Of the metals, iron is easily the most important. In 1928 the world's production of pig-iron was three and one-half times as valuable as that of gold. And with respect to this metal the United States is the most richly endowed among the nations, possessing approximately 25 per cent of the world's resources. According to estimates made in 1910 the actual reserves amounted to more than 4,000,000,000 and the potential reserves to 75,000,000,000 tons. Of the nine major iron deposits of the earth two are situated in the United States—one in the region of Lake Superior and the other in Alabama. The remaining seven are widely distributed—Northern Sweden, Lorraine, Western France, Newfoundland, Cuba, Brazil, and

[6] C. K. Leith, *World Minerals and World Politics* (New York, 1931), 48.
[7] Recent discoveries, particularly of iron, in the Soviet Union may make necessary a revision of this statement.

India.[8] The Lake Superior reserves include the "incomparable Mesabi Range of Minnesota," the richest and most easily mined deposits in the world, "where vast pockets of soft rich ore can be worked in open cuts with steam and electric shovels."[9] The Alabama region is unique among the iron centers of the earth because of the presence in the same locality of rich stores of iron ore, coal, and lime. The United States also contains other important stores of iron. The Great Valley of the Appalachians holds significant reserves from Alabama to Lake Champlain. Then there are the relatively accessible supplementary deposits of Cuba and Newfoundland. And the United States is somewhat nearer than Europe to the mines of Brazil.

In the case of the non-ferrous metals the country is also unusually well supplied. The deposits of copper, by far the most valuable of these metals, are extremely rich and extensive. In North Michigan the ores were originally the richest in the world; in Butte, Montana, nature conspired by means of molten lava to concentrate great stores of copper; and in Utah veritable mountains of proven ore have been found. Large reserves are also known to exist in Arizona and Alaska. Lead is relatively abundant in Virginia, Wisconsin, Colorado, Idaho, and Utah; zinc appears in considerable quantities in Missouri, Oklahoma, Kansas, and New Jersey; bauxite in moderate amounts exists in Arkansas, Alabama, Mississippi, and Georgia; large deposits of molybdenum have been located in Colorado; great reserves of silver have been found in the Rocky Mountain region; and in California and Alaska the United States was given its share of the gold of the world.

In spite of its general richness, however, the country suffers from certain deficiencies among the minor metals. According to present knowledge of reserves and needs there are inadequate supplies of nickel, tin, manganese, platinum, chromium, mercury, antimony, cobalt, bismuth, tungsten, vanadium, and

[8] Recent reports from the Soviet Union suggest the possibility of enormous deposits there.

[9] F. G. Tryon and Margaret H. Schoenfeld (unpublished manuscript).

radium. For these metals the United States apparently will always be more or less dependent on other districts of the world.

In the sphere of non-metallic minerals America is also strangely fortunate. Sulphur, the most important of these minerals for industry, is found in huge masses in the salt domes of the Louisiana and Texas coasts. Here by all odds are the greatest known deposits of sulphur in the world. So abundant is the mineral that the ratio of American to European output per miner is forty-nine to one.[10] The reserves of phosphates in the western states, the greatest of the commercial fertilizers, are the largest on record. Additional deposits of this valuable mineral are found in Florida and Tennessee. Recent discoveries of potash in the Permian rocks of the southwest, a resource in which the country was long thought deficient, may make the United States independent of other nations. America is also well supplied with feldspar, rock asphalt, sheet mica, and the important building materials—cement rock, brick clay, sand, slate, building stone, lime, and gypsum. The deficiencies include cryolite, asbestos, barite, magnesite, talc, graphite, fluospar, nitrate of soda, and the better grades of china clay; but these minerals are all of secondary importance and can be procured by importation.

Energy Resources. In its stores of energy the United States holds an absolutely unrivalled position among the nations of the world. Although a fertile soil, acted upon by wind and rain and frost and the rays of the sun, is a matchless fountain of energy, attention will be directed here to those other sources of energy on which industrial society increasingly rests and from which comes the motive power to quicken the tools and machines of man's contriving. Of these the most important are coal, petroleum, gas, and water. The first three are the product of æons of time and consequently when once used are practically gone forever. The fourth is perpetually renewed and

---

[10] F. G. Tryon and Margaret H. Schoenfeld, *op. cit.,* 44.

may be expected to continue in undiminished strength for ages, and perhaps as long as the world endures.

The most important single source of mechanical power in the contemporary world is coal. Severely limited in amount, incapable of appreciable increase, and unevenly distributed over the world, it constitutes the foundation of the power age. For at present coal is the most dependable force with which to turn the wheels of industry, drive the ships across the sea, subdue the chills of winter, and generally relieve the arms and legs and backs of men. The share of this resource belonging to the nation is therefore of peculiar significance. Without it the full development of industrial civilization lies beyond the realm of possibility, unless and until new and unknown sources of energy are discovered.

The concentration of so large a part of the coal reserves of the earth within the borders of the United States is one of those strange tricks which nature has played upon mankind. Approximately one-half of the known coal of the world was deposited in that region bounded by the Atlantic and Pacific and by the Great Lakes and the Gulf of Mexico. These truly fabulous stores have been estimated at somewhere between two and three-quarters and three and one-quarter trillion metric tons and are widely distributed over the country. The American people possess four great coal fields, any one of which would seem to be a just share of the world's supplies for a single nation. The first underlies the Alleghany Plateau and extends in horizontal seams from Alabama almost to the northern boundary of Pennsylvania. Because this same district was endowed with rich supplies of petroleum and natural gas, it has been called "the power house of the richest nation in the world." But this nation has other power houses. In the middle west is a vast bed reaching from Indiana to Kansas and Oklahoma and said to contain more coal than all Europe. A third deposit, consisting of lignite and sub-bituminous coal, is found in the region of Wyoming, Montana, and North Dakota. The whole of this field, including reserves located in the neighboring Canadian provinces of Saskatchewan and Alberta, is reported to contain three times the coal wealth of Appalachia. Also huge stores of coal, which are probably of greater ultimate value than all the high-priced metals of the region, are known to exist in the southern Rockies. Finally, the Gulf states, the Pacific coast, and Alaska are by no means entirely devoid of this resource. Nowhere else in the world has nature placed so much power at the disposal of man.

And these incomparable stores of coal are supplemented by exceptionally rich reserves of petroleum and natural gas. While any estimate of America's share of the world's endowment of these fluid fuels would be extremely untrustworthy, because of the incompleteness of the data, the United States unquestionably holds an extremely favored position among the nations. Rich and extensive oil fields have been found in many parts of the country—the Alleghany Plateau, the Ohio Valley, Oklahoma and Kansas, central and north Texas, the Gulf Coast, Wyoming, and California. The amount of petroleum in the natural reservoirs of these fields, originally, has been estimated at approximately 40,000,000,000 barrels. Then there are the oil-bearing shales of Kentucky and the central Rocky Mountain Region which probably contain more than twice the oil of the reservoirs. Of natural gas, a truly matchless fuel, the United States was equally well-endowed. Being associated with oil, where the strata have not been disturbed, it has approximately the same geographical distribution as petroleum. It is interesting to note that western Europe, from which came the inspiration for the development of industrial civilization, is almost totally deficient in both of these perfect fuels. Petroleum it must import from other regions of the earth; natural gas it must practically do without.[11]

Water, as it flows down to the sea, provides a final great source of energy. Since the power of river and stream may be

[11] See E. L. Rauber, "The World's Power Resources," in L. C. Marshall, *Industrial Society*, Part II (Chicago, 1929), 329-334.

used perpetually and never be consumed, a peculiar significance attaches to its development. The extent of this resource, however, is not unlimited, as so many seem to believe, but clearly depends on rainfall and land elevation. In both of these respects the United States is well situated, although somewhat less so than parts of Africa and Europe: rainfall is relatively abundant over wide areas and two great mountain systems, as well as numerous smaller ranges and isolated units of rugged terrain, give the country an average elevation of more than 3000 feet. The fact that the heavier precipitation occurs in the regions of lower altitude is unfortunate. Yet according to the conservative estimates of the United States Geological Survey, the rivers and streams of the United States are capable of developing 38,000,000 horse power. And through the construction of storage dams this amount might be greatly increased and perhaps even multiplied several fold.[12] The full development of the water power of the country would proportionately lengthen the life of the coal, oil, and gas reserves of the nation.

Natural Beauty. Not the least of the resources of the United States, though not capable of scientific measurement, is its natural beauty. While every region, even the deserts of Arabia and the ice fields of the Arctic, has charm for those who have made it their home for generations, the æsthetic endowment of the middle portion of North America is unusually rich and varied. The fertility of the soil, the abundance of the vegetation, the number of the lakes and streams, the irregularity of the topography in many regions would in themselves make this a beautiful land. But of equal significance is the factor of variety that characterizes every manifestation of nature. Within the borders of the United States may be found almost any type of landscape that the temperate zones of the earth can fashion: from the perpetual verdure of Florida and southern California to the everlasting snows of the Rockies, from the low-lying

[12] F. G. Tryon and Margaret H. Schoenfeld, "Mineral and Power Resources," Chapter II, Part I, in The President's Research Committee on Social Trends, *Recent Social Trends in the United States* (New York, 1933), I, 73.

shores of the Gulf region to the lofty summits of the High
Sierra, from the rugged coastline of the north Pacific to the
gently sloping beaches of the south Atlantic, from the soft
contours of the hills and valleys of New England to the titanic
peaks and deep gorges of the western ranges, from the narrow
pastures of the eastern seaboard to the broad prairies of the
middle west, from the short grass of the Great Plains to the
towering sequoia of the Calaveras grove, from the burning
sands of the Mojave to the dripping swamps of the Everglades,
from the gentle flow of the Hudson to the rushing cataracts of
Niagara, from the gray fogs of Puget Sound to the brilliant
colors of the "Great American Desert," from the mud flats of
Louisiana to the solid carpets of Alpine flowers in the upland
parks of Montana.

Among the treasures of American scenery are the great natural spectacles or curiosities which always attract the attention
of the traveller: the falls of the Niagara where for ages the
waters of Lake Erie have plunged over a hundred-foot preci-
pice on their journey to the sea; the natural bridge of Virginia,
strange product of nature's caprice, which spans a ninety-foot
chasm 215 feet deep; the Mammoth Cave of Kentucky, whose
Stygian chambers extending for miles through limestone strata
are everywhere adorned with beautiful and fantastic forma-
tions; the charmed Valley of the Yosemite, which shelters a
grove of the giant sequoia, nourishes a luxuriant growth of
trees, shrubs, and grasses, and in a matchless setting of rock and
foliage and flower drops its waters in three successive falls to
a river bed 2500 feet below; the basin of the Yellowstone with
its more than 100 geysers, its 4000 springs of every description,
its great canyon, lakes, streams, and waterfalls, its rich stocks
of fish, bird, and beast, and its generally unrivalled position as
the child of nature's most whimsical moods; and finally the
Grand Canyon of the Colorado whose 125-mile gorge cleaves
through the high plateaus of Utah and Arizona to a depth of
2000 to 5000 feet, whose bastions, towers, cliffs, and terraces,

marked by red, white, green, brown, and black strata, rise in fantastic but always impressive compositions, and whose immensity so moved Coronado, the first white man to behold it, that he reported banks reaching "three to four leagues into the air" and broken "into pinnacles higher than the tower of the Cathedral of Seville."

But of far more significance than these rare spectacles of nature, however beautiful and picturesque they may be, are the scenes amid which the great masses of people must live. Few indeed are the regions in the United States, where life is tolerable, that are altogether lacking in charm. The eastern portion of the country, dominated by the Appalachian highlands from the Gulf of the St. Lawrence to Georgia and Alabama, is one of the most beautiful parts of the earth. In New England the Berkshires, the Green Mountains, and the White Mountains; in New York the Adirondacks and the Catskills; and in the regions to the southwest the Blue Ridge, the Black Mountains, the Great Smokies, and from Pennsylvania to the Gulf Coastal Plain the parallel ranges of the Alleghanies, give character and variety to the landscape. In the northeast the country is studded with innumerable lakes of glacial origin; and, because of the abundant rainfall, the entire Appalachian country is traversed by streams and rivers. The Hudson, flowing between its high and heavily wooded valley walls, has few rivals among the rivers of the world.

The beauty of this part of the United States is greatly enhanced by the luxuriance of the vegetation. Everywhere in summer, except on the rocky summits of the White Mountains of New Hampshire, the land is draped from highest peak to water's edge with a green mantle of forest. In the north and the south the dominant tone is given by the dark needles of the conifer; in the middle regions, by the lighter foliage of the hardwoods which in autumn assumes the most brilliant hues of red and yellow and orange. In much of this region, moreover, the land is blanketed with a covering of flowers which changes its color and pattern from season to season; and in many places the slopes of the Alleghanies are clothed in a thick growth of mountain laurel and rhododendron which in June and July burst into blossom and bathe the entire landscape with their loveliness. Here truly is a paradise for the artist or lover of natural beauty.

The impression which these forests in their primeval state made on a sensitive mind is revealed in De Tocqueville's account of his journey through parts of New York and Michigan in 1831:

"We pursued our way through the woods. From time to time a little lake (this district is full of them) shines like a white tablecloth under the green branches. The charm of these lonely spots, as yet untenanted by man, and where peace and silence reign undisturbed, can hardly be imagined.

"I have often climbed the wild and solitary passes of the Alps, where Nature refuses to obey the hand of man, and, displaying all her terrors, fills the mind with an exciting and overwhelming sensation of greatness. The solitude here is equally deep, but where, as in Milton's paradise, all seems prepared for the reception of man, the feelings produced are tranquil admiration, a soft melancholy, a vague aversion to civilized life, and a sort of savage instinct which causes you to regret that soon this enchanting solitude will be no more. Already, indeed, the white man is approaching through the surrounding woods; in a few years he will have felled the trees now reflected in the limpid waters of the lake, and will have driven to other wilds the animals that feed on its banks. . . ."[13]

Originally these forests of which De Tocqueville speaks reached far beyond the Appalachian highlands. In changing form, responding to differences in soil and climate, they draped the valleys of the Ohio and the Mississippi, covered half of Texas and Oklahoma, embraced practically the whole of Mis-

[13] Alexis de Tocqueville, "A Fortnight in the Wilderness," in *Memoirs, Letters and Remains* (London, 1861), II, 179.

souri and Wisconsin and the major part of Illinois and Minnesota, and extended long fingers up the water-courses into the prairies of Kansas, Nebraska, and Iowa. Beyond the forests lay the vast reaches of the plains with their cloak of long and short grasses, pierced here and there by clumps of willow and cottonwood. While this region conveys an impression of unbroken monotony to the casual traveller, to those who have come to know it by long residence the open sky, the great distances, the heroic mold of the landscape, the soft colors of dawn and sunset, the untempered fury of storm and blizzard, the direct exposure to the clashing of the elements, hold an ineffable charm.

Out of the plains rise the eastern outposts of the Cordilleras, a system of mountain ranges that reaches from central Colorado to the Pacific, passes northward into Canada and Alaska to the borders of the Arctic and sweeps southward through the tropics and on to the tip of South America and Tierra Del Fuego to plunge beneath the chill waters of the Southern Ocean. Within the United States this system includes numerous rugged ranges, steep-walled canyons, sheltered valleys, and intermontane plains and plateaus. Here is one of the great natural playgrounds of the continent partitioned by the barren majesty of the Rocky Mountains, the awe-inspiring grandeur of the Sierra Nevada, and the forest-clad ridges of the Cascade and Coast Ranges. To describe the natural beauty of this vast empire of forest and flower and mountain and gorge is impossible. Even the "Great American Desert" lying between the Rockies and the Sierra is a land of bewitching beauty—a region of riotous coloring, of brown and yellow and tawny reds tinted with blacks and grays, where "the brilliant colors of midday turn to violet in the softer lights of dawn or sunset." Beyond the Coast Range the continent falls rapidly and, in many places, precipitously into the Pacific. In the Northwest, from Washington to the Gulf of Alaska, the union of land and water conveys a sense of the everlasting power of nature. Deep fiords, flanked by cliffs 2000 to 5000 feet high, cut great gashes one or two hundred miles in length into the coastline, mountain walls two miles in height rise in silent might out of the ocean, and ageless glaciers pour immense ice streams down the valleys to the sea. And thus the North American continent dips beneath the waves of the western waters.

UTILIZATION OF RESOURCES

The foregoing account, which deals for the most part with the original natural endowment of the United States, reveals a land peculiarly equipped for the building of an industrial civilization, capable of producing within its own borders practically all crops not dependent on tropical conditions, possessing in extraordinary quantity nearly all of the more important minerals, and endowed with enormous stores of mechanical energy. While during the past three centuries the American people have greatly reduced the fertility of the soil in large areas, felled or burned approximately seven-eighths of the original forests, wasted enormous quantities of the mineral riches of the country, and marred the natural beauty of the land in many places,[14] the resources are still sufficient to place America in a unique position among the nations of the world.

The point should also be made that advances in science and technology will enevitably make for a more efficient and complete utilization of natural resources, at least if such advances are not set at naught by inherited economic and social practices. Through the development of chemistry innumerable synthetic products may be expected to supplement or displace the goods of nature. Also the discovery of new forms of energy may greatly diminish man's dependence on coal and oil and water-power. But these prospects, however alluring, must always be subjected to critical appraisal. According to Tryon and Schoenfeld, there exist slight grounds for optimism on this score at the present time:

"There is little recent progress to record in the utilization of

14 See Isaiah Bowman, *op. cit.*, pp. 96–97; and below, Part II, Chapter II, "Economy."

the other [than water] inexhaustible sources of power. A decade of speculation on the fascinating idea of atomic energy finds physicists skeptical of proposals to harness it and leaves the impression that the power of the future must be obtained directly or indirectly from the sun. The use of windmills is declining. Power from the tides lies still in the future although an 80,000 horsepower project at Passamaquoddy Bay is now before the Federal Power Commission. Solar motors and Claude's experiments with the warm waters of the tropics have served chiefly to emphasize the low grade character of these resources. Like the low grade iron and aluminum which together make up 10 per cent of the crust of the earth, the low grade energy resources exist in stupendous amounts, but by any techniques now known are available only at prices far above what we are accustomed to pay."[15]

Clearly, although revolutionary discoveries and developments may be reported at any time, it would scarcely be the counsel of wisdom to assume them. In spite of much experimentation and discussion coal remains the major source of mechanical energy. The economical administration and efficient utilization of all the power resources of the country would therefore seem to be imperative. The time has not yet arrived when the American people, along with the rest of mankind, may issue a declaration of independence from the accustomed fountains of energy.

[15] F. G. Tryon and Margaret H. Schoenfeld, *op. cit.*, 73–74.

Chapter III

TECHNOLOGY

The American people have received from the hands of nature one of the most richly endowed regions of the earth. In its combination of climate, soil, flora, fauna, minerals, and energy resources this area is suited, perhaps above all others, for the building of an industrial civilization at the present juncture in human history. Nature has thus placed at the disposal of the nation materials and energy in extraordinary quantity and variety for the attainment of its purposes. Certainly, if the people of the United States fail to achieve their ideal of providing a rich and abundant life for ordinary men and women, they cannot place the responsibility for failure on the poverty of their material resources. Their lot has been cast amid uniquely favorable natural surroundings.

It should be observed, however, that there is another basic factor to be taken into account. The natural endowment conditions, but does not determine, the work and forms of society. Indeed it can be said to be rich only if men are equipped to develop and exploit it. Nothing is more obvious than the fact that primitive peoples have lived for centuries and even millennia in lands abundantly supplied with coal, iron, and other minerals, without ever rising above the level of dependence on hunting and fishing and crude agriculture. Others have lived on the shores of wide oceans for equally long periods of time, observing daily the rise and fall of the tides, and yet have never built great ships and set out on long voyages of trade and discovery. As Mr. Bowman says, "the physical world changes constantly in its *meaning* to man because of the constant change in his technology. Earth and man toss the ball back and forth. We require, therefore, a technique of re-

54

search with respect to man and a technique with respect to the earth and a third or regional technique that is adapted to the study of diverse man living upon a diverse earth."[1]

All that can be said with safety, then, about the physical environment is that it establishes certain limits to human action and offers certain potential materials and resources to peoples capable of using them. Yet these so-called limits are difficult to discover and the ultimate borders of these potential materials and resources are not now, perhaps never can be, known. What is done by a nation within a given enviroment depends upon its ideas, energies, and interests, which in turn are intricately related to the whole movement of civilization called world history. No formula less catholic than this is admitted by modern knowledge. Without some kind of physical environment no civilization can flourish; but without some elements of civilization, the primitive arts at least, so-called natural riches are of slight consequence.

From the standpoint of the achievement of purposes, therefore, the arts with which the physical endowment is developed are quite as important as the endowment itself. In fact the two are but aspects of a single unity. Among these practical arts technology is the most powerful and dynamic. Through it old resources can be developed more fully and efficiently and new resources discovered and utilized. For convenience technology has been defined as "the art of applying science and mechanics to the various departments of human economy." While this definition, like all definitions, is not wholly satisfactory, it will be employed as a point of departure in the present chapter. It suggests clearly that technology, being thoroughly practical, is an instrument of purpose. But, as the ensuing pages will show, it is not merely an instrument of purpose; it also transforms the conditions out of which purposes grow. It thus becomes increasingly a creative factor in the evolution of culture.

The repercussions of technological advance are already ap-

[1] Isaiah Bowman, *Geography in Relation to the Social Sciences* (New York, 1934), 37.

parent in every division of life. In this chapter, however, no effort will be made to give a complete account of the role of technology in American society. Rather will the analysis be presented in highly abstract form, with the attention directed toward certain of the larger considerations involved and with the presentation organized about the subjects of the growth, the power, the inner nature, and the impact on civilization of technology. But since this mighty force penetrates and influences every department of social life, it cannot be confined to a single and separate chapter. On the contrary, it must appear as a disturbing and transforming factor, directly or by implication, on practically every page of the present volume.

THE GROWTH OF TECHNOLOGY

For various reasons that need not be recorded here, technology has advanced farther and permeated the social fabric more deeply in America than elsewhere. This fact may be observed in the countless outer manifestations of technology, in the growth of machines and laboratories,[2] in the succession of inventions, in the changing occupations of the people, in the new processes and instrumentalities by which men hunt and fish, breed animals, cultivate the soil, harvest crops, fell forests, delve in mines, fabricate goods, exchange commodities, communicate with one another, travel from place to place, and engage in armed conflict. Here the story will be confined altogether to a few facts regarding the growth of mechanical invention and the changing occupations of the people.

In its outer manifestations technology advanced relatively little from the days of Cæsar and Pompey down to the nineteenth century. During all of these centuries the work of the world was done mainly by human beings, supplemented by domestic animals and to a very limited extent by fire and wind and water. From time to time tools had been improved so that men might lift heavier burdens or do more or finer

2 See below, Part II, Chapter VII, "Science."

work with the same effort; but the development of implements and machines proceeded with exceeding slowness. Plows in Washington's day were little if any better than those of the ancient world. Though the scythe was a great improvement over the primitive sickle, it opened up no new vistas of agricultural advance. When about the middle of the seventeenth century Joseph Jenks began to manufacture at Lynn, Massachusetts, an improved scythe similar to that now in use, by lengthening and strengthening the blade without adding to its weight, his invention constituted an important technological improvement.[3] However, the amount of grain a farmer could raise was still limited, not only by the amount of land he could cultivate with a very primitive horsedrawn plow, but also by the area the available men could mow with scythes during the short harvest season.

A similar restriction was placed on the usefulness of the short-staple upland cotton, which now constitutes the bulk of the crop, because of the labor required to separate the fibre from the seed. Eli Whitney's cotton gin, which made its appearance in 1793, although a very simple piece of mechanism requiring no great amount of power, revolutionized agriculture in the South, enabled that region to become the world's greatest producer of cotton, accelerated the growth of the textile industries of England and New England, gave a new lease of life to the institution of Negro slavery, accentuated the tendency of the South to produce a staple crop, and helped bring on the Civil War. The iron plow produced by Jethro Wood and others during the first quarter of the nineteenth century represented a great improvement over the past; and the steel plow made by John Deere and the "chilled" steel plow patented by James Oliver in 1868 completed the evolution of the blade now in use.[4]

In the early thirties several patents were granted for harvest-

[3] W. B. Weeden, *Economic and Social History of New England* (Boston, 1890), I, 183.
[4] Holland Thompson, *The Age of Invention* (New Haven, 1921), 111–1115.

ing machines. Cyrus McCormick of Rockbridge County, Virginia, was not only the inventor of a successful reaper but also a business man of unusual vision and ability. Seeing the suitability of his machines to level prairies, he moved to Chicago and began manufacturing in 1847. When the Civil War transferred farm hands to the army, the consequent shortage of labor greatly accelerated the adoption of the reaper; and the new machines enabled the North to maintain farm production in spite of the diversion of great numbers of workers from their ordinary occupations. As self-binders replaced simple mowing machines, the need for human labor was further reduced. However, until the perfection of the internal combustion engine in the twentieth century, which made possible a practicable farm tractor, the horse and occasionally the ox furnished the motive power for agriculture. But in the factories that built the machinery, time moved more swiftly.

In 1765 James Watt, after repairing a model of the inefficient Newcomen steam engine, conceived the idea which led to the invention of an engine with the reciprocating feature. By the opening of the nineteenth century this improvement had been so far perfected that it could furnish power for industry in considerable quantities. And machines to drive were already at hand. During this same period in England mechanical devices for the spinning and weaving of cloth were invented and developed. Steam soon supplemented or displaced water power in the operation of the textile mills. In 1790 Samuel Slater installed his first spinning machinery at Pawtucket, Rhode Island, and textile factories soon appeared in various parts of New England. This development went forward with particular rapidity during the period from 1808 to 1815, when Jefferson's embargo and the war of 1812 furnished effective protection to the infant industry. The factory system, a most characteristic outer manifestation of technology, was taking root in America.

Meanwhile another important development had appeared. In

1798 Eli Whitney organized a factory near New Haven for the manufacture of firearms and proceeded to devise and perfect a plan for making identical parts of muskets. Under this method a musket could be assembled from parts that had never been fitted together before and any lost part might be replaced without special fitting. Moreover, Whitney found that the machine tools, which he had invented to make the parts, could be operated quite as well by unskilled labor as by men who had served long apprenticeships acquiring the skills of the gunsmith. "So it was in the shops of the New England gunmakers that machine tools were first made of such variety and adaptability that they could be applied generally to other branches of manufacturing; and so it was that the system of interchangeable manufacture arose as a distinctively American development."[5]

In transportation and communication the changes were equally revolutionary. Men living before 1800 had long known how to build ships and sail them against the wind, and to find their way on long voyages; but on land they still followed modes of travel not fundamentally different from those of ancient times: they walked, they rode animals, or they were carried in vehicles drawn by animals. Moreover, few American roads were good in any season, while the great majority were practically impassable during bad weather. In 1807 Robert Fulton and Robert Livingston placed the first commercially successful steamboat on the Hudson; in 1811 a steamboat was built at Pittsburgh; by 1830 steamboats had revolutionized transportation on the western rivers. The application of steam to land transportation followed. In 1830 successful locomotives were running on railroads in both England and the United States: the era of railroad building had begun. Steamboats and locomotives meant more rapid communication as well as improved transportation. The electric telegraph, operated between Washington and Baltimore in 1844, worked another

[5] *Ibid.*, 185.

radical change in this field. The telephone soon followed. Then with the opening of the twentieth century came the automobile, the movie, the radio, and the airplane.

By 1830 the industrial revolution in most of its important phases had begun; at the outbreak of the Civil War it was rapidly gathering momentum. Yet the period following the war was to witness even more striking developments. Before the possibilities of an age of iron, broadened through the use of anthracite coal and later of coke in the smelting of iron, had been fully realized, the Bessemer process ushered in the age of steel. Steam and water turbines, the internal combustion engine, and electricity placed new forms of energy, in practically unlimited amounts, at the disposal of man. As a consequence of new discoveries and processes the basic industries, most of which had been steadily increasing their use of power and machinery since the thirties or forties, grew at a constantly advancing rate down to the end of the century. By that time the frontier was closed and America had entered irrevocably the age of industrialism. Thereafter invention continued yet more rapidly; and the union of mechanics and electricity produced first the automatic machine, then the automatic factory, and profoundly altered the role of human labor and skill in the productive process.[6] But of even greater significance for the future was the systematic organization of research[7] on an ever-widening scale. Some conception of the resulting changes in industry may be gathered from the following graphic description by Stuart Chase:

"Standard gauges in actual use are now accurate to three-millionths of an inch. . . . The first power lathe, built in 1800, could be lifted up and carried around by a man. The largest boring mill in the United States can now gnaw a hole 60 feet in diameter through solid steel. . . . Hydraulic presses that will flatten a mass of steel into a thin plate may be so regulated

6 Walter N. Polakov, *The Power Age* (New York, 1933), 67 ff.
7 See below, Part II, Chapter VII, "Science."

that the moving parts may come to rest against an egg shell without cracking it. . . . With the slackening of immigration and the crude labor supply after the War, management was forced to devise machines for handling materials—work formerly done by the muscles and backs of hunkies. Behold those new monsters: belt conveyers, locomotive cranes, spiral chutes, tier lift trucks, overhead carriers, bucket conveyors, truck tractors, gravity chutes. . . . Here is a press like a rearing Brontosaurus thirty feet in height, just installed by a company manufacturing motor cars. It exerts a pressure of one million pounds. A piece of raw steel is fed to it. Crunch! Out comes a finished fender."[8]

This whole story of the growth of invention during the past century, one of the most striking outer manifestations of technology, is summarized by W. F. Ogburn. In the table[9] on the following page he has assembled the facts for the United States from 1840 to 1930 and for Great Britain from 1751 to 1931.

The first impression gained from an examination of the table is that mechanical invention has experienced a phenomenal growth in both of these countries during the last two or three generations. In the United States the number of patents issued increased approximately one hundred-fold in eighty-five years, while in Great Britain the number multiplied about eighteen hundred times in one hundred seventy years. Moreover, discoveries in physics in France, England, and Germany, which may be said to underlie mechanical invention and the general advance of technology, increased from 59 for the five years ending in 1815 to 917 for the five years ending in 1900.[10]

The second and even more significant impression is that the era of mechanical invention is not over. Indeed the number

[8] Stuart Chase, "The Heart of American Industry," in *America as Americans See It,* edited by Fred J. Ringel (New York, 1932), 26, 28.

[9] W. F. Ogburn, with the assistance of S. C. Gilfillan, "The Influence of Invention and Discovery," Chapter III in The President's Research Committee on Social Trends, *Recent Social Trends in the United States* (New York, 1933), I, 126.

[10] *Ibid.*

of patents issued for each country was highest for the latest period reported; and, with very few exceptions, each five or ten years represents an advance over the immediately preceding interval. These facts suggest that the peak of invention has

Patents Issued in the United States by Five-Year Periods		Patents Issued in Great Britain by Ten-Year Periods	
FIVE YEARS ENDING	NUMBER OF PATENTS	TEN YEARS ENDING	NUMBER OF PATENTS
1845	2,425	1761	100
1850	3,517	1771	234
1855	6,143	1781	309
1860	16,997	1791	535
1865	20,779	1801	722
1870	58,833	1811	947
1875	61,024	1821	1,119
1880	64,496	1831	1,576
1885	97,357	1841	3,002
1890	110,493	1851	4,679
1895	108,465	1861	19,188
1900	112,325	1871	22,356
1905	143,791	1881	33,495
1910	171,560	1891	87,623
1915	186,241	1901	130,197
1920	197,644	1911	160,386
1925	203,977	1921	138,909
1930	219,384	1931	182,782

not yet been reached and even that, if ever to be attained, is still far in the future. In the degree that mechanical invention is a basic factor in producing social change, it may consequently be expected that the remaining years of the twentieth century will be marked by changes quite as disturbing as any that the world has seen during the past three or four generations.

To any who may feel that the inventions of the future will be less revolutionary in nature than those of the past the point should be made that many of the recent discoveries in the fundamental sciences of physics, chemistry, and biology have by no means been fully applied to human affairs. Moreover, there seem to be excellent grounds for believing that these sciences will continue their steady advance from year to year.

Also certain basic inventions are only beginning to be exploited today. The development of the transmission of electrical power, a branch of engineering science still in its infancy, should result in an enormous reduction in the number of power houses in the country. According to competent authorities, the whole of the United States might be served by as few as five hundred great central stations. The resulting changes in social arrangements would be almost incalculable. The marked improvement of contraceptive devices, which seems as certain as anything can in this world, may be counted upon to affect yet further the family and the relations between the sexes. And the photo-electric cell, when fully perfected and applied, seems capable of displacing great multitudes of men in industry, in transportation, and in almost every realm to which the machine can penetrate. Consider the following highly restrained statement by Mr. Ogburn:

"The photo-electric cell is old but became practically useful only when vacuum tube amplifiers were made available. Its use with the amplifier is so recent that its social effects will be largely in the future, although even today an unusual variety of uses has been found for this mechanical eye, which never knows fatigue, is marvellously swift and accurate, can see with invisible light, and co-ordinates with all the resources of electricity. It sorts beans, fruit and eggs, measures illumination in studios and theatres, appraises color better than the human eye, classifies minerals, counts bills and throws out counterfeits, times horse races, counts people and vehicles, determines thickness and transparency of cloth, detects and measures strains in glass, sees through fog, records smoke in tunnels and chimneys, and is indispensable in facsimile telegraphy, television, and sound-on-film pictures. Other of its uses are to direct traffic automatically at less frequented crossings, to open a door at the approach of a waitress and to serve as an automatic train control."[11]

[11] *Ibid.*, 133.

The rapidly expanding role of technology in American life during the past century is clearly revealed in the changing occupations of the people. In 1840, the first year for which data of any value are available, only an insignificant fraction of the population was engaged in pursuits that might in any sense be said to represent this new interest. In that year the federal census reported but 65,255 persons under the single broad category of learned professions and engineers, at least four-fifths of whom must have been physicians and teachers. Not until the following decennial census, however, does a genuinely illuminating picture appear. In 1850 the country could boast but 591 architects, 189 draftsmen, 512 civil engineers, 1614 surveyors, 465 chemists, and 943 college professors. In 1860 the list of technical occupations is lengthened: 12 electricians, 51 assayers, 2 astronomers, 2 explorers, and 3 geologists are reported. In 1870 metallurgists appear for the first time; in 1890 mechanical, electrical, and mining engineers; and in 1920 aeronauts. During the eighty-year period from 1850 to 1930, while the general population was growing from 23,191,876 to 122,775,046, the number of engineers of all kinds grew from 2126 to 226,249, the number of architects from 591 to 22,000, the number of draftsmen from 189 to 79,922, the number of chemists, assayers, and metallurgists from 465 to 47,068, and the number of college professors and presidents from 943 to 61,905.[12]

THE POWER OF TECHNOLOGY[13]

Perhaps the most striking characteristic of technology is the power which it places in the hands of men. Thus it emancipates the human body from natural physical limits by substituting metal fingers, arms, and legs for human organs and by multiplying them indefinitely for the performance of functions

[12] Probably includes some teachers in schools below collegiate rank.

[13] For the ideas contained in the remainder of this chapter the author is indebted largely to William Beard. See his *Government and Technology* (New York, 1934).

in the discharge of services and in the production and transportation of goods. Also, it emancipates the human body from its energy limits, by substituting the forces of organic and inorganic nature for human brawn and muscle. Likewise, in an increasing measure, it emancipates mankind from the limits of material nature as originally presented to the primitive mind, by creating new chemical substances and new forms of plant and animal life. Finally, it offers an increasing emancipation from the limits of space, by providing swifter and ever swifter means of transport and communication. In other words, under technology, the production of commodities and services is no longer limited by the number of human beings at work and by crude nature as seen by the untutored eye. The possibility of indefinite extension in application and use lies open to intelligence.

The fact that technology is an instrument of extraordinary power is altogether obvious. The point therefore need not be labored here. Man has become interested in the advance of technology primarily because he has gradually learned that it is capable of multiplying his strength immeasurably and even of displacing his labor altogether. The perspectives which it has already opened to human eyes surpass the dreams of antiquity. At last apparently men may be freed from grinding toil, and a life of material security and relative abundance may be provided for all. At least this seems to be possible in those favored regions of the earth, like America, where nature has provided the necessary resources.

Something of the nature and magnitude of the revolution precipitated by technology may be disclosed by a reference to the data on energy consumption in America since the founding of the Union. Prior to the writing of the Declaration of Independence, according to the estimates of engineers, the rate of energy consumption per capita nowhere in the world exceeded 4000 or fell below 2000 kilogram calories a day. Within these narrow limits men lived and died, civilizations rose and fell, age followed age. In the United States in 1929 the daily per capita consumption of energy stood at the fantastic figure of approximately 160,000 kilogram calories. From 1840 to 1929, when the population of the country was growing from slightly over 12,000,000 to 122,000,000, the number of British Thermal Units, derived from coal, oil, natural gas, and water power and consumed in the economic process, increased from 75 trillion to almost 27,000 trillion. And the greater part of this increase took place after 1900.[14] "Public utility plants alone," says a recent report of a committee of the Society of Industrial Engineers, "have increased wholesale sale of energy from 3,254,000,000 KWH in 1912 to 44,326,-000,000 KWH in 1929, or 1360 per cent."[15]

The change in the rate of energy consumption is due of course to the tapping of new sources of power. From the days of the cave-dwellers down to 1830 the basic source of power in all societies was the human engine, whether enslaved or free. To be sure, here and there man used fire to soften ores and metals, put wind and waterfall in crude harness, and forced beasts of burden—the ox, the camel, the horse, the carabao, the dog—to work for him; but all of these forms of assistance probably only succeeded in doubling the total consumption of energy. With his own strength man everywhere cultivated the soil, harvested the crops, built houses and cities, and fabricated garments, tools, and weapons. Today all but a tiny fraction of the burden has been shifted from human shoulders to the sturdy and tireless back of the iron horse. The feeble instruments for the transversion of energy which nature placed at man's disposal are being superseded and have already practically vanished from the picture. Out of the mines of America alone have come 1,000,000,000 mechanical horses or 10,000,000,000 mechanical slaves who require neither

[14] Stuart Chase, *Technocracy* (New York, 1933), 19–23.
[15] Report of the Committee on the Significance of Technocracy of the Society of Industrial Engineers, *Economic Significance of Technological Progress* (New York, 1933), 11.

rest nor sleep. A single giant turbine can in twenty-four hours do the work of nine million men.

When harnessed to machines these modern engines are capable literally of showering men with goods and services. At least such is the testimony of the engineer, the most competent witness in the field. Ralph E. Flanders, Vice-President of the American Society of Mechanical Engineers, has thus succinctly outlined the possibility: "The engineer knows— all engineers know—that, if some omniscient dictator were installed as ruler of the United States, they could provide for him raw materials, machinery, and trained labor sufficient to flood, bury, and smother the population in such an avalanche of food, clothing, shelter, luxuries, and material refinements as no Utopian dreamer in his busiest slumbers has ever conceived."[16]

In another place the same authority has written as follows:

"For much less expenditure of physical and nervous energy than he is now putting forth, it (engineering) offers the common man far more of goods, in the way of food, shelter, garments, travel, books—material satisfactions of all kinds—than he has ever hoped to have. This does not depend on some future engineering development—it is within reach now. Present mechanical and engineering processes are producing an unparalleled flow of goods, with a surprisingly small fraction of the population engaged in the work really necessary to their production and distribution. . . . Engineering has so tremendously multiplied the effectiveness of the individual workman that material plenty with moderate toil becomes possible for the first time in human history."[17]

Charles R. Stevenson, head of a New York firm of management engineers, has spoken in similar vein:

[16] Ralph E. Flanders, "Pandora's New Box," *The Forum* (December, 1930), LXXXIV, 336.
[17] Ralph E. Flanders, "The New Age and the New Man," Chapter I in Charles A. Beard, *Toward Civilization* (New York, 1930), 26–27.

"We have in the United States one hundred and twenty million people living in a country that is capable of producing with its present productive equipment everything that is necessary to allow all of us to have everything we need to eat, everything we need to wear, houses to live in, automobiles to ride in, schools, theatres, churches, athletics and other recreational facilities. All this could be had and no one would have to work more than thirty-five hours a week."[18]

In summarizing an enquiry into the operating efficiency of American industry conducted by a committee of engineers, Walter N. Polakov has outlined in striking phrase the perspectives disclosed to mankind by recent advance in technology. "If we take an arithmetic average," he says, "of the most efficient and least efficient groups given in the Alford and Hannum report, we find that the productivity of our present Power Age industries could be increased 40 times, using existing technological and managerial means. This would mean that instead of the 25,000,000 workers ordinarily employed we could satisfy all the demand for goods that existed in 1929 with only 625,000 workers."[19] This statement suggests that technology has placed within the grasp of the American people the vision of Aristotle: "If every tool when summoned, or even of its own accord, could do the work that befits it, just as the creations of Daedalus moved of themselves, or the tripods of Hephaestus went of their own accord to their sacred work, if the weaver's shuttles were to weave of themselves, then there would be no use either of apprentices for the master workers, or slaves for the lords." Today tools of surpassing complexity and power, of their own accord, can actually do the work that befits them and thus render obsolete both slaves and lords.

---

[18] Charles R. Stevenson, *The Way Out* (New York, 1931), 5.
[19] Walter N. Polakov, *op. cit.*, 136. Also see L. P. Alford and J. E. Hannum, "Measuring Operating Performance by the Kilo Man-Hour," in *Mechanical Engineering* (December, 1932), LIV, 821–822.

Technology, however, is not merely a slave, ready and willing to do the bidding of man. It is also a master, making demands upon its creator. Indeed, if not properly managed, it may turn its power to destructive ends and spread misery through the nation, as the experience of recent years fully demonstrates. At any rate, if the promise of technology is to be fulfilled, its own inner nature must be recognized. And society must be organized so that it may function in accordance with its laws. Bassett Jones, in speaking of the productive mechanism that has been fashioned by technology, makes this point clear:

"The production end of our economy, as it now exists, has been built during the past century in more or less strict accord with such principles of engineering. It is a machine, but it is a mechanism of great complication, which nevertheless must perform, and can perform only, in accordance with hard and fast natural laws. It is futile to expect it to violate such laws, and if the demand made upon it, or the control of its operation is such as to require impossibilities in performance, the machine will either cease to function properly or cease to function at all, quite irrespective of what men may wish it to do or try to make it do."[20]

When broadly conceived technology manifests six basic, but closely interdependent, characteristics: it is rational; it is functional; it is planful; it is centripetal; it is dynamic; and it is efficient. Each of these characteristics will be examined.

In the first place, technology is essentially rational. If given free rein, it liberates the human mind from the slavery of precedent and over-rides long-established barriers to thought. This is due to the fact that it embraces a complex of immediately relevant ideas and methods which serve human purposes

[20] Bassett Jones, *Debt and Production* (New York, 1933), 9.

and at the same time profoundly influence the formulation of
those purposes. Instead of bowing to authority, however venerable or universally accepted, it observes, inquires, describes
accurately and mathematically. It proceeds according to the
known and measured characteristics of forces and materials.
It rejects rule-of-thumb assumptions and decisions—it overthrows prejudices, whims, vulgarisms, and traditions and
brings the phenomena of its observation to the test of quantitative reasoning and predictable outcome. The engineer
does not guess or hope that his operations in the realm of
physical relationships will have a certain result: he *knows* that
they will. Otherwise he is not an engineer but a charlatan.
As technology occupies ever larger areas of economy and the
engineering élite increases in numbers, the rationality of science is thrust deeper and deeper into the operation of social
functions.

In the second place, technology is functional rather than
academic. By its very nature it is concerned with applications
and outcomes, not with contemplation and speculation on the
nature of things. Any branch of humanistic study and
thought may be completely sterile, that is, conducted for the
pleasure and entertainment of the person involved, without
any consideration of use, indeed even with contempt for the
very idea of applicability and utility. Not so with technology;
it is studied and taught with constant reference to use. Those
who master it can apply it with assured results, and do so
apply it as long as they remain active technologists. Achievement in the realm of practical affairs, not amusement or the
mere accumulation of ideas, is the supreme goal of technology.

In the third place, technology, conceived and directed with
respect to action, is necessarily planful. The engineer cannot
take a single step without formulating a purpose, without
determining direction in advance, without a blueprint of the
work to be accomplished. The plan may be large or small,

according to the undertaking in hand, but it must be definite and based upon positive knowledge of ends to be realized. On this account, the spirit of technology runs counter to the impulsive and capricious actions of individuals, which are the central drives of economy in the pre-machine age and are treated as such by classical economics. It insists upon prevision and excludes guess-work from its field of operations. So the area of plan and design widens with the area of industry occupied by technology.

In the fourth place, technology is centripetal in nature. Dominated always by the necessity of design, technology is continually pushing plan outward into adjoining regions of economy ruled by guess-work and is ever drawing chaotic procedures within its embrace of order. Having established plan in one place, it is not content with disorder on the periphery of its immediate operations, but tends by its logic and thought to unite and arrange neighboring operations around a common focus. Thus standardization advances in every direction throughout economy, bringing many and diverse departments under the rule of the center. In this way technology facilitates the process of consolidation in industry —the process which has already brought 38 per cent of the business wealth of the United States (apart from banking) under the direction of 200 giant corporations.[21]

In the fifth place, technology is dynamic. It acts. It explores. One new discovery or invention suggests another. The solution of a single problem in physics or chemistry usually raises a second or a cluster of problems. The dynamic character of technology is illustrated in the growing number of patents issued by the government of the United States, to which reference has already been made. If the frequency of basic discoveries and inventions declines, as often suggested by observers, doubtless refinements, adjustments, and adaptations may continue to multiply. For instance, man may

[21]See below, p. 176.

now travel on land, in the air, on the water, and under the water, by mechanical contrivances. No other medium of travel is open to invention, unless it be in the earth, through the stratosphere, or through inter-stellar space, but the airplane, train, automobile, ship, and submarine may be indefinitely refined and improved by technology. Even totally new instrumentalities may be devised. Should refinements diminish in number, adaptations to human purposes will doubtless continue, at least until the human spirit becomes quiescent. It is this dynamic character of technology which accelerates social change and especially differentiates modern society from all preceding social orders.

In the sixth place, technology is efficient. This is its crowning and perhaps most pervasive conception—the performance of the largest possible amount of work—the accomplishment of the greatest possible result—with the least expenditure of energy. It is also a most revolutionary conception. Practically it is first applied to the elimination of wastes due to loss of heat and to friction in engines and machines. Here a knowledge of the mechanical equivalent of heat makes possible measurements and determinations of amazing refinement. From the machine itself, the idea of efficiency is extended to labor— to a consideration of the human element in industry, to the elimination of fatiguing operations, to physical movements best adapted to the accomplishment of results with the least wear and tear on the body. From the sphere of labor it is extended to the community. Very appropriately the engineer asks, what does it avail to reduce losses of heat in engines, in machine set-up, and in labor methods, and then permit a loss of vital energies through unfavorable housing, travelling, and living conditions? In answering this question some manufacturers, especially in England, set up model industrial communities designed to unite efficiency and beauty in living arrangements. Thus in the end the quest for efficiency leads to æsthetics.

The concept of efficiency also places an ever-growing premium on professional competence. In a technological society good intentions are not enough; expert knowledge is absolutely indispensable. Without such knowledge a machine, a plant, an industry, or even the entire economic system may be thrown into disorder and wrecked. Because of the amount of energy involved, mistakes may be far more costly than they were in the simple farming communities of a hundred years ago. By careful experiment the engineer finds "the one best way" of operating a particular mechanism. To operate it in any other way leads to waste and sometimes to disaster. This means that in certain large areas, which will no doubt increase as technology pushes its conquests into new territory, the pooling of inexpert opinions will have to give way to trained intelligence. The judgment of one competent man is worth far more than the combined judgments of an ignorant multitude. In fact in the realms governed by technology the registering of uninformed opinion is simply irrelevant.

THE IMPACT OF TECHNOLOGY ON CIVILIZATION

With the growth and application of technology has come a veritable revolution in the structure and functions of Western society. An agrarian or feudal civilization has been transformed into an industrial and mechanical civilization. The story of this transformation has been told with more or less fullness and accuracy in many works.[22] It need not be repeated here, even in outline. But one caution is appropriate. It is customary for historians to say that an invention has *caused* this or that change in society. For example, owing to the fact that setting-up exercises were once extensively broadcast over the radio, a sociologist states that such exercises taken by listeners "were an effect of the radio." This is an oversimplification. The radio in itself is a dead instrument. Why were

[22] See Lewis Mumford, *Technics and Civilization* (New York, 1934); and William Beard, *Government and Technology* (New York, 1934).

exercises broadcast? By what inducements were owners of radio apparatus led to broadcast exercises? Why did listeners pay any attention to them? Then why did the broadcasting of exercises go out of fashion? The radio is still here, as a cause, if it was one, but the effect has ceased. Inventions alone do not *cause* social changes. They are not things outside of man which force a pattern of conduct upon him. They are themselves the product of the human mind working in society. They make possible new forms of behavior, such as swifter travel, but they do not compel them. Introduced into a society marked by a given level of civilization, an invention offers an instrumentality to existing morality and intelligence, and changes follow in time. Science cannot explain "why"; it can but report and describe.

Instead of being regarded, then, as the cause or as a collection of causes, technology must be assimilated in thought to the movement of interests and ideas which make up the substance of society in change. It is with such reservations that the "influence of technology on modern society" must be considered. As a growing array of machines and physical operations and a body of ideas, it has penetrated all departments of modern life and, in the process, age-long methods, customs, and organizations have been destroyed or profoundly modified. No branch of economy, medicine, education, recreation, communication, government, or international relations has escaped the sweep of this revolution. Nor have architecture, the arts, letters, morals, and philosophy gone unscathed during the wide-reaching upheaval and reconstruction. Illustrations in detail are presented in the chapters which follow, but certain broad principles may be stated here.

Among the chief economic consequences which have flowed from the introduction of technology, perhaps the most significant for society and for the educator or the statesman seeking to chart his way have been specialization and integration in industry. Specialization on the one side has split the few simple crafts of early times into thousands of occupations. These occupations are constantly changing; some are being destroyed completely; others are in process of transformation. No classification is valid for any considerable period of time. Independence in production, security in craft skill, and precision in requisite education and training tend to disappear with the advance of technology. And automatic machinery is not only taking over the skills of the past but is even absorbing the function of attendance. Thus men become increasingly and collectively dependent on the machine.

Specialization, in turn, is accompanied by integration through transportation and exchange: California farmers specialize in growing oranges and live by exchanging their produce in distant markets for innumerable necessities and luxuries. With specialization on such a scale economic independence for the individual, the family, and even the community disappears. The functioning of one specialty hangs upon the functioning of others. Individual responsibility is supplemented by and is dependent upon corporate responsibility. This is one of the fundamental outcomes of the technological revolution.

A closely related outcome is the production of enormous quantities of goods for enormous masses of people, as distinguished from limited production for selected buyers belonging to an upper class. Mass production for the masses accompanies machine industry everywhere. Otherwise the machines could be kept busy for only a few hours a week. A single commodity, turned out in immense quantities, cannot be sold in the immediate community; its sale must spread throughout the country, perhaps the world. Correlated with mass production is mass consumption. Unless the masses can and will buy the numerous commodities manufactured by the ton and carload, technological industry comes to a standstill or is slowed down to a fraction of its capacity. Whereas in the day of agriculture and handicrafts, the great majority of the population had to be content with the barest subsistence, now the functioning of the whole industrial mechanism depends upon buying power and rising standards of life among the people. Exclusiveness in the possession and use of standard commodities becomes impossible, if machine industry is to function. Since the distribution of buying power involves at bottom the distribution of income, the basic problems of collective economy come into purview in any consideration of the efficient operation of technological industry.

Finally, the independent role of technology in society should be noted. Though associated, in its practical applications, with capitalist enterprises in the exploitation of natural resources and the promotion of industry, as a body of ideas and methods it works independently in the development of thought respecting economy and social organization. Rational, functional, planful, centripetal, dynamic, and efficient by its inner logic and necessities, technology brings its methods to bear on all relevancies which are irrational, formal, chaotic, dispersive, static, and wasteful. Already this intellectual operation, which is both critical and constructive, is manifest in journals of engineering, in the proceedings of technical societies, and in the writings of individual technologists. It runs in every direction—through conceptions of exploitation connected with oil, minerals, timber, and water power; through industrial management; through production and transportation; through city, regional, state, and national planning and administration. As technology advances in application, its thought gains in momentum and overrides political and economic barriers established in a pre-technological age. It destroys the individualistic economy of Washington and Jefferson and creates the framework of a thoroughly integrated society. In the chapters that follow this transformation will be described, the accompanying tensions noted, and the failures and potentialities of the epoch developed.

PART TWO

SOCIAL TRENDS AND TENSIONS

FAMILY

In the first federal census, taken in 1790 at the very beginning of the national history of the American people, the family was made the unit for the gathering of data and the name of the head of each family reported. This practice was continued for two generations or until 1850, when the family was displaced by the individual. These facts are of more than superficial significance. They not only tell of a marked advance in census enumeration; they also register a profound change in social organization. During the colonial period and well into the nineteenth century the family was the basic social unit. Thereafter, under the impact of strange forces family walls began to crumble and family functions to disperse, while the individual severed ancient domestic ties and became increasingly a member of an ever growing and ever expanding society. In this revolutionary shift are contained or implied the major social trends of the age.

THE PRE-INDUSTRIAL FAMILY

Although the situation varied from place to place and changed from decade to decade, and although the authority of the pre-industrial family was tempered by the church, chartered companies, community organizations, colonial legislatures, royal governors, state and federal governments, and modes of migration and settlement, the family was the dominant factor in the conquest of the new continent. Before the rise of industrial civilization in America this institution performed most of the functions necessary to the maintenance and perpetuation of society. In characterizing colonial life at the close of the seventeenth century, James Truslow Adams concludes that "we thus have to deal with a widely scattered and mainly agricultural population leading a hard-working, narrow, parochial and sometimes dangerous existence in solitary farms, tiny hamlets, or at most in what would now be considered small villages."[1] And conditions changed but slowly during the eighteenth century. This was the world which the fathers of the Republic faced in the Constitutional Convention of 1787—a world of families living on isolated farms.

The isolation and the low level of technology forced the family to be practically self-sufficient on the economic side. Property in land was the chief form of wealth and source of income. With a few acres the individual family could be or could soon become relatively self-sustaining. In the farm household, supplemented by the surrounding community, industry and agriculture were united in a closely integrated round of activities. Of commerce there was little. Henry P. Hedges, writing in 1885, has described the self-sufficiency of the farm family in Suffolk County, New York, in the eighteenth century:

"From his feet to his head the farmer stood in vestment produced on his own farm. The leather of his shoes came from the hides of his own cattle. The linen and woolen that he wore were products that he raised. The farmer's wife or daughter braided and sewed the straw hat on his head. His fur cap was made from the skin of a fox he shot. The feathers of wild fowl in the bed whereon he rested his weary frame by night were the results acquired in his shooting. The pillow-cases, sheets and blankets, the comfortables, quilts and counterpanes, the towels and table cloth, were home made. His harness and lines he cut from hides grown on his farm. Everything about his

[1] James Truslow Adams, *Provincial Society 1690–1763* (New York, 1927), 23.

ox yoke except staple and ring he made. His whip, his ox
gad, his flail, axe, hoe and forkhandle, were his own work.
How little he bought, and how much he contrived to supply
his wants by home manufacture would astonish this generation."[2]

As this quotation suggests, the farm family, and at this time
the farm family was the typical family, practically clothed itself.
The eighteenth century was the age of homespun. "If we could
have examined the wardrobes of the farm men and women
piece by piece," write P. W. Bidwell and J. I. Falconer, "we
should have found everything of household manufacture, except a few bits of Sunday finery, hard-earned and long-treas-
ured, a broadcloth coat, a beaver hat, shoe-buckles, a silk gown,
or a few ribbons."[3] In his *Report on Manufactures,* in 1790,
Alexander Hamilton tells of this reliance on homespun:

"Great quantities of coarse cloths, coatings, serges, and flan-
nels, linsey woolseys, hosiery of wool, cotton, and thread, coarse
fustians, jeans, and muslins, checked and striped cotton and
linen goods, bed ticks, coverlets and counterpanes, tow linens,
coarse shirtings, sheetings, towelling, and table linen, and
various mixtures of wool and cotton, and of cotton and flax,
are made in the household way, and, in many instances, to an
extent not only sufficient for the supply of the families in which
they are made, but for sale, and even, in some cases, for
exportation. It is computed in a number of districts that two
thirds, three fourths, and even four fifths of all the clothing of
the inhabitants are made by themselves."[4]

The dependence of the household on its own food supply
was equally complete. Henry S. Nourse has thus described

[2] Henry P. Hedges, "Development of Agriculture in Suffolk County," in
Bicentennial History of Suffolk County (New York, 1885), 42.
[3] Percy Wells Bidwell and John I. Falconer, *History of Agriculture in the
Northern United States 1620–1860* (Washington, 1925), 128.
[4] *The Works of Alexander Hamilton,* edited by Henry Cabot Lodge (New
York, 1904), IV, 128–129.

the diet of the Massachusetts farm family in the latter part of the eighteenth century:

"The ordinary food of the farmer's family, though abundant, was of the simplest, demanding the sauce of good appetite and sound digestive powers. Tables 'groaned,' but chiefly under the weight of 'bean porridge hot and bean porridge cold,' brown bread, hominy or hasty-pudding and milk, pork, salt beef boiled, salt and fresh fish, succotash and the commonest vegetables in their season. Molasses and honey sufficed for sweetening, sugar being costly, and rarely used except in sickness or in entertaining guests. The top shelf at the village store held a row of white cones wrapped in purple paper. One of these 'loaves,' weighing eight or ten pounds, was about a year's supply of sugar to the ordinary family. The paper wrap was carefully saved and utilized in the dyeing of yarn."[5]

Of these items of diet all but the salt, the sugar, and perhaps the molasses were supplied by the family. Meal and flour, to be sure, though derived from the farmer's grains, were ground at the local grist mill. The men slaughtered the animals and the women cured the meat. The latter also made butter, cheese, and lard. Maple syrup and sugar were often produced on the farm, where nature furnished the raw materials. Tea, coffee, and chocolate were but little used prior to the Revolution.[6]

Within the family, as already suggested, there was a careful division of labor, tasks being allotted to all members according to sex, age, strength, and special ability. Moreover, being comparatively independent of the outside world, the family could organize its energies and resources with some degree of rationality. Within the limits set by productive capacity it could co-ordinate production and consumption and

[5] Henry S. Nourse, *History of Harvard, Massachusetts* (Harvard, 1894), 100.
[6] Percy Wells Bidwell and John I. Falconer, *op. cit.*, 127.

transmute economic gains into leisure, security, and cultural improvement. An over-supply of non-perishable goods would have been unthinkable. A surplus merely made it possible for all to go fishing. Abundance meant an easing of the physical struggle, unless the individual or family cared to devote itself to mere wealth-accumulation, as no doubt often happened. But the point to be emphasized is that at this time in American history the economy was fairly self-contained, and elementary planning, on the scale and in the terms required, was the common practice. The fact that the economy of the household was extremely simple and easily manageable by crude methods of calculation and control does not alter the situation. Economic planning is no new thing in American or human history. The scope of its operations has merely been immeasurably widened.

Being comparatively self-contained in its economy, the pre-industrial family was equally self-contained in most other things. In the physical care of its members it relied for the most part on its own resources. Standards of consumption and living conditions were not only a strictly family concern, but were also quickly and easily responsive to family energy, talent, and industry. The relevant factors were in large measure within the range of family control, as limited by the level of contemporary knowledge. Questions of sanitation, of guarding food and water and milk supply from pollution, of securing air and sunshine and protection from noise and smoke and ugly surroundings did not trouble men in that age. The Indian was perhaps less dangerous than the automobile. Sickness and accident were usually treated by "home remedies" of folk origin or by the nearest clergyman who in early colonial times was supposed to minister to the needs of the body as well as to those of the soul.[7] Even on the southern plantation "each family had its own medicine-chest, and its own recipes and prescriptions handed down from genera-

[7] James Truslow Adams, *op. cit.*, 60.

tion to generation, and brought oftentimes from across the sea."[8] The state of medical science was backward; the provision for medical training was in its infancy; hospitals were practically unknown; and physicians "were few and far between." According to one report "a list of prominent citizens in Baltimore in the eighteenth century, includes a barber, two carpenters, a teacher, a parson, and an inn-keeper, but no doctor," unless the category is made to include midwives.[9] Says Francis R. Packard, "It has been estimated that at the outset of the War for Independence there were upward of three thousand five hundred practitioners of medicine in the colonies, of whom not more than four hundred had received medical degrees."[10] The family assumed directly the larger part of the burden of caring for the sick. Also it provided protection for the weak and an asylum for the aged.

A third major function discharged by the family was the education of the young. Although in colonial Massachusetts the state sought to establish primary schools at public expense as early as 1642, the masses of the people enjoyed little schooling in America prior to the nineteenth century. Even in Puritan Massachusetts the laws designed to secure school support and attendance were honored more frequently in the breach than in the observance, at least after the spiritual zeal of the early colonists had cooled. Moreover, in this commonwealth definite educational responsibilities were placed upon the family. During the period of 1660 to 1672 families were ordered to teach "their children and apprentices so much learning as may enable them perfectly to read the English tongue and knowledge of the capital laws."[11] But before the rise of industrial civilization the need for schooling was extremely limited. Education was overwhelmingly non-scholas-

8 Maud Wilder Goodwin, *The Colonial Cavalier* (Boston, 1894), 277.
9 *Ibid.*, 277.
10 Francis R. Packard, *History of Medicine in the United States* (New York, 1931), I, 273.
11 Arthur W. Calhoun, *A Social History of the American Family* (Cleveland, 1917), I, 72.

tic in character and, except for the moral and religious education of the church, was provided almost exclusively in the
home and neighborhood.

In the wider sphere of cultural activities the family discharged other important social responsibilities. It was the
chief agency for providing recreation for the population. In
country districts the great distances and the primitive means
of communication tended to limit social contacts and to force
the family to rely upon its own resources for amusement and
entertainment. The high birth-rate, resulting frequently in
families of ten or twelve children and occasionally in families
of even twenty or twenty-five, added to these resources. Also,
and particularly among the Puritans, the family performed
essential religious functions. Likewise it tended to transmit
from generation to generation its cultural possessions, its
artistic traditions, its moral standards, and its general outlook
upon life. It thus served to perpetuate itself with considerable
fidelity. Little wonder therefore that Samuel H. Smith,
an ardent democrat and a writer on education in the early
days of the republic, viewed parental authority as a major
obstacle to the building of a better society. "Error is never
more dangerous than in the mouth of a parent," he said.
"Prejudices are as hereditary as titles."[12]

The status, privileges, and duties of the several members
of the pre-industrial household were those of the patriarchal
family which the American people had inherited from their
European forebears—an institution derived from feudal society and designed to transfer family name and landed estate
from father to son through a line of legitimate heirs. The
husband and father, as chief provider and head of the
family, was entitled to honor, respect, and obedience from the
other members of the household. It was the duty of the
wife to rear the children, keep the home, perform innumer-

[12] Samuel H. Smith, *Remarks on Education* (written 1796) (Philadelphia, Printed for J. Ormrod, 1798), 64.

able industrial tasks, and generally minister to the needs of the husband. While her comforts varied with social and economic status, her position with respect to man was much the same in all ranks. If unmarried, the woman was customarily forced into a subordinate role in the household of some male relative. Children were required to be industrious and obedient to the will of the father, even in such matters as education, choice of occupation, and selection of a companion in marriage. Although practice and equity often softened the rigors of the common law, within the family circle there was none to dispute legally the rule of husband and father. The double standard of morals was generally accepted: woman was expected to be the flower of virtue—virgin before and chaste after marriage; man might sow his wild oats and even violate the nuptial bond without fear of disgrace. While this patriarchal tradition changed slowly during the colonial period and presented different facets in the several colonies, it remained substantially unimpaired to the last quarter of the eighteenth century.

THE IMPACT OF NEW FORCES

The period that witnessed the founding of the republic also saw two powerful movements gain momentum—movements which, though radically unlike and in some respects antagonistic, contained common elements and re-enforced each other at certain points. The one was the westward expansion which swept from the Alleghanies to the Pacific in a single century, rather than the one thousand years predicted by Jefferson. The other was the rise of industrialism, the march of the machine, the growth of cities, the close integration of life on a large scale. Both of these movements tended to modify, to disorganize, and eventually to destroy the relatively self-sustained, patriarchal family of the pre-industrial age.

The Westward Expansion. The distinctive American contribution to the family pattern came with the movement beyond the Alleghanies and the consequent growth of the spirit of democracy and individualism. The very fact that the family was the major vehicle for carrying European civilization across the continent was profoundly significant. Undoubtedly the frontier encouraged the high birth-rate which prevailed in the United States until the middle of the nineteenth century; and the high birth-rate in turn made possible the rapid advance of the frontier to the Pacific. When land could be had for the taking, when life was simple and hard, when labor was scarce, a large progeny was deemed both an asset and an evidence of the favor of God. But it was the general condition of equality and the absence of all hereditary ranks, so emphasized by De Tocqueville, that most affected the traditional family. Where economic differences were small and property could be easily acquired, the mercenary marriage was destined to disappear. Similarly, where women were scarce and where the spirit of democracy prevailed and class distinctions were frowned upon, the question of the social rank of the contracting parties rapidly lost its significance. Also, where the individual was capable of challenging the authority of the group, parental restraint and community control were weakened. Banns were abolished and the requirment for publicity dropped. Under the impact of the frontier the individuals directly concerned came to regard marriage as their exclusive affair. A necessary corollary of this attitude was the demand for easy divorce. And Indiana, a pioneer state, allowed the courts to dissolve a union for any cause they saw fit. The vicissitudes of life on the frontier encouraged the formation of unions on slight acquaintance and the frequent and prolonged separation of the partners to the marriage bond.

Scarcity of labor and freedom of movement altered the status of the child. The early assumption of economic responsibilities led to rapid maturity and emancipation from prolonged parental control. Boys became men and girls became women at an unbelievably early age. Moreover, in a country of boundless resources, inviting youth to seek their fortunes in the west, patriarchal exactions could not be enforced. The consequent laxness of family discipline and the boldness and impudence of children naturally called forth considerable unfavorable comment. Some critics even contended that the stability of the nation was menaced by the decay of government in the home. Although many parents continued to exhibit traditional zeal in the training of their children and although the old religious influence was by no means extinct, the spirit of individualism was gaining ascendancy and heralding that emancipation of the child which was to grow to ripe fruition in the early years of the twentieth century.

Along with other forces at work in the first half of the nineteenth century, the westward expansion tended to destroy the unity of the family. European travelers during this period often commented on the absence of affection in American life. Indubitably the weakening of the economic bonds of the family led to some loosening of sentimental attachments. As already observed, the abundance of opportunities in the new land moderated the dependence of children on their parents and the migrations toward the setting sun from generation to generation almost established a tradition of the severance of family ties. The growth of individualism, the urgent demands of practical affairs, and the equal division of property among children combined to undermine, not only the foundations of the patriarchal system, but even the unity of the family itself. The development of public education reduced the role of the home in an important sphere; religious and political differences often turned son against father and brother against brother; and the spirit of independence, nurtured by the frontier, fostered the substitution of the court for the family council in the adjustment of grievances. Despite these weakening tendencies, however, home life was often marked by a large measure of mutual respect, esteem, and affection.

The Rise of Industrial Civilization. The growth of industrial civilization with its system of factory production and urban conditions re-enforced at some points the influence of the frontier. Although this development may be said to date from the establishment of a cotton mill in Rhode Island by Samuel Slater in 1790, the household was still the center of manufacturing at the beginning of the nineteenth century. In 1816 the great majority of the 2512 looms and 2700 spinning wheels in Indiana were in private cabins. Even in Massachusetts most of the articles in domestic use before 1836 were made from materials grown on the farms and fabricated in the homes of the state. Since industrialism took to the factories work that had previously been done in the home, the majority of the earlier mill workers were the daughters of yeomen. Many wives continued to labor in their homes, while taking their products to the mills. "The processes carried on in the first factories," writes Edith Abbott, "were those of carding and spinning, and the women and girls, therefore, who went into the factories to operate the new machines, were doing what had always been women's work. They had taken over no new employment, but the manner of carrying on the old had been changed."[13]

One of the early arguments for the introduction of the factory system into America, an argument supported by no less a man than Alexander Hamilton, was that it would make possible the utilization of the labor of women and children who might otherwise be idle. This line of reasoning appealed strongly to the Puritan mind. The labor force of the first factory consisted wholly of a woman and her children. At this time there was no thought that men would go into the mills, except as foremen and directors. Since, with the abundance of free land, every man might become an independent

[13] Edith Abbott, *Women in Industry* (New York, 1909), 45.

freeholder, most men preferred to live by agriculture. In the Lowell mills in 1827,[14] nine-tenths of the employees were girls and young women from the surrounding country who worked for a few years and then returned to their homes to marry or went west to teach. Women found employment, moreover, not only in the cotton mills but also in establishments for the making of straw bonnets and the manufacture of buttons. And by 1850, according to the census, they had entered numerous other occupations such as cigar making, the clothing trades, the boot and shoe industry, and printing and publishing. In that year, 225,922 women and 731,137 men were employed in the manufacturing industries of the country.[15]

The effect of these developments on the family life of the masses was pronounced. In Connecticut and Rhode Island the father commonly sent his children into the factory and then collected a dollar or two a week for the services of each. The hours of labor were long, often from twelve to fifteen hours a day; and after men entered industry they were forced to compete with women and children. The situation was aggravated by the fact that many women were not wholly dependent on their jobs, but worked for "pin-money," while awaiting the day of marriage. In this competition men were forced to accept reduced wages, and then to enlist the support of wife and children to maintain a minimum standard of living. After a long day in the factory congenial home life was practically impossible. The position of woman became increasingly difficult. If she went into industry, she was subject to severe fatigue and overwork; if she remained in the home, she could bring little economic return to the family.

The progress of industrialization was accompanied by urbanization and the growth of the bourgeoisie and the

14 *Ibid.*, 121.
15 *Ibid.*, 81. Harriet Martineau cites only five occupations open to women in America in the early thirties. They were teaching, needlework, mill work, work in printing offices, and the keeping of boarding houses.

aristocracy of capitalism. Among these classes, from the eigh-teen-thirties on, a rage for luxury and conspicuous consump-tion developed. Female apparel became a source of great ex-travagance and women were encouraged to lead a more or less parasitical existence. The affectation was fostered that the feminine sex is fashioned from a finer clay and should be protected from the world. Thus woman assumed the form of a lovely, but expensive, ornament to embellish the estate of the successful male. As a result, among the aspiring classes, marriage, being extremely costly, was discouraged. Economic alliances increased and fortune hunters appeared in the land. Because of the high rents, the servant problem, and the de-cline of domesticity, those who did marry were reluctant to establish homes and often were to be found living in hotels and boarding houses. Under such conditions the old family life was impossible; and the children, being turned over to servant girls, suffered from malnutrition, excitement, and promiscuous associates.

In large cities during the second half of the nineteenth cen-tury, fecundity showed a marked decrease and the practice of abortion became common. In New York City premature and still-births multiplied more than twenty-seven times while the population grew but six-fold.[16] While these figures may be accounted for in part by improvement in registration, they also mark the beginning of "race suicide" among the more favored classes. The dangers of female parasitism and the question of giving women a means of livelihood independent of marriage were discussed in the press. It should be noted that among the poor circumstances had forced wives and mothers into industry long before the opportunities of higher education and access to the professions were really opened to the daughters of the middle classes. Although the tenden-cies observed were far from universal among urban dwellers, after the Civil War the forces of the rising industrialism were

[16]Arthur Calhoun, op. cit., II, 210.

of greater significance in shaping matrimonial institutions than the independent spirit of democracy that had been generated by the frontier. The city was already well on its way to dominion in the United States.

THE MODERN FAMILY

The early twentieth century has seen the fulfillment of the prophecies of the preceding generations. The patriarchal family brought from beyond the Atlantic has been all but destroyed. The democratic individualism of the frontier served to emancipate both women and children from tradition; and the forces of industrialism shattered the self-sufficient domestic economy, reduced the prestige of husband and father, widened the gap between parent and child, and even threatened to disrupt the home. The pressure of earning a livelihood, or of achieving an ever higher standard of living for their families, has left many men little time to keep in touch with their children, while opportunities for higher education, increased leisure, and economic independence among women of the favored classes have increased the influence of the mother in the household. At the same time the state has declared that the father is no longer master in his own family and has forced him to send his children to school, to submit to various health regulations, to accept the ruling of the juvenile court on the treatment of a delinquent child, and to keep his sons and daughters out of the labor market until early or even later adolescence. Also his wife is often in revolt. Increasingly she refuses to promise obedience in the marriage ceremony and asserts her individuality by keeping her own name and working outside the home. And in most states the law has decreed that she is mistress of her property and earnings.[17]

17 *Survey of the Legal Status of Women in the Forty-Eight States,* National League of Women Voters (New York, 1930), 9–19.

Changes in Family Function. The family, moreover, has not only lost its ancient authority; it has also lost many of its former functions. With the growth of industrialism and the division of labor, numerous economic activities have departed from the home never to return. This process may be said to have begun with the transference of spinning and weaving to the mills. Later, in varying measure, candle-making, soap manufacture, canning, cooking, washing, and sewing took the road to the factory. The extent of this shift of function is revealed in the statistics on the growth of the industries which have taken over the household tasks of earlier times. Thus the figures show that bakeries, canning factories, and power laundries have increased much more rapidly than the population. Similarly the growth of restaurants is evidence of the decline of the family kitchen; and the reduced popularity of the sewing machine, combined with an expansion of the women's clothing industry, is evidence that less garment-making is being done in the household. According to a sample study, baker's bread is being used in two-thirds of the farm homes, three-fourths of the town homes, and in 90 per cent of the urban homes of the country.[18] Laundering is done in only 33 per cent of the city households, though it is still carried on in 88 per cent of the rural homes.

These data indicate not only that domestic industry is declining, but also that it is declining much more rapidly in the city than in the country. An investigation of the time devoted to housekeeping duties showed that most of the tasks covered by the study received slightly more time in the city than in the farm homes, while the number of children was lower for the urban family. The significance of this inquiry lies in the fact that it reveals homemaking still to be an important function in many households, with the home-maker spending an

---

[18] W. F. Ogburn, "The Family and Its Functions" in The President's Research Committee on Social Trends, *Recent Social Trends in the United States* (New York, 1933), I, 664.

average of forty-five hours a week on her job. These facts suggest that despite the great changes enumerated, the family continues to discharge important economic obligations.

The economic functions of the home, however, have been greatly altered. Under the agrarian regime they were primarily productive in character: today they have to do largely with consumption. The task of purchasing goods and services for the household, a task that scarcely existed in the day of the relatively self-sufficient family unit, has taken the place of production as the central economic interest. Moreover, not only are the goods formerly produced in the home now bought in the market, but many things are demanded that the colonial matron knew nothing about. A study of the net per capita output[19] of a number of selected commodities from 1919–1931 reveals some of the changes which have taken place recently in the field of consumption. In even so brief a period striking shifts appeared in the production and use of different types of food. The consumption of such staples as grain products and potatoes—foods requiring a considerable amount of preparation—gradually declined. At the same time the use of dairy and bakery products, fresh fruits and vegetables, and canned and prepared foods of all kinds, such as fish, meats, fruits, soups, and vegetables, expanded. As a consequence of these changes, the amount of time and energy going into mere preparation of food must have been considerably reduced. The increased consumption of flavorings, ice cream, chocolate, and cocoa products no doubt reflects the substitution of the soda fountain lunch for the mid-day meal at home. The growing sales of all forms of electrical equipment and particularly of those that lighten the burden of cooking, register further changes in the economic functions of the family.

The consumption of other classes of household goods shows similar trends.[20] Thus the sale of living room furniture has

19 R. S. Lynd assisted by Alice C. Hanson, "The People as Consumers" in *ibid.*, II, 902–906.
20 *Ibid.*, 904.

risen sufficiently to offset the decline in the use of practically all other types of furnishings. Combined with an enormous increase in the purchase of window draperies, this shows a tendency toward the "dressing up of the living room as the most socially conspicuous part of the house." The buying of clothes has also changed greatly during the past generation. The mania of style, which now controls the market, has created a demand for more dresses and the ensembling of outfits, and has accelerated the rate of obsolescence of women's apparel. And the spread of advertising and high-pressure salesmanship has made intelligent buying imperative, at a time when intelligent buying is all but impossible. In making the choices involved in the purchase of the multitudinous goods used in the modern home, the housewife has little to guide her through the maze created by ingenious advertisements, changing fashions, and the bewildering number of local and national brands. Here is a tremendous task of economic education that the rise of industry, founded on the institutions of private capitalism, has placed upon the home.

Another important function that the family has discharged from primitive times, and particularly under conditions of pioneer life in America, is that of providing protection and security for its members. In modern society this function is being transferred to other agencies. Life and property are now guarded by police, detectives, watchmen, soldiers, firemen, and numerous inspectors and officials employed by the state. Also institutions for the care of the sick and the mentally and physically defective are maintained increasingly under both public and private auspices. In urban communities child-birth is being transferred more and more to hospitals; and everywhere the aged who have been struck down by poverty are being cared for by special homes or annuities. Industrial laborers are protected by workmen's compensation laws or employer's liability acts; widows are aided in the support of their children by mothers' pensions and family aid societies; while minors are protected by juvenile courts and child labor laws.

The fickleness of fortune has caused many individuals to seek security from old age and death in insurance and trust companies. In the thirty years from 1899 to 1929, endowment policies increased 800 per cent.[21] Family budgetary studies[22] also show that 87 to 94 per cent of the working class and clerical families investigated were paying substantial premiums on life, accident, and health insurance. However, under normal circumstances the family remains the main support of its members and bears chief responsibility for future security through savings, investment, and insurance. An investigation of 506 families of government employees[23] revealed that in 288, or more than half, expenses exceeded income, in 112 income exceeded expenses, and in 106 the account was balanced. These facts, as well as others to be presented in a later chapter, show how inequalities in the distribution of income unfit many families to discharge the traditional responsibilities toward their members. Poverty in the home makes impossible the achievement of the American ideal of equality of opportunity.

Certain educational functions were early taken over by the state. First through schools for paupers' children and later through free public schools, extending from the kindergarten through the university, the state has trespassed upon the territory of the family. Today a parent who wishes to teach his child at home may find himself thwarted by the compulsory education laws; and the school is gradually extending its sway. When reading and writing and arithmetic were being taught in "the little red school house," the family continued to train its younger members in the practical arts of the house, the farm, and the shop. But in recent generations even the vocational preparation of the young has been

21 W. F. Ogburn, *op. cit.*, 673.   22 R. S. Lynd, *op. cit.*, 894.
23 Bureau of Labor Statistics, *Monthly Labor Review* (Washington, August, 1929), 41.

assumed in considerable measure by the state and corporate industry. Instruction in cooking, sewing, and laundering is given in courses of home economics, while the mechanic arts and the science of agriculture are taught in high school and college. Yet the point should be emphasized, that in spite of loss of function the family remains the most powerful educational agency in society. While it may not teach certain special skills and knowledges that have become identified with "education" in the popular mind, it still is almost entirely responsible for the mental and moral development of the child during the first six years of life. It should be recalled, however, that in the sphere of education the family is an agency, not for improving society, but rather for the perpetuation of the existing order with all of its inequalities.

In the sphere of religion the influence of the home has also probably tended to decrease. Certainly the American people are less pious and less given to ecclesiastical enthusiasms than were their colonial ancestors. The declining church attendance has no doubt been followed by relaxation of all forms of family worship. Even in homes that perpetuate the strong religious tradition of the past, much of the teaching of Bible verses and religious precepts has unquestionably been transferred to the Sunday School and confined to the Sabbath day. According to a recent study of pupils in the seventh, eighth, and ninth grades of public schools, only one American-born white child in eight participates in family prayers. There is evidence, however, of a large difference between the rural and the urban family. The former is almost twice as likely to send its children to church as the latter. In country districts the institutions of the older America still persist.

Another area in which the family has lost ground is that of recreation. Although the growth of commercial amusements may be traced in part to the reduction of hours of labor, the increase of wealth and income, and the conversion of Sunday into a day of play, it also represents a decline in the influence of the home. Among the competing recreational agencies which have developed with great rapidity during the past few decades are municipal parks, bathing beaches, athletic clubs, public playgrounds, schools and colleges, the cinema, and the radio.[24] The fact that a large part of recreation is now being provided by public, co-operative, and commercial enterprises, however, does not mean that the family is wholly out of the picture. Indeed radio, though commercially sponsored, tends to take recreation back into the home, even though it may place control in other hands. According to the 1930 census, 40.3 per cent of the families of the country possessed receiving sets. The family, moreover, may still exercise some control over recreation pursued outside the home. An investigation of group activities carried on by parents and children showed that family walks and attendance at the movies were twice as frequent in the city as in the country.[25]

That the changes enumerated have greatly weakened the family is obvious. The decline in the productive functions of the home has meant a corresponding decline in the economic value of housewife and children and an increase in family expenditures for the purchase of goods and services. In other words the household has been swallowed up in a vast and intricate pecuniary economy. At the same time the opening of numerous occupations to women has emancipated them from financial dependence on marriage. The family has lost or is losing its ancient economic supports. It no longer rests on the solid foundations of property interests.

Changes in Family Structure. Changes in family functions have naturally led to changes in family structure. Particularly basic is a decrease in the size of the household. The census reports that the average size of the family has decreased from 4.7 in 1900 to 4.5 in 1910, to 4.3 in 1920, and to

24 See below, Part Two, Chapter VI, "Recreation."
25 W. F. Ogburn, *op. cit.,* 675–676.

4.1 in 1930.[26] "In 1900 each one hundred households had 63 servants, relations, lodgers and boarders, but in 1920 the number had dropped to 49 and in 1930 to only 44, . . . which may perhaps be indicative of the declining economic functions of the family."[27] The greatest changes in family structure are of course to be found in the city, where the institution has been most fully exposed to the impact of industrialism. There the reduction of the birth-rate and the increase in the number of childless marriages have been most marked. Two-thirds of the families studied in New Haven contained no child under five years of age, one-half no child under ten, and one-third no child under twenty-one. The small household of the city may of course be due to a tendency on the part of people with children to move to the suburbs. "Standards of family life in suburban communities," says E. C. Lindeman, "tend to conserve the rural ideal whereas other types of activity tend toward the urban pattern. It may be said, therefore, that the suburban community is a kind of family community brought into existence because of the strength of the family impulse, and in opposition to the urban trend."[28]

Reduction of family size and function has in turn affected the housing pattern. Changes in dwelling arrangements are particularly evident in rapidly growing urban and metropolitan areas where style is more responsive to demand. It is reported from Denver that "the smaller number of children per family, lessened interest in the home as a social center . . . the transfer of space-using kitchen and laundry activities to commercial enterprises, and the decreased portion of the family income available for home purchase and maintenance are typical changes which lead to the insistent demand

[26] News Release, Department of Commerce, Bureau of the Census (Washington, November 30, 1931).
[27] W. F. Ogburn, op. cit., 682.
[28] E. C. Lindeman, "Sociological Backgrounds of Family Life" in Parent Education, White House Conference on Child Health and Protection, III A (New York, 1932), 5.

for smaller and smaller living units."[29] At present over 50 per cent of the new homes in cities are in multi-family dwellings. In Chicago and New York trends in housing have been very similar. Whereas 45 per cent of the apartments constructed in Chicago from 1913 to 1917 contained less than five rooms, the corresponding figure for the years 1927 to 1931 was 75 per cent.[30] In New York the average number of rooms per apartment declined from 4.19 for apartments built in 1913 to 3.34 for those built in 1928.[31] Also in this same city new apartments with less than four rooms constituted 33.6 per cent of total construction in 1918 and 77.3 per cent in 1928.

These drastic changes are affecting family habits in many respects: the lawn and garden have disappeared, heating and lighting are handled by specialists, odd jobs about the home are hard to find, and the cultural resources of the family lie increasingly beyond the apartment walls. The personal home is passing.[32] With it is also passing the pride in appearance and ownership which in former times was of great importance in giving status to the family. Fine houses are being replaced by standardized dwellings. And with the increasing mobility of the population the family refuses to form enduring attachments anywhere.

The impact of social mobility on the family merits extended analysis. The phenomenon has numerous and varied manifestations. In its most conspicuous form it is simple territorial mobility, that is, the movement of individuals from place to place in pusuit of business, pleasure, or personal cultivation. Other types of mobility are the shifting of individuals from job to job and factory to factory; the change of occupation

[29] Quoted from *Denver Business Review*, by R. S. Lynd, *op. cit.*, 865.

[30] W. F. Ogburn, *op. cit.*, 667.

[31] T. S. Adams and W. D. Heydecker, "Housing Conditions in the New York Region," in *Regional Survey of New York and Its Environs* (New York, 1931), VI, 238.

[32] *New York Times*, April 18, 1932. Release of report on Housing and Architecture prepared for the Report of the President's Research Committee on Social Trends, by L. B. Holland.

within the lifetime of the individual; the failure of the son to follow in the footsteps of the father; and the climbing and descending of the social ladder. Each of these forms of social mobility is peculiarly manifest in the United States.

Territorial mobility, always characteristic of the American people, has been enormously accelerated by mechanical progress. Undoubtedly individuals in the United States today change their places of residence more often, spend more time in motion, and cover more ground in their travels, than the people of any other epoch or country of recorded history. Whereas formerly territorial migration was limited to a narrow circle around the place of birth, now it encompasses the globe. In 1920, according to the federal census, only 67.2 per cent of the inhabitants of the country were residing in the state in which they had been born. But this figure gives a wholly inadequate measure of the extent of the movement of population within the country.[33] The statistics of street car rides, railway passenger service, and the number and use of automobiles help to fill out the picture.[34] With the shifting of residence from one place to another, either through the nomadic movement from apartment to apartment, from neighborhood to neighborhood, or from community to community, local patriotism fades away and attachment to native soil and hearth loses its strength. Such mobility, moreover, means contact with conflicting mores, the loosening of the controls exercised by the neighborhood group, and the weakening of the influence of the home on the children. When the members of a family disperse to widely separated communities, the sense of unity cannot be maintained. Under modern conditions the family no longer persists through the years but rather forms, breaks up, and re-forms in the lifetime of each generation.

Shifting from job to job is a second form of social mobility

33 Pitirim Sorokin, *Social Mobility* (New York, 1927), 383.
34 See below, Part Two, Chapter III, "Communication."

that is widespread in America and that profoundly affects family life. Investigations have shown that an annual labor turnover of about 100 per cent is normal for industry and that during "good times" it may rise to 400 per cent. According to an investigation made in 1913–1914 only 32.9 per cent of the employees in certain plants had worked on the job for five years or more, while 13.1 had worked three months or less. Four years later the corresponding figures were 27.8 per cent and 18.7 per cent respectively. The tenure of clerks and teachers is almost equally unstable. Among women clerical workers only 24.1 per cent had worked over five years in the same position.[35]

A change in occupation belongs to a somewhat higher order of magnitude than a shift in position because it usually registers a rise or fall in the social status of the individual and family involved. An examination of the records of insurance policy holders showed that 58.5 per cent had changed their occupations during the period following issuance of policy. Only 42.5 per cent of college graduates investigated had not shifted callings some years after graduation. Apparently only the smallest fraction of the population fails to change vocations at least once during a lifetime.[36] While instability varies with occupational level, being highest among unskilled laborers and lowest among business and professional workers, it touches all classes and introduces an element of uncertainty with respect to the future. Practically every family consequently has secret or avowed hopes of wealth and fears of poverty.

The stability of the family from generation to generation is dependent in part on the transmission of occupation from father to son. In the relatively static societies of the past such transmission was the rule; in America today it even seems to be becoming exceptional. It shows greatest strength in those classes in which family status is high and in those occu-

[35] Pitirim Sorokin, op. cit., 394–397.   [36] Ibid., 424 ff.

pations which require technical experience and specialization, which are most highly remunerative, and which are associated with social prestige and privilege. But it seems to have weakened rapidly during the last three or four generations. According to one inquiry, whereas 72 per cent of the grandfathers pursued the occupation of the great-grandfather and 38.9 per cent of the fathers pursued the occupation of the grandfather, only 10.6 per cent of the sons followed in the footsteps of the father.[37] Particularly do the children of farmers seem to abandon the calling of the parent. Clearly the family has far less influence over the life of its members than it did in former times.

Marriage or birth into a particular family today is of much less consequence than in the past. To be sure, family may still mean poverty or riches, shame or honor for the individual, but in the course of a lifetime his own achievements, particularly if he is gifted and fortunate, count for more than status of parent or spouse. The very phenomenon of rapid change, so it has been observed, makes the differences between generations appear greater than the differences btween families, if extremes are disregarded. The growth of the large city and the relative decline of the neighborhood tend to diminish family prestige, except in the case of the very rich and socially powerful, when the reverse seems to be true. As sons and daughters in ever-increasing numbers leave the parental fireside and seek to carve out their fortunes in distant places, the strength of family influence declines. More and more is the individual of ordinary parentage forced to make his own way in the world.

All of these forces tending to alter the family of tradition seem to converge in the steady and rapid growth of divorce, separation, and desertion. Social mobility in its several forms, since it inevitably weakens primary group controls

[37] This doubtless is due in part to the relative decline in agriculture, the increasing complexity of the occupational life, and the phenomenal growth in the number of occupational categories.

and frees the individual from the domination of the environment of his childhood, provides the opportunity for severing the matrimonial bonds. A recent study[38] suggests that frequent change of residence is closely related to divorce. At any rate the control group was found to be more stable than the divorce group, both as to permanence of dwelling and average number of years in the community. Moreover, whereas the latter tended toward areas of higher disorganization, the former inclined toward districts of lower disorganization. The mobility of city life and the disintegration of the family appear to go hand in hand. Ernest R. Mowrer has thus summarized his findings:

"With the breakdown in neighborhood control in the city, resulting from the constant movement from one social situation to another, the individual is freed from the usual social restraints which function so effectively in the country and upon which much of the stability of social organization in the past has been built. And while this may not in all instances result in the production of attitudes in conflict with group standards, it does facilitate the expression of such attitudes by breaking down the repressive and coercive control of the primary group."[39]

The growth of divorce has naturally brought new family types and much matrimonial experimentation. The New Haven study found many households composed of a single parent and children. Divorce statistics, moreover, seem to indicate that broken homes will continue to increase in the immediate future. The United States now has the highest divorce rate in the world, one marriage in every six ending in the domestic relations courts. The data of the federal census reveal broken homes among 14.6 per cent of the families of the country. Among Chicago school children a higher rate has been

[38] Ernest R. Mowrer, *The Family* (Chicago, 1932), 206.
[39] *Ibid.*, 206.

found, and among delinquent children a yet higher rate has been recorded. The rate in the city is twice that of the surrounding country; it is higher among the rich than in any other class, while desertion is most frequent among the poor. In the early years of marriage the most common grounds of divorce are cruelty and adultery, in the middle years neglect, and thereafter desertion and drunkenness.[40] Children seem to be a stabilizing factor in the family: only 8 per cent of the couples having children resort to the courts, while 71 per cent of childless marriages end in divorce.

The disruption of the family accompanying the growth of industrialism and urbanization has raised in the minds of many the question of the future of monogamy. Here perhaps is the most fundamental issue in the whole field of the relations between the sexes. On the one hand, the defenders of tradition hold that monogamy is the basis of organized society and offers the only practicable method of providing for child nurture and responsible parenthood. On the other hand, the critics of the old order argue that monogamy is no longer possible; that the refusal to recognize this fact has led to evasion, hypocrisy, and injustice; and that increasing individualism in personal life requires the social recognition of various types of matrimonial union. They go further, moreover, and contend that divorce, if followed by remarriage, is not compatible with strict monogamy and is in fact a sort of "serial polygamy." It is also well-known, they point out, that other sexual arrangements coincident with marriage are entered into by both sexes. Even while the family group holds together, the wife may practise polite adultery and the husband may visit a prostitute, maintain a mistress, or have a love affair with some woman of independent means. The anonymity of the individual in the complex society of the present undoubtedly tends to foster such relationships. Also the development of increasingly effective contraceptive devices makes possible the partial separation of

[40] Alfred Cahen, *Statistical Analysis of American Divorce* (New York, 1932), 40.

the sexual and reproductive functions, frees woman from fear of the natural biological consequences of the sexual act, and removes the dangers to legitimate inheritance that formerly lurked in illicit practices. Also it has doubtless contributed much to the current rapid trend toward a stationary population.

Attempts to deal with this situation have led to cults of free love, trial marriages, and companionate unions. All of these proposals are founded on the practice of birth control and on the principle that the relation should be contingent on the duration of affection. Free love would dispense with the marriage ceremony and all bonds enforced by society; trial marriage would stress the importance of successful sex adjustment and would make the permanent union depend on a mutually satisfactory trial of sex relations; companionate marriage would emphasize the value of common interests and provide for entrance into marriage in the normal legal manner but with the understanding that the bearing of children should await the testing of the relationship.

This threefold challenge to monogamy has been called forth largely by the harshness of divorce and alimony laws that seek to perpetuate the marriage relation beyond the wishes of the parties involved. Proposals for meeting it involve the adoption of more strict marriage regulations, the passage of more lenient divorce laws, and provision for the responsible use of contraceptive devices. The period immediately ahead is certain to witness extensive and radical changes in the sphere of matrimonial relationship. The family of the pre-industrial era has already passed away.

THE CHANGING POSITION OF WOMAN

The forces that have altered the functions and structure of the family have at the same time changed the position of woman. Her economic duties were modified both by life on the frontier and by the rise of industrialism. The former

placed heavy responsibilities on the shoulders of wife and
mother; the latter took women in increasing numbers out of
the home and gave them a degree of financial independence.
But this shift in economic position was only a part of a vast
movement which led to the overthrow of the traditional conception of the nature of the female sex and to the emancipation
of woman from numerous disabilities under which she had suffered through the ages. She has not only abandoned in part the
ancient role of child-rearing, housekeeping, and servant of
man; she has also refused to be physically weak, intellectually
inferior, and emotionally unstable. She has tried her hand with
success at practically all of the occupations, shown proficiency
in most of the "manly" sports, taken honors in the institutions
of higher learning, made political conquests of a revolutionary
character, and carved out a place for herself in literature and
the arts. While the struggle is still in progress, it has proceeded far enough to make any return to the old order unthinkable.

The Eighteenth-Century Ideal. The nature and the extent
of the changes already recorded may be indicated by reference
to the past. As late as the early nineteenth century the status
of woman in the common law was akin to that of a chattel
who worked without wages and had no career in prospect outside of wedlock. As a child her services belonged to her father;
with marriage they were transferred to her husband. "Marriage," says Arthur W. Calhoun, "reduced her to a subordinate and cramped position. She was expected to embrace her
husband's religion, to confine her activities to the home, and
to make her husband's pleasure her guiding star."[41] The life
of a spinster, making her a dependent in the household of
some male relative, had nothing to recommend it. The education of woman, which was suited to her humble sphere, was
in close accord with Rousseau's view that "the whole education
of women ought to be relative to men. To please them, to be

[41] Arthur W. Calhoun, *op. cit.*, II, 83.

useful to them, to make themselves loved and honored by them, to educate them when young, to care for them when grown, to counsel them, to console them, and to make life agreeable and sweet to them—these are the duties of women at all times, and what should be taught them from their infancy."[42] Early attempts to broaden the education of woman were opposed on the grounds that they would beget in her a distaste for the pleasures of domesticity and unfit her for the duties of family life.

In supporting the traditional conception of the status of woman in society the force of religion was brought into service. The following document, which represents the attitude of the orthodox clergy of Massachusetts toward the early woman's rights movement, outlines the traditional ideal of woman and gives some notion of the distance travelled since 1837:

"We invite your attention to the dangers which at present seem to threaten the female character with widespread and permanent injury.

"The appropriate duties and influence of women are clearly stated in the New Testament. Those duties and that influence are unobtrusive and private, but the source of mighty power. When the mild, dependent, softening influence of woman upon the sternness of man's opinions is fully exercised, society feels the effect of it in a thousand forms. The power of woman is her dependence, flowing from the consciousness of that weakness which God has given her for her protection, and which keeps her in those departments of life that form the character of individuals, and of the nation. There are social influences which females use in promoting piety and the great objects of Christian benevolence which we cannot too highly commend.

"We appreciate the unostentatious prayers and efforts of woman in advancing the cause of religion at home and abroad; in Sabbath schools; in leading religious inquirers to the pastors for instruction; and in all such associated effort as becomes

42 J. J. Rousseau, *Emile*, translated by William T. Payne (New York, 1926), 263.

the modesty of their sex; and earnestly hope that she may abound more and more in these labors of piety and love. But when she assumes the place and tone of man as a public reformer, our care and protection to her seem unnecessary; we put ourselves in self-defense against her; she yields the power which God has given her for her protection, and her character becomes unnatural. If the vine, whose strength and beauty is to lean upon the trellis work, and half conceal its clusters, thinks to assume the independence and overshadowing nature of the elm, it will not only cease to bear fruit, but fall in shame and dishonor into the dust. We cannot, therefore, but regret the mistaken conduct of those who encourage females to bear an obtrusive and ostentatious part in measures of reform, and countenance any of that sex who so far forget themselves as to itinerate in the character of public lecturers and teachers. We especially deplore the intimate acquaintance and conversation of females with regard to things which ought not to be named; by which that modesty and delicacy which is the charm of domestic life, and which constitutes the true influence of woman in society, is consumed, and the way opened, as we apprehend, for degeneracy and ruin. We say these things not to discourage proper influences against sin, but to secure such reformation as we believe is Scriptural, and will be permanent."[43]

The Battle for Equal Rights. The nineteenth century witnessed rapid and profound changes in the status of woman. In the early part of this period intelligent members of the sex became keenly aware of the indignity of their position and looked about for remedies. They soon saw that the crux of the problem was economic. So long as they were cut off from remunerative employment they would remain in a condition of dependence and servitude. Entrance into all vocational

[43] Extract from a Pastoral Letter of the General Association of Massachusetts to the churches under their care in 1837. From *The History of Woman Suffrage*, I, 81-82.

ranks, moreover, called for educational opportunities, legal rights, and political equality.

With increasing vigor, as the century advanced, the battle was waged on all fronts. Gradually gains were made. Ancient barriers to occupations were broken down. Oberlin College in the frontier state of Ohio opened its doors to men and women alike in 1833; modern statutes guaranteeing legal rights to women were enacted by state legislatures. A convention meeting at Seneca Falls in 1848, that famous year of revolution throughout the western world, drew up a declaration of the rights of women. In 1869 the National Woman Suffrage Association was founded; in the same year the territorial legislature of Wyoming gave women the vote; and in 1920 the Nineteenth Amendment to the Federal Constitution, granting women equal suffrage with men, was ratified and became a part of the supreme law of the land. Yet, as Miss Grace Abbott has pointed out, remarkable as this record of achievement is, the progress of women "during the past century must be measured less by their contributions than by the removal of legal, social, or economic barriers which have prevented them from making their contribution to our common life."[44] The ripe fruits of this struggle would therefore seem to lie in the future.

Economic Gains. Woman's battle for economic opportunities is only partly won: home-making, though under changed conditions, is still very generally regarded as her natural vocation. In the early years of the struggle the champions of the old order implored woman to pause and consider what would become of the home and of her own finer nature, if she were to take her place beside man in every field of labor. "The fatuity of these arguments," Mr. Calhoun points out, "was that while woman was depicted as the tender, clinging vine or as the presiding genius of the home, the census of 1860 showed one million women working by the side of men in various

[44] Grace Abbott, "The Changing Position of Women," in *A Century of Progress* (New York, 1933), 254.

domains of 'coarse, rough toil.' "[45] Apparently men who opposed the inexorable march of events were not interested in those members of the "gentler sex" who were forced out of the home by economic necessity.

Despite the opposition of conservative influences, women entered industry, the trades, and the professions in increasing numbers. Although in some callings they are still reluctantly accepted and are subjected to severe discrimination, they are now found in practically all vocations. The census of 1930 revealed 22.1 per cent of the female population ten years of age and older pursuing gainful occupations. Of the whole number thus employed 29.2 per cent were engaged in domestic and personal service; 22.4 per cent in manufacturing and mechanical industries; 16.4 per cent in professional service; and 15.9 per cent in trade.[46] Moreover, since 1880 the trend of employment has been definitely away from domestic occupations and toward store, office, and professional work.[47]

The position of the married woman employed outside the home is of peculiar interest. Although her number has increased steadily in the face of strong prejudice, her right to work is only grudgingly acknowledged. This perpetuation of prejudice is clearly revealed in the rules against the employment of married teachers in the majority of public school systems and in the widespread demand that married women should give up their positions during hard times.[48] Such practices would seem to indicate that women are welcome in the labor market only as a surplus to be drawn upon when needed. They also give evidence of the lingering of the tradition that the female should be dependent on the male. Since 29 per cent of the gainfully employed women are married and since each

[45] Op. cit., III, 86.
[46] News Release, Department of Commerce, Bureau of the Census (September 9, 1931).
[47] S. P. Breckinridge, "The Activities of Women Outside the Home," in Recent Social Trends in the United States, I, 717.
[48] Ibid., 715–716.

decennial period has seen a gradual increase in this ratio, the married woman is clearly in industry to stay. The percentage working outside the home varies of course in different sections of the country, being lowest in the agricultural states where to a considerable extent the family persists as a productive unit and highest in the District of Columbia where peculiarly urban conditions prevail most completely.[49] But everywhere the new dispensation gradually extends its sway.

Numerous studies point to economic pressure as the principal cause of the entrance of married women into the industry.[50] In the higher occupational groups this motive, unless it is made to include the desire for a higher standard of living for the family, is probably less controlling. An investigation of a small group of professional women, who were successful home-makers and mothers, revealed that in only 8 per cent of the cases was economic pressure the sole reason for working, while in 38 per cent financial necessity shared responsibility with other factors. Surplus energy was the only assigned cause for 48 per cent of the women and was part of a complex set of conditions for 39 per cent more. Some of them worked outside the home merely to enrich the content of their own lives. Along with other considerations this motive was cited in 22 per cent of the replies.[51] The eagerness for careers is particularly significant in view of the fact that the wife can seldom shift all household duties to other shoulders. Among the more poorly paid workers she must often carry two jobs: laboring in shop or factory during the day and looking after the home mornings and evenings. In the more favored callings she may be able to employ competent help and thus be permitted to choose work that is in harmony with her talents. But at whatever cost it is secured, gainful employment gives

---

49 *Marital Condition of Occupied Women, Fifteenth Census of the United States: 1930,* Department of Commerce, Bureau of the Census (Washington, 1932).
50 *Ibid.,* 714–715.
51 Virginia M. Collier, *Marriage and Careers* (New York, 1926), 13.

woman economic independence, destroys the foundations of
the patriarchal tradition, and tends to make marriage a partnership between equals.

Political Gains. Woman's political gains have been perhaps
the most spectacular of her triumphs. The winning of the
right of suffrage, however, has not meant equality in this
sphere. With something of the fervor with which they fought
for enfranchisement, women are still battling for jury service
and for the removal of such legal discriminations as remain
on the statute books of a number of states. Women, moreover, have not failed to take advantage of the opportunities
offered to them by their new status. They have gone into
public office in steadily advancing, if not in great, numbers.[52]
Fifteen have inscribed their names on the roll of the Congress
of the United States. Women have worked in the consular
and diplomatic service and have held cabinet office in the
federal government. In the sphere of state government 146
women have served in thirty-nine legislatures; and they have
filled the posts of supreme court judge, governor, lieutenant-
governor, secretary of state, attorney general, state auditor, and
treasurer. Also thousands of women today are serving town,
county and city in various appointive and elective positions.
In the future they may be expected to enter politics in increasing numbers.

Following the ratification of the Nineteenth Amendment
women have concentrated their efforts on the removal of the
remaining political and legal disqualifications.[53] In promoting the passage of needful legislation they have worked
through political parties and non-partisan organizations. In
1930 the League of Women Voters reported[54] that during the
ten years following the inauguration of national suffrage 130

[52] *A Survey of Women in Public Office,* compiled by National League of
Women Voters (New York, 1931).

[53] *The Legal and Political Status of Women in the United States,* National
League of Women Voters (New York, 1927).

[54] *The Achievements of Ten Years,* reproductions of charts prepared by the
National League of Women Voters (New York, 1930).

laws had been enacted in thirty-two states and the District of Columbia for the abolition of legal discrimination against women. This legislation covered the subjects of marriage, property rights, office-holding privileges, guardianship of children, and many others. Substantial success was also reported in the passage of laws relating to education, child welfare, women in industry, living costs, social hygiene, and efficiency in government. The organization, moreover, feels that its work will not be done until the heritage from the patriarchal system is completely liquidated. The Woman's Party hopes to achieve this end through an equal-rights amendment to the Constitution that will establish a condition of legal equality between the sexes throughout the jurisdiction of the United States. The League of Women Voters places its reliance on the slower process of individual enactment in the separate states.

Cultural Gains. In the domain of cultural opportunities the advance has been extremely rapid. Particularly in the sphere of higher education have women achieved a new status. They have increased their enrollment in colleges and universities from 54,000 in 1890, to 356,000 in 1928,[55] and from 35 per cent of the total registration in 1900 to 42 per cent in 1930. In the professional schools women increased their enrollment until 1924, after which, probably because of attempts to limit the number entering certain callings, a slight recession took place. The influence of this incursion of woman into the academic realm is already being felt in various departments of life. College women are demanding work that will give a richer meaning to existence than does domestic service. That a large percentage of these women do look forward to work outside the home is illustrated by the newspaper report that every graduate of Smith College in 1931 sought the aid of the college placement bureau in obtaining a position.

In 1930, women could claim more than 600,000 teachers, more than 13,000 librarians, more than 10,000 college presidents

[55] *Bulletins* of the United States Bureau of Education, No. 20 (Washington, 1932), II, 339.

and professors, more than 7000 surgeons and physicians, and nearly 6000 editors and reporters. It is significant, however, that they have entered those professions in greatest numbers in which they have encountered the fewest artificial obstacles.[56] In the sphere of scholarship they have long since demonstrated their proficiency. But here their achievements have been only grudgingly acknowledged and then attributed to their tendency to become bookworms, to be pleasing to their instructors, and to refrain from striking out along independent lines. In this criticism, as Miss Abbott observes, there is an element of truth: "Women have been trained to conform from childhood —which does not mean that they are by nature more timid in their convictions, in their selection of interests or in their pursuit of an objective than men. For many years one objective of college women has been to prove that they were not unequal mentally and physically to performing the tasks that were set for college men. And in their eagerness they have perhaps more than proved it."[57]

Women are also beginning to make contributions to the arts. But it is too early to evaluate their achievements in this field. The occasional awarding of prizes to women suggests that they are doing some work of distinction. The time, however, during which they have been able to work without being on the defensive, simply because of their sex, has been too brief. Perhaps in this sphere more than in any other they have fallen short of their powers because of hostility and closed doors. In her brilliant essay, *A Room of One's Own,* Virginia Wolfe shows the effect of this opposition on women in literature. She points out that the woman writer of the nineteenth century assumed the tone of voice of one expecting criticism: "She was admitting that she was 'only a woman,' or protesting that she was 'as good as a man.'" She was not encouraged to become an artist: she was snubbed, slapped and exhorted. To face the criticism of a patriarchal society and to be true to her own vision re-

[56] Grace Abbott, *op. cit.*   [57] *Ibid.*, 269.

SOCIAL FOUNDATIONS OF EDUCATION

quired integrity and genius of the highest order. Only after women have gained economic security and moral assurance can they be expected to make their normal contribution as artists. Thus far they have been handicapped by poverty, dependence, and absence of creative tradition.

The Present Situation. Because of these great changes in status women today face a new world. They are growing to maturity under a new dispensation. The battle for rights has passed its peak. No longer are girls being reared in an atmosphere of repression, conflict, and rebellion. Argument about the nature of woman and her ability to excel in the fields of masculine endeavor is giving way to a recognition of the achievement of women throughout the ages[58] and to a consideration of the opportunities open to women in the modern world.[59] Mary R. Beard has observed that "thought about women has been derived from partial history and partial experience colored by the passions of conflict," and that the balance necessary for understanding women can be attained only by making history embrace the whole course of civilization. "Woman and her work in the world," she says, "can best be understood in relation to the total process that has brought mankind from primitive barbarism to its present state. Her moods and aspirations have their roots in the very beginnings of society and they have been well nourished through the centuries by opportunities of her own making as well as by those of man's contrivance. . . . It is only by attempting to comprehend the wide course of civilization, therefore, that we can hope to understand women."[60]

Looking behind the scenes of history, Mrs. Beard found "women helping aggressively to shape the play in every act of life." She found them assuming chief responsibility for the perpetuation of the race, inventing the domestic arts that enrich life and lie at the root of civilization, patronizing and

58 Mary R. Beard, *On Understanding Women* (New York, 1931).
59 "Women in the Modern World," *Annals* (May, 1929), CXLIII.
60 Mary R. Beard, *op. cit.,* 32–33.

assisting in the development of new branches of learning, participating in movements for social amelioration, directing the affairs of state and kindling the fires of revolution, enduring the hardships of the frontier and the struggle for empire, and sharing with their fathers and husbands and brothers and sons in the task of building the nation. In concluding her survey of woman's role in the past she writes as follows:

"If this analysis of history is approximately sound and if the future like the past is to be crowded with changes and exigencies, then it is difficult to believe that the feminism of the passing generation, already hardened into dogma and tradition, represents the completed form of woman's relations to work, interests and society. In so far as it is a sex antagonism, even though based on legitimate grievances against exclusions or discriminations in employment, it is and has been partial and one-phased, not fundamental. The converse is true with respect to man's hostility to the presence of women at the center of every sort of activity. Women have always been alive to everything that was going on in the world. They always will be. If, as our engineering writers are constantly telling us, society is to be increasingly technical in nature, then competence, not sex, will be the basis of selection and women will have to stand that test with men. Feminism as sex antagonism bearing the wounds of many honorable battles may then drop out of sight. Masculinism as sex monopoly may then yield to concepts of expertness."[61]

The release of middle-class woman from domestic toil has raised in an acute form the question of the utilization of her time. All too frequently today she fails to make a wise use of her new-found freedom. The tradition that the wife should work only in the home and that the mark of a successful husband lies in his ability to support his family single-handed continues to linger in the mores of the people. As a result, many

[61] *Ibid.*, 521–522.

a man, in order to keep his wife in the home, shoulders the
economic responsibility formerly borne by both, while the
emancipated woman idles away her days, develops a thirst for
luxuries, engages in a game of conspicuous consumption with
her neighbors, and vainly seeks one sensation after another.
Under these circumstances the husband may have little or no
time to devote to cultural interests. Although the hours of
work have been shortened, the increased intensity of labor and
the commercialization of recreation have conspired to fill man's
free moments with culturally unprofitable amusements. The
real difficulty, however, lies in the uneven distribution of
leisure between the sexes. "Women are the inheritors of the
Industrial Revolution," writes Lorine Pruette. "Many of the
tasks of the home have been lifted from their shoulders, with
the result that some women are without any job at all, some on
no better than a quarter- or a half-time job, while some are
working double time."[62] Their free hours may be consumed
in window shopping, playing bridge, attending tea parties,
patronizing the cinema, or assuming the guardianship of a
superficial culture. At the same time their sisters among the
laboring classes may be struggling without success under intolerable economic burdens.

This situation is further aggravated by the decrease in the
birth rate. In a modern family of two or three children the old
function of child-care can occupy but a small part of the
long span of a woman's life. Moreover, increasingly children
and even infants are turned over to schools, kindergartens, and
nurseries. And among the more favored classes they often
spend their summers in camps and go off to boarding schools
and colleges at an early age. In many instances child rearing is
thus a full-time job for but a few years and thereafter a part-
time job for perhaps fifteen years more. Census data show
that only about one-fifth of the women beyond the age of ten
are gainfully employed. Another fifth constitute girls in school

[62] Lorine Pruette, *Women and Leisure* (New York, 1924), xi.

or persons too old to work. Most of the remaining three-fifths are housewives, many of whom employ domestics.[63] During at least a part of their lives these women present a problem of social waste and of social injustice of large magnitude. Unfortunately it is those who have received the most training and the greatest privileges at society's expense that are most likely to be kept in idleness. According to an analysis of census data for 1907, occupied women fall into two large classes: in the first the individual on marriage is likely to abandon employment; in the second she is not. The former group is composed largely of teachers, artists, stenographers, and other office and professional workers; the latter of factory operatives, agricultural laborers, and actresses. Women in the first category give up their occupations because the superior earning power of their husbands permits them the luxury of following outworn mores; while those in the second category, with the exception of actresses, cling to their jobs because of economic necessity. But whatever the explanation of the facts, the adventitious position of great masses of women in contemporary society is clearly apparent. It is a vestige from an era that has passed away, a reminder of social arrangements long since discarded.

THE EMERGENCE OF A NEW CONFIGURATION

The foregoing analysis shows that the forces released by science and technology have profoundly disturbed the configuration of family and sex relationships evolved to meet the conditions of the pre-industrial age. The family has lost many of its functions and altered its structure. It has been robbed of much of its one-time authority. The ancient division of labor between the sexes has been shattered. A return to the domestic institution of the eighteenth century is as impossible as the restoration of the colonial period in American history.

Before the rise of industrial civilization the family was

[63] *Ibid.*, 49–50.

to a considerable degree a social microcosm, performing most of the functions necessary for the maintenance of social life. On the economic side it was largely self-contained; also it provided education for the young, an asylum for the aged, and protection for all of its members. It even planned the social economy on the small scale required. Today its isolation has been removed; its unity destroyed; its continuity broken. It can no longer maintain the semblance of an independent existence. As a rule it holds title to no productive property of any consequence. It cannot even insure employment to its members. The individual family has been absorbed into a vast industrial society and its fortunes identified with the fortunes of millions of other families. A new configuration is forming in which the household will play a much weaker role than in the past. If men are to have economic security, medical attention, adequate educational opportunities, suitable housing and living arrangements, and appropriate facilities for play, recreation, and cultural development, responsibility will have to be shifted to some larger social unit. Indeed the shift is already far advanced. The close interdependence of men has moved beyond the circle of domestic relationships. Technology has widened the boundaries and integrated the texture of human association. The time has passed when the rational ordering of the economy can be achieved within the limits of the family.

Chapter II

ECONOMY

In its original meaning among the ancient Greeks economy was household management. In colonial times in America the term could have been used in much the same sense. As the preceding chapter reveals, the ordinary family of the pre-industrial age was practically self-contained. Consequently, except for the payment of taxes, the liquidation of mortgages, and the purchase of a few staple articles of trade, economy was primarly a domestic matter. The intervening generations have witnessed the dissolution of this early unity and the evolution of a radically different system of economy marked by specialization, differentiation, integration, and mass production on a vast scale. The nation today is scarcely more self-contained than was the typical farm family of the North or the representative plantation of the South when Washington was born. This transition from a domestic to a national, or even world, economy has created difficulties and opportunities of great magnitude.

UNION OF AGRICULTURE AND MANUFACTURE

It has often been remarked that the economy of pre-industrial America was founded on agriculture. This observation is true, but it tells little or nothing. In the last analysis practically every complete economy above the level of barbarism rests on the farm, because from the soil come indispensable food-stuffs and a major portion of the raw materials of manufacture. Without agriculture, and the cognate industry of forestry, such materials would be confined almost altogether to mineral and maritime products. So the distinctive characteristic of the colonial and early nineteenth-century economy was not that it was agricultural, but rather that it represented a union of agriculture and manufacture within the smallest social integer —the family with its supporting neighborhood. The so-called farmers and farmers' wives and sons and daughters were also carpenters, blacksmiths, masons, millers, cobblers, weavers, spinners, dyers, butchers, and food preservers.

In concluding their study of the northern farmer of this period Bidwell and Falconer state that he was "a jack of all trades":

"Besides taking his part in many of the harder tasks of the household industries, such as breaking, swingling, and hatcheling flax, the farmer applied himself more or less regularly to a diversity of other tasks according to his especial 'bent' and opportunities. On the sea-coast, he was frequently a sailor or a fisherman for part of the year. In inland towns he often plied some trade or other and was classed as an artisan as well as a farmer. Every farmer did a multitude of odd jobs for himself, such as repairing old buildings, and building new, laying walls and stoning up wells, butchering pigs and cattle, making axe-handles and brooms, splitting staves and shingles, tanning leather, and cobbling shoes. Occasionally he performed some of these tasks for a neighbor, who either had not the requisite skill or was too busy with strictly agricultural operations. Such service was more often repaid in kind than in currency."[1]

In the South the situation was not very different. Although the southern planters grew certain staples for both colonial and over-seas trade, their isolation forced them to be relatively self-contained. The plantation, to be sure, being a kind of enlarged household, had somewhat greater resources than the northern family and could achieve a larger measure of differentiation

[1] Percy Wells Bidwell and John I. Falconer, *History of Agriculture in the Northern United States 1620–1860* (Washington, 1925), 130–131.

of function. The whites provided management and direction; the negroes both skilled and unskilled labor—the women sewing, knitting, weaving, spinning, and housekeeping; the men working as blacksmiths, carpenters, masons, millers, shoemakers, and farmers.[2] T. J. Wertenbaker, moreover, has proved conclusively that the typical southern planter of colonial days was not a great landholder and owner of many slaves but rather was a small farmer who worked for himself.[3]

This turn toward a self-sufficient economy in the American settlements was not of course the intention of those who promoted colonial ventures. The London Company had expected to procure needed raw materials from Virginia and to tap rich "supplies of pitch, tar, soap ashes, resin, flax, cordage, iron, copper, glass, and timber for shipbuilding and other purposes." Not wholly dissimilar motives lay back of the establishment of the other settlements. But conditions in the new land were not particularly favorable to the fulfillment of these plans. Necessity forced the colonists to become farmers rather than tradesmen, many-sided in their economic activities rather than specialists. Questions of food, clothing, and shelter eclipsed all other considerations. The distances were so great and the coming and going of ships so uncertain that they could not depend on imports from the mother country.[4]

The conclusion, however, should not be drawn that there was no trade in the pre-industrial economy. As a matter of fact there was a great deal. The isolation was only relative, and as a rule the self-sufficiency of the farm was by no means complete. There were large variations from region to region. Maryland and Virginia grew much tobacco for the European market; the Carolinas and Georgia tended to specialize in rice, cotton, and indigo; and the inhabitants of the New England coast,

[2] See Wilson Gee, *The Social Economics of Agriculture* (New York, 1932), 33. Also Letitia M. Burwell, *A Girl's Life in Virginia Before the War* (New York, 1895), 1–2.
[3] T. J. Wertenbaker, *The Planters of Colonial Virginia* (Princeton, 1922).
[4] See Wilson Gee, *op. cit.*, 28–29.

finding the soil comparatively thin and barren, turned to the sea and to the development of fishing, ship-building, and ocean commerce. Also trading centers sprang up all along the Atlantic seaboard and at the junction points of trails, highways, and water courses. Finally, as communities became established, differentiation of function began to appear. This tendency was observed by Tench Coxe, an Englishman who visited America toward the close of the eighteenth century and was particularly impressed by the union of agriculture and manufacture:

"Those of the tradesmen and manufacturers, who live in the country, generally reside on small lots and farms, from one acre to twenty; and not a few upon farms from twenty to one hundred and fifty acres; which they cultivate at leisure times, with their own hands, their wives, children, servants, and apprentices, and sometimes by hired labourers, or by letting out fields, for a part of the produce, to some neighbour, who has time or farm hands not fully employed. *This union of manufactures and farming* is found to be very convenient on grain farms; but it is still more convenient on the grazing and grass farms, where parts of almost every day, and a great part of every year, can be spared from the business of the farm, and employed in some mechanical, handycraft, or manufacturing business. These persons often make domestic and farming carriages, implements, and utensils, build houses and barns, tan leather, and manufacture hats, shoes, hosiery, cabinet-work, and other articles of clothing and furniture, to the great convenience and advantage of the neighbourhood."[5]

A dominant feature of this pre-industrial economy was the practical absence of the market in the modern sense. Both farmer and manufacturer produced primarily for *use* and not for *sale*. In the case of the self-sufficient family this was obviously true. Here, since communal conditions prevailed,

5 Tench Coxe, *View of the United States of America* (London, 1794), 442.

there could be no market. Each produced according to his strength and consumed according to his need, due allowance being made for the vagaries of human nature. And even when the artisan or craftsman labored at his special calling he produced in response to clearly formulated demand, if not to definite prescription. Also he produced for his neighbors with whom he had lived for many years and with whom he doubtless hoped to live for many more. Moreover, he customarily received as compensation for his goods, not money, but other goods produced in similar fashion. Under such circumstances certain standards of justice and fairness, not to say humanity, tended to control and suffuse economic transactions. Indeed to the ordinary citizen of the period the separation of economics and ethics would have seemed incongruous.

The standard of consumption under this system was of course extremely modest, if compared with twentieth-century conditions. The economy was based on a low level of energy transversion; human labor was the main source of power; and machines in the modern sense were yet to be invented. The farmer used tools that the ancient Roman would have understood—the wooden plow with clumsy wrought-iron share, the wooden shovel with iron-shod edge, the harrow with wooden or iron teeth, the sickle, the flail, the scythe, the axe, the hoe, the bill-hook and the pitchfork.[6] The craftsman or manufacturer employed tools equally primitive in character. Life was hard and luxuries few. Men, women, and children worked long hours to beat back the forest and wring a scanty living from nature. And yet the family of that day enjoyed a large measure of material security. While men could not expect much, they at least understood the terms in the economic equation. They knew that, due allowance being made for the whims and caprices of nature, effort and industry would bring their reward. To be sure, economic depressions appeared at intervals, urban workers were thrown out

[6] See Percy Wells Bidwell and John I. Falconer, *op. cit.,* 123–126.

of work, farm mortgages were foreclosed, and "squatters" were driven from their lands, but for the great masses of the people unemployment was without meaning and no great financial disaster could sweep away in a day or an hour the savings of a lifetime. It was this economy that created the tradition of the *independent farmer*.

SPECIALIZATION AND THE MARKET

During the last decades of the eighteenth and the early decades of the nineteenth century, forces that had long been gathering overwhelmed the household and community economy. Under the impact of invention, technology, and an appropriate philosophy the homogeneous economy of the pre-industrial age went through a process of differentiation not unlike the development of an embryo, with its successive metamorphoses and its fixing of specialized organs and tissues. By the close of the century, except for survivals in remote and inaccessible parts of the country, the loosely organized nation of semi-independent families and communities, which had met the gaze of Hamilton and Jefferson, was transformed into a closely-knit society resting on economic foundations of unexampled scope, complexity, and power.

During the century the family lost its independence, manufacture drew away from agriculture, and a complicated system of exchange came into being. Moreover, within each of the major branches of economy, with the exception of farming itself, labor was divided, subdivided, and divided again until the entire system was marked by the most minute specialization. The occupations of the people, particularly after 1870, lost their former stability and began to change and multiply with great rapidity.[7] In the eighteenth century, callings could be counted by scores or hundreds; in 1920 the Census Bureau found it necessary to compile an index of

[7] See Ralph G. Hurlin and Meredith B. Givens, "Shifting Occupational Patterns," Chapter VI in The President's Research Committee on Social Trends, *Recent Social Trends in the United States* (New York, 1933), I, 269.

"20,000 or more occupational designations." This differentiation also proceeded geographically and created division of function among regions, districts, and even city quarters and blocks. And all of these specialties and particularities were bound together by new forms of transportation and by the market. The entire story cannot of course be recited here. It has already been told in many works. The more revolutionary lines of change, however, will be indicated by tracing the development of agriculture—the industry out of which the contemporary complex has evolved.

At the time of the founding of the nation the great majority of the population were living on farms and plantations; agriculture was not only the main source of livelihood, but was also the dominant mode of life. In 1790 only 3.3 per cent of the people of the country were living in cities of 8000 or more inhabitants. The remainder lived in smaller cities, towns, villages, hamlets, and strictly rural districts. Also this population was scattered over a vast area extending from Georgia to Maine and from the Atlantic coast to the distant boundaries of the Northwest Territory.

The breaking down of the isolation of the individual family and the creation of conditions permitting division of labor and specialization of function were clearly dependent on the improvement of transportation and communication. This of course came gradually throughout the colonial period. As the density of population increased, the number of connections grew and trails were transformed into roads and highways. At the same time river and ocean transportation advanced in both quantity and quality. And as a part of the process both internal and external trade expanded. Bidwell and Falconer show that the export of foodstuffs to Britain, Ireland, Europe, and the West Indies increased significantly during the period from 1770 to 1794.[8] Also in the later decades of the eighteenth century the currents of internal

[8] *Op. cit.*, 134–137.

trade grew appreciably in volume. The back country sent to the cities and seaports firewood, potatoes, poultry, pork, beef, cattle, cheese, butter, lard, cider, corn, wheat, flaxseed, barley, rye, oats, beans, potash, hay, and timber, and received in return rum, salt, dry goods, iron, tea, and molasses. At the same time a coasting trade flourished which gradually brought about a threefold differentiation along the Atlantic seaboard. New England developed grazing, dairying, fruit-growing, manufacturing, and the maritime pursuits; the Middle Colonies, grain production and a varied agriculture supported by commerce and manufacturing; and the southern colonies, the growing of grain, tobacco, rice, indigo, and cotton.[9] Thus the year 1800 saw the regions east of the Alleghanies exhibiting a considerable measure of economic specialization and integration. The mercantile, financial, and manufacturing interests were making their appearance in the national life.

In the early decades of the nineteenth century the West was gradually drawn into the integration. Even the first settlements in this region carried on an intermittent and slender trade with the east and south, exchanging pork, beef, grain, and whiskey for salt, sugar, cotton, and manufactured goods. Soon after 1800 the western farmers drove cattle over the mountains to eastern markets. But prior to the building of the Erie Canal and the construction of railroads the natural outlet for the products of this region was the Ohio River, the Mississippi, and New Orleans. In 1811 the first steamboat appeared on the Mississippi; by 1820 steam navigation was well established.[10] Trade consequently flourished and the business enterpriser appeared on the scene. "There is a class of men throughout the western country called 'merchants,'" wrote H. B. Fearon in 1818, "who, in the summer and autumn months, collect flour, butter, cheese, pork, beef, whiskey, and every species of farming produce, which they send in flats and

[9] *Ibid.*, 137–144. [10] *Ibid.*, 171–174.

keel-boats to the New Orleans market. The demand created by this trade, added to a large domestic consumption, insures the most remote farmer a certain market. Some of these speculators have made large fortunes."[11]

The New Orleans market, however, was far from satisfactory. The river transportation was slow and uncertain; and New Orleans was poorly equipped to handle ocean trade. The great market for western produce was in the east beyond the mountains; but overland transportation was tedious, difficult, and even hazardous. The water routes in this direction were interrupted and "the so-called roads were merely narrow avenues through the woods from which the trees had been felled and rolled away, leaving the brushwood and stumps a foot or a foot and a half high."[12] According to estimates, the cost of land carriage in the western region ranged from a cent to a cent and a half per mile for one hundred pounds. "At such rates," say Bidwell and Falconer, "corn could not stand the expense of moving 20 miles, even though produced at no cost, and wheat could not be profitably transported by land more than 50 or 75 miles."[13] In his study of trade on the Great Lakes and neighboring rivers during this period, Israel D. Andrews reports that "the expense of transportation from Buffalo to New York was stated at $100 per ton, and the ordinary length of passage *twenty days;* so that, upon the very route through which the heaviest and cheapest products of the West are now sent to market, the cost of transportation equalled nearly *three* times the market value of wheat in New York; *six* times the value of corn; *twelve* times the value of oats; and far exceeded the value of most kinds of cured provisions."[14] Clearly the commercial union of the east with the west, and the consequent differentiation of function, waited upon a radical cheapening of transportation.

[11] H. B. Fearon, *Sketches of America* (London, 1818), 201.
[12] Percy Bidwell and John I. Falconer, *op. cit.,* 180.   [13] *Ibid.,* 181.
[14] Israel D. Andrews, *Report on the Trade and Commerce of the British North American Colonies and Upon the Trade of the Great Lakes and Rivers* (Washington, 1854), 234.

This came with the opening of the Erie Canal in 1825. Although the trade down the Mississippi continued to grow more rapidly than the trade through the canal until 1850, eventually it helped to turn the tide toward the east. Immediately freight rates from the Great Lakes to the Atlantic dropped from one hundred to fifteen or twenty-five dollars a ton.[15] The era of canal building was on. By 1855, with the completion of the locks at Sault St. Marie, navigation was open "from the western end of the Great Lakes to the Atlantic seaboard," and the northern half of the country from the Mississippi to the coast was covered with a system of waterways.

But in the meantime a new and more rapid form of transportation had appeared. The railroad spread over the land, and particularly in the north, with amazing speed. In 1840 the country could boast "only a little more than 2000 miles of railroad." Ten years later this mileage had grown to over 7000 and by 1860 to 30,626, crossing the Mississippi and pushing into the fertile prairies of Iowa. The railroad rapidly superseded the waterway for many kinds of traffic. Thus, "of the exports from Chicago in 1858, $21,000,000 worth was sent by lake vessels, $1,000,000 worth by canal, and $60,000,000 worth by railroad. Twenty per cent of the flour, 70 per cent of the packinghouse products, and all of the livestock were shipped by rail, while nearly all of the wheat went by way of the lakes. Of the livestock received at Chicago in that year all the hogs came by railroad; of the 140,000 cattle received, 9 animals came by way of the lake, 21,000 were driven in, and the remainder came by railroad. It was estimated in 1862 that two-thirds of the freight to and from the West was moved by railroads."[16] In 1869, the completion of the Union Pacific linked the Atlantic with the Pacific and signalized the triumph of modern forms of transportation. Thereafter the expansion of the railroads, the building of trolley systems, and the develop-

[15] Percy Wells Bidwell and John I. Falconer, *op. cit.*, 306.
[16] *Ibid.*, 307–308.

ment of motor vehicles and airways merely filled in lines of growth already marked out and increased the speed with which goods could be moved.[17]

The development of cheap, rapid, efficient, and reliable means of transportation, which has placed its revolutionary stamp upon the past one hundred years, quickly destroyed the self-sufficiency of the rural family, made the practice of agriculture assume a more and more specialized form, and undermined the economic foundations of the "independent farmer" of tradition. Thereafter the tiller of the soil might continue to boast of his freedom from external restraints, while in actual fact he was being drawn ever more remorselessly into a great complex of economic relationships. His change of status is clearly reflected in the decline of household industries which has been summarized as follows by Bidwell and Falconer:

"At the beginning of the nineteenth century the typical northern farmer was still clad in homespun cloth made of wool sheared from his own sheep, spun, dyed, and woven in his own home by the women of his household. Many other articles of household furnishing, such as blankets, sheets, and towels, were also made by these hardworking women. Before 1840, however, the household textile industry had been largely transferred to the new cotton and woolen mills, the graceful spinning wheels and the noisy handlooms were being relegated to the attics of the farmhouses, there to accumulate dust and cobwebs until rescued and restored to posts of honor by the antique-collectors of our own generation."[18]

This decline of household manufacture implied of course a correlative growth of factory manufacture. In his Report on Manufactures in 1790 Alexander Hamilton described seventeen industries that had developed to a point involving the use of raw materials transported from different localities, the division of labor in the process of fabrication, and the sale of the

[17] See below, Part Two, Chapter III, "Communication."   [18] *Op. cit.*, 250.

product in more or less distant markets. The articles thus manufactured or converted to human use included leather, iron, tools, textiles, pottery, paper, hats, spirits, oil, sugar, tobacco, hardware, carriages, and gun-powder.[19] It should also be remembered that at this time manufactured goods were being imported in considerable quantity and variety from England. By 1808, according to E. L. Bogart, American industrial independence, in terms of the technical level of the age, was established.[20] In the years that followed, the development of manufacturing in the United States proceeded with great rapidity, making conquest after conquest and robbing household industry of one commodity after another. By 1927 manufacture, carried on outside the home, was capitalized at close to fifty billion dollars, employed almost nine million wage-earners, had at its disposal about forty-three million horse-power, and produced goods valued at more than seventy billions. Even the art of bread-making seems to be disappearing from the home.

This great trend has commonly been viewed from the standpoint of the advance of factory production, the growth of cities, and the creation of a great industrial proletariat. Its repercussions in the field of agriculture and rural life have been equally impressive. The prophecy of Horace Bushnell in 1851 that "this transition from mother and daughter power to water and steam power is a great one, greater by far than many have as yet begun to conceive—one that is to carry with it a complete revolution of domestic life and social manners,"[21] has already been more than fulfilled. As the rural household produced fewer and fewer things, but in larger and larger quantities, economic success "no longer depended on the unremitting efforts of the farm family, aided by Providence, but to a large extent also upon the unpredictable wants and labors of

19 See Ernest Ludlow Bogart, *An Economic History of the United States* (New York, 1922), Chapter X, 146–156.
20 *Ibid.*, 59.
21 Horace Bushnell, *Work and Play* (New York, 1864), 376.

millions of persons in the industrial villages and in the newer farms to the westward."[22]

The changed situation required new traits of character. The ancient "virtues of self-reliance and independence, of frugality and thrift" ceased to be adequate. If not combined with the virtues of the market-place, with "shrewdness in buying and selling," they might lead the farmer into a species of economic serfdom. And the country has often witnessed the spectacle of embattled farmers suffering from the movements of distant markets, hurling defiance at Wall Street, and still nursing the illusion of independence. The fact is that during the past century the individual farmer, by abandoning the industries on which his self-sufficiency rested and by even adopting some narrow specialty within the field of agriculture, such as cotton growing, wheat raising, or dairying, has lost control over many divisions of the economic process and has been drawn into an economy that is enormously complex and clearly corporate in character. His present plight is unquestionably to be traced to the inadequacy of his adjustment to the new conditions.

The rise of factory industry, however, should not be regarded as an alien force descending upon the rural household from the outside. The whole of modern economy, from the standpoint of its basic functions, was contained in and has evolved out of that household. In a very genuine sense manufacture is the child of agriculture; the city is the offspring of the country; and factory workers are the children of husbandmen. Moreover, when farmers' daughters migrated to the textile mills of Massachusetts in the first part of the nineteenth century, they merely continued to do under altered circumstances and in a more highly specialized way what their mothers and grandmothers had done before them. And so today the millions of men and women engaged in manufacturing and other industries divorced from the land may be regarded as farmers

[22] Percy Wells Bidwell and John I. Falconer, *op. cit.*, 252.

who have taken and followed numerous economic functions out of the one-time self-contained rural household.

The specialization of function has been attended by an extraordinary advance in productive power and efficiency. Along with specialization has gone an extension of the market for each commodity produced; an extension of the market has made possible large-scale production; and large-scale production has stimulated the standardization and mechanization of processes of manufacture. Industry, by placing machines of ever-increasing power at the disposal of agriculture, has released in corresponding proportion great numbers of the population from the raising of food and raw materials and shifted them to other departments of the economy, there to produce innumerable goods and services unknown a few generations ago. At its best the eighteenth-century economy could provide but an extremely meagre living for the masses of the people. And to get this it compelled them to work long and hard. The economy of today would seem to be capable of placing material security and abundance within the reach of the entire population.[23]

Perhaps the most revolutionary of all the changes that followed the break-up of the self-contained domestic economy was a change in the purposes controlling production. With the rise of the new economy men tended more and more to produce for *sale* rather than for *use*. And now the infinitely varied economic activities of the American people are given direction and goal by a market that is always more than local in character and that is often world-wide in scope. Industry and agriculture, with all of their differentiations, are bound together by a system of exchange that is of surpassing intricacy and complexity. The magnitude of the burden borne by this system may be revealed in part by reference to commercial statistics. In 1929 wholesale trade employed 1,605,042 persons and recorded net sales of $69,291,548,000. Corresponding figures for

[23] See above, Part One, Chapter III, "Technology."

retail trade were 3,833,581 and $49,114,654,000 respectively. In the same year 2,179,015,000 short tons of revenue freight were carried by the railways of the country. Also the domestic water-borne commerce of the United States amounted to 456,290,000 short tons, and the foreign commerce to 127,510,000. Today in America everybody is engaged in selling something, perhaps even himself, to somebody else.

THE TRADITION OF LAISSEZ-FAIRE

During the latter part of the eighteenth century, when the family economy was beginning to lose its functions, when the tendency toward differentiation was gaining strength, and when the market for an increasing variety of goods was transcending the boundaries of the local community, there gradually took form in the industrially advanced parts of the western world a theory of economy and government that reflected the temper of the rising middle classes and that seemed to harmonize with the trends of the age.[24] This theory, which was given most complete and felicitous expression by Adam Smith in his *Wealth of Nations*, published in 1776, came to be known under the name of *laissez-faire* and proved to be peculiarly congenial to the conditions of life in the young republic, with its enterprising population, its abundance of natural resources, and its freedom from restraining influences. The result was the development in America of a body of maxims, opinions, ideas, and institutions that persist today under vastly changed circumstances. The core of this heritage consists of three parts—a money and price system, the rationale of gain-seeking, and the institution of private property in land and capital goods.

In the price system the movement toward an extended and integrated economy found an indispensable instrument—an instrument for binding together the various specializations

[24] See below, Part Two, Chapter X, "Government."

that appeared and multiplied with the growth of transportation. According to the theory, some form of money, whether cattle, tobacco, silver, or gold, makes possible or at least greatly facilitates the division of labor and provides for an automatic adjustment of price relationships. And the specialization, which is constantly carried to new intensities in individual work, in single plants, in great industries, and even in localities and regions, achieves enormous gains in productive efficiency, as the historical record plainly shows. Indeed, without specialization the use of modern machinery and technology would be severely limited. Through "the market," a device for attaching numerical tags to all forms of goods as they are passed on to later processes or to consumption, the differentiation of economic function is co-ordinated and integrated.

Under a price system, if all restraining influences are removed, pressure or weakness of demand for any commodity in relation to supply, immediately or presently available, raises or lowers the denomination of the numerical tag. In sensitivity and nicety of organization markets for different kinds of goods vary from the informed bidding of the raw cotton exchange to the unenlightened search for "bargains" of retail shopping, or to the monopoly arrangements in the pricing of aluminum. But for most commodities change of supply or effective demand will sooner or later find expression in change of price. Under *laissez-faire* the controls of the economy lie hidden in this fact. High prices for a given commodity tempt the application of labor and capital to its production; low prices squeeze labor and capital to curb the supply or to shift to the production of some other commodity whose supply is shown by price to be inadequate. Deviously but inevitably, the rent of natural resources, the interest on capital goods, and the wages of labor are all determined by the fluctuations of prices at the time of the exchange of goods. Profits, as a reward over and above interest, arise whenever supply falls below demand, continue as long as this condition persists, disappear when equilibrium has been established, and turn into losses as the pendulum swings on to excess production.

Ideally, these separate returns of rent, interest, wages, and profits are supposed to constitute measures of productive worth to the total economic process of natural resources, capital goods, labor, and management. To its expounders therefore the price system, besides facilitating specialization, provides an automatic adjustment of the consuming power of the various economic classes to their several economic contributions, and so, evidently, an automatic adjustment of production to the total command over consumption. Thus the economic mechanism operates justly and efficiently under its own power and direction without the interference of government or collective action. For the state to attempt regulation of any kind would be to violate immutable economic laws and court economic disaster.

The second feature of this body of doctrine which was received so hospitably by the American people, as they emerged from the self-contained family economy, is the rationale of gain-seeking. The thirst for private profit is made the motive power that drives the wheels of all industry and gives coherence to the system of price relationships. The theory assumes that every man is supremely devoted to his own pecuniary interest, that he knows best what that interest is, that he himself can guard and advance that interest most effectively, and that, since the whole is equal to the sum of all its parts, if he will but mind his own business and dutifully think only of what is good for himself, then the greatest social good will be achieved. And as laborer, landlord, capitalist, and entrepreneur each drives his hardest bargain, the largest total product or income is assured and the prices of commodities are fixed at levels which guarantee highest total well-being. It will be observed that this represents a complete reversal of the assumptions underlying the household economy that was passing away.

It is not strictly true, however, to say that government plays no part in this process. Indeed, in the third and most important feature of the system of *laissez-faire,* the institution of private property in the instruments of production, the state in a sense sets the stage and orders the conditions for the play of economic forces. It clearly stipulates that the weapons to be used in the struggle will be the weapons of the merchant, and not those of the soldier, the priest, or the scholar. In the words of John Locke, the seventeenth-century spokesman of the middle classes, which were then ascending to power in England and which were destined to espouse these doctrines of economic individualism, "the great and chief end, therefore, of men uniting into commonwealths and putting themselves under government, is the preservation of their property." Thus by guaranteeing to the individual the fruits of his labor and of his ingenuity, the state placed its seal on the outcome of the battle for material goods and on the whole rationale of gain-seeking. As a matter of historical record, of course, it went much further and became the more or less pliant tool of those who had been most successful in this contest.

The crucial and characteristic application of this principle, after the coming of large-scale enterprise, proved to be private ownership and administration of productive capital. According to the theory, this arrangement, if founded on the principle of self-interest, insures the placing of the ablest individuals in positions of economic power and the most efficient utilization of the material resources of the nation. It is thus the duty of both landlord and capitalist to win the maximum of rent or interest for the use of these possessions. Under strictly competitive conditions, which the doctrine assumes will prevail, exactions in either form cannot exceed the worth to the entrepreneur of the resources in question: if rents are too high, the less productive lands will remain idle; and if the interest on capital is unreasonable, management will employ labor in place of machines or even retire from the field.

All of this seems to have been an easy eighteenth-century assumption. And if the assumption be granted, a rugged individualism, even though it may over-ride humane sentiments, becomes the essence of patriotism in times of peace and must pervade all economic relationships. Since only in his personal pursuit of gain can man be counted upon to apply himself closely, and hence effectively, to the task of winning wealth from the earth, government must confine itself to the exercise of police power, the enforcement of contracts, and the protection of property rights. The competitive spirit is thus made sacrosanct and individual selfishness is raised to the level of a public virtue. Any losses which may accrue as a result of inco-ordination and absence of general planning are presumed to be more than offset by the superior drive of gain-seeking in the total production of wealth.

Such in barest outline are the basic principles of that body of economic thought which took root in American institutions at the time of the break-up of the family economy. In its simplified and pure form, however, it has never existed outside the realm of social theory. In every so-called capitalistic economy departures from the principle of competitive self-regulation have been frequent. In fact, as the political history of the United States reveals,[25] the principle has commonly been invoked in practice for the purpose of defending some vested interest or obtaining some gainful opportunity; rarely indeed has any individual or group endeavoured to live by its precepts. Almost invariably the ardent champions of competition, once having grasped power, have refused to live by their own professed doctrines. Through the institutions of government they have consolidated their position and sought special privileges; through the institution of inheritance they have transferred their power, not to the most competent among their successors, but to their own offspring. When men are encouraged to engage in profit-seeking, they are prone to employ any methods that may enable them to achieve their ends. Moreover, as time has worn along, private enterprise has received check after check at the

[25] See Charles A. Beard, *The Myth of Rugged American Individualism* (New York, 1932).

hands of government or collective action. This trend has reached its culmination for the moment in the measures of the Roosevelt administration enacted in 1933.[26]

THE RESULTS OF LAISSEZ-FAIRE

In view of the unrivalled richness of the natural endowment of their country and the unprecedented power placed in their hands by the advance of technology during the past century, the American people might reasonably be expected already to have disposed of the economic question and to have turned their energies to the more difficult and human tasks of cultural development. Certainly, if life was tolerable at all, or even possible, to their pioneering ancestors, before the rise of the machine and the conquest of mechanical power, it would seem that at least they should have achieved a high degree of economic security. And since they are avowedly committed to the democratic ideal, it would seem further that they should have distributed the benefits derived from technical advance fairly evenly among the masses of the population. The extent to which these goals have been attained should provide a partial measure of the adequacy of the doctrines of *laissez-faire* and the inherited economic institutions.

Wealth and Income. During the past one hundred and fifty years, under the reign of an ever more tempered *laissez-faire*, the American people have made a material advance without precedent in history. Within this brief span of time they have taken possession of half a continent, organized a closely knit economic system, achieved the highest *average* standard of consumption ever known, and become the richest nation in the world. From the founding of the Union down to 1929, a period of five generations, the actual wealth of the nation, as measured in dollars, grew from an estimated $620,000,000, over three-fourths of which was in land, to more than 360 billions[27]

26 See below, Part Two, Chapter X, "Government."
27 National Industrial Conference Board, *Bulletin* No. 51 (March 20, 1931), 406.

and the total annual income from a fraction of a billion to approximately 90 billions.[28] Moreover, with but 6.2 per cent of the population of the globe the United States produces and consumes annually about 50 per cent of the world's mechanical energy. These figures, which might be multiplied endlessly, suggest that the American people have prospered mightily under the inherited economic system.

A further examination of the facts, however, reveals another side to the picture. The purpose of an economy, against which the efficiency of its operations must be measured, would seem to be the distribution of security, goods, and services among the population in the greatest possible abundance, due allowance being made for the wants of men and the welfare of future generations. Data regarding wealth and income in the United States will illuminate this question.

The vast material wealth which the American people have created in the course of their history is very unevenly distributed. Perhaps the most dependable, though limited, study of the question is contained in a report of the Federal Trade Commission in 1926.[29] This body gathered data on the estates of deceased persons, as recorded in the probate courts of twenty-four carefully selected counties in thirteen states during the years 1912 to 1923 inclusive. Of the 184,958 decedents twenty-one years of age or over, only 43,512 had estates sufficiently large to probate. This means that more than 75 per cent of the persons dying in those counties within the twelve-year period had practically no property, although in arriving at its general estimates with respect to the distribution of wealth the Commission assigns to each of these decedents property valued at $258, the average value of the estates of the lowest category (under $500) included in the probate records. The study concludes with the statement that "about 1 per cent of the esti-

[28] W. I. King, *The National Income and Its Purchasing Power* (New York, 1930), 75. Also National Industrial Conference Board, *op. cit.*, 406.
[29] The Federal Trade Commission, *National Wealth and Income* (Washington, 1926), Chapter III, 56–69.

mated number of decedents owned about 59 per cent of the
estimated wealth and that more than 90 per cent was owned by
about 13 per cent of this number."[30] And the Commission
might have added that the forty-four largest estates ($1,000,-
000 or over), approximately one-fourth of one-tenth of one per
cent of the total number, embraced 18.5 per cent of the total
wealth involved. If these figures may be taken as representative
of the country, only the smallest fraction of the people own
sufficient property to give them a sense of security and independence. The remainder would seem to be dependent for the
opportunity of earning their livelihood on the will of this nu-
merically insignificant minority. Apparently the practice of
the "rugged individualism" of American tradition must be
confined to a very favored few.

To many, however, the question of ownership of wealth is
far less important than income. Attention will therefore be
directed to the distribution of income in the United States, as
indicated by the income tax returns. Although these figures
do not report the earnings of individuals and families at the
lower levels, they are sufficiently complete to give a fairly clear
picture of the situation. In a recent pamphlet[31] Stuart Chase,
using the data for 1927 (a year of mild recession) and adding
an estimate of the income of those not filing reports, has arrived at the following summary table:

INCOME CLASS	NUMBER OF PERSONS	TOTAL INCOME PER CLASS	AVERAGE PER PERSON
Over $5,000,000 per year........	10	$ 89,000,000	$8,900,000
$1,000,000 to $5,000,000........	273	497,000,000	1,800,000
$100,000 to $1,000,000..........	10,784	2,222,000,000	206,000
$10,000 to $100,000..............	332,789	7,298,000,000	22,000
$5,000 to $10,000...............	543,509	3,759,000,000	6,900
Reporting income under $5,000...	3,235,000	8,708,000,000	2,700
No income report..............	41,000,000	62,500,000,000	1,500
Total (about)................	45,000,000	$85,000,000,000	$ 1,900

[30] *Ibid.*, 58.
[31] Stuart Chase, *Poor Old Competition* (New York, 1933), 7.

This table requires little explanation. The wide differences in income are evident. At the top of the pyramid are 283 persons each receiving more than one million dollars a year and averaging approximately two millions. And among them are ten who receive on the average almost nine millions each. At the bottom are 41,000,000 persons, the great body of the American people, among whom the average income per worker is $1500. This figure, however, shelters a wide distribution ranging from zero to $3500. Between the two extremes covered by the returns, which means from $1500 or $3500 (depending upon marital state) to $1,000,000, are a few more than 4,000,000 people. Moreover, as Mr. Chase himself has observed in commenting on the table, "about 350,000 individuals receive $10,000 or more, taking in the aggregate over ten billions of the total national income. Thus less than one per cent of the American income-receivers secure 12 per cent of all income." M. A. Copeland,[32] also using the income tax data, estimated that the percentage of the total income received by the wealthiest 10 per cent of the population, during the nine years from 1918 to 1926 inclusive, ranged from 28.9 in 1920 to 35.3 in 1921 and maintained an average for the period of 33.0.

The naked figures, however, do not tell the whole story. Before their meaning in terms of the satisfaction of human needs can be made apparent, they must be translated into standards of living. This has been attempted by Paul Nystrom[33] for the year 1927. The table given below, adapted from his study by George Soule,[34] provides a rough estimate of the proportion of the population falling into each of ten economic classes.

This table presents a striking contrast to the glowing accounts of the abundance of natural resources, the miracles of technology, and the automatic beneficence of *laissez-faire* in

[32] M. A. Copeland, "Marketing," Chapter V in The President's Committee on Recent Economic Changes, *Recent Economic Changes in the United States* (New York, 1929), 836.
[33] Paul H. Nystrom, *Economic Principles of Consumption* (New York, 1931), 279–298.
[34] George Soule, *A Planned Society* (New York, 1932), 236.

economy and government. As Henry George pointed out in his *Progress and Poverty* in 1879, during the early stages of industrial development in the United States, in spite of the centuries of so-called progress, great masses of people continue to live in poverty. Even in years when the country was said to be

	APPROXIMATE POPULATION OF GROUP	PER CENT OF TOTAL POPULATION
Public charges..............................	1,000,000	.8
Tramps, work-shy, etc....................	2,000,000	1.7
Poverty level..............................	7,000,000	5.9
Bare subsistence...........................	12,000,000	10.1
		18.5
Minimum for health and efficiency..........	20,000,000	16.8
Minimum comfort........................	30,000,000	25.2
Comfort...................................	20,000,000	16.8
Moderately well-to-do.....................	15,000,000	12.6
		71.4
Well-to-do................................	10,000,000	8.4
Liberal standards of living.................	2,000,000	1.7
		10.1
Total population...........................	119,000,000	100.0

enjoying unexampled prosperity and when every citizen was supposed to have two chickens in the pot and at least one car in the garage, certain great industries, such as agriculture, coal, and textiles, were badly depressed, more than one-sixth of the population were living below the minimum for health and efficiency, and over one-third of the men, women, and children of the nation were denied the most elementary comforts.

What the condition of the masses may be during a period of profound depression, such as opened in 1929, when the total social income was diminished by an amount ranging from one-fourth to one-half, when from twelve to fifteen million people were thrown out of work, and when additional millions had both hours and wages reduced, must be left to the imagination. Thus far only partial accounts have been attempted by the sociologists.[35] Yet sufficient data are available to show that the depression bears very unevenly on the different elements of the population. The following table is illuminating:[36]

YEAR	INDUSTRIAL DIVIDENDS AND INTEREST IN MILLIONS OF DOLLARS
1919	579.16
1920	601.70
1921	542.20
1922	524.69
1923	541.46
1924	566.19
1925	596.06
1926	664.38
1927	1,555.50
1928	1,703.00
1929	2,725.20
1930	3,080.10
1931	2,664.00
1932	1,831.20

In commenting on the table the Committee says: "These figures disclose the unexpected fact that *industrial dividends and interest, even during the third year of the depression, were over twice as great as they were at any time prior to 1927.*" A fact somewhat more generally known is that "payrolls declined approximately 60 per cent from the second quarter of 1929 to the second quarter of 1932, while the number employed declined approximately 40 per cent."[37] Clearly those who control American industry are fully committed to the principle of gain-holding, as well as gain-seeking.

But the impression should not be given that the economic

[35] See James M. Williams, *Human Aspects of Unemployment and Relief* (Chapel Hill, 1933). Also Mauritz A. Halgren, *Seeds of Revolt* (New York, 1933).
[36] Report of the Committee on the Significance of Technocracy of the Society of Industrial Engineers, *op. cit.,* 15.
[37] Emmett H. Welch in Bulletin of the Taylor Society (New York, 1932), XVII, 169.

problem is merely one of achieving a more equal distribution of income. Even if the total goods and services produced were divided equally among the inhabitants of the country, the result would still be out of harmony with the productive power of the economic mechanism. At the very peak of prosperity in 1928 and 1929 when the system reached the highest level of productivity ever attained anywhere on the earth, the average per capita income amounted to no more than $750.[38] While this is relatively large, if compared with the position of other countries, it is scarcely sufficient to maintain a high level of health and comfort.

Efficiency of Operation. The failure of the inherited system of ideas and arrangements to provide economic security for the masses of the people is apparent. The inevitable conclusion is that it works badly. And an examination of its functioning reveals at least six major forms of waste or inefficiency; first, it is unable to keep the economic mechanism in steady and continuous operation; second, it seems incapable of coordinating production and consumption; third, it encourages the irrational use of energy and materials; fourth, it exploits natural resources without regard for the future; fifth, it places the economic interests of special classes above both moral and æsthetic considerations; and sixth, it fails to utilize science and technology fully and in the interests of society as a whole. Each of these six forms of inefficiency will be briefly reviewed.

Interruptions of production. That private capitalism has been unable to keep the productive and distributive mechanism in steady and continuous operation is entirely patent today. Indeed since the great tulip crash in Holland in 1637 society has been shaken to its very foundations from time to time by severe crises or depressions that stop the wheels of industry, throw millions of men out of employment, and bring misery and privation to whole populations. For the United States men-

38 W. I. King, *op. cit.,* 87. Also National Industrial Conference Board, *op. cit.,* 406.

tion need only be made of the major disasters of 1837, 1857, 1873, 1893, 1921, and 1929.

These periodic crises seem to inhere in *laissez-faire* economy, to express cumulative disharmony within the system, and to increase in scope and intensity with the rise of industrial society. So persistent are they that many have come to regard them as part of a natural economic order and economists have sought to discover the laws of their operation. Apparently the irrational forces of competition tend steadily toward a condition of extreme inco-ordination between production and consumption. According to the contentions of certain students of the question, depressions reflect the growing clash between technology in production and profit-seeking in distribution and the use of ox-cart methods of control in an age of high-powered automobiles and airplanes.[39] But whatever their causes, they reveal the gross inefficiency of the present economic order and point to the necessity of fundamental reform. Until they are checked, further advances of technology in the sphere of production will doubtless bring misery and insecurity. At any rate the transmuting of such advances into corresponding economic gains for the masses of the people cannot be expected.

Besides the great cataclysms that visit society at irregular intervals, there is the ebb and flow of activity inherent in seasonal change. The result is more idle labor and machinery, and failure to draw from the equipment the wealth that it is capable of producing. In such fields as clothing and coal mining the wastes involved in keeping the plant ready for intensive production during the busy season are increased by the competitive structure of industry. Since small units are unable to provide the capital or carry the risks involved in storage, their consequent readiness to supply at the peak of demand prevents the growth among consumers of more regular purchasing habits.

[39] See Bassett Jones, *Debt and Production* (New York, 1933); and Thorstein Veblen, *The Theory of Business Enterprise* (New York, 1927), and *The Engineers and the Price System* (New York, 1921).

A third source of interrupted production is the struggle between labor and capital that has come with large-scale enterprise
and that grows out of the conflict of interests between workmen
and the representatives of property. With the actual stoppage of
industry by strikes and lockouts everyone is only too familiar,
although as Wolman and Peck have pointed out, industrial calm
has reigned for fairly long periods, as for example during the
ten years following the great battles of 1922.[40] Of equal, if not
of greater, importance from the standpoint of efficiency is the
spread of the practice of voluntary restriction of output among
both organized and unorganized workers. "Restriction," says
Stanley B. Mathewson, in summarizing an extensive investigation of the question, "is a widespread institution, deeply
intrenched in the working habits of American laboring people."[41] Feeling that efficiency will not be rewarded and that it
may even be penalized through the lowering of piece rates or
the hastening of unemployment, the workman may exercise
vast ingenuity in achieving a high degree of inefficiency.

Finally, quite apart from periodic depressions, seasonal fluctuations, and labor struggles, stoppage of production in particular enterprises or industries may arise from a number of
causes. Due to the sensitiveness of the money and credit economy, accidents of finance may close factory doors. Peculation
by the management of a company, struggles for "control" by
moneyed interests,[42] temporary price changes, bank failures
may all result in waste of productive capacity. In addition,
since every industrial country has become a more or less
integral part of a great world economy, events taking place
beyond the national boundaries may have the most profound

[40] Leo Wolman and Gustav Peck, "Labor Groups in the Social Structure,"
Chapter XVI in *Recent Social Trends in the United States,* II, 840.
[41] Stanley B. Mathewson, *Restriction of Output Among Unorganized Workers* (New York, 1931), 146.
[42] See *They Told Barron,* edited and arranged by Arthur Pound and Samuel Taylor Moore (New York, 1930); J. T. Flynn, *Graft in Business* (New
York, 1931); Max Lowenthal, *The Investor Pays* (New York, 1933).

effects on the domestic credit structure and thus alter the pace of production.

All of these forces working together give to the economic system an extreme measure of instability and insecurity. Any retardation of the rate at which the productive mechanism operates brings about unemployment, with its incalculable human wastes, its reduction of consuming power, its spread of fear and uncertainty, and its interruption of the flow of business. The extremely volatile character of the system is clearly revealed in *The Annalist's* index of business activity for the month of June in each of the last six years:[43]

1928	98.7
1929	108.9
1930	89.0
1931	76.5
1932	52.9
1933	76.9

In the production of individual commodities the same index shows the following levels for June of 1933:[44]

Pig iron production	39.9
Steel ingot production	57.5
Freight car loadings	58.9
Electric power production	70.4
Bituminous coal production	65.6
Automotive production	63.6
Boot and shoe production	125.9
Zinc production	51.0

Inco-ordination of production and consumption. A second charge of inefficiency against the existing system is that it seems incapable of co-ordinating production and consumption. Wholly aside from, though closely related to, the recurring fortuitous failures to make use of its equipment, the competitive order tends steadily toward the installation of excessive

[43] *The Annalist*, XLII (July 21, 1933), 79.
[44] *Ibid.*, LXII (August 11, 1933), 185.

machinery. Competing enterprises and even competing industries, trusting in the gods of chance and not knowing with any precision what quantity of their product will be demanded, equip themselves for the peak loads which at any time they may carry or hope to carry. Shifts in the fortunes of the economic struggle may leave particular firms or entire industries "over-expanded." Shoes, soft coal, and cotton textiles may be offered as examples on a large scale today. Stuart Chase, using the early post-war figures, when over-capacity was unusually high, estimated the average plant-excess of the country's industries at 30 per cent.[45] According to A. D. Whitside, President of the Woolen Institute, the consumption of woolen fabrics in 1927 "amounted to approximately $656,000,000 as compared with a maximum manufacturing capacity of $1,750,000,000 at current prices."[46] And the President of the National Coal Association, speaking of conditions in the bituminous coal industry, estimated a total capacity for 1928 of 750,000,000 tons, whereas the average production for the three years of 1927–28– 29 was but 517,000,000.[47]

Under the present system there is an automatic tendency toward an unequal distribution of wealth. This in turn leads directly to the devotion of too much of the social income to investment and too little to consumption. As a result the system, if not out of balance at the moment, is always tending toward a state of disequilibrium. According to the testimony of the committee of industrial engineers, the "purchasing power of the majority of the population of the U. S. A." remained "practically unchanged" from 1919 to 1929 and "productive capacity" outran "buying ability." During this period, while the index of physical production advanced from 119 to 134, the index of distribution to the consumer increased from 100.9 to only 104.3.[48] Thus it would seem that the practice of gain-

---

[45] Stuart Chase, *The Tragedy of Waste* (New York, 1926), 189.
[46] Scoville Hamlin, *The Menace of Overproduction* (New York, 1930), 27.
[47] *Ibid.*, 4, 5. See also 160, 161.   [48] *Op. cit.*, 13–14.

seeking on the part of the owners and managers of capital, the corner stone of classical economic thought, leads inevitably to depression and disaster.

Powered machinery, when privately owned, gives to its possessors the right to a portion of the wealth produced. If an adequate share of the income thus received were immediately consumed, whatever social injustice might be involved in the process, a proper balance could be maintained. But the fact is that a disproportionate amount of it goes into investment and thus increases the claims of ownership on goods to be made in the future. As these claims mount in volume, they compel a progressive decline in the share of the total income that can go, through wage payments, into immediate consumption. The breach between buying and productive power consequently grows ever wider. To be sure, through the steady liquidation of the claims of ownership, due to badly conceived or knavishly induced investment, the system itself tends to generate its own correctives. According to W. L. Stoddard,[49] the annual loss occasioned by simple frauds amounts to two billion dollars. Even more colossal must be the amounts lost in the failures of "respectable" investment houses to gauge conditions at home or abroad accurately.[50] On the other hand, the growth of the claims of property is stimulated by the rationalization of industry, the introduction of automatic machinery, and the general decline in the role of human energy in the productive process. If proportionately less and less is to go to labor, because of the reduction in the hours of labor or the number of workmen employed, the instability of the system will be increased. Successful and continuous operation of the modern mechanism for the production and distribution of goods and services requires the systematic translation of gains in efficiency into lower prices and higher wages. The strain which it thus places on

[49] W. L. Stoddard, *Financial Racketeering and How to Stop It* (New York, 1931).

[50] See Fred C. Kelly, *How to Lose Your Money Prudently* (Philadelphia, 1933).

the business mentality and the mores of rugged individualism is doubtless too great to be borne.

The presence in industry of excessive productive capacities leads to a perpetual conflict of interest between hard-pressed firms, which wish to use their equipment to the fullest and sell the product even at ruinous prices, and the more solidly established companies which would benefit from a restriction of production. That the rapid growth and elaboration of trade associations in the country, not to mention various forms of racketeering in retail business, is largely the result of conflicts of this kind seems highly probable. The statistical information about market trends, circulated by many of these associations to their members, and the encouragement given to more exact methods of cost accounting look directly toward limitation of production. The sterner measures of semi-monopolistic combinations frequently operate so smoothly as to escape public notice. In a price economy these efforts at adjustment of production to effective demand probably operate to retard the abandonment of obsolescent or unwisely located equipment and so prevent losses of wealth and undesirable social dislocations which would accompany strictly competitive operation. Few of these quasi-controls, however, have been able to exert much influence on limiting the entry of new capital into the industries involved. And it is in the absence of such directives that one of the chief weaknesses of the present system lies.

The sorry plight of agriculture is closely related to this tendency of competition to over-capacity. From 1900 to 1930, because of the rapid spread of the use of farm machinery and power and the wholesale shift[51] from the worn lands of the eastern and southeastern states to the newer soils of the western regions, productivity per worker on the farms rose 30 per

[51] Between 1919 and 1929 approximately 32,000,000 acres, almost entirely in the states east of the Mississippi, were taken out of harvested crops, while an increase of 33,000,000 acres devoted to such crops occurred west of the river.— O. E. Baker, "Agricultural and Forest Land," Part 2 of Chapter II, "Utilization of Natural Wealth," *Recent Social Trends in the United States*, I, 108–109.

cent.[52] As a consequence, in spite of some decline of the rural
population in recent years, the total productive capacity of the
farms of the country has shown an enormous increase. At the
same time the market for products of the soil has not grown in
proportion. In agriculture as a whole, competition is still pris-
tine; and nowhere is the failure of this principle to achieve
stability better illustrated. Until recently efforts to form co-
operative associations, for the most part marketing agencies
only, have made little headway. Since farmers have been unable
to combine to limit production, much marginal land has remained in cultivation and agricultural prices have been driven
to levels ruinous to the rural population. The situation is further complicated by the weight[53] of farm mortgages which
compels farmers to produce cash crops rather than subsistence
for themselves; and the influence of the tariff, which raises the
cost of manufactured goods without providing compensation
through the protection of the prices of farm products. But in
the main agricultural difficulties may be traced to excess capacity occasioned by free competition. A dreary and tragic
road of liquidation of marginal and submarginal lands would
seem to lie ahead. And with respect to the future the problem
is greatly aggravated by the fact that the application of technology to agriculture is still in its early stages, and by the
further fact that the country faces a stationary population
within the course of a generation or two. This means that
vast areas will have to be taken out of cultivation and the number of farmers, or the amount of farming done by the individual, greatly reduced.

The point should be emphasized, however, that the competitive system has not really created a general condition of
over-production, as is so often claimed. Facts already given
regarding the distribution of income among the American

[52] *Ibid.,* 99.
[53] The interest charges on these mortgages have been estimated at $700,-
000,000 a year. Lawrence Dennis, *Is Capitalism Doomed* (New York, 1932),
133.

people show with unmistakable clarity that the real difficulty lies elsewhere. While industry has no doubt in some cases produced too much of a given commodity or even produced commodities that are individually and socially harmful, on the whole it has produced far too little and far less than it is capable of producing. The charge against the system, therefore, is not that it tends to over-produce, but rather that it creates a chronic condition of under-consumption. Even in times of greatest prosperity severe privation prevails among great masses of the people; and in days of adversity starving men, women, and children must witness rich foods rotting on the wharf or in shop windows.[54] Thus far private capitalism has failed to distribute steadily and continuously sufficient purchasing power among the population to take from the shelves the goods that the productive mechanism is able to place on the market.

This failure has given rise to a number of strange phenomena. Among other things it has led to the practice, to be outlined in the next section, of forcing goods upon the consumer. Through various devices, such as installment buying and the assumption of mortgages, the individual is encouraged to live beyond his means. He is even made to believe that the purchase or consumption, even wasteful consumption, of goods is a patriotic duty. Then, when the domestic market is exhausted, the scene is shifted to foreign countries and an effort is made to find consumers in other lands. The extension of credits abroad to finance foreign consumption of American natural resources and of goods produced by American labor may be hailed as a great economic victory. On the other hand, the importation from abroad of raw materials, of which the United States is inadequately supplied from the standpoint of the long-time needs of the country, such as wood pulp and manganese, may be bitterly opposed. Finally, after all else fails, and the market continues to be glutted, commodities may be destroyed on a huge scale. Thus, when in the summer of

[54] See Harper Leech, *The Paradox of Plenty* (New York, 1932).

1933 the cotton-growers, under government leadership, agreed to plow up 9,000,000 acres of cotton and so destroy one-fourth of their crop, George N. Peek, chief administrator of the adjustment program, hailed the event as "the greatest achievement in the history of American agriculture."[55] One can only imagine how such an achievement would have been viewed by the self-contained farm family of the pre-industrial age.

Irrational use of energy and materials. A third basic weakness of the present system is the encouragement which it gives to the irrational use of energy and materials. Although changes in consumption habits are inevitable and desirable, *laissez-faire* resorts to exceedingly wasteful methods of discovering the wants of the population. Indeed it complicates the problem by teasing consumers to demand many extravagant, silly, and useless wares, and even seeks to arouse desire for much that is downright injurious. Competition among producers multiplies indefinitely the variety of goods produced. While the resulting multiplicity of brands and patterns has considerable novelty and some artistic value, the method employed to this end is undoubtedly a very costly one. Recently the federal Department of Commerce has taken the lead with remarkable success in a movement for the simplification of practice and the elimination of useless and worthless distinctions in certain fields. In nearly all luxury and semi-luxury goods, however, since minor differences are necessary as selling points, the number of varieties marketed continues to be very large. The attendant waste is partly in the needless duplication of investments and partly in the increased cost of production caused by the frequent setting and scrapping of machinery.

Moreover, since the guide to production is the hope of profit, as influenced by a possible market demand, a not inconsiderable portion of the energies of the country has been turned to the making of goods intended to play upon human fallibilities. Stuart Chase, after exploring the traffic in harmful drugs,

[55] *The New York Times,* July 15, 1933.

adulterated goods, patent medicines, distilled spirits, commercialized vice, crime, quack professional "services," gambling and speculation, super-luxuries and fashions, and advertising, has estimated that the calculable wastes involved consume a man-power of some seven millions.[56] In order to protect itself against the more extreme abuses of this type society has imposed such minor controls as laws prohibiting fraud or license, motion-picture and radio censorship, taxation of luxuries, the Pure Food and Drugs Act, and the Federal Trade Commission. Such measures, however, are far too few and feeble to counteract the powerful drive for profits.

Resources are wasted, moreover, not only in the making of socially undesirable goods, but also in forcing these and other goods upon the consumer. Unintelligently conceived or badly managed production, arising out of the desire for gain, becomes dependent on the artificial arousal of demand. And since the general welfare requires the continuous operation of the productive mechanism, a curious doctrine of waste is promulgated as the essence of economic wisdom. Every citizen is told that he should consume copiously and extravagantly, leaving the morrow to take care of itself; and every salesman is taught that the forcing of more and more goods upon the public is a cardinal virtue and the road to "progress." Society thus arrives at the strange reversal of logic: men produce not in order that they may consume; on the contrary, they consume in order that they may produce. Commodities must not even be made too well, lest they wear too long and thus slow up the expansion of industry. Consequently products commonly carry extravagant charges, accumulated in the search for purchasers. Indeed the costs of production in many cases may be far less than the costs of distribution and sale. The entire system of retail marketing, with its innumerable competing units, each with a heavy burden of overhead charges, is lavish in its use of the nation's energies. Although the growth of department and

[56] Stuart Chase, *The Tragedy of Waste* (New York, 1926), 106.

chain stores has achieved certain economies, M. A. Copeland regards as "probably true" the statement that "marketing costs, in contrast to production costs, have been tending to rise, in ratio to sales, over a period of years."[57] The same writer says that "from 1921 to 1927, the total annual expenditures for advertising in the United States probably increased about 50 per cent."[58] It has also been estimated that installment selling adds as much as 10 per cent to the retail price of commodities sold under its provisions.

The wide differences in income levels, so characteristic of capitalism, are undoubtedly an important factor in promoting the wasteful employment of the resources of the country. Purchasing power being concentrated disproportionately in the hands of a small class, the productive and distributive system tends to revolve about the desires and standards of this class. As a consequence, the steady purveying of goods to the poor proceeds unnoticed and with relatively little improvement from time to time, while industry devotes itself assiduously to inciting and capturing the rapidly changing tastes of the bourgeoisie. The domination of this class in the sphere of consumption is clearly revealed in advertisements. Only rarely do these reflections of the business mind direct their appeal to members of the laboring classes. The masses, lacking purchasing power, except for the necessities, receive comparatively little attention.

Waste of natural resources. In the fourth place the inherited economic order tends to disregard the long-run interests of society. The regime of free competition, operating through a price system, can be counted upon to protect those interests only when such action is thought to be financially profitable to private enterprise. This fact is illustrated in the exploitation of the material riches of the country. No doubt the sight of a continent to be possessed and the very abundance

[57] M. A. Copeland, "Marketing," Chapter V in *Recent Economic Changes in the United States,* I, 421.

[58] *Ibid.,* 424.

of the opportunities to be grasped increased the intensity of the struggle for wealth. At any rate a powerful tradition of despoliation, going back to pioneer days, has become deeply rooted in the mores; and the destruction of game and timber and soil, practised by the early settler, has been followed by succeeding generations and continues even to the present day. In the midst of seemingly indefinite plenty and inexhaustible resources there appeared to be no need to save. "Here's a fine animal," said the frontiersman, "let's kill it. Here's a big tree, let's cut it down. Here's a thick sod, let's plow it up."[59] Such was the motto of the rugged individualist in his rapid trek across the continent. And the growth of science and technology has multiplied his primitive strength a millionfold.

The destruction of animal life, while perhaps not greatly significant from the standpoint of the welfare of the nation, reveals the disregard of the future and of humane instincts so characteristic of a strongly competitive economy. The bison, which at the time of the discovery roamed over almost the entire continent and numbered, according to rough estimate, 150,000,000 head, is today practically extinct. Following the completion of the great continental railroads after the Civil War the vast herds of the Great Plains literally melted away before the white man's gun. Lieutenant-Colonel Richard I. Dodge has thus described the annihilation of the southern herds by men brought into the region in the seventies by the Santa Fé, each intent on getting-rich-quick through the hunt on buffalo hides:

"By wagon, on horseback, and a-foot, the pot-hunters poured in, and soon the unfortunate buffalo was without a moment's peace or rest. Though hundreds of thousands of skins were sent to market, they scarcely indicated the slaughter. From want of skill in shooting, and want of knowledge in preserving the hides of those slain, on the part of these green hunters, one hide sent to market represented three, four, or even five

[59] J. Russell Smith, *North America* (New York, 1925), 26.

dead buffalo. . . . In the beginning . . . the hunting parties organized themselves on any haphazard basis. Every man wanted to shoot; no man wanted to do the other work. Buffalo were slaughtered without sense or discretion, and oftentimes left to rot with the hides on."[60]

As the months and years passed the slaughter became organized into an industry and the career of the American bison drew rapidly to a close. The last cargo of hides was shipped east over the Northern Pacific in 1884; and the last buffalo hunt within the United States was conducted in 1886.

The story of the buffalo was repeated with many other forms of animal life. The fur seal, both male and female, were killed in their rookeries during the breeding season and their helpless offspring left to die. The alligator of the streams and lakes of the southeast was pursued with such ruthless zeal that it is now almost extinct and its native waters are being re-stocked by the Fish Commission. A survey conducted in 1909 by William T. Hornaday, Director of the New York Zoological Park, showed that bird life had decreased from 50 to 70 per cent in many states and as much as 77 per cent in Florida. Birds at one time plentiful, such as the swan, the wood-duck, and the wild turkey, are now extremely rare. The white heron, so numerous along the coasts of Florida and the Gulf states at the beginning of the nineteenth century that a single tree would harbor fifty to one hundred nests, was exterminated to satisfy the fashion in millinery. During the nesting season both sexes "become adorned with delicate spraylike plumes. . . . In order to secure these plumes at their best, the hunters concealed themselves into one of the breeding grounds or 'heronries' and killed the parent birds as they returned with food for their young."[61] But perhaps the most thorough and merciless campaign of destruction was waged against the passenger pigeon. With

60 Richard I. Dodge, *The Plains of the Great West* (New York, 1877), 131, 134.
61 Rudolph Cronau, *Our Wasteful Nation* (New York, 1908), 89.

nets, fire, and whiskey this bird was trapped by the million
and shipped to the city market from 1840 to 1880. Hear the
testimony of Pikagon, a converted Pottawattamie chieftain:
"In my youth, the countless numbers of the pigeons led me to
believe that they were almost as inexhaustible as the great ocean
itself. Yet notwithstanding their incredible numbers, great
endurance and long life, they have entirely disappeared from
our forests. We strain our eyes in spring and autumn in vain
to catch a glimpse of these pilgrims."[62] The same greed, waste,
and improvidence have marked the exploitation of the fish
resources of the country. Through the disregard of the spawn-
ing season, the use of fine-meshed nets, and the pollution of
waters by refuse from factories and mills, various species of
fish have been threatened with extinction. Only the interference of a federal commission has prevented the complete
destruction of the salmon. And so the account could be indefinitely prolonged to include the beaver, the sea otter, the pronghorn, the whale, the manatee, the shad, the lobster, the green
turtle. Under the system of individual enterprise, when profits
are at stake, no form of wild life can be secure.

The treatment of the forests was of the same order as that
of the buffalo, the salmon, and the passenger pigeon. To the
pioneer, trees were an obstacle to be removed, a foe to be vanquished. And man finally won his battle with the forest. "The
settlers," says Rudolph Cronau, "felled it, smashed it, burned it,
till they got all the room they wanted. Their children followed
this example and destroyed the forest with the same reckless-
ness they would have used against their worst enemy."[63]

The pioneer, however, was fighting a bitter struggle with
nature for land and home and family. Also he was merely interested in removing the timber from fertile regions. But with
the growth of the lumber trade, occasioned by the settlement of
the country, the possibility of making huge fortunes out of the
forests led to destruction on an enormous scale. Lumber com-

[62] *Ibid.*, 86.   [63] *Ibid.*, 11.

panies fought among themselves and bribed legislatures for possession of the choicest timber lands of the nation and then proceeded to extract from those lands the largest amount of profit in the shortest possible time. The methods employed in the eastern lumber camps are described in a passage from "a leading magazine" quoted by Mr. Cronau:

"In the Maine and New Hampshire forests thousands of men spend the winter cutting the forests of the choicest lumber and destroying young growing trees on every hand in their haste to get ready for the high water in the spring. All the big sound trees of a desirable species are cut without regard to their surroundings; withdrawing the necessary shelter from a crop of seedlings in one place, killing others in the fall and removing of the timber; here felling all the seed trees, so that there will be no reproduction; there clearing the way for a worthless species that will promptly choke out the valuable ones; cutting the best sections from the fallen timber, and leaving the tops and boughs and parts of the trunks to dry and rot and litter the forest floor with highly inflammable rubbish. Those parts of the timbered forest that do not degenerate into mere brush, grow a thin second crop of very inferior lumber, and sooner or later the inevitable spark, dropped by the locomotive or the camper or the lumberman himself, finds its way into the dry refuse, and what is left of a thousand acres or a thousand miles, as may be, of woodland, goes up in flame."[64]

As a consequence of these methods, applied with variations to one region after another from the Atlantic to the Pacific, the primeval forests of unrivalled extent and quality have gone "the way of all flesh." Only one-eighth of the original 822 million acres of forest has escaped the ravages of axe and saw and fire. The present situation has thus been summarized by George P. Ahern:

"Virgin timber in every forest region but the Pacific North-

64 *Ibid.*, 12–13.

west is about to disappear. . . . Second growth timber, our sole remaining hope for wood, is deteriorating because of destructive logging practices, uncontrolled fires, and unreasonable and uncertain local taxation. . . . Forest depletion in the United States amounts annually to the equivalent of sixty billion board feet. The annual growth . . . is estimated at not to exceed ten billion board feet.[65]

"The colossal area which continues to be burned over annually in the United States seems almost unbelievable in this modern age. . . . But the ghastly record is irrefutable. During the five year period from 1925 through 1929, an average of 45 million acres of forest land was burned over annually. During 1930 some 191,000 fires swept over 52 million acres. Thus in one single year ten per cent of the total forest area of the United States was destroyed or seriously reduced in productivity by these largely avoidable conflagrations.[66]

"Lumbermen interested in continuing the profits they make from forest devastation have spent great sums in propaganda intended to make people believe that the future of American forests is safe. Many have been deceived, but the fact is that nothing could be farther from the truth. Propagandists say that forests reproduce themselves and that we will soon have timber crops like cotton, corn, and wheat. It is true forests reproduce themselves if fire is controlled, seed trees left, and Nature given a chance; but Nature is balked by man at every turn.

"Much is said of our reforestation operations, but as a matter of fact we replant on public and private woodland areas about 155,000 acres annually. In contrast, Japan, although staggering under a colossal debt and not much larger in area than California, plants trees each year on more than twice the entire area planted in the United States."[67]

The supply of certain of the finest woods, such as white pine

65 Lt. Col. George P. Ahern, *Forest Bankruptcy in America* (Washington, 1933), 13.
66 *Ibid.*, 17.   67 *Ibid.*, 308–309.

and black walnut, which not so many years ago was regarded
as inexhaustible, has almost vanished from the market; and
whole regions once covered by forests of unforgettable majesty
give the appearance of having been struck by a cyclone or
visited by some terrible blight. The destruction of the forests,
moreover, has upset the delicate balance of nature and seriously
affected the flow of water from the highlands to the sea. With
the cutting of the trees many springs and streams have disappeared altogether; others dry up in the summer and overflow
in the spring. Thus the Ohio River, formerly one of the most
regular of waterways and in itself a natural resource of great
value, has lost much of its usefulness and at certain seasons
of the year has even become a menace to both life and property. Because of the removal of the forests covering its water-
shed in the Appalachians, the spring rains rush down the
mountain slopes in torrents, raise the river out of its banks,
inundate great districts of cultivated land, and carry off the
richest elements of the soil.

This suggests that the American people have had no more
regard for their soil than for their other resources. And such
is the case. Through leaching and erosion great areas, particularly in the east and south, have been rendered unfit for
agriculture. According to H. H. Bennett of the United States
Bureau of Chemistry and Soils, "something like 17,500,000
acres of land which were formerly cultivated in this country
have been destroyed by gullying, or so severely washed that
farmers cannot afford to attempt their cultivation or reclama-
tion."[68] This exceeds the total acreage of arable land in the
whole of Japan.[69] "In the Piedmont of Georgia, the Carolinas
and Virginia," says Mr. Bennett, "probably not less than 60 per
cent of all the upland . . . has lost from 4 to 18 inches of its
soil . . . many of the gullies have cut down to bed rock."[70]

[68] Quoted by O. E. Baker, "Agricultural and Forest Land," Part 2 of
Chapter II, "Utilization of Natural Wealth," in *Recent Social Trends in the
United States*, I, 95.
[69] *Ibid.*, footnote.   [70] Quoted in *ibid.*, 95–96.

This same authority also declares that a fourth of the cultivated land in the United States has lost perhaps a third of its top-soil, and that another fourth has been robbed of a sixth or more of this fertile stratum. Unregulated grazing on unfenced pub-lic ranges has destroyed vegetation, exposed the soil to wash-ing, increased the violence of floods, and filled the rivers with silt. Then the single-crop method of farming, practised by both the pioneer and the commercial farmer, has seriously depleted the fertility of much of the land of the country. Mary Huston Gregory has thus described this process of soil exhaustion:

"In the early days of farming in this country, it was the custom to grow a single crop, which had been found to give good results, year after year in the same field. In Virginia and other near-by states nearly all the best land was given every year to the cultivation of tobacco, which exhausts the soil rap-idly. In the states farther north other crops were planted in the same way. As a result, some of the most fertile soil in Virginia, the Carolinas, Massachusetts, and other eastern states has been so exhausted that it is no longer worth cultivating. Everywhere throughout the New England states are to be found these worn-out farms, and, while they were never so fertile as the lands of the Mississippi Valley, each one was rich enough to support a family in comfort, with something left to sell; but because they were required to produce the same crops, and so take the same element from the soil, year after year, they have be-come so lacking in one of the essential elements that they are unfit for cultivation, and have been abandoned."[71]

In some respects the waste of mineral resources, which has flourished so vigorously under the regime of *laissez-faire,* is most serious of all. These resources, in a peculiar sense the foundation of industrial civilization, are all limited, and many severely limited, in extent. Also, unlike the animal life, the forests, and even the soil, they are incapable of being renewed

[71] Mary Huston Gregory, *Checking the Waste* (Indianapolis, 1911), 18.

except in terms of geological ages. The mode of their exploitation consequently serves as an excellent measure of the long-time efficiency of an economic system.

The entire story cannot be re-told here. It must suffice to point out that the mineral riches of the country have been looked upon primarily, not as a valuable material heritage to be utilized and conserved with careful regard for the needs of the remote future, but rather as opportunities for the accumulation of private wealth. The result has been a serious neglect of the interests of society as a whole. The cream has been skimmed from the mines of the nation, whether mention be made of iron or copper or coal or oil or the precious metals.[72] In getting the cream, moreover, much good milk has been spilled and lost forever. The fact that the reserves of all of the more important minerals are still sufficient to meet the requirements of the country for many years to come does not justify the practices of the past. In addressing the Conference of Governors meeting in Washington in May, 1908, at the call of President Theodore Roosevelt, I. C. White, State Geologist of West Virginia, had this to say regarding the exploitation of the nation's fuel resources: "The wildest anarchists determined to destroy and overturn the foundations of government could not act in a more irrational and thoughtless manner than have our People in permitting such fearful destruction of the very sources of our power and greatness."[73]

In the mining of coal, Mr. White pointed out that methods wasteful in the extreme have been employed and that from 40 to 70 per cent of the total deposits have been left underground.[74] Competitive enterprise opens too many pits, depresses the price, and leads operating companies to work only the richest and most accessible seams and leave secondary sup-

[72] See F. G. Tryon and Margaret H. Schoenfeld, *op. cit.*, 77–85.
[73]*Proceedings* of a Conference of Governors in the White House, Washington, D. C., May 13–15, 1908 (Washington, 1909), 27.
[74] *Ibid.*, 32. Also see Mary van Kleeck, *Miners and Management* (New York, 1934).

plies abandoned and unworkable. Tryon and Schoenfeld thus summarize the situation:

"The economic losses are by this time a familiar story. Here we must stress the waste of resources that such destructive competition compels. After field examination of hundreds of mines in all the major eastern districts, the engineers of the United States Coal Commission placed the average loss in mining bituminous coal at 35 per cent, of which 15 per cent is classed as unavoidable and 20 per cent as avoidable under present known practice. In the agricultural states of the middle west, the loss averages from 37 to 53 per cent, nearly half the coal being left underground in pillars and stumps without attempt at recovery. The engineers of the Coal Commission were careful to refer to the tonnage sacrificed as a 'loss' and not a 'waste,' and in justice to the coal operators it must be made plain that they had no choice in the matter. Sheer abundance of resources and competition in an over-developed industry forced them to adopt such practices or go out of business. But from the social viewpoint the fact remains that 150,000,000 tons of minable coal is left underground every year under circumstances which render its recovery highly improbable. The avoidable loss is as great as the entire bituminous production of post-war Germany."[75]

In the case of petroleum the situation is even more arresting. Competition has caused rival firms to tap the same reservoir, relieve the pressure on the oil, and thus place large quantities of this precious fuel beyond recovery. But natural gas affords the most extreme illustration of the wastefulness of *laissez-faire*. This extraordinary gift of nature, found in quantity in no other great industrial nation, has been permitted to escape into the air in almost unlimited quantities. "There can be no doubt," Mr. White told the Conference of Governors in 1908, "that for every barrel of oil taken from the earth there

[75] *Op. cit.*, 86.

have been wasted more than 10 times its equivalent in heating power, or weight even, of this best of all fuels; and that much more than half of this frightful waste could have been avoided by proper care and slight additional expenditures in oil-production."[76] According to Wilbur and DuPuy, "in California . . . it is estimated that the loss of natural gas alone has been sufficient to have paid the national debt. Every day for years in that State enough gas has been going off unused into the air to do the work of 25,000 tons of coal. The same sort of gas losses has taken place in Oklahoma, and notably in Texas. And these losses still go on. New fields have been brought in when there was already too much oil above ground. They have been produced when they were not needed. They have depressed the market and hurt the industry. They have been depleted without serving any useful purpose. . . . There has been no time to stop, to estimate the situation, to map out a proper course of action."[77]

Disregard of moral and æsthetic interests. A fifth weakness of *laissez-faire* lies in its tendency to place the economic interests of special classes above both moral and æsthetic considerations. This may best be illustrated by reference to the influence of business on government. It has been charged that private ownership of industry must be held accountable for corrupting the local, state, and national governments. Admittedly American political institutions were devised in the eighteenth century to represent the more prosperous elements in agriculture and commerce. As these earlier economic interests were superseded by industry, political institutions were forced into new molds.[78] The transfer of power was achieved through the wholesale corruption of officials by industrial combinations, through the pressures of special interests, and through the deception of electors by governmental bodies. The evidence

[76] *Op. cit.,* 27.
[77] R. L. Wilbur and W. A. DuPuy, *Conservation in the Department of the Interior* (Washington, 1931), 52.
[78] See below, Part Two, Chapter X, "Government."

brought forward by numerous investigators[79] on this point can scarcely be refuted.

In every industrial country the interest on the part of private enterprise in tariffs, franchises, concessions, exemption from the laws, and special privileges of every description has led to the prostitution of government to the promotion of strictly private ends. Certainly in the United States, in local, state, and national politics, the record is continuous from the period of the Civil War down to the organization of the Reconstruction Finance Corporation of the Hoover Administration and the investigation of the great banking houses in 1933. In speaking of municipal administration, Charles J. Bullock remarked on one occasion that "behind the boodle alderman one finds the eminent banker and respectable financier." Woodrow Wilson once said that "the masters of the government of the United States are the combined capitalists and manufacturers of the United States." And Max Lowenthal in his study[80] of the receivership of the Chicago, Milwaukee and St. Paul Railway—the largest receivership in the history of American finance—shows how the courts may be manipulated by rich men bent on adding to their riches. Even the House of Morgan, with its carefully cultivated reputation for probity, engages in the practice of extending favors to persons high in the political councils of the nation and to members of both the old political parties. The common but erroneous belief that politicians are more corrupt than business leaders is doubtless due to the fact that they are judged by higher standards. In fact, corruption of a kind is the essence of business, sanctified by a long tradition. In their relations with government business men merely apply the code of their calling.[81] When occasionally they are

[79] For example see Charles A. Beard, *Economic Interpretation of the Constitution of the United States* (New York, 1914); Matthew Josephson, *The Robber Barons* (New York, 1934); Harry W. Laidler, *Concentration of Control in American Industry* (New York, 1931); Lincoln Steffens' *Autobiography* (New York, 1931); Carl D. Thompson, *Confessions of the Power Trust* (New York, 1932).

[80] Max Lowenthal, *The Investor Pays* (New York, 1933).

[81] See John T. Flynn, *Graft in Business* (New York, 1931).

called to book by an irate and exasperated public, it is only
natural that they should feel themselves victims of mob hys-
teria. They know that they have merely been caught doing
what all of their confrères have been doing for generations.
There is doubtless much truth in the dictum of Plato that:
"Ruin comes when the trader, whose heart is lifted up by
wealth, becomes ruler."

Few students of social institutions have enjoyed better opportunities for witnessing the process of the corruption of politics by business than Sir Arthur Salter. After ten years of the
most intimate contact with the governments of the world, he
speaks of government "failing because it has become inmeshed
in the task of giving discretionary, partial, preferential privileges to competitive industry, by methods which involve detailed examination and subject it to sectional pressure."[82] In
another place he points out that "those interests which are so
organized as to exercise the strongest political pressure get
protection, or the highest rates of protection, at the expense of
the rest of the community. . . . The evil consequences are
illimitable. Time, energy, attention, money that should be
devoted to improving processes, are devoted to persuading
politicians. The system offers the highest rewards, the richest
spoils, to those who can most successfully corrupt the Government. The machine of Government itself—in the widest
sense, including the Ministry, the Civil Service, the Parliament,
and the Electorate—cannot under these conditions, and does
not, remain honest and competent enough to perform its primary tasks."[83] Thus economic interest, pursued by men who
seek private gain by destroying the moral fiber of government, has made almost superhuman the task of applying to the
wastes and maladjustments of the present order the correctives
which social welfare requires.

In similar fashion the urge for private profit overrides
æsthetic considerations.[84] This is shown clearly in the subordi-

[82] Sir Arthur Salter, *Recovery* (New York, 1932), 341.
[83] *Ibid.*, 210.   [84] See below, Part Two, Chapter VIII, "Art."

nation of the beauties of the natural landscape to the motive of wealth accumulation. Only where such beauties can be exploited for purposes of personal gain are they conserved, unless the public takes a hand. Also the evanescent and particularistic interests of business enterprise have shown themselves incapable, in the large, of achieving an ordered and efficient arrangement of the physical *mise en scene*. The city pattern of blocks and streets, designed for easy speculation, has given little of comfort, even less of beauty, and at a terrific cost of waste and congestion. According to the Regional Plan this cost amounts to $500,000 a day for New York City and $1,000,000 for the entire metropolitan area. It is of course true that the lines of urban development were set in the age of steam power; and steam demanded concentration. New types of industrial communities, based upon electricity and gasoline, are already appearing in the Piedmont of the Carolinas and Virginia, in the south of England, and elsewhere. But these communities, though less congested than the cities of an earlier generation, have discovered no way to conserve the permanent interests of their inhabitants without the substitution of local or regional planning for land speculation.

The struggle for private gain seems to compel all who engage in the contest either to descend to the practices of their competitors or go to the wall. As bad money drives out good, so in business ethics, unless collective action intervenes, the low tends to displace the high. This tendency is noted particularly in the cultural agencies, such as the press, the movie, and the radio, which are run for profit. Almost a generation ago, Edward Bellamy perceived the dilemma of the socially minded business man and remarked that under competition there was no free play whatever allowed for the capitalist's better feelings, even if he had any. He could not be better than the system. If he tried to be, the system would crush him. He had to follow the pace set by his companions or fail in business. Whatever rascality or cruelty his rivals might devise he must imitate or drop out of the struggle. The very wickedest, mean-est, and most rascally of the competitors—the one who ground his employees lowest, adulterated his goods most shamefully and lied about them most skilfully—set the pace for all the rest.[85] In his radio address to the nation on July 24, 1933, Presi-dent Roosevelt directed attention to the same difficulty. "It is obvious," he said, "that without united action, a few selfish men in each competitive group will pay starvation wages and insist on long hours of work. Others in that group must either follow suit or close up shop."[86]

But since the entire population is now drawn into the pecuniary economy, the ethics of gain-seeking permeates the whole economic fabric. The laborer applies the principle of self-interest to his job and engages in a game of deliberate withdrawal of efficiency; and everywhere the tradition seems to be making headway among the youth that one need not work for a living, or at least that one should seek out some easy berth in the economic system and live by his wits. This tendency reaches its logical conclusion in racketeering. The following apology by a labor leader turned racketeer re-veals a type of mentality that is by no means uncommon in the present age:

"As to the other 'rackets' (besides bootlegging liquor), as you call them—we call them 'business'—they're a damn sight more moral than most of the rackets that usually go by the name of corporation. Let us admit that we, the so-called racketeers, do 'extort' money from so-called legitimate business establish-ments—what of it? Doesn't every other gang of business men do the same thing, one way or another? Isn't practically every-thing that is sold in America sold for more than it is worth—first by the manufacturer, then by the wholesaler, finally by the retailer? Business is a hold-up game from top to bottom. Those on top exploit those beneath them economically. Capi-

[85] Edward Bellamy, *Equality* (New York, 1898), 79–121.
[86] *The New York Times,* July 25, 1933.

tal exploits labor. . . . Big business screws small business. Of course they have made it legal and moral."[87]

In his commencement address delivered on June 6, 1933, President Nicholas Murray Butler spoke of the exaltation of the gain-seeking motive in contemporary society as a "pathologic phenomenon." This motive, he told the graduating classes at Columbia University, "has been running riot throughout the world for several generations, and nowhere more violently or with more shocking results than in the United States. It has been found not only possible but easy for men to explain and to defend acts undertaken through the dominance of the gain-seeking motive which, when fully revealed and clearly understood, have amazed and shocked thoughtful men and women everywhere. . . . If the gain-seeking motive is to be exalted to the highest place, then morals disappear and life becomes a struggle for the survival of the most unfit." In referring to the corrupting power of money he attacked the very citadel of the present economic system. "Control of money and constant association with money," he said, "is perhaps the most demoralizing of human occupations. Small wonder that in the ancient world it was thought to be a fit occupation for slaves! There is something about this contact and control which obscures moral principles and human values, and tends to develop a stiffly legalistic attitude toward every human relationship."

Failure to utilize science and technology. A sixth and final defect of the inherited order is its failure to make full use of science and technology. To be sure, as is demonstrated in a later chapter, the past generation has witnessed an unprecedented growth of industrial research.[88] But society at large is not receiving benefits commensurate with the development. In the field of consumption this is perhaps best illustrated by the refusal of the federal government to place the

[87] Louis Adamic, *Dynamite* (New York, 1931), 369–370.
[88] See below, Part Two, Chapter VII, "Science."

findings of the Bureau of Standards at the disposal of the ordinary consumer. Characteristically the function of getting and disseminating dependable information regarding the quality of goods is left to a co-operative body such as Consumers' Research. While production is free from the deliberate obfuscation which advertising injects into consumption, it has its own methods of restraining the spread of knowledge. Through protection given to "business secrets" artificial barriers, designed to hold technical information closely, are erected everywhere. The time-honored defense, justifying this procedure on the grounds that the inventor or investigator would not put forth his best efforts if he were not assured of monopoly privileges, has been proved false by the experience of industry itself. The great majority of scientific workers today receive regular salaries that bear no relation to the value of their discoveries. The latter are the property of the employing firms and may or may not be developed technically, depending upon the policies of the holders of the patent rights. Often they are locked in the safe and held as a form of legal protection against the claims of rival companies.

Under the current relationship between science and industry, however, knowledge may not only be suppressed or not fully used. It may be devoted to something less than the promotion of the common welfare. The object of much of the research carried on under the auspices of industry is neither the disinterested pursuit of truth nor the general improvement of the material lot of men, but rather the advancement of the pecuniary fortunes of private persons or companies. The scientist, the technologist, the engineer is forced into the role of the docile servant of business. In the degree that the interests of business and society coincide, the relationship may not work badly; but to the extent that these interests diverge, it can only result in substituting the lesser for the greater good. The fact that they do diverge is brought out clearly in the report of the committee of industrial engineers, already referred to.

In concluding its discussion of the question of technological unemployment the committee states succinctly "that we are suffering *not* from technological unemployment but from THE UNEMPLOYMENT OF TECHNOLOGY."[89]

THE END OF LAISSEZ-FAIRE

This conflict between business and technology was pointed out some years ago by Thorstein Veblen[90] and recently has been developed in more detail by the engineers themselves.[91] It has also been sensed by Harold J. Laski in the following passage:

"The significance of the foundation of industrialism in the technical sciences seems to have escaped the business man. As these sciences have developed, they have become organized into professions; they have created within themselves a spirit of their craft, of which the essence is a refusal to be governed by the mere motives of private gain. They display, in fact, standards, habits, and purposes which escape the control of the business man because they are outside the range of the knowledge his specialty confers upon him. Just as the lawyer and the doctor have always been more than men who gain a living by the practice of law or medicine, so the engineer, the chemist, the architect, to take only obvious examples, have developed a sense of service to an ideal in which money-making has no necessary part."[92]

The foregoing analysis makes abundantly clear the inefficiency of the inherited economic order. However well its basic institutions and ideas may have functioned in the loosely knit

[89] *Op. cit.*, 25.
[90] See Thorstein Veblen, *The Engineers and the Price System* (New York, 1921).
[91] See Bassett Jones, *Debt and Production* (New York, 1933), and Walter N. Polakov, *The Power Age* (New York, 1933).
[92] Harold J. Laski, *Democracy in Crisis* (Chapel Hill, 1933), 59. Also see Fred Henderson, *The Economic Consequences of Power Production* (London, 1931), *passim*.

pioneering society of a century ago founded on agriculture and handicrafts, it functions badly today. It has failed to use in the interests of the masses of the people the economic power that has come with the advance of technology. In spite of the creation of a truly miraculous mechanism for the production of goods, men feel less secure than they did in the days of the frontier and free land. At all times the majority of the population live in a condition of more or less uncertainty, while in periods of crisis even the favored economic classes know not what the future will bring. That the doctrines and practices of *laissez-faire* therefore should have been modified is to be expected. Already they have been profoundly altered by the impact of the forces of industrialism. A review of four dominant trends of the past several generations will show this to be the case—the trend toward consolidation of business enterprise, the trend toward co-operation in agriculture, the trend toward organization of labor, and the trend toward government intervention in economy.

Consolidation of Business Enterprise. The tendency toward consolidation of business enterprise early made itself manifest. As the fixed charges of capital grew in relation to the total cost of production, the possibility of investment losses in any single undertaking through competition mounted proportionately. Cobblers cannot long work at prices which do not yield a living for all competitors; low prices will quickly drive some from the field. But shoe factories will operate for years at prices which yield only a driblet or even a negative return on the investment. With heavy outlays in plant and machinery and high overhead costs of management, any concern is under pressure to sell its product in volume regardless of price. Obviously, advances in power-machine production have carried this pressure to ever new intensities. The inevitable response has been a general linking of units within each industry in order to reduce in so far as possible the perils of competition. Of the numerous devices which have been used for this purpose (pools, trusts, interlocking directorates, holding companies, mergers, trade associations) some have sought regulation of supply and adherence to fixed prices, while others have worked mainly for economies in operation and have been content to see prices fall with increased volume of sales. The effect in either case has been to confirm the habit of co-operation among enterprises in the same industry and to bring into being autonomous quasi-controls.

In recent years the movement toward consolidation has advanced with great rapidity. According to Willard L. Thorp[93] the number of mergers in the field of public utilities grew from 22 in 1919 to 1029 in 1926; and during the period from 1919 to 1928 no less than 7249 firms in mining and manufacturing were merged with or acquired by others. Since credit has been an indispensable instrument in the building of many of these combinations, power has tended to gravitate into the hands of the great investment houses. Lewis Corey has estimated that control over one-fourth of the corporate assets of the United States "is concentrated in 167 persons in the Morgan combination who hold more than 2450 interlocking directorships in corporations."[94] On the other hand, Berle and Means find that on or about January 1, 1930, two hundred non-financial corporations controlled 49.2 per cent of the corporate wealth (other than banking), 38.0 per cent of the business wealth (other than banking), and 22.0 per cent of the total wealth of the nation.[95] In commenting on this concentration of power these same authors say: "If roughly half of the corporate wealth is controlled by two hundred large corporations and half by smaller companies it is fair to assume that very much more than half of industry is dominated by these great units. This concentration is made even more significant when it is recalled

93 Willard L. Thorp, "The Changing Structure in Industry," Chapter II in *Recent Economic Changes in the United States* (New York, 1929), I, 187. Also see Harry W. Laidler, *Concentration in American Industry* (New York, 1931).
94 Lewis Corey, *The House of Morgan* (New York, 1930), 448.
95 Adolf A. Berle and Gardiner C. Means, *The Modern Corporation and Private Property* (New York, 1932), 32.

that as a result of it, approximately 2,000 individuals out of a population of 125,000,000 are in a position to control and direct half of industry."[96] In some industries, such as steel, aluminum, and woolen textiles, protection afforded by the tariff has doubtless been a factor in the organization of large units.

The growth of the modern corporation has also tended to separate ownership and control. As the "number of stock holdings and especially of modest ones" has increased, a marked trend of the age, actual power has passed into fewer and fewer hands.[97] Not infrequently today one per cent of the investment of a corporation will exercise control. Consider the significance of the following sentences taken from Berle and Means:

"In each of these types, majority control, minority control, and management control, the separation of ownership from control has become effective—a large body of security holders has been created who exercise virtually no control over the wealth which they or their predecessors in interest have contributed to the enterprise. . . . New responsibilities towards the owners, the workers, the consumers, and the State thus rest upon the shoulders of those in control. In creating these new relationships, the quasi-public corporation may fairly be said to work a revolution. It has destroyed the unity that we commonly call property—has divided ownership into nominal ownership and the power formerly joined to it. Thereby the corporation has changed the nature of profit-seeking enterprise. . . . This dissolution of the atom of property destroys the very foundation on which the economic order of the past three centuries has rested. Private enterprise, which has molded economic life since the close of the middle ages, has been rooted in the institution of private property . . . self-interest has long been regarded as the best guarantee of economic efficiency. It has been assumed that, if the individual is protected in the right both to use his own property as he sees fit and to receive the full fruits of its use, his desire for personal gain, for profits, can

[96] *Ibid.*, 33.   [97] *Ibid.*, 69–118.

be relied upon as an effective incentive to his efficient use of any industrial property he may possess. . . . In the quasi-public corporation, such an assumption no longer holds. As we have seen, it is no longer the individual himself who uses his wealth. . . . The explosion of the atom of property destroys the basis of the old assumption that the quest for profits will spur the owner of industrial property to its effective use. It consequently challenges the fundamental economic principle of individual initiative in industrial enterprise. It raises for re-examination the question of the motive force back of industry, and the ends for which the modern corporation can be or will be run."[98]

Even the opposition of the federal government has not been able to halt the trend toward consolidation. Following the Civil War the "trust movement" drew attacks from the smaller business interests threatened by it—attacks which bore fruit in the Sherman and Clayton Acts designed to destroy or prevent monopolistic combinations. Although the ingenuity of highly paid legal talent, the secretiveness of corporate officials, and the general tolerance of the Department of Justice have made possible the circumvention of these legislative measures, statutory disfavor has set its mark on the resulting organizations. "Our industrial structures," says R. G. Tugwell, "are reminiscent of weeds grown in the dark, and even those new co-ordinative features, which have grown in the somewhat brighter twilight of mere suspicion, present strange and unnatural features to be understood only by admission that the functions they profess to be organized for are less important than those which are hidden and unprofessed."[99] The half-century of effort to force competition upon the large corporations has failed. Paradoxical as it may seem, even the authority of the state has not been able to maintain the principles of laissez-faire in the face of technological changes. Moreover,

98 *Ibid.*, 5, 6–7, 8, 9.
99 R. G. Tugwell, "The Principle of Planning and the Institution of Laissez-Faire," *American Economic Review* Supplement (March, 1932), XXII, 77.

according to Berle and Means the trend of the recent past indicates that the great corporation "will become increasingly important in the future." It appears "to have been growing between two and three times as fast as all other non-financial corporations."[100]

With the passage of the National Industrial Recovery Act in the summer of 1933, forces that had been gathering for generations, as technology transformed the basic factors in the economy, overwhelmed the barriers erected in an earlier age. In this act government abandoned the established policy of striving to prevent the consolidation of business and frankly recognized the inevitable trend toward the organization of industry into its natural functional divisions. Under its provisions private enterprise was not only permitted to combine, but was actually ordered in the name of the public welfare to combine, to form for each industry a nationwide organization, to draw up a code governing wages, prices, hours of labor, working conditions, and numerous operating conditions. The aim was a complete co-ordination of the productive resources of American industry. Thenceforth the process of the consolidation of business enterprise went forward rapidly.

Co-operation in Agriculture. Agriculture has seen no such trend toward consolidation as that which has marked industry. Even the size of the farm seems not to have increased markedly since the eighteenth century. According to Bidwell and Falconer, the "typical farm in New England in this period ranged from 100 to 200 acres," the average farm in the older settlements of the Middle Colonies was about 135 acres, and in the back country somewhat larger.[101] In 1925 the Federal Census reports 145.1 acres in the average farm in the United States. Five years later, however, this figure had increased to 156.9.[102] Whether this change represents the beginning of a

---

[100] *Op. cit.*, 40.
[101] Percy Wells Bidwell and John I. Falconer, *op. cit.*, 115–116.
[102] Edmund de S. Brunner and J. H. Kolb, *Rural Social Trends* (New York, 1933), 48.

genuine trend remains to be seen. Although very small and very large farms both appear to be growing in numbers, and although corporation farming has made its appearance, agriculture remains today a sphere for the operation of small enterprise.[103] As at the time of the founding of the nation, the cultivation of the soil is in the hands of the family. Yet the trend toward specialization, which has been going on throughout this whole period, continues today and is binding the farmer ever more closely into the economy of the country.[104]

In certain directions, however, farmers are abandoning the individualistic or family tradition of the past. Since the middle of the last century they have co-operated here and there in making butter and cheese, in the buying of many kinds of goods, and in the marketing of grain, livestock, fruits, vegetables, wool, cotton, tobacco, hay, broomcorn, honey, nuts, rice, eggs, poultry, and other products.[105] "The rapid rise to a position of power of the movement for the co-operative marketing of agricultural products," write Brunner and Kolb, "has been one of the most pronounced trends affecting rural America in the last fifteen years. It has been a rise, not without its dramatic aspects, especially when the individualistic character of the American farmer, in whose veins flows the blood of the pioneer, is considered."[106] From 1915 to 1930 the number of co-operative marketing associations grew from 5,424 to 12,000, the gross membership from 651,186 to 3,100,000, and the volume of business from $635,839,000 to $2,500,000,000.[107] Thus, while the farmer has generally refused to co-operate with his fellows in production, except in the form of a neighborly exchange of labor and machinery, he seems to be moving rapidly toward co-operation in the sphere of marketing and buying.

This refusal to co-operate in production, at a time when large-scale consolidation was taking place in business, doubtless

103 *Ibid.*, 50–51. 104 *Ibid.*, 52.
105 R. H. Ellsworth, *Agricultural Cooperative Associations*, Technical Bulletin No. 40, U. S. Department of Agriculture, 1928, 4–6.
106 *Op. cit.*, 53. 107 *Ibid.*

tended to prevent the spread of technology in this field and certainly placed agriculture in an unfavorable position in its relations with other forms of industry. As a consequence of this and many other conditions, including the over-expansion of farming, the decline in population growth, the increase of productive efficiency, the reduction in the role of the horse in the American economy, the shifting of the dietary habits of the people, and the closing of certain foreign markets, the farmer found himself in increasingly difficult circumstances following the World War. All efforts to relieve the situation failed. The available purchasing power was simply incapable of absorbing the products of the farm. The resulting plight of the farmer has been summarized by Louis M. Hacker:

"In 1919, the total farm property of the nation had been valued at $78,000,000,000; by 1932, this value was $44,000,000,-000. In 1919, the total farm income was $15,000,000,000; by 1932, $5,200,000,000. In June 1932, farm commodity prices were at 52 per cent of the prewar level while the prices of the things the farmer bought were at 110 per cent of the prewar level. . . . Mortgage indebtedness had increased from $3,300,000,000 in 1910 and $7,900,000,000 in 1920 to $9,500,000,000 in 1931; in the last year interest and other costs on mortgage debts ate up fully eight per cent of gross farm income, as compared with three per cent in the prewar years. In 1931, taxes absorbed 11 per cent of gross farm income as compared with four per cent in the prewar years. So onerous were these fixed charges that during the five years ended March 1, 1932, 9.5 per cent of the farms of the country changed hands through forced sales . . . while 3.5 per cent of the farms were sold for tax delinquencies."[108]

The downward tendency of farm prices reached its nadir in February, 1933. So, if the year 1920 and the month of February, 1933, be taken as points of comparison, the index number of

[108] Louis M. Hacker, *The Farmer Is Doomed* (New York, 1932), 20–21.

grains declined during this interval from 231 to 34, of fruits and vegetables from 249 to 57, of cotton and cottonseed from 248 to 44, of meat animals from 173 to 53, of dairy products from 188 to 62, of poultry products from 222 to 57, of all groups from 205 to 49, and the ratio of prices received to prices paid from 99 to 48.[109] The "independent farmer" of tradition has had to pay dearly for his venture into the domain of commercialized agriculture, while clinging to his heritage of economic individualism.

The impact of these powerful economic forces on the farmer led to a rapid change in rural psychology. In various one-time rich agricultural regions farmers struck, halted by collective action the movement of agricultural produce, and even combined to interrupt the administration of the law of contracts in the foreclosure of mortgages. Then on May 12, 1933, an act was passed by the Congress of the United States providing for the control of production of cotton, wheat, corn, hogs, dairy products, tobacco, rice, and beet and cane sugar, and the re-establishment of the relation existing during 1909–1914 between the prices of agricultural and manufactured products. It was in connection with the administration of this act that Mr. Peek made the statement, already quoted, regarding the significance of the agreement of the cotton growers to destroy one-fourth of their crop. By way of explanation he went on to say that this achievement demonstrated the fallacy of the contention that "the farmer does not know how to co-operate." However this destruction of produce may be regarded, it would seem to indicate the close of an era in American agriculture that reaches back to colonial days. The farmer is beginning to acknowledge the interdependent character of industrial economy.

Organization of Labor. In the sphere of labor the trend toward organization has been under way for a hundred years.

109 The Bureau of Agricultural Economics, *The Agricultural Situation* (Washington, May 1, 1933), Vol. 17, No. 5, p. 16.

It was implicit in the rise of the factory system and large-scale production, in the separation of the workman from his tools involved in the growth of machinery, in the appearance of impersonal relations between employer and employee in corporate enterprises, in the conflict of interest between labor and capital engaged in a common undertaking, and in the decline in the bargaining power of the individual laborer that accompanied the concentration of employing power. Throughout the western world, though less in America than elsewhere, the industrial proletariat created by the advance of the new order of production tended toward collectivism in both action and mentality.

Although the conditions of labor in an occasional textile mill in early New England were as nearly ideal as a benevolent capitalistic paternalism could make them, the great majority of manufacturers were in business neither for their health nor for the welfare of their employees. Moreover, by the middle of the century, when native girls were largely displaced by Irish and French Canadians, the more humane spirit generated by the life of a simple agrarian community rapidly lost its vigor. Consequently workmen, finding exploitation inherent in the system and learning that the only dependable guardian of their interests lay in their own strength, proceeded to band together. Labor organizations appeared sporadically in the thirties and again in the fifties, some of them attaining temporary prosperity; but it was not until after the Civil War that organized labor developed sufficient strength to maintain itself through a period of depression. Then two types of labor organizations achieved national prominence. The Knights of Labor, founded by a group of Philadelphia garment cutters in 1869, followed geographical lines in their organization and opened their ranks to workmen of all trades and all degrees of skill. Farm laborers, as well as industrial workers, were invited to participate in a grand crusade to establish the "co-operative commonwealth" in America. The Knights took an active part in politics, grew in numbers until the middle eighties, and then declined and disappeared from the scene.

Meanwhile trade or craft unions had been developing on a national scale. In 1882 these unions formed a loose federation which was reorganized in 1886 under the name of the American Federation of Labor. This organization gradually replaced the Knights of Labor as the most powerful labor force in the United States, representing about four-fifths of the total membership of American unions,[110] although other organizations, such as the Industrial Workers of the World, the Railroad Brotherhoods, the Amalgamated Garment Workers, and the International Ladies Garment Workers, have appeared and exerted influence out of proportion to their numbers. Between 1890 and 1914 the membership of all unions grew "from no more than 300,000" to 2,700,000. Then under the favorable economic and political conditions generated by the World War the ranks of organized labor expanded rapidly, passing the five million mark in 1920. Thereafter, because of the reversal of governmental policies, the hostility of business, the depression of 1921, the mediocrity of leadership, and the displacement of labor by machinery, a contrary trend set in.[111] By 1931 the membership had declined to 3,298,000.

In 1933 the general trend of a century reached its culmination in the National Industrial Recovery Act of the Roosevelt administration. According to the provisions of this act every code drawn up for the governing of a particular industry must definitely stipulate:

"(1) That employees shall have the right to organize and bargain collectively through representatives of their own choosing, and shall be free from the interference, restraint, or coercion of employers of labor, or their agents, in the designa-

110 Leo Wolman and Gustav Peck, "Labor Groups in the Social Structure," Chapter XVI in *Recent Social Trends in the United States*, II, 831.
111 *Ibid.*, 831–833.

tion of such representatives or in self-organization or in other concerted activities for the purpose of collective bargaining or other mutual aid or protection;

"(2) That no employee and no one seeking employment shall be required as a condition of employment to join any company union or to refrain from joining, organizing, or assisting a labor organization of his own choosing; and

"(3) That employers shall comply with the maximum hours of labor, minimum rates of pay, and other conditions of employment, approved or prescribed by the President."[112]

Government Intervention in Business. Since the founding of the Republic, and particularly since the close of the Civil War, government—local, state, and national—has rapidly increased its functions and intervened in the operation of the economy. It has engaged in the control of banking and credit, the erection of tariff barriers, the conservation of natural resources, the rendering of numerous services to business, the extension of assistance to agriculture, the protection of urban workers, the regulation of corporate enterprise, the levying of taxes on income, and the actual performance of many strictly economic functions. The trend, however, will not be analyzed here, because the facts are summarized in systematic fashion elsewhere in the present volume.[113] Suffice it to say at this point that, with the coming of the administration of Franklin D. Roosevelt, the separation of politics and economics underlying the practice of *laissez-faire* was definitely and deliberately, though perhaps not finally, at an end.

A MANAGED ECONOMY

The American economy of today bears little resemblance to that of a hundred or a hundred and fifty years ago. Out of the

[112] Benjamin S. Kirsh, *The National Industrial Recovery Act* (New York, 1933), 150.
[113] See below, Part Two, Chapter X, "Government."

relatively self-contained agricultural household and rural community has emerged a new economy of vast complexity. In the overthrow of the old order the practice of a more or less rugged individualism served a useful purpose. Yet the earlier unity was no sooner on the road toward disintegration than another and far more comprehensive unity began to manifest itself. That very technology which private enterprise had nurtured in its drive for profits apparently contained the seed of a managed economy. At any rate the mechanism for the production and distribution of goods, of which it was the parent, seems incapable of efficient administration by the irrational methods of the competitive system. Moreover, being planful in nature, technology introduces the principle of design, prevision, and control into ever wider areas of the economy.

It was not surprising, therefore, that following the disaster of 1929, men rapidly lost faith in a system of control that had become outmoded by technological advance. Even President Hoover, ardent disciple of "rugged individualism" though he was, observed that "we are passing from a period of extremely individualistic action into a period of associational activities." Suggestions for the introduction of some form of central planning began to pour in from various sources—from labor leaders, industrialists, university professors, publicists, and statesmen.[114] More than thirty plans found their way to the press. The present Commission in formulating its Charter declared unanimously that one of the goals "which must of necessity shape instruction in the social studies" is "national planning in industry, business, agriculture and government to sustain mass production of goods on a high level of continuity and to assure the most economical and efficient use of our material resources."[115] And in their review of findings, the President's Research Committee on Social Trends, after sug-

114 See Charles A. Beard, *America Faces the Future* (New York, 1932). Eleven of these plans are reprinted in this volume.
115 Charles A. Beard, *A Charter for the Social Sciences* (New York, 1932), 79.

gesting the need for some form of social planning, closed their argument with the following statement:

"The alternative to constructive social initiative may conceivably be a prolongation of a policy of drift and some readjustment as time goes on. More definite alternatives, however, are urged by dictatorial systems in which the factors of force and violence may loom large. In such cases the basic decisions are frankly imposed by power groups, and violence may subordinate technical intelligence in social guidance.

"Unless there can be a more impressive integration of social skills and fusing of social purposes than is revealed by recent trends, there can be no assurance that these alternatives with their accompaniments of violent revolution, dark periods of serious repression of libertarian and democratic forms, the proscription and loss of many useful elements in the present productive system, can be averted.

"Fully realizing its mission, the Committee does not wish to assume an attitude of alarmist irresponsibility, but on the other hand it would be highly negligent to gloss over the stark and bitter realities of the social situation, and to ignore the imminent perils in further advance of our heavy technical machinery over crumbling roads and shaking bridges. There are times when silence is not neutrality, but assent."[116]

In November, 1932, the American people went to the polls and voted overwhelmingly for the "new deal" of Franklin D. Roosevelt. That this vote was a vote of negation rather than a vote of affirmation is unquestionably true. Yet it did reveal a readiness on the part of the country for a sharp shift in policy. Certainly many intelligent citizens, when they heard the President's radio address to the nation on July 24, 1933, appealing for popular support of the National Recovery program, felt that he was reporting the progress of their own thinking when he said: "Long before Inauguration Day I became convinced that

[116] *Op. cit.,* "Introduction," I, lxxiv–lxxv.

individual effort and local effort and even disjointed Federal effort had failed and of necessity would fail and, therefore, that a rounded leadership by the Federal Government had become a necessity both of theory and fact."[117]

The American economy is thus launched on a new course. The conclusion, however, should not be drawn that the road to the future is clearly marked out. The contrary is unquestionably true. The way is uncertain and full of pitfalls. In the field of social policy and program only the first steps have been taken. The areas of sharpest conflict, involving changes in the distribution of wealth and income, lie ahead. The most that can be said is that the way is being cleared for the definition of issues and the rational alignment of political forces. The assumption underlying the present program that the solution of the economic problem lies in the direction of the establishment of a partnership between business and government may well prove to be false or even destructive of the ideals of American democracy. The question of whose interests are to be considered paramount in the reorganization of the economy remains still to be answered. Moreover, in neither ideas nor dispositions are the American people equipped to deal with the changed situation in which they find themselves. The consequent educational task called forth by the conflict between the popular mind and the realities of life is without parallel in the history of the nation.

[117] *The New York Times,* July 25, 1933.

Chapter III

COMMUNICATION

The fundamental rôle played by agencies of communication in the development of industrial civilization has already been clearly indicated. The household of the eighteenth century was compelled to be self-contained by the sparseness of the population and the primitive character of the means of transporting goods and persons from place to place. The disintegration of this household proceeded hand in hand with the growth of new forms of communication—improved highways, canals, steamboats, railroads, automobiles, airplanes, telephones, and radio. And simultaneously these same agencies laid the foundation for the grand social integration of today, founded on specialization and differentiation of economic function. In the absence of such inventions the population of the United States would of course have grown more dense and institutions would have suffered some change, but the basic social pattern, expressing the intimate life of family and neighborhood, would have persisted. The growth of communication, however, has not only made possible mass production and the exchange of commodities on an enormous scale. It has also complicated the problems of government and profoundly affected the cultural life of the people. It is to this question that the present chapter will be devoted.

THE PATTERN OF AGRARIAN SOCIETY

In the agrarian society of the colonial era and the first decades of the republic the agencies for conveying news to the people were comparatively few in number and primitive in character. The average citizen was cut off, for the most part, from the outside world. If he was fortunate enough to be able to read and write with facility, which was improbable, he might carry on an intermittent correspondence, by means of an irregular and untrustworthy mail service, with friends or relatives in distant parts of America or even beyond the sea. He might visit the village store and there at more or less regular intervals hear meager news read from papers published perhaps weeks or months before. He might listen to gossip brought into the community by the driver of the stagecoach or by passengers who had risked their necks riding over the rough roads. But he could depend on no well-organized agencies to keep him informed on the course of events in the nation and the outside world.[1]

Likewise the various cultural and educational institutions to be found in the ordinary community could be expected to contribute but little to an understanding of world problems. The cultural level of the home was not high. Books were few in number, even in the most refined of American house-holds. Traditions were handed down chiefly by word of mouth. Fortunate was the family which contained a grand-parent or other aged relative who, from his position at the fire-place, would relate some of the happenings of his own life-time and of preceding generations. And fortunate was the occasion that brought a guest who could be persuaded to re-main for a leisurely stay, while he told the news-hungry family of life beyond the horizon. The school at this time imparted little of authentic and useful knowledge regarding human society and institutions. Its primary emphasis was on the acquisition of the tools of learning—reading, writing, and arith-metic. The church gave less information about this world than the next. Certainly it devoted much more attention to informing its congregation concerning the living conditions in heaven and hell than about the operation of the government at Washington.

[1] See Seymour Dunbar, *A History of Travel in America* (Indianapolis, 1915).

This analysis suggests that the ordinary citizen in the days of the agrarian order was far less well-equipped to deal with his world than he is today. The contrary, however, seems to be the case. The dominant fact of pre-industrial society was the relative simplicity of life. The burden of informed opinion to be borne by the individual therefore was not heavy. The social world in which the average man "lived and moved and had his being" was extremely constricted. He engaged either in an agriculture that was largely self-sufficient or in some occupation intimately related to the farming economy. Also he either owned his establishment and worked for himself, or was saving money with the expectation of becoming independent at an early date. Large-scale enterprise, minute division of labor, distant markets, collective bargaining, social insurance, complicated systems of exchange, were practically outside his experience. Hours, wages, and conditions of labor he regarded as strictly his own affair, or as an affair between himself and his employer. Certainly these things were of no concern to the government. If dissatisfied with his present condition, he could seek another employer, or load family and household goods upon a wagon and set out for the West. Under such conditions heaven and hell might seem much nearer than the Capitol on the Potomac.

Into this narrow world of family and neighborhood activities national and international affairs occasionally obtruded themselves. Every four years after the adoption of the Federal Constitution the country rang with such cries as "Old Hickory" and "Tippecanoe and Tyler too"; and political campaigns were conducted by means of parades, barbecues, bonfires, and public speeches and debates. These incursions, however, were merely breaks in the monotony of existence. The conduct of federal and even state government affected but little the life of the ordinary man. The essence of government was local. And for dealing with the local situation the citizen was fairly competent. Through personal contact he came to know the candidates for office and through hours of discussion with neighbors across the rail fence, at the village store, or around the town pump he became familiar with issues. Although local elections were sometimes influenced by the obscure fortunes of state and national politics, the voter commonly had or thought he had fairly clear reasons for casting his ballot for one person rather than another. Life was still so simple in its relationships that man could tackle its problems with a fair degree of understanding and assurance.

NEW FORMS OF TRANSPORTATION AND COMMUNICATION

During the past one hundred years this simple agrarian life has been overwhelmed and transformed by the development, at an ever more rapid tempo, of the instrumentalities of transportation and communication. During the first half of the nineteenth century, as observed in the preceding chapter, these instrumentalities were being constantly improved and extended. New roads were being built, old roads regraded, and additional stage lines put into operation. The government enlarged the mail service. More newspapers were launched; weeklies became dailies; eastern journals found their way in larger numbers into the West. Increased attention was given to the establishment and maintenance of schools. Through the use of steamboats on rivers and lakes and through the building of canals commerce was binding the distant sections of the country together. And by the middle of the century the railroads and the telegraph were creating a wholly unprecedented social unity. A quantitative analysis of the growth of the more important of the new agencies will give some measure of the transformation wrought in this sphere by technology and invention.

The development of locomotive transportation was rapid. In 1842 there were but 4000 miles of railroad in the country. By 1860 this figure had increased to 31,000, by 1880 to 93,000, and by 1900 to 193,000, when the main outlines of railroad trackage were practically completed. This figure rose "to a maximum of 254,037 in 1916, and declined by 1930 to 249,052."[2] Although the peak of railway passenger traffic was reached about 1920, when 1,269,913,000 passengers were carried 47,369,-906,000 passenger-miles,[3] great improvements in this form of transportation have continued down to the present. The time required for making long trips has been shortened steadily from year to year, increasing the ease of maintaining contacts between widely separated sections of the country. Comforts have been introduced that relieve the tedium of the transcontinental journey and transform into a pleasure what was once an exhausting ordeal. Air-cooled cars, now provided by certain lines in summer, furnish a type of luxurious accommodation that is found but rarely in homes, hotels, factories, or office-buildings.

It was the automobile, however, that played the central rôle in the disintegration of the rural community. The growth and spread of the motor vehicle constitute one of the most striking and revolutionary phenomena of the age. "In 1900," say Willey and Rice, "there were 8000 'horseless carriages' in the United States, according to estimate. On January 1, 1931, the number of motor vehicles registered was 25,814,103. It is probable that no invention of such far-reaching importance was ever diffused with such rapidity or so quickly exerted influences that ramified through the national culture, transforming even habits of thought and language."[4] And the greater part of this development took place after the close of the World War. In 1930 the automobile gave to the American people a total of 332,000,000,000 passenger miles of service.[5] This same period saw an enormous amount of highway construction for the comfort and convenience of motor traffic. More than 660,000 miles

[2] Malcolm M. Willey and Stuart A. Rice, "The Agencies of Communication," Chapter IV in *Recent Social Trends in the United States*, I, 169.
[3] *Ibid.*, 169.   [4] *Ibid.*, 172.   [5] *Ibid.*, 177–178.

of surfaced roads now penetrate into all sections of the country; and other thousands have been improved beyond recognition over their horse-and-buggy days. The number of car licenses from distant states, which are to be seen on the interstate highways, give some measure of the influence of the automobile in overcoming ancient geographical barriers.

Since the time of Fulton the development of the steamship and water transportation has gone steadily forward. By 1929 water-borne domestic commerce, utilizing a great system of routes embracing coastal waters, the Great Lakes, rivers, canals, and connecting channels, reached the figure of 527,535,000 short tons. Corresponding advances in ocean transportation have brought the nation increasingly into relations with the other countries of the world. But this question will receive consideration in a subsequent chapter.[6]

Having made a conquest of the land and water, man turned to the air. As a result, the airplane, which is but carrying further the function of the locomotive, the automobile, and the steamship has been advancing rapidly. Indeed, scheduled air service in the United States is said to date practically from 1926. In that year there were but eighteen airways in operation with 3715 miles of passenger route. Five years later, in 1931, the number of services had grown to 126 and the mileage to 45,704. The daily average miles flown advanced from less than 12,000 to 129,825 and the number of passengers from 5782 to 522,345.[7] While the airplane presumably will never supplant the more slow-moving agencies of transportation, it will no doubt continue to take over certain types of services requiring great speed.

The agencies of transportation have been supplemented by a vast network of instruments of point-to-point communication that even bind the nations together. The cable and telegraph have been followed by wireless. In 1927 there were 256,809

[6] See below, Part Two, Chapter XI, "World Relations."
[7] Malcolm M. Willey and Stuart A. Rice, *op. cit.*, 183.

miles of telegraph pole lines in the United States. In this same year the number of land messages amounted to 215,595,000 and of ocean cable messages to 13,987,000. Through the use of recent inventions the accuracy of these messages has been greatly increased and their delivery expedited. Wireless messages transmitted by commercial agencies rose from 154,617 in 1907 to 3,777,538 in 1927.[8]

The extension of telephone service has been even more rapid. The number of telephones in the country grew from 1,355,911 in 1900 to 20,201,576 in 1930, and the number of telephone calls from 5,071,000,000 in 1902 to 29,196,000,000 in 1927.[9] During each year of the nineteen-twenties from five to seven millions of miles of wired line were added. Long distance service is much more adequate than formerly, and conversations with persons on other continents are now not only feasible but matters of daily occurrence. Both business and diplomatic relations with foreign countries are being modified and facilitated by the increasing use of telephone services.

Radio perhaps represents the most striking extension of communication facilities in recent years. "The dramatic evolution of the radio within one decade," write Willey and Rice, "from a mysterious curiosity to a widely diffused and universally accepted instrument of entertainment, business, learning and mass communication, has few if any counterparts in social history."[10] Commercial broadcasting was begun only in 1920. Now the country is dotted with broadcasting stations and the total capital investment in all branches of the radio industry is said to be three billions of dollars. In January, 1932, the number of receiving sets in use in the United States was estimated at 16,026,620 and the total daily radio audience at 37,442,869 persons.[11] Thus millions of homes resound daily with a strange medley of voices coming over the air from the most distant places.

[8] *Ibid.*, 195–196.
[9] *Ibid.*, 198, 199.
[10] *Ibid.*, 211.
[11] *Ibid.*, 211, 214.

Though relatively ancient in origin the press is largely a product of industrial civilization. Just prior to the depression of 1929, the publication and sale of books rose to unprecedented figures. The same thing may be said of magazines and periodicals. The number of monthlies, the largest single group, increased "from 2328 in 1900 to 3804 in 1930, and quarterlies, the next largest class, more than tripled."[12] The daily press has grown to huge proportions. While the number of newspapers has been slowly declining, the total circulation has been increasing rapidly. In 1931 there were 2268 newspapers in the country with a total daily circulation of approximately forty millions.[13]

Another powerful agency of communication, though developed primarily as a form of amusement, is the cinema. First known as the "nickelodeon," it advanced so rapidly in popularity and price of admission that its original name soon became obsolete. With the talking feature, which was perfected in very recent years, it has come to play an enormous rôle in the life of the American people. The number of motion picture houses in the country on January 31, 1931, has been estimated at 22,731, with a seating capacity of 11,300,000. To provide these houses with pictures 500 feature films with about 200 prints of each were made in 1930. And in the same year, according to competent opinion, the weekly admissions to cinemas amounted to 100,000,000.[14]

This of course by no means gives a complete account of the agencies of communication now operating in the United States. Only the more striking developments have been mentioned. Nothing has been said of the electric railway which reached its culmination in 1922, of the postal service whose "per capita gross revenue grew from $0.17 in 1846 to $5.29 in 1931,"[15] of the great newsgathering agencies which reach to the farthest corners of the globe, and of various other new instrumen-

[12] *Ibid.*, 205.   [13] *Ibid.*, 204, 205.
[14] *Ibid.*, 208. See below, Part Two, Chapter VI, "Recreation."
[15] *Ibid.*, 191.

talities that serve to bind the nation together. At the same time the more primitive forms of transportation and communication, characteristic of the pre-industrial age, continue to have their influence. Thus the platform, though suffering from the competition of new agencies and from changes in popular tastes and attitudes, still holds an important position. The theatre survives, but is subject to the severe competition of the movies. The church also carries on amid great difficulties, as the range and frequency of stimuli playing on the public mind increases. In politics and at the chautauqua the old-fashioned spell-binder has given way to the more sober and less leisurely speaker. And through amplifiers and the radio the patronage of the platform has been enormously extended.

As a result of these changes in the realm of transportation and communication, and various other factors that need not be mentioned here, the structure of American society has been transformed. The United States has become the most mobile and closely integrated society in history. From coast to coast and from the Great Lakes to the Gulf, in spite of geographical differences, cultural diversity, and conflicting economic interests, the forty-eight states have been welded into a single great community. The unifying forces released by technology have even refused to halt before the boundaries of the nation. Already America has moved out into the world to become increasingly dependent on the fortunes of the other peoples of the earth.

ADMINISTRATION AND CONTROL

The new agencies of communication have played a fundamental rôle in bringing into existence a society of extreme complexity. They are also the major dependence of man in his effort to follow and understand the course of events in this highly dynamic and enlarged world. The question of the administration and control of these agencies is therefore a matter of crucial importance from the standpoint of both citizenship and cultural enrichment. While this question cannot be examined here in all of its details, there are three features of the present situation that will be subjected to analysis: the trend toward centralization of control, the widespread domination of commercial motives, and the development of the art and practice of propaganda.

Centralization of Control. In the sphere of communication, as in practically all other areas of social life, the past generation has witnessed a powerful trend toward consolidation and centralization. This trend may be observed in the newspaper, the cinema, and the radio.

As already noted, although the increase in daily newspaper circulation was continuous down to the beginning of the depression in 1929, the number of daily newspapers in the country reached its maximum in 1917. In the case of weekly publications an even more pronounced trend is discernible. The number of such papers declined from 16,323 in 1915 to 12,636 in 1931. During this period many country newspapers ceased publication and others disappeared through consolidation.[16] At the same time chains of newspapers have been established under central management. Of similar import is the extension of the circulation and influence of great metropolitan dailies, which has been made possible by the increased speed of transportation. Thus the circulation of *The New York Times* or *The Chicago Tribune* is aided by every reduction of train schedules in the vicinity and by the development of airplane service. Under such competition local publications, representing local points of view, are gradually forced to the wall and the great population centers increasingly place their impress upon the cultural life of the nation. The practice of syndicating articles works in the same direction.

In the moving picture industry, probably because of the large financial outlays involved, the trend toward consolidation has moved with striking swiftness. Of the 2500 or more pic-

16 *Ibid.*, 203–204.

tures produced annually in the United States, including "short subjects," 98 per cent are made in Hollywood.[17] From this world-renowned movie center come mass standards for speaking, for gesturing, for travel, for furnishing homes, for choosing and wearing clothes, for making love, for breaking the law, for committing robbery, arson, and murder. From Hollywood come conceptions of foreign lands, peoples, and cultures, as well as prejudices and propaganda regarding innumerable domestic issues.

In the field of radio broadcasting the country is dominated by the metropolitan centers and particularly by New York. The great broadcasting chains all center in the city at the mouth of the Hudson and send out programs performed largely by New York artists and sponsored by New York advertisers or at least by business men having close New York connections. So the radio tends to disseminate the culture of New York and, to a very much smaller degree, Chicago and San Francisco. Moreover, chain programs are allotted an ever-increasing percentage of time on the air throughout the country.

Particularly since the World War has this trend toward centralization been noticeable. According to Willey and Rice these years have witnessed "increased utilization coupled with concentration of facilities. For his news, the reader of the paper is dependent largely upon the great news gathering agencies; for his motion pictures, there is dependency upon a group of well organized producers; for his radio, he comes more and more in contact with large and powerful stations, dominated increasingly by the nation wide broadcasting organizations. Mass impression on so vast a scale has never before been possible. . . . Greater possibilities for social manipulation, for ends that are selfish or socially desirable, have never existed."[18]

A caution, however, should be uttered here. The common

[17] William H. Short, *A Generation of Motion Pictures* (Unpublished Manuscript), 75.
[18] *Op. cit.*, 215.

view is that these centralizing tendencies in the sphere of agencies of communication involve a complete standardization of life for the individual. As a matter of fact, the individual has a far greater number of choices than ever before. To be sure, the small communities of the past were widely different, since they were isolated from each other; but the individuals within any one of these communities were expected to conform fairly closely to its standards of thought and conduct. The disintegration of this community has freed him from the coercion of the family and the neighborhood to a degree that can scarcely be grasped today. He is now becoming a member of a vastly larger community in which standards of thought and conduct manifest the most extraordinary diversity. He may consequently make choices today where yesterday he was expected to follow in the footsteps of his fathers and heed the voice of Mrs. Grundy.

Domination of Commercial Motives. In each of its important divisions the press is dominated by commercial motives. Thus the publication of books is a form of business enterprise and, like all other business ventures, is conducted primarily for purposes of material gain. The ephemeral and trashy books which flood the market are written, printed, and sold, neither to improve nor to corrupt the popular taste, but simply and solely to make money. As a rule they are published because, in the competition for the consumer's dollar, they are thought to be more profitable than books of high intellectual or artistic quality.

The position of magazines is not unlike that of books. The number published and sold has increased phenomenally in recent years. They also have catered to the desires of purchasers. Some of them, reflecting the interests and tastes of comparatively small groups of readers, maintain a high standard of both form and content. But the great majority sold at typical news stands, such as motion picture magazines, and many others, are so written and illustrated as to appeal chiefly to persons whose reading habits are confined to nourishing their more primitive desires and impulses.

The gathering and publication of news is becoming more and more a gigantic business rather than a profession. This tendency is illustrated by the vast circulations of particular papers, by the competition of books, magazines, radio, and other means of communication, by the speeding up of the processes of news gathering, of publication and of distribution, and by the growth of space devoted to gossip, scandal, and sport, and the dwindling of the prestige and influence of the editorial page. No ordinary newspaper can survive without receiving huge sums from advertising; no newspaper can receive huge sums from advertising unless it has extensive circulation; no newpaper can secure extensive circulation unless its columns interest potential readers. It is widely believed, amply illustrated, and only in special instances disproved, that in order to reach the masses a newspaper must appeal to a relatively low level of taste. At any rate, this seems to be true in a society in which newspapers must compete for patrons in order to survive. Under such conditions even the most conservative publications cannot afford to neglect the latest murder, the latest kidnapping of an important personage, or the latest trial involving sex scandal, unless the individual or family involved has sufficient power to buy or frighten off the editors. The only solution yet reached by publishers desiring to issue a superior newspaper is to present both the good and the bad, in the hope that readers with diverse interests will select according to taste.

The decline of the editorial page can be attributed in part to the recognition of the fact that appeals to the masses of readers must be made through the presentation of sensational material in the news columns. Also it is due in part to the fact that today the editorial page is rarely under the control of one man who has a vital interest in the problems of his community and who at the same time has the power to gamble with the circulation of the paper by printing editorials which might arouse the wrath of readers. This is but another illustration of the generalization that the printing of both news and editorials, which was once a profession, is now a business and must be conducted according to the rules of business. On no other hypothesis can one explain the effort on the part of the newspaper management to play up the prejudices of the public and the general aversion to printing anything calculated to provoke hostility among patrons or potential patrons.

The change that has come over the daily newspaper during the past generation, because of the twofold trend toward centralization and commercialization, was recently described by Robert Lincoln O'Brien, former editor of *The Boston Herald,* at a meeting of the League of Women Voters of Cambridge, May 6, 1929:

"Old-time newspapers were simple affairs, growing out of the thought of their communities, unrelated to other investments of their owners, representing chiefly the local spirit and aspirations, often typified in the editorship of some one outstanding man like Greeley or Raymond or Dana. That was the old order.

"With it I intended to contrast the big groups of chain newspapers now operating, as impersonal in their control, for the most part, as a gasoline company; with editors transferred from city to city and post to post as would be the executives of any corresponding commercial organization. This is the new idea. In consequence of it such considerable cities as Pittsburgh, Denver, and our neighboring Albany possess no newspaper which is not a part of somebody's chain, and so responsive to the mechanism of a great organization. . . .

"These changes from the newspapers of the old time, focusing about a personal editor, to a cog in the great chain of modern business, certainly constitute one of the most momentous economic and cultural overturns of our era. With it has come the amazing growth of syndicate features, or those contributions of literary geniuses, or picture-making experts, which appear simultaneously in a hundred different newspapers. The Associated Press itself has undergone a not dissimilar transformation. A generation ago it was the vehicle of official reports, and a usually staid recital of the undisputed things of a serious character. Today there is hardly anything in a daily paper which the Associated Press is not furnishing, or seemingly on its way to furnish—pictures, special-feature departments, and gossipy material of every sort, until the time seems not far distant when a newspaper which enjoys membership in the Associated Press could get along with this service supplemented by a single editorial writer and a few reporters."[19]

The cinema seems to be even more completely commercialized than the press. For the purpose of attracting the largest possible audience, pictures are adjusted to the intelligence and untutored taste of the masses. For the most part the producer is sensitive to neither intellectual, nor moral, nor even æsthetic values. He is genuinely concerned with these things only as they affect box-office receipts. He is not interested in the elevation of cultural standards, unless it serves to stimulate business. Society endeavors to enforce upon the cinema traditional ethical conceptions by setting up boards of censors, who pass judgment on all pictures and strive to eliminate scenes which are regarded as immoral. No doubt some good results are occasionally achieved. The usual effect, however, is to mar pictures which are not necessarily bad by fitting them into the mold of tradition. Moreover, no censorship, however intelligent, can guarantee that the movies will perform their function adequately, since they are to be criticised less for content that is positively bad than for lack of content that is positively fine in ethical, intellectual, and artistic perception. Censorship cannot give direction, inspiration, and vision: it can merely perform the negative function of voicing disapproval.

[19] Quoted in Carl D. Thompson, *Confessions of the Power Trust* (New York, 1932), 287–288.

The case of the radio is peculiarly interesting. Although it is potentially a powerful instrument of popular enlightenment, its primary concern today certainly is neither the educational nor the cultural elevation of the masses. It is operated in the interests of commercial sponsors, engaged in the sale of almost every conceivable commodity from coal and real estate to cures for constipation and halitosis. Hence in the competition for the attention of the largest possible number of purchasers, the appeal of the programs is generally aimed at the present level of the education and the interests of the masses of the people. The radio thus becomes an instrument for the perpetuation, if not the further degradation, of the prevailing standards of taste and culture. Under the current system of operation, moreover, an individual sponsor is forced to capitulate to the crowd, even against his own desires. Being in business for private gain, he can scarcely be expected to finance the broadcasting of a lecture to be heard by hundreds, or a symphony to be enjoyed by thousands, if millions of possible customers are waiting eagerly to follow the fortunes of cheap comedians. As a consequence, service to the public is definitely subordinated to the motive of material profit.

It should be said, however, that while the radio is largely dominated by commercial interests, the devotion of occasional programs to the ends of public enlightenment is not to be ignored. It has proved itself an invaluable instrument for teaching music appreciation to school children. The weekly addresses arranged by certain well-known civic agencies and delivered by men and women of genuine competence reach audiences of considerable magnitude, even though they may not be comparable to the great multitudes tuning in regularly for Amos 'n' Andy. The increasing use of radio by political leaders is rendering ineffective the time-worn tricks of the platform speaker. The broadcasting of programs, spoken or musical, from foreign countries is exploding the myth of American isolation.

Finally, the point should be emphasized that, because of the great expense involved, the press, the cinema, and the radio tend increasingly to fall under the control of the financial interests of the country. Such a condition means that in case of a conflict or controversy involving the perpetuation of the present economic system, the weight of all of these agencies is likely to be thrown on the side of the maintenance of the *status quo*. Moreover, when the privileges of powerful groups are involved, commercial motives are either subordinated or molded to the protection of the more fundamental interest. Also it may be commercially profitable to spread misunderstanding among the masses of the people. This brings the analysis to the question of the art of propaganda.

The Art of Propaganda. The present age might well be called the age of propaganda. The various agencies of communication that have been invented, developed, and extended during the past century have become powerful instruments for the molding of public opinion. To be sure, they might conceivably be employed primarily for spreading knowledge among the people and for equipping the ordinary citizen for the intelligent discharge of his civic responsibilities. That they are used for this purpose to some extent is true. Yet the fact remains that they are very commonly employed by special interests in pleading special causes. And since their services normally go to the highest bidder, this means that the great inequalities in the distribution of wealth are reflected in the molding of public opinion. Rarely does the battle for popular approval go against the party with the larger purse.[20]

Examples of the use of the agencies of communication for propaganda purposes are innumerable. They may be observed in every issue of a newspaper, in many a cinema film, and in practically any radio broadcast. They may also be seen in every political campaign and in every struggle carried on

[20] For a thorough treatment of this entire question of propaganda see F. E. Lumley, *The Propaganda Menace* (New York, 1933).

among the countless groups, sects, and interests that compose American society. The publicity agent and the public relations counsel have become a part of the social fabric. Individuals, corporations, and government practise continuously the art of cultivating the good will and shaping the mind of the public. The process will be illustrated by the campaigns carried on by government during the World War, by the efforts of the electric power industry to mold popular opinion in the nineteen-twenties, and by the program of advertising which is carried on perpetually by business.

Regimentation of public opinion during the World War. The power of the new agencies of communication in molding the public opinion of entire nations was clearly and conclusively demonstrated in the World War. "During the war-period," says Harold D. Lasswell, "it came to be recognized that the mobilization of men and means was not sufficient; there must be a mobilization of opinion. Power over opinion, as over life and property, passed into official hands, because the danger from license was greater than the danger of abuse. Indeed, there is no question but that government management of opinion is an unescapable corollary of large-scale modern war."[21] And the lessons learned in the war have not, and probably never will be, forgotten.

From the very outbreak of the war, agents of both the allied and the central powers were busily at work in the United States, using every available technique to secure support for their respective countries and to arouse hostility toward their enemies. The American government endeavored to check the activities of both groups, but with only partial success. In addressing their appeal to the American people the Central Powers proved themselves less successful than their opponents and month after month lost ground in the struggle for prestige and

[21] Harold D. Lasswell, *Propaganda Technique in the World War* (New York, 1927), 14–15. Also Sir Phillip Gibbs, *Now It Can Be Told* (New York, 1920); Bertrand Russell, *Free Thought and Official Propaganda* (New York, 1922).

sympathy. Yet during the first two years of the war the majority of the population were apparently opposed to active participation in the conflict; and in 1916 the incumbent president
was re-elected on the slogan: "He kept us out of war."

When a battle is on bystanders receive little consideration
from the principals in the struggle. The rights and interests
of the United States were violated many times by both contending parties. Consequently, as the struggle wore on, active
alliance with either side became preferable to neutrality. Besides lacking skill in propaganda, the Central Powers were unfortunate in the fact that through loans great private interests
in America gradually bound themselves to the Allied cause.
Hence, more and more the instruments of propaganda in
the United States—the instruments which theoretically provide the data for the formation of enlightened opinion—fed
the people with suggestions and data calculated to prove that
Germany and Austria were the champions of barbarism, while
the Allied Powers were the defenders of civilization. In due
time the American people, with vast enthusiasm, entered the
war to carry the ideals of democracy around the world.

Once the die was cast, many persons who in times of peace
would have been vigorously opposed to misrepresentation of
any kind, now feeling the necessity of offering a united front
to the enemy, thrust aside their scruples. The Allied governments eagerly and quickly provided the means for "educating" the American public regarding the issues of the war.
The mass of material furnished the press played its intended
rôle. Even more dramatic in execution and effect was the
utilization of soldiers on leave from the armies, usually men
who had been conspicuously wounded and conspicuously decorated for gallant services. Mutilated and distinguished apostles
of the Allied cause spoke from the platforms of churches, colleges, and municipal auditoriums portraying vividly the atrocities said to have been committed by the common enemy. There
were stories of soldiers crucified; of Belgian women violated

wholesale; of babies twirled by their heels and dashed against the trees; of carloads of bodies of dead soldiers transformed into soap and fertilizer.

Thousands and millions were "converted" by these missionaries from the front. The truth of statements made was rarely questioned. If any one doubted their authenticity, he was suspected of German ancestry. To say anything good about or in defense of the enemy, or anything that cast reflection upon the name of the Allies, became almost prima facie evidence of treason. "One hundred per cent Americans" wrote books and articles, made speeches, organized drives, and in innumerable ways demonstrated their ability to sift, select, and correlate facts so as to prove true whatever the situation demanded. College and university professors, with occasional exceptions, ran with the crowd. Even ministers of religion, the avowed disciples of the Prince of Peace, prayed and lobbied for the prosecution of the war. Political, academic, and clerical propagandists collaborated in an endeavor to give high moral sanction to the struggle by calling it a "war to end war" and by declaring that its purpose was to "make the world safe for democracy." Never was there a more effective use of slogans in an effort to control the beliefs and activities of the people. The notion of a "war to end war" appealed even to a large percentage of the pacifists; and the idea of making the world safe for democracy touched the hearts of all Americans who had been taught to accept an unthinking patriotism.

The Allied governments even succeeded in considerable measure in propagating their ideas among the enemy, as well as among their own people. The President of the United States sought in various ways, and with marked success, to get word to the German people that war was being made, not on them, but on their leaders. Use was even made of that new vehicle of transportation and communication, the airplane, to deluge central Europe with literature to prove that the American people had no quarrel with the German masses and that the

German rulers were the common enemy of all mankind. Whether or not this propaganda was essentially true or false, at least it left much of the truth untold. It said nothing of the secret treaties and understandings among the Allied powers.

All parties to the conflict developed great skill in reporting events at the front. When the enemy retreated, he was routed by gallant forces; when the Allies retreated, they merely moved back to previously prepared positions. However, in order that the utmost of support might be secured for the army, the precarious nature of the situation had to be brought home to the people. But this had to be done in such a way as not to frighten unduly or destroy morale. Again, the report had to be so worded that the enemy could not twist it into a confession of defeat and thereby raise the morale of his own forces. Hence the seriousness with which every phrase was considered before any official statement was given out. Public opinion was built up and shaped for the achievement of particular purposes. It was not the ordered judgment of the masses derived from complete or unprejudiced reporting of the relevant facts. The people were the tools and not the masters of their military and political leaders. To be sure, opposition appeared here and there and occasional individuals refused to suppress their convictions, their economic interests, or their conceptions of welfare. Furthermore, the enemy, even in the United States, was able to disseminate sufficient facts and rumors to create considerable dissension. On the whole, however, a united front against the foe was maintained until the signing of the armistice.

As military fervor died down, scholars began to delve into the archives of the war period. The result has been a radical transformation of the picture of the causes and the conduct of the war. The great majority of competent students of the question have become convinced that no one nation and no one group of men caused the war. And the stories of atrocities, when exposed to the light of persistent investigation, have one by one faded away. It is now generally admitted that these stories were the products of fevered imagination and that they were disseminated primarily because of their propagandist value and with little regard for their authenticity. The World War was the occasion of the greatest and most successful campaign of propaganda ever attempted in human history. By means of the press and other agencies of communication the minds of the masses were regimented and made to respond to the wishes of governments. And the first world war was waged without the use of the radio.

The campaign of the power industry.[22] During the nineteen-twenties the managers of the power industry set out, at public expense, to persuade the American people that public utility corporations are benevolent agencies which serve the public with a maximum of efficiency and which, because of the regulation of their rates by state governments, do not operate for private profit as do other forms of business enterprise. The campaign of "education" was conducted on many fronts.

Indeed when the Director of the Information Department of the National Electric Light Association was asked in court whether he knew of any means of publicity that had been neglected by his organization, he replied: "Only one, and that is sky writing. I don't believe we have tried that with airplanes."[23] Among the means employed were leaflets, pamphlets, booklets, and bulletins; advertising, editorials, press service, clip sheets, and cartoons for newspapers; weekly and monthly news bulletins for press, public officials, public libraries, and influential people; schools, colleges, universities, and all educational institutions; speakers and speakers' bureaus to provide addresses generally; billboards, radio, and moving pictures; envelope stuffers or small folders in monthly bills of customers; and activities among chambers of commerce, Kiwanis, Rotary, Lion, and service clubs, labor and farm organi-

[22] See Ernest Gruening, *The Public Pays* (New York, 1931); Jack Levin, *Power Ethics* (New York, 1931); Carl D. Thompson, *op. cit.*
[23] Carl D. Thompson, *op. cit.,* 270.

zations, municipal leagues and civic societies, women's clubs and organizations, Boy and Girl Scouts, and various religious bodies including church clubs and the Y. M. C. A. As a result of this gigantic effort, in the course of four years much was done "to change and direct the economic thought and economic practice of the American people."

School textbooks dealing in any way with the subject of electric power or of public utilities in general were carefully examined. Those making adverse criticisms of these interests or in any way approving public ownership or control were blacklisted and excluded from the schools where possible. In order that books of the "right" kind might be available specialists were subsidized to write them. Whether these authors, not a few of them college professors, were actually bribed to suppress their own views on the subject may be open to question. Doubtless many teachers saw and still see the welfare of the public in terms of the welfare of the independent business interests of the country. Consequently, when they wrote books agreeable to the public utility companies, they were merely expressing their own convictions. Much of the material published was biased and the selection of facts was biased, but this would probably have been true had the same persons written on the same subjects without subsidies. The gist of the matter is that only persons with the proper bias were chosen to do the writing and that their works were urged upon the schools and upon the public by interested parties for the purpose of creating sympathy for the private power industry and antagonism toward the idea of public ownership.[24]

A nationwide campaign of propaganda was carried forward through the daily press. Immense quantities of material favorable to the utilities were sent to newspapers throughout the country. Many editors were perfectly willing to fill their columns with the carefully written dispatches and articles

[24] See Bessie Louise Pierce, *Citizens' Organizations and the Civic Training of Youth* (New York, 1933), 242–275.

which came to them without expense. Others, though seeing and resenting the propagandist purpose of the material,
printed it because they wanted the advertising of the public
utility companies, which amounted to "something like $25,000,-
000 to $30,000,000 per year."[25] Refusal would have meant a seri-
ous loss of revenue. As a result the press deluged the country
with articles glorifying private ownership, demonstrating the
fairness of the rates charged, and attacking as "socialistic,"
"communistic," or "bolshevistic" all proposals for public interference. And the same note was often sounded on the editorial
page.

But teachers, authors, and editors did not stand alone in
having their thinking done for them by experts of the power
industry. Masters of chautauqua were paid to deliver addresses
throughout the country on appropriate occasions. Women's
clubs of one kind or another proved particularly fruitful fields
for the exercise of utility evangelism. Indeed, the "educational"
process was carried so far that local club officials consented
to send to local newspapers, over their own signatures, propaganda blurbs prepared in the offices of the utility companies.
The expense of all of these propagandist activities, of course,
was not paid out of the coffers of the industry. "Don't be
afraid of the expense," urged the managing director of the
National Electric Light Association, "the public pays the expense."

The efforts of the power industry to mold public opinion
through the schools, the press, and other agencies, were exposed
by the investigations of the Federal Trade Commission. As a
result of the disclosures, public resentment was aroused and
the activities were curbed for a time; but publicity organizations are still maintained and the indoctrination of the
utility point of view, even if now done in a more covert
fashion, is still carried on. Moreover, let prosperity return and

25 Carl D. Thompson, *op. cit.,* 310.

the investigation be forgotten, and the campaign will no doubt soon be in full swing again.

The use of communication facilities by the power interests to create a favorable public opinion is only one example of a type of social conduct that is widespread in the United States. Whenever an organization is formed to advance any special interest, it sets the wheels of propaganda in motion. Thus for years the forces of prohibition, in an effort to make the production and sale of alcoholic drinks illegal, used every means available to arouse public sentiment against the saloon. And arrayed against them were the great liquor interests of the country. The same phenomena may be observed when shipbuilders oppose the reduction of the navy, when manufacturers extol the merits of high tariffs, and when bankers with investments in foregn countries demonstrate the wisdom of free trade. Also when missionaries of radical doctrines, communist or fascist, use every available technique to make converts; and when the apostles of "one-hundred-per-cent-Americanism" strive by similar methods to prove the menace of radicalism and the excellence of inherited institutions. The list of propagandist movements might be extended indefinitely to embrace almost every activity in which the welfare of one group or class is affected by the conduct of another. America is a nation of promoters. Few indeed are the individuals who are not more or less active members of a considerable number of organizations which are trying to "convert" other people to their way of thinking. Modern communication facilities are superbly adapted to the conduct of these reciprocal propaganda activities. And they are still being constantly improved, with television almost here and probably with other new developments "just around the corner."

Advertising and salesmanship. It is perhaps in the immediate field of business that the most intensive use of propaganda techniques may be found. "Advertising," says J. F. Hull, editor of *The Maryville* (Missouri) *Tribune,* "is the Thor of modern civilization. And just as the thunder god of the old Norse mythology made the valleys and plains by the strokes of his giant hammer, so publicity in this day makes its mark upon the affairs of this old world and shapes the thought and molds the opinions of all men."[26]

Rare is the article sold competitively which is not thrust upon the potential customer with every wile and trick of the salesman's art. Newspaper, billboard, and radio tell incessantly of the superior merits of various makes of cigarettes, point to the pleasure to be derived from a particular brand, clinch the argument with stirring music or colorful sex appeal. Presumably the real differences among the numerous cigarettes which are widely advertised are insignificant. Yet the belief is widespread that the "education" of the smoking public is not without effect. Certainly it is effective in the sense that no one firm could afford to cease advertising unless its competitors did likewise; and combinations in restraint of advertising do not promise soon to play a significant rôle in American business life. Even if all advertising of cigarettes were stopped and an end made to the clamor of the salesman, campaigns urging the consumer to substitute sweets for cigarettes might cut into the tobacco trade. Under the present business system producers must advertise, not only to compete with other producers of the same or similar products, but in order to compete with goods of quite different kinds.

Tobacco salesmanship is of course only one illustration of the use of propaganda in the sphere of business. It but suggests a vast range of phenomena which are of social and cultural significance, not primarily because they drive the consumer to purchase particular commodities, but rather because they place a terrific strain on his energy and attention. For nobody is the day more than twenty-four hours long; and for all, capacity for attending is limited. No one can read all that

[26] *Ibid.,* 309.

is written or hear all that is said. Either he must choose for himself, or others will choose for him the things to occupy his mind. Under an economic system that places such a premium on the selling of goods, the techniques of salesmanship absorb a disproportionate share of the time of the individual citizen and thus distract his attention correspondingly from matters of civic and social consequence. Business trespasses inordinately upon the premises of other interests. The contrast here with the agrarian economy of colonial times, when salesmanship scarcely existed, is sharp and clear.

THE PRESENT IRRATIONALITY

An analysis of the functioning of the agencies upon which the citizens of industrial society must depend for knowledge of happenings in his world reveals a condition of extreme irrationality. Here, as in the case of material goods, men go without in the midst of possible plenty. In the railroad, the steamship, the automobile, the airplane, the telegraph, the telephone, the radio, the cinema, and the press, technology has placed in human hands instruments for extending immeasurably social contacts and for bringing to the individual dependable knowledge about society and the world.

These instruments, however, are only very incompletely and imperfectly used. Certainly far less thought has gone into their social use than into their mechanical improvement. To a very large extent they are operated by social ideas and institutions that were evolved before the days of technological society. In their general functioning there is little of that rationality which characterizes their operation on the technical side. They are inco-ordinated and forced to work at cross-purposes. They are commonly the tools of business enterprise; and their services as molders of public opinion may be sold to the highest bidder. They may even be employed deliberately to defeat the ends of enlightenment and understanding for which they are ostensibly and avowedly devised. As a result, in spite of the great advances in engineering, the ordinary citizen, subjected to an incessant barrage of contrary stimuli from contradictory and conflicting sources, finds himself entirely bewildered in the presence of both his personal and his civic responsibilities. The elaborate and complicated agencies of communication of industrial society, as administered today, serve him less adequately than the comparatively simple and primitive agencies served his great-grandfather living in the pre-machine age.

The American political system places large responsibilities on the people and assumes their competence to rule. Clearly, if they are to rule wisely and guard the widest and most permanent social interests, they must have sufficient command of the facts underlying governmental action to enable them, or at least the more active and intelligent among them, to form trustworthy and informed opinions on all public questions and to exercise discrimination in arriving at civic judgments. That they are living up to this ideal today, few would have the hardihood to assert. The very scope and complexity of the present social order would seem to make almost impossible demands on the human mind. The world in which the individual lives has become so extended and interdependent that he can observe only the smallest fraction of the events that nevertheless affect him and condition his welfare. For the rest he must depend on the agencies of communication described in this chapter, which report to him what happens beyond the range of his own sense organs. There is thus built up between him and the world which he is expected to manage a mental picture that may grievously falsify the reality.[27] Yet that picture, however inadequate and false, must serve as his practical guide. The task of keeping these channels of information open, honest, and efficient is one of the supreme tasks of democratic society.

[27] See Walter Lippmann, *Public Opinion* (New York, 1922) and *The Phantom Public* (New York, 1925).

CHAPTER IV

HEALTH

From the standpoint of the masses of the people provision for promoting health, vitality, and general physical well-being as a specialized social function is of relatively recent origin. To be sure, primitive men had their shamans and magicians who presumed to combat disease, and the ancient world laid certain foundation stones for the development of medicine. But the science of healing made little solid advance before the dawn of the nineteenth century; and during the colonial period in American history physicians were not infrequently regarded with distrust. Moreover, as pointed out above, the number of practitioners of the medical art was extremely limited as late as the third quarter of the eighteenth century. This meant that the responsibility for treating sickness and preserving health, like most other social functions, was discharged primarily by the family. The development of preventive medicine is a product of the past two or three generations and has attended the rise of industrial civilization.

THE MEDICAL RESOURCES OF THE COUNTRY

The magnitude of this growing interest on the part of the American people in the question of health is reflected in the expansion of the medical resources of the country. Among these resources should be mentioned medical knowledge, institutions for training and research, professional personnel, institutions for diagnosis and care, and agencies of public health.

The primary medical resource is medical science—a resource that has been increasing at an ever more rapid rate since the middle of the last century. Through the co-operative efforts of scientists from many countries the boundaries of medical knowledge have been pushed back progressively. "Within the span of a single lifetime," says the Committee on the Costs of Medical Care, "the widespread utilization of anesthesia, aseptic surgery, bacteriology, physiology, and radiography has revolutionized the practice of medicine. Even during the last decade, medicine's advance in the unending warfare against sickness is little short of miraculous."[1] The unadorned account of this warfare, replete with adventure and sacrifice, makes a thrilling story.

For the advance of medical knowledge and the improvement of medical aids and equipment extensive provision is made. Following the establishment of the Medical Department of the University of Pennsylvania in 1765 the study of medicine has been a recognized part of the program of higher education, although until the latter part of the nineteenth century medical training was provided for the most part by groups of physicians who associated together for the purpose. Practically every great university now has its medical school where research, as well as professional training, is carried on. In these institutions the study of the related sciences is also being vigorously prosecuted. Then there are the scientific institutes, founded by private benefactions, which are making large contributions to experimental and preventive medicine. Among these should be listed the Rockefeller Institute for Infectious Diseases, the Carnegie Institution of Washington, the Phipps Institute for Tuberculosis, the Phipps Psychiatric Clinic, and the William H. Wilmer Institute of Ophthalmology. Millions of dollars are being expended every year in the United States in pushing the inquiry into the causes and conditions of health and disease.

Also in comparison with the past, resources for combatting disease and promoting health are provided on a munificent

[1] The Committee on the Costs of Medical Care, *Medical Care for the American People* (Chicago, 1932), 3.

scale. According to the findings of the Committee,[2] "nearly 1,-
100,000 persons in the United States devote all or a large part of
their time to providing medical service. . . . About one-half are
private practitioners; the other half serve in medical institutions or are engaged in the sale of medical commodities."[3]
Leading this vast army are 142,000 physicians who in growing numbers are devoting themselves to special aspects of medicine, such as internal medicine, surgery, gastroenterology, diet-
otherapy, proctology, obstetrics, gynecology, pediatrics, and
orthopedics. Then there are 195,000 graduate nurses, 150,000
practical nurses, 132,000 pharmacists, 47,000 midwives, and 196,-
000 lay personnel in hospitals, clinics, and public health agencies, as well as varying numbers of student nurses, public health
nurses, optometrists, opticians, osteopaths, chiropractors, chi-
ropodists, pediatrists, naturopaths, electrotherapists, Christian
Science practitioners, and others.

These medical workers are supplied with great quantities
of physical equipment and numerous special institutions for
diagnostic, therapeutic, and preventive treatment. In comparison with the past and other countries America today is unusually well-supplied with hospitals and clinics. In 1873 the
country possessed but 149 hospitals "containing 35,000 beds. By
1931, 6613 hospitals were registered by the American Medical
Association, and there were 974,115 beds. The capital investment for the latter year was over $3,000,000,000."[4] In the case of
the clinic serving ambulatory patients an even more remarkable
development is recorded. Although the first institution of this
kind was organized in Boston in 1786, by the opening of the
twentieth century the number had grown to only one hundred.
Thirty years later, if the term be made to embrace both out-

---

[2] Since frequent reference will be made in this chapter to the Committee
on the Costs of Medical Care, hereafter the title will be abbreviated to the
Committee.

[3] *Ibid.*, 3–4.

[4] Harry W. Moore, "Health and Medical Practice," Chapter XXI in The
President's Research Committee on Social Trends, *Recent Social Trends in the
United States* (New York, 1933), II, 1070.

patient departments of hospitals and independent institutions, there were about 6000 clinics in the country receiving approximately 30,000,000 visits a year. America is also well-equipped to dispense drugs and medicines to the population. In 1931 the country contained 60,000 drug stores, served by a huge staff of licensed pharmacists, assistant pharmacists, and apprentice pharmacists. Moreover, the number of independent colleges of pharmacy increased from one in 1821 to 69 in 1932.

Finally, among the medical resources should be included the various agencies for the promotion of public health. The beginnings of this type of administration have been traced to the Marine Hospital Service for the care of merchant seamen, which was organized in the Treasury Department in 1798 and which in 1912 became the United States Public Health Service. For generations, however, this arm of government developed but slowly. In 1867 "only eleven states and the District of Columbia had boards of health." Today every state in the Union makes some organized effort to safeguard public health. Also recent decades have witnessed a very rapid increase in the interest of counties, municipalities, and other local governments in the health of their citizens. The laws and regulations pertaining to public health adopted by state legislatures during the single year of 1919 fill a volume of 928 pages.

A concluding and summary index of the concern over health and of the extent of the medical resources is found in the sums devoted to the support of the medical program. In 1929 the American people spent $3,656,000,000, exclusive of the cost of hospitalization of communicable cases, "for all forms of medical service, including those services purchased indirectly through taxes and other community funds."[5] For the year involved, this enormous sum exceeded the expenditure on education and amounted to approximately 4 per cent of the entire income of the nation. Clearly the resources of industrial society are being mobilized on a large scale in the war on disease.

[5] The Committee on the Costs of Medical Care, *op. cit.,* 13.

THE ACHIEVEMENTS OF MEDICINE

But an account of the growth of medical science, of the number of medical institutions and agencies, or even of the huge expenditure on medical services fails to deal with the substance of the matter. All of these striking developments can have but one object: the control of disease and the preservation of life. To what extent have they succeeded in their aim? The answer to this question is unequivocal and emphatic. As a result of advance in the knowledge and practice of medicine, men today live in a world that is far safer from the inroads of disease than was the world of their fathers. Various deadly distempers have been conquered, the span of life lengthened, numerous irrational fears banished, and man's sense of physical security in the world greatly increased.

For more than a thousand years bubonic plague periodically ravaged Europe, exacting a heavy toll in human lives and misery. As late as the fourteenth century, so it has been estimated, this disease destroyed over 60,000,000 human beings or approximately one-fourth of the people living on the earth; today it is seldom encountered in Europe or America. In the seventeenth century in England smallpox was so common that the pockmarked face was almost universal; today smallpox has all but disappeared. From 1800 to 1879 portions of the United States were swept annually by yellow fever; today this disease is completely gone. Thirty years ago 35.9 persons per 100,000 died annually of typhoid fever; today the rate is only 4.8 and still going down. During the same period the death rate from diphtheria declined from 43.3 to 4.9.[6] Stephen Smith, after a long life devoted to public health, has thus described conditions which persisted in our cities as late as 1866:

"Smallpox, scarlet fever, measles, diphtheria, were domestic pestilences with which the people were so familiar that they regarded them as necessary features of childhood. Malarial

[6] See Harry H. Moore, *op. cit.*, 1061–1062.

fevers . . . were regularly announced in the autumnal months as having appeared with their 'usual severity.' The 'white plague,' or consumption, was the common inheritance of the poor and rich alike. With the immigrant came typhus and typhoid fevers, which resistlessly swept through the tenement houses, decimating the poverty-stricken tenants. At intervals, the great oriental plague, Asiatic cholera, swooped down upon the city with fatal energy and gathered its enormous harvest of dead. Even yellow fever, the great pestilence of the tropics, made occasional incursions. . . . Failure to improve the unhealthy conditions of the city, and the tendency to aggravate them by a large increase of the tenement-house population, offensive trades, accumulations of domestic waste, and the filth of streets, stables, and privy pits, then universal, caused an enormous sacrifice of life, especially among children."[7]

Not only, however, have particular diseases been brought under control or their virulence greatly reduced. The general death rate has been notably lowered. In New York City the average annual death rate for the five years preceding 1866 was 38 per 1000 population. The corresponding figure for today is about twelve. Studies in other American cities have revealed similar changes. All of these facts mean that the expectation of life at birth has been greatly increased. While reliable data for most parts of the country are lacking, the expectation of life in Massachusetts at the end of the eighteenth century was approximately thirty-five years. In Europe during the Middle Ages the corresponding figure was not far from twenty, and in modern India it is twenty-six. Today in the United States it is fifty-seven years for males and sixty years for females.[8] While the great gains have not affected all ages alike, being particularly significant in the early years of life, these indices furnish unimpeachable testimony to the solid

[7] Stephen Smith, M.D., *The City That Was* (New York, 1912), 19–20.
[8] Edgar Sydenstricker, "The Vitality of the American People," Chapter XII in *Recent Social Trends in the United States,* I, 605.

and brilliant achievements of medical science and the general improvement of living conditions.

The entire question of safeguarding and promoting the health of the American people is being greatly eased by the decline of the birth rate. It is of course well known that for several generations, due to the spread of the use of contraceptives and probably to the operation of certain obscure causes, the birth rate has been falling throughout most of the western world. In the United States this tendency has become so pronounced that, with the continued restriction of immigration which seems probable, a stationary and possibly even a declining population may be expected in the not distant future. In 1930 for the first time in the history of the nation the federal census showed an actual decrease in the number of persons in an important age group.[9] In that year the number of children under five years of age was 128,840 less than it was in 1920. Moreover, the number of births has been declining steadily and rapidly since 1924. As a consequence, in spite of the much larger population, there were approximately 90,000 fewer births in 1931 than in 1910. Just when the population will become stabilized is of course a question that cannot be answered with any degree of assurance. But if present tendencies continue, the point should be reached during the latter part of the present century.

The fact to be emphasized, however, is not that the population is to become stationary in a certain year or decade but rather that man at last has achieved a large measure of control over one of the most powerful of natural forces—the force of human reproduction. The melancholy formula of Malthus, that population always tends to outstrip the food supply, seems about to be laid to rest forever. Under that formula war and famine and pestilence were a part of the order of nature and not to be escaped or controlled. Today men, if they will, may

[9] Warren S. Thompson and P. K. Whelpton, "The Population of the Nation," Chapter I in *Recent Social Trends in the United States*, I, 26.

live under happier conditions. With the moderation of the birth rate the severity of the human struggle can be softened and a secure place in the world guaranteed to all. Though the increasing number of persons surviving to the higher ages will bring special problems and difficulties, the gains from the standpoint of health and physical well-being are incontestable.

THE PRESENT HEALTH SITUATION

If the analysis were to be concluded here, the problem of guarding the health of the population would seem to be near solution. That there has been unquestioned progress cannot be denied. Yet that much remains to be done is equally true. An examination of the present health situation shows much preventable illness, defect, and death, incomplete use of medical knowledge and facilities, and numerous difficult problems raised by industrial civilization.

Preventable Illness, Defect, and Death. In spite of the conquest of certain diseases and the great reduction in the death rate, relatively few individuals live out the allotted span of life. What that span may be is of course unknown. But it is known that, whether the summons comes early or late, great masses of the people are carried off by disease or accident. In an ideal situation the principal cause of death would be old age, or the simple wearing-out of the organism. While old age is of necessity frequently an important contributing factor, only rarely is it recognized as the immediate and direct cause of death. Moreover, the increase in the proportion of the population living to middle and old age as a result of the control of the maladies of childhood, such as diphtheria, measles, scarlet fever, and whooping cough, as well as certain diseases affecting all ages, such as typhoid fever, pneumonia, and tuberculosis, has led to a sharp growth in the number of deaths from other ailments, notably heart disease, cancer, diabetes, and cerebral hemorrhage. Unless effective methods for controlling these maladies of the more advanced years are discovered and generally applied in the coming decades, an increase in the gross death rate is to be expected. This whole question of preventable death has been well summarized by Edgar Sydenstricker:

". . . The point that interests us here is the failure of so large a proportion of the population to reach the end of even a modest life span—say 60 or 70 years. The data already referred to are ample to illustrate the actual failure to survive as well as to indicate some of the principal causes of death at different ages. Table 14, which brings up to date the gross mortality rates for certain causes, shows the rates for the more immediate causes of death. These facts should be interpreted, however, in the light of the impairments and illnesses that have been found to exist and occur long before death comes. If this is done, a conclusion of profound significance to the conservation of vitality is inescapable, namely that the vitality of the American people—whatever it may be if it were measurable in terms of inherited longevity—is impaired to an appalling extent by disease and environmental conditions that result not only in the immediate death of many but also in lowered efficiency, suffering, unhappiness and organic breakdowns which contribute to premature mortality."[10]

The amount of illness, which may or may not result in death, constitutes another measure of the adequacy of the health program. A number of studies made by the United States Public Health Service indicate that according to the lowest rates discovered there are approximately 130,000,000 cases of disabling illness in the country each year.[11] If non-disabling illnesses are added, the figure is more than doubled. Moreover, the disabling illnesses are of such severity that on the average men lose

[10] Edgar Sydenstricker, *op. cit.*, 658.
[11] Alden B. Mills, *The Extent of Illness and of Physical and Mental Defects Prevailing in the United States.* Abstract of Publication No. 2 of the Committee on the Costs of Medical Care (Washington, October, 1929), 5.

seven to eight and women eight to twelve days per year. The situation with respect to school children is very similar. And the diseases chiefly responsible for this vast deal of suffering are relatively few in number and presumably capable of being controlled. In order of frequency they are colds and bronchial troubles, influenza and grippe, digestive diseases and disorders, ailments of the pharynx, tonsils, and larynx, non-venereal diseases of the genito-urinary system, diseases of the skin and cellular tissue, "headache," and "rheumatism." The first is by far the most frequent of the list. The common cold accounts for almost one-half of all disabling illness and probably for a yet larger proportion of all illness.

Equally disturbing is the prevalence of chronic disease in the nation. A study in Massachusetts, where medical facilities are certainly equal to the average of the country, suggests that at any one given moment approximately 12 per cent of the entire population of the state is suffering from some form of chronic disease.[12] The inquiry, moreover, showed that the rate per 1000 persons rose from 17 for those under twenty to 198 for those 50-54 years of age, that about one-fifth of the sick had more than one disease, and that over 8 per cent were completely disabled.

Of peculiar gravity is the persistence of diseases whose cause and cure are understood. Thus at any given time in the United States there are probably 1,000,000 persons sick with malaria and 700,000 suffering from tuberculosis.[13] In the southern states, because of the low standard of living among the masses, several million men, women, and children have their vitality reduced by the hook-worm. Venereal diseases continue to bring sterility to thousands of women and spread paralysis, locomotor ataxia, and mental disorder among the population. And every year records thousands of cases of small-

[12] H. L. Lombard, "The Chronic Disease Problem in Massachusetts," *Hospital Social Service*, XXII (1930). Quoted by Edgar Sydenstricker, *op. cit.*, 657.

[13] Alden B. Mills, *op. cit.*, 12.

pox, typhoid fever, and diphtheria. Practice has failed to keep pace with knowledge.

Physical and mental defect constitute yet another measure of the health of the people. Of the various studies of physical defect that have been made the examination of approximately 100,000 adult males under the auspices of the Life Extension Institute is the most reliable. If the findings of this investigation be applied to the total population of the country of corresponding age and sex, a procedure which would probably give an unduly favorable picture of the situation, the average man is afflicted with more than five physical defects. Fifty-seven per cent of the men examined were suffering from defective vision, 43 per cent from enlarged or diseased tonsils, 37 per cent from hypertrophic rhinitis, 34 per cent from constipation, 20 per cent from thickening of the arteries, 16 per cent from defective hearing, and 15 per cent from carious teeth. The extent of mental defect is difficult to determine, because of the absence of objective standards. Nevertheless various estimates suggest that the number of feebleminded persons in the country is not far from 900,000. And studies in the State of New York indicate that "on the average, approximately one person out of 22 becomes a patient for mental disease during the life of a generation."[14] According to W. J. Mayo neuroses alone are responsible for more human misery than tuberculosis or cancer.

The total situation with regard to disease and death has thus been summarized by the Committee:

"The death rates from cancer, diabetes, and appendicitis are rising threateningly. More babies are dying each year, many of them needlessly, than there were American soldiers killed in the World War. Every year tuberculosis kills its thousands and costs the country more than half a billion dollars. By early application of our knowledge we could double the cured cases

---

[14] Horatio M. Pollock and Benjamin Malzberg, "Expectation of Mental Disease," *Psychiatric Quarterly* (Albany, New York, October, 1928).

of cancer. The venereal diseases still levy a heavy toll of blindness and mental disorders upon the nation. A great army of rheumatics remains untreated without hope of alleviation or cure. Many diabetics still remain without insulin or receive it too late. Human life in the United States is being wasted, as recklessly, as surely, in times of peace as in times of war."[15]

The advance in medical knowledge, the decline of the birth rate, the conquest of certain diseases, and the general practice of protecting the weak, have raised a final problem of fundamental character. Many thoughtful people believe that these changes tend to impair the racial stock. It is pointed out that the birth rate has declined disproportionately among the more gifted strains of the population. As a result, the less gifted increasingly become the progenitors of the race and thus gradually lower the quality of the stock. This tendency toward deterioration is re-enforced, so the argument runs, by the impairment of the rigor of natural selection because of medical advance and the spread of humanitarian impulses. The more ardent advocates of this point of view paint the future in extremely somber colors: they prophesy a race of mental and physical degenerates parasitic on medical knowledge and destined sooner or later to be destroyed by some terrible catastrophe. How seriously these gloomy forebodings should be taken is a matter for conjecture today, owing to the imperfections of the science of heredity. Yet the matter of the biological qualities of the race is of such significance for the future that the whole question merits the most thorough study. Already many states, wisely or unwisely, have enacted laws for the sterilization of defectives and for the enforcement of certain medical standards for marriage.

Incomplete Use of Medical Knowledge and Facilities. The underlying cause of the failures of medicine is entirely patent. On this question there seems to be practically complete agreement among specialists. "We know how to do a lot of things

15 *Op. cit.,* 150.

which we don't do, or do on a wretchedly small scale,"[16] wrote William H. Welch in 1925. "Our failures," says the Committee, "result not only from insufficient scientific knowledge and from human weaknesses, but also from our failure to utilize existing knowledge, techniques, equipment, and personnel."[17] And the Committee concludes its majority report with these words: "Thousands of people are sick and dying daily in this country because the knowledge and facilities that we have are inadequately applied. We must promptly put this knowledge and these facilities to work."[18]

The failure to make full use of the medical resources of the nation is clearly revealed by the studies of the Committee. Although an annual medical examination is ordinarily regarded as necessary for the safeguarding of health, in any one year less than 7 per cent of the population receive this kind of service. And less than 5 per cent are immunized against diphtheria or any other disease. Even in the cases of relatively severe illness a surprisingly large proportion of the population receive no medical care whatsoever. Thus among 11,000 persons disabled by sickness in certain districts surveyed by the Metropolitan Life Insurance Company 25 per cent were not attended by physicians. Of 11,558 cases of sickness studied in Hagerstown, Maryland, in 1921–1924, not including colds, "indigestion," and biliousness, 40 per cent were not attended.[19] A comprehensive study of the situation in Vermont in 1929 showed that 60 per cent of the people of that state did not employ the services of a physician and 70 per cent did not consult a dentist during the year. According to estimates made for the country as a whole 20 per cent of the people do not go regularly to the dentist. And a nation-wide survey of 8639 white families, 1928–1931, found that 38 per cent of the 38,668 individuals involved received no

[16] *State Charities Aid Association News* (New York, December, 1925), XIV, 2.
[17] *Op. cit.*, 146.   [18] *Ibid.*, 150.
[19] *The Five-Year Program of the Committee on the Costs of Medical Care* (Washington, February 13, 1928), 23.

medical, dental, or eye care in the course of twelve consecutive months.[20]

Aside from the underlying factors of ordinary human stupidity and of unhealthful living and working conditions, the improvement of which should be one of the primary objects of all economic and social planning, these shortcomings are to be traced in large part to the inco-ordination of medical facilities, economic inequalities among the population, emphasis on therapeutics rather than preventive medicine, and the ignorance of the public regarding the whole question of hygiene and medical care. A brief elaboration of each of these factors will make clear the nature of the problem which the American people face in the field of medicine. The problem will be found to be fundamentally social and educational in nature.

Inco-ordination of medical facilities. In the first place, a condition of general inco-ordination prevails in the practice of medicine. Here, as in so many other areas of American life, a tradition of *laissez-faire* evolved to meet the needs of a simple, loosely integrated society continues to rule. This tradition persists even though experience shows that "the successes of modern medicine have been achieved for the most part in those fields in which knowledge, techniques, equipment, and personnel have been organized under community leadership. Thus we have made concerted efforts to control infant mortality, tuberculosis, and the acute communicable diseases, and in large measure we have succeeded. Some disorders, on the other hand, have been left to the initiative of the private practitioner and the individual citizen with disappointing and sometimes negligible results."[21]

In general medical facilities "are not distributed primarily according to needs, but rather according to real or supposed ability of patients to pay for service."[22] This is particularly true in the case of therapeutics, a branch of medicine reserved

[20] The Committee on the Costs of Medical Care, *op. cit.,* 9.
[21] *Ibid.,* 146.   [22] *Ibid.,* 4–5.

largely to private enterprise and every kind of voluntary undertaking. Here only the roughest kind of relationship exists
between institution and need. Consider the preparation of
personnel. Physicians are trained in a hundred separate schools,
each more or less autonomous and primarily absorbed in its
own fortunes. The profession, moreover, has developed no
adequate philosophy for the medical needs of society, nor has
it devised any methods for the determination of such needs.
The same may be said regarding nurses, dentists, and all other
branches of the medical personnel. As a consequence, even
though the total number of trained persons may be appropriate,
which is of course very unlikely, the grossest kind of inco-ordination may be found within the medical service. It has been
estimated that "approximately 45 per cent of the physicians of
the country have completely or partially limited their practice
to a specialty, although apparently the needs of the people could
be met adequately if not more than 18 per cent of physicians
were specialists."[23] The maladjustment in the field of hospital
service is of the same order. One community may have an excess
of beds for acute illnesses and a shortage for mental or chronic
diseases, while in another community the condition may be
exactly reversed. Also, although hospital or clinical connections are practically indispensable for effective medical service,
large numbers of physicians do not have such connections. In
1929 one-third of the physicians of Philadelphia were thus hampered in their work.[24]

Within a particular profession inadequate provision seems
to be made for preparing practitioners for the different grades
of service. As a consequence, highly trained persons may devote most of their time to treating the most simple ailments—
ailments that might be cared for by specialists of a much
lower level of preparation and at a much lower cost to society.

[23] Ibid., 5.
[24] Nathan Sinai and Alden B. Mills, A Survey of the Medical Facilities of
the City of Philadelphia: 1929. Publication No. 9 of the Committee on the
Costs of Medical Care (Chicago, 1931), 140.

Dean Alfred Owre, in advocating the organization of dental practice with a stomatologist (a specialist with thorough medical training in the hygiene and diseases of the mouth) in charge of a group of assistants of various types who could be trained in a relatively short time, makes the following statement:

"Two years ago I made a rough comparison, for a typical mid-west County, of the existing thirteen dental practices versus a possible group clinic of twelve trained technicians under the direction of an oral specialist. This was based on figures from an exhaustive published study. Without going into details of the 13 dentists' educational qualifications and of their practices, it may be said that both left a great deal to be desired. . . . Moreover—and here is the vital point—not more than fifteen per cent of the population received any dental care. What they did get was almost wholly emergency and simple routine work. An efficiently organized group clinic of thirteen could do much more work than this, and of infinitely better quality. . . . A comparison of educational costs alone . . . showed a potential saving to society of at least $230,000. A comparison of possible clinic salaries, liberally estimated, with the reported incomes of the thirteen dentists showed a slight balance in favor of the clinic. It is self-evident that economies of operating costs for a single clinic as compared with the 'overhead' for thirteen separate offices, would be considerable. Great as the economic advantage appears, however, the chief benefit to the community would be in the quality and extent of the services rendered."[25]

In the geographical distribution of medical facilities severe maladjustment also exists. Although this is due in part to inequalities of wealth and income, it is to be accounted for in considerable part by other causes. Geographically the medical and other professional personnel is distributed almost of necessity quite at random in so far as the needs of the public are concerned. The reason is to be found in the fact that the prac-

[25] Alfred Owre, unpublished manuscript.

tice of medicine is conducted as a form of private business enterprise and inevitably tends to gravitate to those areas where the largest profits and the most conspicuous opportunities for personal advancement are found. The studies of the Committee show that "many communities are under-supplied with practitioners, hospitals, and other facilities, while others have a surplus. For example, in 1929 there was one physician to every 1431 persons in South Carolina, as contrasted with one to every 571 in California and one to every 621 in New York State. In 1928, there were 19 dentists per 100,000 population in Mississippi, and 101 in Oregon. . . . Wisconsin had one (hospital) bed for community use to each 154 persons, while South Carolina had one to each 749 persons. Similar conclusions are reached from data on other states."[26] Generally the rural community in the United States is under-supplied in this as in so many other departments of life. The better-trained, the more ambitious of every profession drift toward the cities. Even hospitals seem to find the rural atmosphere uncongenial: in 1928, approximately 43 per cent of American counties had no hospitals for general community use.[27]

Economic inequalities. In the second place, economic inequalities among the people of a particular community generate inequalities in the enjoyment of medical care. Here is one of the natural consequences of the operation of the existing economic system. Although the great majority of physicians, following a splendid tradition, customarily respond to the call of distress regardless of the financial status of the patient; and although various forms of service are provided without charge for the very poor, the fact remains that poverty, physical defect, malnutrition, sickness, medical neglect, and premature death all form parts of one great social complex. What rôle sickness plays in this complex no one can say with precision.

[26] *Op. cit.,* 5.
[27] Allon Peebles, *A Survey of Statistical Data on Medical Facilities in the United States.* Publication No. 3 of the Committee on the Costs of Medical Care (Washington, 1929), 38.

It is known, however, that among the poor the frequency of disease is consistently greater, the quality of professional service distinctly lower, and the amount of medical care decidedly less than among the well-to-do.

According to one study made by the United States Public Health Service[28] in 1916 the incidence of illness in the lowest income group was 115.5 per cent greater than in those strata of the population where the adult males were earning wages considered to be adequate. The United States Children's Bureau,[29] investigating 22,967 live births between 1911 and 1916, found that the annual death rate per 1000 births rose from 59.1 for infants whose fathers earned $1250 and over to 166.9 for those whose fathers earned less than $450. In the influenza epidemic of 1918 the rate of mortality among the very poor was 263 per cent of the rate among the well-to-do. An investigator for the Committee estimates that "dependent persons are ill on the average nearly twice as often as persons with incomes considered adequate," and that both "infant and adult mortality rates are from one and one-half to two and one-half times as high among the poorest groups."[30]

The Vermont study in 1930, to which reference has already been made, showed a per capita medical cost of $21.20. Families with incomes above $2500, however, which constituted 36 per cent of all the families of the state, paid 81 per cent of the total medical bill. If dollars may be taken as a measure of the medical care received, this means that the 64 per cent of the poorer families received but 19 per cent of the medical care (not including public health service) provided in the state. Lee K. Frankel in a study of 3281 families holding policies with the Metropolitan Life Insurance Company[31] during a period of six months ending with June, 1929, found an inverse ratio

---

[28] Frank J. Bruno, *Illness and Dependency*. Miscellaneous Contributions on the Costs of Medical Care No. 9 of the Committee on the Costs of Medical Care (Washington, March 1, 1931), 5.

[29] *Ibid.*, 8.   [30] *Ibid.*, 1.

[31] Lee K. Frankel, *Cost of Medical Care* (New York, 1929), 9.

between per capita expenditure for medical care and size of family. For the six months covered by the inquiry families of two averaged $41.24 per capita; families of four $15.57; families of six $11.25; families of eight $10.44; and families of nine or more $6.64. That the spending of smaller amounts by the larger families was due to the pressure of other needs on the family budget may be assumed. In its survey of 8639 white families the Committee found that "the groups with smaller incomes obtain far less service. In spite of the large volume of free work done by hospitals, health departments, and individual practitioners, and in spite of the sliding scale of charges, it appears that each year nearly one-half of the individuals in the lowest income group receive no professional medical or dental attention of any kind, curative or preventive."[32] In the case of sickness the poor face three possibilities: they may accept free medical service, where it is available, and perhaps lose their self-respect; they may assume the financial obligations involved and soon find themselves laboring under an intolerable burden of debt; or, what is most likely, trusting in a kind providence, they will forego proper medical care, seek relief in patent medicines obtained at the nearest drugstore, and thus permit illness to become compounded until health is irretrievably lost. It should also not be forgotten that, because of inferior living and working conditions, the poor face every exposure to disease under a severe handicap. In their case, moreover, such exposure is likely to be both more frequent and enduring.

The meaning of prolonged sickness to the very poor, or even the moderately poor, a category which embraces great masses of the people, can scarcely be understood by members of the more favored classes. A single hospital experience may consume the savings of years or take funds that ordinarily would go for recreation and cultural growth. And if illness visits the bread-winner of a family, the greatest loss of course is not to be charged against the cost of medical care but rather to the

[32] *Op. cit.*, 9.

suspension of the family income. Various studies have shown that at least three-quarters of dependent families present one or more health problems and that each of these families has not less than two members suffering from some physical disability serious enough to require medical service. Frank J. Bruno thus summarizes the situation:

"Serious illness of either a breadwinner or of the homemaker lowers the family standards of living. This often means moving into a poorer neighborhood, living in a less desirable house with fewer rooms, less light and open space, disposing of some of the better or more salable articles of furniture, and curtailing recreation and variety and supply of food. These are circumstances and conditions which entail danger to physical health, and, even more, tend to break the morale of the family and increase overwhelmingly the sense of failure and inferiority characteristic of dependency."[33]

Emphasis on therapeutics. In the third place, under the present regime emphasis is placed on curative rather than preventive medicine. This emphasis is powerfully entrenched in medical tradition and can be traced back to primitive times when practically nothing was known regarding the causes and prevention of disease. Indeed, in the popular mind medicine is still known as the art of healing and the idea of preventive medicine contains an element of incongruity. Also the stress on therapeutics is the natural product of the present organization of medicine as a form of private enterprise. The ordinary physician, trained to cure disease and generally dependent for his livelihood on the practice of this art, has a certain vested interest in sickness and physical suffering. The conscientious member of the profession must constantly feel himself torn between two desires: on the one hand, as a normal human being he can only rejoice at the thought of a completely healthy community; while, on the other, as a guardian of the eco-

[33] Frank J. Bruno, *op. cit.,* 11.

nomic welfare of himself and family in a highly competitive world, he must experience secret satisfaction and relief from financial worries on learning that the amount of sickness among his patrons is on the increase or that some epidemic is about to visit his neighborhood. Until physicians find economic security in rooting out disease and defect of every kind and in positively maintaining the health of the population, the traditional emphasis on curative medicine will continue.

Nevertheless the superiority of prevention over cure is so generally recognized that it has found proverbial expression. It is in this realm moreover that medicine has made its great conquests: the reduction in the general death rate, the checking of the mortality of infants, the control of numerous contagious diseases, and generally the conversion of the world into a safer place in which men may live. But prevention is in large measure a public rather than a private enterprise. It is known today that both disease and defect are commonly social in their origins—products of group life, of living conditions, and even of time-honored institutional arrangements. Consequently, since preventive medicine must deal with these things, it has been obliged to make its way in the face of powerful opposition from traditional forces.

By far the most important branch of preventive medicine is the public health service. And yet, while practically every investment in this field has brought enormous returns in the safeguarding and the improvement of the health of the population, the American people have extended to it only the most meager support. According to the Committee, communities in the United States "have been pitifully backward in utilizing modern public health procedures. Of the entire $30 per capita spent for the prevention and care of disease, only $1 has been used for public health service, Federal, state, and local."[34]

The development of public health services, however, has encountered not only the apathy of the public: in its early

34 *Op. cit.*, 13.

years it even met hostility at the hands of the medical profession. To be sure, Edward Jenner, the discoverer of vaccine for smallpox, Joseph Lister, the pioneer in antiseptic surgery, Louis Pasteur, the brilliant student of micro-organisms, Robert Koch, the founder of practical bacteriology, and Walter Reed, the conqueror of yellow fever, were all physicians. Yet they worked in the sphere of sanitation more than in the realm of curative medicine. Moreover, many of the pioneers in sanitary engineering were medical laymen. Thus Lemuel Shattuck, one of the earliest Americans in the field, was a school teacher and lay student of public health. In 1851 he reported to the Sanitary Commission of Massachusetts on the need in that state of pure water, adequate drainage, and a state board of health. He was ignored by the public and scorned by the medical profession. In 1842 Sir Edwin Chadwick, an economist and political scientist, published a report on "Sanitary Conditions of the Labouring Classes in Great Britain" in which he attempted to convince London of the hazard of drinking polluted water from the River Thames. He received little encouragement from the physicians and was roundly denounced by the private water companies. Under the existing state of affairs, the defender of the public, whether in the sphere of health or of scientific research, may expect to meet with the opposition of the private interests involved. Even in the realm of promoting the physical well-being of the population, American society tends to uphold the principle of profit-making.

Ignorance of the public. In the fourth place, the general public is unprepared to make intelligent use of the medical resources of the nation. This perhaps is the most basic difficulty of all and is well illustrated by the way in which the people spend their money. While the total amount allocated to health may be adequate to keep the population reasonably free from disease and defect, it is not spent wisely in its details. All but an insignificant fraction of the total expenditure is devoted to curative and corrective measures. As already noted, prevention receives but little support and public health is scarcely accorded serious consideration. The American people spend more on "osteopaths, chiropractors, naturopaths, and allied groups, and faith healers" than on public health, and three times as much on "patent medicines." There even seems to be little reason exercised in the allocation of public moneys derived from taxation. Thus in 1929 the State of Vermont spent ten times as much for the care of persons suffering from mental defect and disease as for official public health work. In this same state the investigators found that "at least 30 per cent of the total expenditure for the care of illness is practically wasted because spent for self-medication or inferior types of practitioners." Throughout the country numerous superstitions reminiscent of the pre-scientific age of medicine persist among the masses. "Denver Mud" and "nanny tea" are still widely used in rural America; and such books as Doctor Chase's *Third, Last and Complete Receipt Book and Household Physician,* published in 1890, continue to be treasured. Here is a vestige of the time when medical care was a household function.

The consumer of course cannot be held entirely responsible for his irrational behavior. Untrained in such matters, the ordinary individual can scarcely be expected to make intelligent use of modern medicine. Moreover, his income is often precarious and inadequate to his needs; high pressure salesmen urge him to live beyond his means; clever advertisers seek out every weakness in his defensive armor; easy roads to health, marriage, and fortune assail him from every bill-board and magazine; and his friends tell him of miraculous cures obtained from this or that remedy or cult. Having been the victim of some sort of charlatanry at the hands of an unscrupulous member of the medical profession he is both profoundly skeptical and extremely gullible. Knowing that his faith has been exploited in the past he is profoundly skeptical; but being grounded in no understanding of principles he is at the same time extremely gullible.

Problems Raised by Industrialism. The situation with respect to health and disease has been profoundly altered by the rise of industrial civilization with its great cities, its close integration, its highly specialized occupations, its system of machine production, its new forms of transportation and communication, and its strange mode of life. This whole question will be illuminated by a brief examination of a number of problems that have been raised, rendered more acute, or forced into new molds by industrialism.

Water supply and waste disposal. Foremost among the problems raised by the coming of a closely integrated society is the problem of water and sewage. City populations have of course always paid dearly for inadequate knowledge about water supply and waste disposal; but today the entire society assumes increasingly the aspect of one vast city. Where man lives next to nature the purity of the water supply generally takes care of itself, but a congested population must resort to the arts in order to safeguard its health. The major difficulty arises out of the fact that water is used for both drinking and cleansing purposes. Thus the water which carries away the waste of one community may flow on unpurified into the drinking supply of the next.

Numerous classic examples of the unholy union of sewage and water supply may be given. For many years Chicago used Lake Michigan both as a means of sewage disposal and as a source of water supply, dumping its sewage along the shores and taking in its water a short distance out. Later the city dug a drainage canal, reversed the flow of the Desplaines River, and thus constructed an "open sewer" leading to the Mississippi. While this arrangement improved Chicago's water supply, it constituted a serious menace to the health of the cities to the south. As a consequence the great metropolis has been ordered to find other means of disposing of its sewage and garbage. But its problem may still remain unsolved, because the State of Indiana makes no effort to prevent Gary and other cities along the Hoosier shore from dumping their wastes into Lake Michigan.

Jean Broadhurst[35] cites other examples of the effect of pursuing the *laissez-faire* policy of agrarian society in dealing with the water and sewage problems of neighboring cities. An epidemic of typhoid fever in Lowell, Massachusetts, which discharged its sewage into the Merrimac, was followed by an epidemic in Lawrence, nine miles down the river. The latter city used the unfiltered water from the Merrimac for drinking purposes. This sequence of epidemics was repeated until Lawrence constructed a plant to filter the river water. Niagara Falls, sixteen miles below Buffalo, receives the latter's sewage in a few hours. As a result, before the institution of filters and chemical treatment, Niagara Falls had the highest typhoid rate in the United States.

The case of New York City is of peculiar interest. Contrary to the present condition, for more than a century this city was a very unhealthful place in which to live. Plagues and epidemics returned each summer with such regularity that the abandonment of the lower part of the city during the hot weather by the well-to-do classes became an annual custom. In time it was discovered that these visitations were the result of a general use of well water and a faulty disposal of waste. The cholera plague of 1866 was traced to piles of garbage and offal stored on vacant lots and along the river fronts. After these many years, although an ample supply of pure water has been procured, the disposal of the city's sewage and garbage remains a baffling problem. The practice of emptying sewage into the harbor and rivers has polluted all of the local bathing beaches. Garbage, taken on scows far out to sea, floats back to

[35] Jean Broadhurst, *Home and Community Hygiene* (Philadelphia, 1929), 104–105.

befoul the Jersey coast. Following much litigation the courts have ruled that New York City must find other methods of waste disposal. This means the erection of gigantic reduction and incineration plants which, if properly managed, should be a source of wealth to the city.

Milk and food supply. A second health problem of enormous import raised by the coming of the industrial regime has to do with milk and food supply. In a simple agrarian society both milk and food are produced for the most part for use by the family or the small local community; in the great society of today they are commonly produced at a distance for pecuniary profit and by total strangers. It is not surprising therefore that government has interested itself increasingly in milk and food inspection. The real wonder perhaps is that government has done so little.

Most large cities are content, through their health departments, merely to inspect in the local markets the solid foods— meats, vegetables, fruits, and cereals. The health hazards of the food supply are usually greater in the restaurants and kitchens than in the shops and stores. In many cities, however, the handlers of food, as well as the conditions under which food is prepared and served, are subjected to considerable scrutiny.

The importance to the health of a community of a safe and ample supply of milk can scarcely be over-emphasized. Perhaps no other food is so responsive a carrier of disease or so indispensable to the welfare of children and the sick. This is so generally recognized that even the suggestion of impure milk may cause a panic among consumers, and any suspicion of unscrupulous tampering with the milk supply may lead to a public scandal. The city consequently sends its inspectors to distant dairies to observe sanitary conditions, to look into the health of the cows, and to supervise the transportation of milk. Then the milk is again inspected at the point of distribution in the city. Concern over the health of the people has even led to the regulation of the price of milk. On occasion the milk companies, in pursuit of profits, have so raised prices that poor consumers have been forced either to reduce their consumption or resort to milk of inferior quality. Some students of the question, arguing that a large city should own and control its milk just as it does its water supply, see no solution to the problem short of the recognition of this service as a public utility. In 1933 certain states created milk boards and thus put milk on a public service basis.

The interest of the government in food inspection will doubt-less increase as the processes involved in the preservation, trans-portation, and preparation of food become more completely industrialized. Already in the Pure Food and Drug Act the federal government has taken measures to safeguard the public interest in the preservation of food. As the practice of using prepared foods from cans, bottles, and other containers grows, the vigilance of the representatives of the public in sanitary control and inspection will no doubt be tightened.

Noise and smoke. A third problem of large importance is raised by those twin evils of the early stages of industrialism —noise and smoke. The very word machine calls to mind the discordant jangling of iron against iron, the screeching of fac-tory sirens, and the general din and roar of the city. In the course of municipal development the noise problem has as-sumed different aspects. In its early stages unnecessary noise was merely regarded as a nuisance. It was for this reason that the old custom in New York City of tolling all the church bells during a funeral was suppressed. For a similar reason ordinances were passed at other times against the street cries of peddlers. Today, however, the charge is much more serious. A recent study by the New York Health Department reports that the harsh noises of the great city place a severe strain upon the nervous system and lead to neurasthenic and psychasthenic states "necessitating frequent recuperation in the country to maintain mental efficiency and alertness." The correction of the evil is at bottom an engineering problem.

The smoke evil is a closely related aspect of the problem of making life livable in the age of science and technology. The economic and æsthetic costs of smoke and soot and dust—the augmented cleaning, laundering, and painting bills, the blackened buildings, the dingy streets, the anæmic shrubs and trees, the clouded atmosphere—are known to all. People are only beginning to realize that the fumes from countless combustion engines and other impurities in the air constitute an important health hazard—a hazard that in greater or smaller measure is faced by more than one-half of the population. The irony, if not the tragedy, of the situation becomes apparent when the fact is recognized that smoke is in itself evidence of the uneconomical use of valuable and often irreplaceable natural resources. Henry Obermeyer has recently estimated that the elimination of smoke would have the following beneficent results: "Reduction by one-sixth of the total death rate . . .; 20 to 50 per cent more sunlight in urban and industrial communities; household cleaning expenses cut by more than half; half a billion dollars saved annually in preventable property damage; wasted fuel reclaimed to the extent of 20 per cent of the country's fuel bill; chemical by-products added to our national wealth to an extent that staggers imagination."[36]

Occupational diseases and hazards. Although practically every occupation since the beginning of time has had its peculiar ailments, the development of modern industry has vastly increased the magnitude of the problem. "A few decades ago," according to Carey P. McCord, "the number of occupational diseases known to the average practitioner of medicine could be counted on the fingers of one hand. They were poisoning from lead, arsenic, mercury, phosphorus, and caisson disease. Other occupational diseases existed, but were known to meager numbers of physicians. At the present time the number of such conditions is so large and increasing so rapidly as to force themselves irresistibly upon the attention of both medical and engi-

36 Henry Obermeyer, *Stop That Smoke!* (New York, 1933), 268.

neering groups. With few exceptions, all industries and occupations provide exposure to the causes of abnormal states that are termed trade or industrial or occupational diseases."[37]

Among the more dangerous industries are painting, white and red lead production, storage-battery making, china and earthenware industries, the phosphorus match industry, the felt hat industry, sand-blasting and emery-wheel grinding, and numerous industries involving exposure of workers to compressed air, wood alcohol, carbon monoxide, sulphuretted and arseniuretted hydrogen, carbon bisulphide, anilins, and nitrous compounds.[38] Mr. McCord enumerates 507 agents "that have proven to be the source of occupational diseases, or else are so closely related (chemically) to these hazards that toxicity may be expected."[39] According to this same author, "it has been estimated that approximately 9 per cent of those abnormal states detected among adult patients in general hospitals in industrial communities are related to work as a cause."[40] Then there is the question of industrial accidents. "Every year," writes this authority, "approximately $250,000,000 are paid out by compensation boards because of injuries in this country. Every year nearly 25,000 industrial workers are killed in the course of their work duties. Every year 2,000,000 other workers suffer nonfatal accidents of varying degree, but of significant severity."[41]

Authority in health control. There are many other health problems that have appeared or assumed new forms in industrial society: the problem of adjusting old age to a rapidly changing world and to the disintegration of the patriarchal family; the problem of protecting the masses from the crushing burden of funeral costs; the problems of promoting temperance in the use of alcoholic beverages and of suppressing

[37] Carey P. McCord, *Industrial Hygiene for Engineers and Managers* (New York, 1931), 53.
[38] W. Gilman Thompson, *The Occupational Diseases* (New York, 1914), 28.
[39] *Op. cit.,* 58–95.   [40] *Ibid.,* 57.   [41] *Ibid.,* 151.

traffic in narcotics. Each of these problems might very profitably be treated at some length, but space does not permit. One problem remains, however, which is so fundamental to the whole question of health that it cannot be ignored. This is the problem of authority in health control.

In the sphere of health control, as in many other fields, it is becoming increasingly apparent that American society is outgrowing the molds set by political conventions in the eighteenth and early nineteenth centuries. Attention has already been directed to the struggle between Chicago and neighboring cities over the use of the waters of Lake Michigan. Even Canadian municipalities have taken part in the controversy. Mention has also been made of a similar dispute between New York City and other urban centers in the same region. In both of these cases competent authority to make decisions was lacking. As a consequence, problems that should have been disposed of by sanitary engineers were settled in the courts at great cost and after much wrangling by opposing lawyers. Because of greatly changed conditions the breadth of governmental authority is often much narrower than the responsibilities to be discharged. The advance of technology has made ancient political boundaries antiquated.

In a study of health and sanitary control in the Chicago region R. F. Steadman[42] found, not a single authority as would seem natural, but 101 different public agencies pursuing different policies and programs. Among these agencies were the United States Public Health Service, 39 other federal health and sanitary services, four state health departments, 55 other state agencies, and two county health services. Within this area, moreover, are 41 cities, 21 towns, 140 villages, and 119 townships, all of which are involved to some degree in the regulation of health. Also the Chicago region contains 11 sanitary districts, 4 county tuberculosis sanitarium districts, and 1 munici-

42 R. F. Steadman, *Public Health Organization in the Chicago Region* (Chicago, 1930), 9–10.

pal sanitary district—not to mention 150 drainage districts, 3 mosquito abatement districts, and a large number of school and park districts. Frequently these various districts, while keeping quite within their rights as autonomous democratic communities, pursue separate and even contradictory aims. The inefficiency of such a condition of affairs requires no comment. In its organization the health service of the American people has simply not kept pace with the growth of industry and knowledge, and with changed ways of life.

THE TREND TOWARD SOCIALIZED MEDICINE

The trend toward a comprehensive and co-ordinated attack on the problem of health has become increasingly marked with the rise of industrial civilization. In the days of the agrarian order medical service was still in the pre-scientific stage, facilities for the training of the medical personnel were comparatively meager, the primitive character of the means of transportation made specialization impossible, and the sparsity of population fostered an individualistic or family tradition in medicine, as in economics and politics. In a society without great cities, dependent on a simple form of economy, and lacking close social contacts, many of the most difficult problems which medicine faces in contemporary society scarcely existed. Consequently the inherited system of medicine has proved itself incapable of coping with the new conditions.

In the changed situation an increasing body of opinion in America and in other parts of the world is coming to favor some form of socialized medicine. That the present system of private medicine is not working efficiently is clearly indicated by facts already presented. It is failing to perform the function for which it exists: it is failing to put medical science at the service of the masses of the people. Also it even seems incapable of providing the physician with that security of income which is his inalienable right as a useful member of society.

This last point perhaps deserves special emphasis. While under the system of private competition for the fees of the well-to-do a small number of physicians may expect to receive princely incomes, the lot of the great majority is far from satisfactory. The competition for patients, moreover, undoubtedly tends to promote unprofessional tendencies within the calling. The individual is forced more and more to respond to the window-dressing imperative. No longer can the physician follow the simple and unostentatious way of the old family doctor. There are too many competitors for the consumer's dollar and the ideal of material success is making deep inroads into the profession. The modern physician must appear opulent, drive a high-priced car, maintain an expensive office, employ a nurse and sometimes a secretary. Although he still obeys, in the letter, the old rule forbidding him to advertise, he knows that he will fare badly if he fails to display himself to advantage. The consequent excessive spending to achieve recognition and maintain status leads to the charging of excessive fees. Thus is established a vicious circle which the individual physician is helpless to break.

The medical profession in its organized capacity, however, is vigorously opposed to every form of socialized medicine. The American Medical Association has gone on record against any further extension of the authority of the state into the field of medicine. Such a pronouncement is of course to be expected and should not be regarded too seriously. The profession at large opposed the development of sanitary engineering and public health agencies. It also persecuted William Morton for his experiments in the realm of anæsthetics and at one time was hostile to all efforts to relieve the pains of childbirth. Physicians, moveover, like all specialists, have ever been extremely jealous of any invasion of their domain. Thus they have taken the position that even trained social workers are not competent to determine whether a particular family of low income should receive free medical treatment. On October 13, 1925, the Chicago Medical Society[43] took exception to the view, which apparently was being advanced by social workers, "that a family receiving less than $125 monthly is entitled to free medical service." Then in a resolution dealing with the matter the following statement may be found: "Any member of the Chicago Medical Society, whether through a hospital, social agency or health department, or as a private physician, who shall aid such institutions in pauperizing the public may be brought before the Ethical Relations Committee to determine whether or not he has been guilty of unethical conduct." Also, medical associations have actively opposed the organization of free clinics and similar institutions.

Experience may prove that state medicine is not the proper solution of current medical troubles. Nevertheless the general trend of the past generation or two would seem to point in the direction of the socialization of medicine. Through various public agencies the state has taken a rapidly increasing interest in the health of its citizens. While the expenditures in this field are comparatively small, the list of services includes public health departments, governmental diagnostic laboratories, the manufacture and distribution of biological products, governmental clinics, public hospitals, school health work, public health nursing, and workmen's compensation laws. The growth of public hospitals has proceeded so rapidly in recent years that 73 per cent of all hospital service was provided by governmental agencies in 1931.[44] Moreover, the growth of numerous forms of institutional medicine is forcing the purely private physician into a rapidly diminishing rôle. Finally, the majority report of the Committee on the Costs of Medical Care points vigorously and unequivocally in the direction of the further socialization of medicine.[45]

[43] Resolution passed by the Chicago Medical Society on October 13, 1925.
[44] Harry H. Moore, *op. cit.*, 1092.   [45] *Op. cit.*, 103–144.

THE POSSIBILITY

In conclusion a word should be said regarding the possibilities of a more abundant physical life resident in the power released by science and technology. For the first time in history, as data already presented in this volume prove, the great burden of exhausting labor can be lifted from the shoulders and backs of men. If the social arrangements necessary to permit the full use of the energy of the machine can be devised, crushing toil may be rendered unnecessary, an adequate material basis of life may be provided for all, and the blessings of medicine may be made available to the masses. Today, because of the heritage of institutions adapted to an age that is gone, the medical system, like practically every other social service, fails to function at full capacity. Here, as elsewhere, men go without in the presence of plenty. Everywhere may be seen the strange anomaly of physicians wanting work and millions of men, women, and children in need of medical attention. "The health field," declared William H. Welch in 1925, "has a woefully ineffective distribution service, as compared with its marvelously effective production service in the laboratories of the world."[46] Whether the number of trained personnel is sufficient for the task is a question without point so long as physician and patient cannot be brought together. Moreover, whatever may be the medical needs of the population, industrial society has made possible their complete satisfaction. Disease and defect are tolerable today only when knowledge of their nature lies beyond the limits of science. And those limits are being pushed forward continuously and irresistibly.

The major possibility, however, does not lie in the direction of the development of the professional service of medicine. Rather is it to be found in the improvement of the living habits and conditions of the masses of the people. Multitudes of men and women know little about the laws of keep-

[46] William H. Welch, *op. cit.*, 2.

ing well, about questions of air, food, drink, and exercise. Then the rise of industrialism, at least in its early stages, tended toward extreme congestion of population and the destruction of the physical conditions necessary to health. With the coming of new forms of transportation and communication a strong trend toward decentralization of cities and industries has set in. Also a growing interest in parks and playgrounds has appeared. And the development of city, state, and national planning makes possible the rational ordering of life and the deliberate creation of those conditions which promote the general physical well-being of the people. With their present resources the American people might make their country a far more healthful place in which to live than it is today.

CHAPTER V

EDUCATION

Mass education, says Clark Wissler, is one of the three "dominant characteristics" of contemporary American culture.[1] Certainly the growth of the school is one of the most striking trends of the age that has witnessed the rise of industrial civilization. Although the true school conceived as an institution designed to provide for the more or less prolonged and systematic instruction of some portion of the younger generation may be traced back three or four or perhaps five thousand years, only in the most recent times has it touched directly any large part of the population dwelling in any part of the globe. The great masses of men and women who have lived and died on the earth never went to school. And at the time of the founding of the nation only a very small fraction of the American people had enjoyed the advantages of the meager schooling of the period.

This of course does not mean that men received no education in early times, but rather that they received their education without the intervention of the school. The perpetuation of any human society is dependent on the process of education. The evolution of culture would be impossible if the spiritual acquisitions of one generation could not be transmitted to the next by the twofold process of teaching and learning. Although methods and agencies necessarily vary from society to society, in some fashion or other each new generation must be inducted into the life of the group, mastering its skills, knowledges, and philosophies and becoming sensitive to its welfare. Otherwise the group perishes. In the case of the more advanced peoples, a complete interruption of the stream of

[1] Clark Wissler, *Man and Culture* (New York, 1923), 5.

cultural transmission at any time would result in disaster. According to Graham Wallas, they might, under such conditions, "die out altogether":

"If the earth were struck by one of Mr. Wells's comets, and if, in consequence, every human being now alive were to lose all the knowledge and habits which he had acquired from preceding generations (though retaining unchanged all his own powers of invention, and memory, and habituation) nine tenths of the inhabitants of London or New York would be dead in a month, and 99 per cent of the remaining tenth would be dead in six months. They would have no language to express their thoughts, and no thoughts but vague reverie. They could not read notices, or drive motors or horses. They would wander about, led by the inarticulate cries of a few naturally dominant individuals, drowning themselves, as thirst came on, in hundreds at the riverside landing places, looting those shops where the smell of decaying food attracted them, and perhaps at the end stumbling on the expedient of cannibalism. Even in the country districts, men could not invent, in time to preserve their lives, methods of growing food, or taming animals, or making fire, or so clothing themselves as to endure a northern winter. An attack of constipation or measles would be invariably fatal. After a few years mankind would almost certainly disappear from the northern and temperate zones. The white races would probably become extinct everywhere. A few primitive races might live on fruit and small animals in those fertile tropical regions where the human species was originally evolved, until they had slowly accumulated a new social heritage. After some thousands of generations they would probably possess something which we should recognize as a language, and perhaps some art of taming animals and cultivating land. They might or might not have created what we should call a religion, or a few of our simpler mechanical inventions and political expedients. They probably would not have re-created such general ideas as 'Law' or 'Liberty'; though they might have created other general ideas which would be new to us."[2]

In pre-industrial society in America, this task of inducting the child into the life of the group was largely the responsibility of the family,[3] supplemented by the institutions of neighborhood or community. In the case of the masses of the people there was little demand for those abilities which the school, even in its more elementary forms, has traditionally sought to develop. The discharge of the ordinary economic and social obligations scarcely required proficiency in reading, writing, and arithmetic, or extensive knowledge of distant places and peoples. In its more advanced forms the school was monopolized by ruling and specially privileged classes. Both secondary and university education were a badge of aristocracy. In many influential quarters, moreover, schooling for the common lot of men was regarded as undesirable and mischievous, tending to put dangerous and "unsound" notions of social equality into their heads and encouraging them to forget their place and manners. When, under the impact of democratic forces during the second quarter of the nineteenth century, the tide for free schools set in, not a few estimable citizens of the higher ranks predicted certain disaster. "The peasant," wrote the editor of the *National Gazette* of Philadelphia, "must labor during those hours of the day which his wealthy neighbor can give to abstract culture of his mind; otherwise, the earth would not yield enough for the subsistence of all: the mechanic cannot abandon the operations of his trade, for general studies; if he should, most of the conveniences of life . . . would be wanting; languor, decay, poverty, discontent would soon be visible among all classes."[4]

[2] Graham Wallas, *Our Social Heritage* (New Haven, 1921), 16–17.

[3] See above, Part Two, Chapter I, "Family."

[4] Arthur M. Schlesinger, *New Viewpoints in American History* (New York, 1922), 90.

In the family the individual received the major part of his vocational, civic, and moral training. Almost from the time he was able to walk about the house or yard he was expected to play some rôle in guarding family interests and promoting family welfare. And as he grew in strength and understanding new responsibilities were placed upon his shoulders. The boy performed innumerable chores having to do with fuel and water-supply, the care of animals, the tilling of fields, the harvesting of crops, and the practice of manual arts; the girl helped to prepare the meals, wash the dishes, do the laundry, preserve fruits, vegetables, and meats, and perform the diverse industrial activities carried on in the home. Gradually, as the youngster matured, and as a part of the process of maturing, he acquired all the occupational skills and knowledges appropriate to the sex. At the same time, as he worked and played and lived in the family circle he received civic and moral training. While this education inevitably reflected the cultural standards of the home, it was marked by a quality of genuineness that is rarely found in the school. It was intimately related to life. Indeed it was an integral part of the process of living.

The family, however, was not the only educational agency of pre-industrial society. In spite of the primitive character of the means of transportation and communication and the relative absence of village life in many parts of America, the individual had many contacts outside the home. The farming community, though commonly vague in outline and amorphous in structure, was nevertheless a genuine social force. The neighborhood was a reality. There were numerous picnics, socials, festivals, and hunting and fishing parties for all ages. The exchange of labor among the farmers, moreover, was a common practice. The church, with its ancient traditions, its organized services, and its sacred ceremonies marking and solemnizing the great crises of birth, marriage, and death, occupied a central position in the moral life of the people. The district school, weak though it was, challenged the authority of parents at certain points and served to promote extra-family relationships for the young. Even the press sent occasional books, magazines, and newspapers into an occasional home. Yet the fact remains that for the most part education was carried on without the directing influence of formal agencies. The individual received his education primarily as a by-product of the life of family and neighborhood.

THE COMING OF INDUSTRIAL SOCIETY

The coming of industrial society changed most profoundly the educational situation. It weakened or impaired the inherited educational agencies; it increased the magnitude of the educational task; it created new educational forces and institutions; and it stimulated enormously the growth and elaboration of the school. In a word the industrial revolution precipitated a revolution in the realm of education. Each of these four major changes will be briefly outlined.

That the advance of industrialsm has weakened or impaired certain of the older educational agencies is patent. For a very large proportion of the population the family is no longer a productive unit in the economy; the compactness of the agrarian household of the past is gone; father and mother and children no longer work together in a common economic enterprise. Rather, unless they remain at home and live a life of dependence and even of parasitism—a common practice among the favored classes—they go their separate ways securing employment where they can. Certainly in the case of the urban masses, the lives of father, mother, and older children have been woven into a vast economic fabric in which the family has practically ceased to function as a unit. To be sure, in spite of all of these changes the home is still charged with greater educational responsibilities than the school or any other agency. Yet in comparison with the past it has suffered greatly at the hand of technology.

In similar fashion other old agencies have been impaired. The church, though holding its membership fairly well, has lost its one-time grip on the life and thought of the people. Even in the realm of morals, not to mention the domain of science, it speaks today with far less authority and has much less power to compel obedience than in former times. In the sphere of secular affairs the voice of the clergy is rarely heeded. Also as a result of the spread of the railroad, the automobile, the telephone, the radio, the motion picture, and other forms of communication, neighborhood lines have been greatly extended and weakened, if not erased altogether. Except in the earliest years of life, the individual is able to escape the watchful and disciplinary eye of parents, relatives, and neighbors and come under the influence of relatively distant places and mores.

It is the change in industry itself, however, that has most influenced education. Throughout human history, work, serious work undertaken in the interest of some group, has been a major and even central educational force. As a rule, whether the child labored with his parents and the elder members of his family or as an apprentice under the direction of a master craftsman in the neighborhood mattered but little. In either event work occupied a large share of his waking hours. After the invention of power-driven machinery this ancient tradition continued for a time. Boys and girls of tender age, unable to find employment at home, followed the industries into the factory to labor long hours at meager wages. The conditions of work, however, had been fundamentally altered. Instead of laboring in a family enterprise or under the tutelage of a neighbor, probably with the leisurely habits of the artisan, the child now worked for a stranger who was engaged in the single-minded pursuit of material gain and who probably felt himself a member of a superior social class. The abuses which appeared under the factory system need not be retold here. They are familiar to all who read history. Suffice it to say that a reaction soon set in, not to humanize machine industry, of course, but rather to keep the child away from the factory. In 1836 Massachusetts enacted the first child labor law in the United States, a law prohibiting the employment in manufacturing establishments of children under fifteen years, unless they had attended school at least three months the preceding year. The movement thus inaugurated has proceeded until "at the present time all but two states have adopted a nominal age minimum of at least fourteen for full time employment in industry."[5] The point to be emphasized here is merely that industrialism, as developed on the foundation of capitalism, has seriously weakened one of the oldest and most powerful educational institutions. Increasingly children grow to manhood and womanhood without engaging, except casually, in socially useful labor.

As the educational agencies of the pre-industrial age were being impaired, the magnitude of the educational task was being increased. One of the most striking changes of this period was the expansion of the social world in which the individual lives and acts and assumes responsibilities. In agrarian society life is of necessity highly circumscribed by the primitive and inefficient means of communication. As a consequence, the individual need not know what is happening beyond the horizon, because for the most part it does not affect him. But in industrial society the situation assumes a radically different aspect. With the coming of modern forms of communication old barriers and boundaries are pushed back relentlessly until the individual finds that his life and fortune may be profoundly affected, not only by what happens over the horizon, but also by what occurs beyond seas and mountain ranges and in the farthest corners of the globe. The task of inducting the child into this great world complex has little in common with the task of preparing the individual to pass his years in the small farming community of a few generations ago.

[5] Raymond G. Fuller, "Child Labor," *Encyclopædia of the Social Sciences* (New York, 1930), III, 418.

Of similar import is the growth of knowledge that has accompanied the rise of industrial civilization. At an ever more rapid rate the spirit of science has been prosecuting its researches in one field after another. In similar fashion invention has followed invention and discovery succeeded discovery. The preservation of the consequent huge and growing store of knowledge requires that it be transmitted, provision being made for the necessary division of labor, from generation to generation. Moreover, a not inconsiderable proportion of this knowledge, organized into the various technologies, is fundamental to the operation of the economy. Without engineers the present social structure would collapse and overwhelm millions of human beings. Man is becoming increasingly dependent on modes and systems of thought that can be mastered only by rigorous application and study on the part of the most gifted minds. The institution of apprenticeship, at least in its inherited form, proved incapable of meeting this situation.

The discharge of the heavy educational tasks of industrial society required great changes in educational practices. Various old agencies, such as the press, have been enormously developed and expanded. Also many new agencies have been created. The instruments of communication that made possible the growth of closely knit nations and even a world society also serve as powerful educational forces. It would appear that through such inventions as the automobile, the telephone, the radio and the cinema, when combined with the press, man might be equipped to deal with some degree of effectiveness with the complexities of modern civilization. Yet, as an examination of the operation of these agencies shows, this goal is far from attainment today.[6]

The primary concern here is with that institution which is exclusively and deliberately devoted to the formal process of education. With the advance of industrial society the school has expanded with great rapidity until today it occupies the

[6] See above, Part Two, Chapter III, "Communication."

position of a major social institution. As old agencies weakened and new educational tasks appeared, larger and larger burdens were placed upon the school. As a result, organized education has gained vast prestige and has probably become one of the fetishes of the American people. It is now commonly regarded as a certain cure for practically every human ill, from marital troubles to international conflict. If the social structure works badly at any point, the customary recourse is to the school and the next generation. William Graham Sumner remarked this tendency almost a generation ago:

"Popular education and certain faiths about popular education are in the mores of our time. We regard illiteracy as an abomination. We ascribe to elementary book learning power to form character, make good citizens, keep family mores pure, elevate morals, establish individual character, civilize barbarians, and cure social vice and disease. We apply schooling as a remedy for every social phenomenon which we do not like. The information given by schools and colleges, the attendant drill in manners, the ritual of the mores practiced in schools, and the mental dexterity produced by school exercises fit individuals to carry on the struggle for existence better."[7]

This popular faith in organized education, which dates back to the great battles for free schools of the thirties and forties of the last century, is reflected in the changes which have swept through public education in the past fifty or sixty years. These changes have recently been summarized by Charles H. Judd:

"Since 1875 the educational system of this country has undergone a transformation. Better equipped elementary schools have been erected; free secondary schools have been established in large numbers; public normal schools for the training of teachers have been organized by the states; and the opportunities for college education have been enlarged and made accessible to young people from all classes of society. Furthermore,

[7] William Graham Sumner, *Folkways* (Boston, 1906), 628–629.

schools have assumed responsibility for many phases of child care and training which formerly were thought of as belonging wholly to the home. Schools are doing much to promote the intelligent care of health. They are training youth in the proper use of leisure. They are adopting special devices to equip everyone whom they can reach for success in vocations and participation in community activities."[8]

Owing to the fact that the school has emerged into a dominant position, attention will now be concentrated on this institution, even though the great power of other agencies is recognized. The account, moreover, will be confined for the most part to the present situation—to the current school program, to the more pronounced trends of the age, and to the uncertainties and confusions growing out of the effort to adjust a scholastic tradition evolved under the conditions of a simple pioneering and agrarian society to the realities of industrial civilization. The facts can best be presented under the heads of school plant, educational opportunity, administration, curriculum, teaching, and purpose.

School Plant. Since the middle of the last century the American school plant has grown from insignificant to Gargantuan proportions. A veritable network of schools of all grades has been spread over the country from the Atlantic to the Pacific and from the Lakes to the Gulf. In 1930 there were reported to the Office of Education at Washington 247,581 elementary schools, 26,690 high schools, 1,078 universities, colleges, and professional schools, 331 teachers colleges and normal schools, 1,844 nurse-training schools, 651 private commercial schools, and 372 schools for the deaf, the blind, the feeble-minded, and the delinquent.[9] While the returns cited here are not entirely com-

[8] Charles H. Judd, "Education," Chapter VII in the President's Research Committee on Social Trends, *Recent Social Trends in the United States* (New York, 1933), I, 325.
[9] *Biennial Survey of Education 1928–30* (Washington, 1931), II, 2.

plete, they give a fairly adequate picture of the situation. Working in these institutions were 1,037,605 teachers, or "2.1 per cent of the number of persons 10 years of age and over who were gainfully employed as reported by the Bureau of the Census."[10] The cost of operating this huge plant in 1930 amounted to \$3,234,638,567;[11] and the value of all school property and endowments for the institutions reported was computed to be \$11,216,704,000, or "7.2 per cent of the assessed valuation of all property in the United States in 1928 subject to general State property tax."[12] These facts give some measure of the growth of the school since the establishment of the great state systems of public education in the middle decades of the nineteenth century.

Educational Opportunity. The extension of equal educational opportunities to the children of all the people, regardless of the accidents of birth or fortune, has been a cherished ideal of the American people for generations. The development of the tradition and practice of free and even compulsory public education at the lower levels, which can be traced back to the laws of 1642 and 1647 of the Massachusetts colony, is one expression of this ideal. Perhaps an even more striking assertion of the democratic principle was the abandonment early in the nineteenth century of the dual educational system of the old world, which reflected the class organization of European society, and the development of a single educational system composed of elementary school, secondary school, and college or university and legally open to all classes alike from the kindergarten to the last year of the graduate school.

An uncritical examination of the statistics of school attendance would suggest that the ideal has been realized. Certainly no society in history ever extended the opportunities of schooling so widely and so fully to the general population. "Approximately 30,000,000 students," says the official summary of the Office of Education, "were enrolled in day schools in

[10] *Ibid.*, II, 7.   [11] *Ibid.*, 11.   [12] *Ibid.*, II, 12.

1930. Of these about 23,500,000 were on the elementary-school level, 4,800,000 on the high-school level, 1,100,000 on the college level, and 500,000 on various levels in special schools."[13] Thus one person in every four in the United States is attending school. In comparison with the past and other societies the enrollments in secondary and higher institutions are peculiarly notable. Mr. Judd's comment is not exaggerated: "In 1930 one of every seven persons of college age was in college and one of every two persons of secondary school age was in secondary school. Never before in the history of the world has there been such a development at the upper levels of an educational system."[14]

In spite of this striking growth of the school, however, particularly at the secondary and higher levels, educational opportunity has by no means been equalized in the United States. Class and other forms of discrimination still operate. In the first place, vestiges of the dual system of Europe may still be found. In the private schools of the country, except where they are conducted by religious denominations or under unusual circumstances, the tradition of class rule, class privilege, and class superiority persists. At any rate the students in these institutions are drawn almost wholly from the favored cultural and occupational groups.[15] This seems to be particularly true of those private secondary schools that are designed primarily to prepare students for certain highly select eastern colleges of great age, prestige, and endowment. To these institutions the families already entrenched in the economic and social system, and also those aspiring to such a position, send their children.

In the second place, even in the system of public education poverty unquestionably plays its part. While compulsory education laws tend to keep the great majority of children in school during the elementary period, beyond the reach of these laws

---

[13] *Ibid.*, II, 3.   [14] *Op. cit.*, 329.
[15] See George S. Counts, *The Selective Character of American Secondary Education* (Chicago, 1922), 135–140. Also see L. V. Koos, *The Junior College Movement* (Boston, 1925), 158.

elimination begins. Thus in 1930 but one-half of the youth of appropriate age were enrolled in the high school and only one-seventh in the college. While various factors contribute to this condition, family influence is not to be discounted. Free tuition does not guarantee equality of educational opportunity. After a child has reached the age of possible self-support, the major cost of schooling is the luxury of leisure. Certain it is that very few boys and girls whose parents are engaged in the rougher and less remunerative forms of labor complete the secondary school. For them to graduate from a college or university of the first grade is in the nature of a miracle.[16] According to Edward J. Sparling, "One of the chief questions asked by ad-missions officers in medical schools is, 'Are you economically independent?' If a student replies in the negative, he is often refused admission, as many medical schools disapprove of out-side work and discourage it."[17] At the secondary level many American communities are beginning to recognize the practical denial of educational opportunity, occasioned by economic in-equalities, and are extending various forms of material and financial aid to indigent students.[18]

In the third place, the principle of equality of educational op-portunity is not applied to certain racial and cultural minorities. Throughout the major part of American history the Indian was scarcely treated as a human being; the newly arrived immi-grant has always been subject to more or less discrimination; the oriental peoples have found unusual barriers placed in their way; and the Jew has often had the doors of certain private schools closed against him. But the harshest treatment has been accorded the Negro. In his case the discrimination has been severe, prolonged, and general. Nathan R. Margold states that "the study financed by the American Fund for Public Service

[16] See George S. Counts, *op. cit.;* L. V. Koos, *op. cit.;* Grayson Kefauver, *Guidance in Secondary Schools* (New York, 1932).

[17] Edward J. Sparling, *Do College Students Choose Vocations Wisely?* (New York, 1933).

[18] Verna A. Carley, *Student Aid in the Secondary Schools of the United States* (New York, 1933).

made by the National Association for the Advancement of Colored People revealed that in South Carolina more than ten times as much was expended for the education of white children as for Negro children; that in Florida, Georgia, Mississippi and Alabama, more than five times as much; in North Carolina, Virginia, Texas, Oklahoma and Maryland, more than twice as much."[19] The same author thus summarizes the educational opportunities of Negro children:

"The right of Negro children, under the 14th amendment, not to be discriminated against with respect to such public education as the state provides for its residents, is one whose existence and propriety is nowhere disputed in theory while, at least in southern states, it is consistently violated in practice. Although the right to equal accommodations seems never to have been sanctioned conclusively by the Supreme Court of the U. S., and seldom by any other court, the dearth of decisions is due only to the scarcity of attempts hitherto to combat the discrimination through litigation; and the same reason probably accounts in large measure for the persistence of the discriminatory practices."[20]

In the fourth place, the extension of educational opportunity varies from place to place. In 1930 the average number of days attended by each pupil enrolled in the public schools varied from 97.7 in Mississippi to 163.4 in New York; and the enrollment in the fourth year of the high school ranged from 4.5 per cent of the enrollment in the first grade of the elementary school in Mississippi to 43 per cent in Washington. Also there is the greatest diversity in the material support of education. The annual cost per pupil in average daily attendance varied from $31.89 in Georgia to $137.55 in New York and the average value of school property per pupil enrolled, from $72 in Georgia

[19] Nathan R. Margold, *Preliminary Report to the Joint Committee Supervising the Expenditure of the 1930 Appropriation by the American Fund for Public Service to the N.A.A.C.P.* (unpublished manuscript).
[20] *Ibid.*

to $407 in New York.[21] There are also great differences from locality to locality within a state. The rural areas in particular suffer from very severe discrimination. As Mr. Judd points out, "the distribution of the burden of taxation and expenditure in different school districts is so unequal as to make impossible adequate education of many young people, especially those living in sparsely settled areas."[22]

In the fifth place, during periods of economic depression, while cultural services tend to be reduced everywhere, the shock is borne very unevenly by the different classes of the population and the different parts of the country. In general the educational opportunities of the well-to-do are not impaired. The opportunities of the poor, on the other hand, are seriously curtailed. In April, 1933, John K. Norton described the situation for the country as a whole:

"A survey of both city and state systems shows that everywhere schools are going on short rations. Teachers' salaries are being cut. In some rural areas teaching positions are allotted to the lowest bidder irrespective of qualifications. The size of classes has been increased and the supply of books and teaching materials decreased. . . . Much needed repairs of school buildings are being neglected in many instances. School building construction is practically at a standstill, dropping 29 per cent in 1931–32, and 47 per cent in 1932–33 in large cities of the country. . . . In many instances essential parts of the schools have been eliminated, such as kindergartens, health service, and night schools. . . . School terms in some urban and in many rural districts have been radically shortened. In some states, whole counties have closed their schools because of lack of funds."[23]

The ravages of the depression among the schools of Alabama

21 Data for these comparisons are taken from the *Biennial Survey of Education 1928–1930*.
22 *Op. cit.*, 373.
23 John K. Norton, "What the Depression is Doing to the Schools" (unpublished manuscript).

at about the same time have been reported by F. Raymond Daniell:

"The State of Alabama is confronted with a financial crisis which threatens the very life of its free public schools. With 85 per cent of its elementary and secondary schools closed already, the people of the State are facing the prospect of utter collapse of their educational system or, at best, a drastic curtailment of its functions."[24]

Administration. The administration of American schools is marked by an incongruous union of practices derived from agrarian and industrial civilization. The agrarian heritage is found in the tradition of local initiative particularly at the lower levels of the educational system and the practice of institutional autonomy among the institutions of higher learning. The contribution of industrialism is manifested particularly in the management of the great city systems and the larger universities.

The tradition of local initiative in the administration of the common schools was largely a product of the method pursued in the settlement of the country. In the new territories the westward migrations moved ahead of the organization of government. As a consequence, the responsibilities for carrying on the various public functions, of which education was one, devolved upon the local communities as they conquered the wilderness. The boundaries of the unit for school administration were fixed by such factors as the topography of the land, the primitive state of transportation, the high birth rate, the poverty of material resources, the low level of cultural standards, and the prevailing conception of educational needs. The result was the district system with its one-room school which, though greatly modified in certain states and regions, still gives the pattern to rural education. Thus in 1930, according to the report of the Office of Education, there were 148,711 one-room

[24] F. Raymond Daniell, "Crisis Threatens Alabama Schools," *The New York Times,* April 23, 1933.

school-houses in the United States. These districts, each with its controlling committee of perhaps three citizens and more or less autonomous in educational matters, belong to a world that has passed away.

A major consequence of the persistence of this tradition of local initiative, tempered though it is by county and state authority, is gross inequality of educational opportunity—a condition already observed. There are poor and rich districts, poor and rich counties, and poor and rich states in the country. Yet, however distinct they may have been at the time their boundaries were drawn, today they are all so bound together in close economic union that the lines separating one political division from another have become supremely arbitrary. Moreover, no one can say with assurance how much of the wealth resident for taxable purposes in a particular region is a product of the efforts of the people living in that region. Thus what proportion of the wealth of New York State, which in 1930 was credited by the National Industrial Conference Board with holding title to almost eleven and one-half per cent of the wealth of the nation, is due to the position that the state occupies with reference to the rest of the country is a question that the rise of industrial civilization has made acute. Certainly the assumption underlying present practice in the support of education has been rendered obsolete by the advance of technology. The anomalies in the situation have been concisely stated by Mr. Judd:

"Much of the inequality in educational support is traceable directly to the small size of many school districts. Frequently a small district includes only property of very low assessable value. A neighboring district, on the other hand, may include an industrial plant or a railroad and be amply able to support schools. Furthermore, the numbers of children in neighboring districts are often very different. Some examples of the inequalities in ability to raise school revenues may be cited from findings of the Educational Finance Inquiry Commission. A table is presented by this commission which shows that of 1,317 elementary school districts in ten typical counties in Illinois, 352 had full assessed valuations per child of school age of $4,900 or less while at the other extreme were six districts which had valuations per child of $45,000 or more."[25]

The tradition of institutional autonomy at the higher levels of the educational system is also a heritage from the loosely knit society of the past. From earliest colonial times down to the present, but particularly during the nineteenth century, colleges and higher schools were founded in great numbers under the most diverse auspices. Although, beginning with the establishment of the University of Indiana in 1820, the state has tended to play an increasing rôle in this sphere, the burden of higher education in the United States is still borne by private institutions. Thus in 1930, of the 1,078 universities, colleges, and professional schools in the country, exclusive of teachers colleges and normal schools, 832 were classified as private.[26] In these non-public institutions were enrolled approximately 60 per cent of all students in attendance.[27]

In spite of the efforts on the part of certain states to co-ordinate the institutions supported out of public funds, the fact remains that as a general rule every college or university of the country is largely autonomous. Neither state nor nation has a genuinely integrated program of higher education. Each institution tends to go its own way, developing departments and facilities as it sees fit and entering into competition with institutions of the same grade for faculty, students, and funds. The result is duplication of effort, dispersion of resources, irrational distribution of facilities, and often failure to articulate with society. In the sphere of occupational training—and even the purest form of liberal education commonly carries some vocational implications—severe inco-ordination often occurs. While in some fields large numbers of persons are trained for

[25] *Op. cit.*, 373–374.
[26] *Biennial Survey of Education 1928–30* (Washington, 1931), II, 2.
[27] *Ibid.*, II, 345–347.

positions that do not exist, in others occupational needs may be neglected. The point to be noted is that the American people have no program of higher education carefully designed to serve the nation. Here, as in many other departments of life, they place their faith in the irrational processes of guesswork and competition.

In certain areas of educational administration, however, the new forces have made themselves felt. In fact in some places the tradition of weak central control has been completely reversed. This seems to have happened at those points where expansion has been rapid and prolonged. The evolution of great city systems of public education out of the narrow local units of an agrarian society and the development of large universities from small colleges have been accompanied by concentration of power in the hands of administrative officials. Perhaps such a concentration of power was required by the rapidity with which changes were taking place. Decisions had to be made quickly and efficiently. Also since, in both the cities and the universities, general authority, as distinguished from administration, passed into the hands of business men serving as members of boards of control, education came to be regarded in many minds as a form of business enterprise. That the spirit and methods of administration developed in the sphere of commerce and industry should be transferred to education was therefore to be expected. Nevertheless such developments present a curious contrast to the dispersion of authority still found very generally in rural America.

The Curriculum. The curriculum of the school today bears little resemblance to the curriculum of one hundred years ago. This is particularly true in the realm of secondary and higher education. As these institutions opened their doors to ever larger numbers of young people and as they assumed one function after another, new courses, new subjects, and even new departments or faculties were added in rapid succession. This process has continued until at the present time the inquirer may find practically anything taught in the high schools and universities of the country from radio mechanics to Sanskrit. In general the century has witnessed the gradual decline in the relative emphasis given to the classics and mathematics and a corresponding increase in the attention devoted to modern language, natural science, history and social science, technology, and the arts. At the same time innumerable so-called extra-curriculum activities have found their way into the school program. Apparently organized education has made a great effort to meet the diverse needs of the greatly expanded student population.

This expansion or enrichment of the curriculum, however, appears to have been guided by no clearly formulated philosophy. Yet it would seem to be based upon the assumption that the school was under obligation to offer any program of study that the individual thought would help him on the road to success. Even courses in advertising and salesmanship were widely introduced into the curriculum at a time when the consumer was already overwhelmed and bewildered by the appeals of the market. At any rate the school appears to have done little more than respond to various pressures both from within and from without. Many subjects have been added, but few have been dropped. Once a unit of instruction gets into the curriculum a vested interest is created which tends to resist attack. As a consequence, since the educational authorities possessed no integrating principle, they tended to place the responsibility for choice of program on the shoulders of pupil and parent. In order that this entire process might be expedited from the standpoint of administrative efficiency, by some unknown calculus the various subjects were equated and divided into units. Above the elementary level education then became essentially a matter of collecting a sufficient number of these units for graduation. The school assumed the aspect of a machine for the distribution of certificates and degrees among the members of the rising generation.

This situation is further complicated by the pluralistic character of industrial society. In contrast with the farming community supporting the district school, the modern urban center is composed of numerous conflicting groups and organizations. With the exception of the smaller and more isolated places which reflect the conditions of the old order, the American community today lacks unity of interest and ideal. Certainly in the realms of economics, politics, morals, and religion, the most diverse points of view abound. Society is divided into sects, parties, classes, and special interests, each of which, in proportion to its strength, strives to incorporate its viewpoint into the curriculum. And this struggle is sharpened by the phenomenal expansion of public education which has accompanied the processes of industrialization. So long as the school remained an institution of the second or third order of magnitude, which means until the most recent times, it attracted but little attention. In those days its influence was small. But with the adoption of universal elementary education, the extension of the opportunities of the secondary school to one-half of the population, and the rapid growth of the colleges and universities, the school has become a major social institution and one of society's most powerful agencies of propaganda.[28] That rival groups should strive to possess it is entirely to be expected. The curriculum at any moment is to some extent a resultant of the play of these battling forces upon the school— professional educators within and conflicting interests without.

A final point to be noted, however, is that the curriculum as a whole, as well as its separate parts, tends to be remote from life. The unloading of functions upon the school, which has continued now for several generations, has fundamentally altered the conditions of education. The situation may best

[28] See George S. Counts, *School and Society in Chicago* (New York, 1928); Bessie L. Pierce, *Citizens' Organizations and the Civic Training of Youth* (New York, 1933); Jesse H. Newlon, *Educational Administration as Social Policy* (New York, 1934).

be understood by observing that the growth of industrialism placed American society in a serious dilemma. If it permitted the child to follow work and other social activities out of the home or small community, it subjected the child to the dangers of exploitation and moral corruption. On the other hand, if it endeavored to transfer these ancient interests to the school, it removed from education a certain measure of reality —direct contact with industry and family life and responsibility. The American people chose to pursue the second course. But that this represents a wholly satisfactory solution of the problem may be questioned. In earlier times children were inducted into the life of the group by discharging genuine rather than fictitious responsibilities. In industrial society as now organized, the surrender of huge areas of the economy to industries entirely separated from the home has made extremely difficult the education of the younger generation in the actual duties of life and work. Thus education becomes bookish and unreal.

Teaching. As already observed the schools of the nation require the services of a huge staff of teachers—more than one million in 1930. Although it is generally recognized that the quality of any education depends primarily on the native powers, the social insight, and the professional preparation of the teachers, there persists among the American people a tradition that the extended training of the teacher is not necessary. Apparently this tradition was a product of pioneering life and of the methods employed in the establishment and administration of public education in America. Schools were organized, not by ministries of education, but by untutored farmers whose cultural and intellectual standards were relatively low. To these farmers the conduct of a school was quite as much a matter of brawn as of brain. Moreover, in comparison with the tilling of the soil, the harvesting of the crops, and the general conduct of the economy, book learning seemed comparatively unimportant, as in fact it was. Consequently, until quite recent

times, the schools of the United States were staffed by immature and untrained persons.

With the growth of cities and the general advance in the
cultural level of the population attending the development of
industrial civilization this older tradition has been greatly
weakened. Only during the past generation has interest in the
professional training of teachers gained much momentum. Although the first normal school in the United States was opened
at Lexington, Massachusetts, in 1839, the movement progressed
but slowly for several decades. The twentieth century, however, has witnessed an enormous development in this field.
Thus the receipts of teachers colleges and normal schools from
public funds for current expenses increased from $2,786,123 in
1900 to $37,210,645 in 1930.[29] And in the latter year the number
of such institutions stood at 331. During this same period the
average number of courses announced in the catalogues of
fourteen state teachers colleges and normal schools grew from
65 to 321.

The present program of teacher training, however, continues
to reflect the conditions of the past. It still bears marks of the
class organization of education developed in Europe during
the eighteenth and nineteenth centuries. There the masses attended some kind of folk school distinguished by a meager
program and an emphasis on obedience and the acquisition of
skills, while the privileged orders were provided with an extended program of intellectual education embracing prepara-
tory school, secondary school, and university. The teachers in
these two branches of the educational system differed in social
origins and in training. Those in the folk schools came from
the masses and were trained in the normal schools, whereas
those in the secondary schools came from the classes and were
prepared in the universities. The American people, though
repudiating the dual educational system of Europe, preserved
that system in part in their program of professional training.

[29] *Biennial Survey of Education 1928–1930* (Washington, 1931), II, 614.

In general they have prepared their elementary teachers in normal schools and their secondary teachers in colleges and universities.

In their curricula and methods of work the normal schools and their offspring, the teachers' colleges, reveal their ancestry. Although various contrary tendencies have been at work, these institutions have fostered the tradition, congenial to a society divided into governed and governing classes, into working and leisure orders, that method may be separated from the content of thought. They have based their programs partly on the assumption that teaching is chiefly a matter of the mastery of method and that education is to be conceived as independent of the body of a given culture. Clearly methodology, if it revolves about its own center, becomes an intellectual operation akin to that of the Sophists of ancient Greece and the minor Scholastics of the Middle Ages; if it advances to the center of the substance with which it deals, it becomes something else, an aspect of purposeful activity. In the former case it is sterile; in the latter it is submerged in thought and philosophy.

Aside from the operation of the deeper social forces, the responsibility for this divorce of method and thought, for the establishment of separate institutions for the training of teachers, must be borne in part by the trends in the higher learning in America. By disdaining concern with educational practice and by becoming immersed in the development of their own specialties, university professors have practiced a form of deception not unlike that practiced by the methodologists. While scorning methodology, they have unwittingly become methodologists themselves. But since they refused to assist teachers confronted by the urgent problems involved in instructing increasing millions of children, the teachers were compelled to shift for themselves.

Another force contributing to this divorce of methodology and thought was the growth of teacher training as a vested institutional interest. Following what seems to be a kind of natural law, the normal school, once established, became concerned, like the good court, with a declaration of its independence and an extension of its jurisdiction. Also like all established institutions it had positions, salaries, emoluments, honors, titles, and privileges to distribute to those presumably expert in the mystery or craft of methodology. Moreover, since most of the students it trained were in a hurry on their way to teaching and since society was increasing the demand for teachers, the normal school confronted a dilemma. Thorough instruction in subject matter seeming impossible, it chose the course of specializing in certain tricks of the trade which poorly educated teachers could repeat without much difficulty. Thus, a virtue was made of apparent necessity, and a makeshift became a dominant interest. Method assumed the form of a cult. And teachers who knew little of the fact and thought of their subjects were subjected to the tyranny of an instrument.

As scholars become enslaved to specialty and pedagogues to method, both inquiry and instruction were impoverished. Moreover, the scholar generally ignored the difficulties of the teacher. Sometimes with a pride little warranted the former assumed that a person deeply engrossed in such a matter as the mediæval manor or the tun-moot in early England was for some reason superior to a person engaged in leading children along paths of knowledge and good living. Thus many university professors scorned such "elementary," but profoundly significant, problems as the instruction of boys and girls and refused to consider the vital question of the relation of their specialties to the schools. Like the pedagogues they had their vested interests which they wished to guard. If specialty is brought into connection with life, its small stature is exposed. They therefore thought it safer to preserve their cult or mystery unsullied by the world.

As the rift widened, as subject matter specialists turned in upon themselves and their specialties, and as methodologists gained increasing power over teacher training and the schools, the latter took steps to fortify their growing vested interest. They brought pressure upon state legislatures and state and local boards of education and secured the adoption of laws and rules requiring applicants for elementary and high school teaching positions in any field or fields to present credentials stating that they had taken and passed a certain number of courses in "education," variously described, sometimes as "the theory and art of teaching" and sometimes as "the science of education." The proportion of hours in this field to the total number of hours required for certification varies. In some cases it is as high as one-fourth; but whether it is one-fourth or one-tenth or one-fifteenth, it is a positive limitation. No matter how competently and widely trained in subject matter the applicant may be, he cannot obtain a teaching certificate without having taken and passed the prescribed number of courses in pedagogy. Schools and professors offering instruction in "education" are thus given a preferred position with reference to a subject which in both theory and practice is loosely defined.

Perhaps the most characteristic development in the sphere of education since the opening of the twentieth century is the effort to create a science of education. Into this movement a tremendous amount of energy has gone. The quantitative method has been applied to the learning process, methods of teaching, and many aspects of school administration. School systems large and small, state and local, have been surveyed; and so-called objective tests, scales, and score-cards, practically without number, have been standardized for the measurement of intelligence, school attainments, teaching ability, administrative efficiency, and almost every phase of the conduct of education. And the prediction has been confidently made again and again that by means of the scientific method all of the problems of education will submit themselves to speedy and impersonal solution.

The results of this development are difficult to appraise at the present time. A great body of facts pertaining more or less to the task of education has certainly been accumulated. A very large proportion of these facts, however, are either comparatively irrelevant or trivial in nature; and the attention of teachers, administrators, and educational leaders has been directed to those aspects of the educative process that lend themselves most readily to the application of quantitative procedures— the more simple, the more mechanical, the less profound aspects of the problem. It is not too much to say that emphasis on the measurement of the more mensurable concomitants of education, regardless of questions of relevance, has provided the profession with a mode of escape from the larger and more disturbing questions that have been raised by the onward sweep of industrial civilization. When the best minds in education might have been devoting themselves to a consideration of the meaning for education in the United States of the shift from the individualistic agrarian economy, they were actually engaged in the fashioning of spelling scales and score-cards for school buildings.

The devotion to measurement has also fostered the view that education is a branch of thermo-dynamics and is essentially mechanical in nature. All matters involving the selection and rejection of values, which after all must always lie at the center of any educational program, were barred from consideration on the grounds that they were subjective in nature, outside the range of science, and therefore unworthy of consideration by educational science. The consequence of this narrowing of the field of interest and of inquiry was quite generally the acceptance of the traditional framework of institutions, ideas, and values. When that framework crumbled in the great depression beginning in the summer and fall of 1929, those engaged in the scientific study of education were therefore caught wholly unawares. The foundations on which they had been building, without really being aware of the fact, were found to be in a process of disintegration. They had regarded education as primarily a question of method and more or less independent of the course of cultural evolution.

The mechanical conception of education resting on the quantitative method also favored the elaboration of the technique of education. This in turn tended to alter the rôles of teacher and administrator. If education is largely a matter of tests and scales and classification, then the process can be guided by persons seated at the center of a given school system. By manipulating the proper levers at the proper time they can direct efficiently the course of learning and teaching throughout the area under their jurisdiction. One need not even know the content of a particular subject which he is supervising, if he has at hand objective tests which, when administered according to carefully outlined directions, reveal as unerringly as a thermometer in its field the precise condition of the learner. If the tests are supplemented by a knowledge of method, the supervisor can pass judgment not only on the product but also on the process of instruction. All of these tendencies have resulted in the reduction of the rôle of the teacher and the elevation of that of the administrator or supervisor. Under such a regime, for a genuinely gifted person to engage in teaching would appear to be a waste of talents.

Purpose. The American people have manifested a profound faith in something that they think goes on in the school and that is called education. This faith is revealed in the great school plant they have built, in the huge sums of money they devote to its maintenance, and in the vast numbers of children they send to its classrooms and laboratories. But when the question is raised regarding the purpose of this vast enterprise no convincing answer is forthcoming, beyond the response that it is engaged in the education of the younger generation. The assumption is widespread that education has its own purposes and that these purposes are above examination and criticism.

Having assumed that education is its own justification, the American people naturally tend to measure its advance in quantitative and physical terms. This fact has been remarked by native and foreign critics alike for decades. A striking instance of the tendency appeared in connection with the retirement of the president of the oldest and most renowned university of the country at the end of the academic year in 1933 —a university that is popularly regarded as the custodian of the cultural life in America. In an appraisal of his administration, covering a quarter century, a column in the New York *Times* for June 25—a newspaper that prides itself on the intellectual quality of its clientele—carried in its headlines the statement that he had "doubled the enrollment, increased the endowment, and expanded the buildings" of the institution. Doubtless in the mind of the writer of the article and in the minds of the great majority of the readers, these accomplishments were sufficient to make the administration notable. That the purpose of the university and the quality of instruction could be taken for granted, was confidently assumed. For was the institution not devoted to the *education* of the youth of the nation? If this was so, then nothing else mattered.

Absence of purpose in American education, however, is only apparent. Careful examination shows that the school system from top to bottom is dominated by a purpose that has changed but little in the course of a century—a purpose that has survived the expansion of the public school, the development of public high schools and state universities, the coming of junior high schools and junior colleges, the addition of innumerable subjects and courses to the curriculum, and the invention of countless pedagogical terms and devices. Indeed, in large measure these developments, adaptations, and innovations have been inspired by this purpose. That it is rarely made the subject of discussion shows how profoundly it is held. Besides teaching loyalty to inherited practices, institutions, and ideals—an aim of education in every society—the American public school has been supremely devoted to the ideal of helping the individual, fortunate enough to reach the higher levels of the system, to get ahead of his fellows in the struggle for economic advantage. "I wonder if it isn't a fair statement," said Harold L. Ickes, Secretary of the Interior, in addressing the National Education Association at Chicago on July 6, 1933, "that while we have indulged ourselves liberally in education, we have not done this so much for the sake of education itself or to add to the culture and graciousness of life, but because of the general belief that by educating ourselves and our children we have been making it more possible to win in the race for acquisition of wealth."[30]

The situation can best be understood by reference to educational practices that reach far back into the past. The American people inherited from Europe the tradition that secondary and higher education are a badge of aristocracy and point toward preferred occupations and social status. With the establishment in the United States of a system of publicly supported schools, reaching from the kindergarten through the graduate and professional schools of the university, this ancient tradition was not abandoned. On the contrary, it was applied with vigor and enthusiasm to the new arrangements. The "educational ladder," most appropriately named, was viewed, like the natural resources of the country, as a way of escape for the individual from the hardships and degradation of manual labor and of entering the easier and more "respectable" life of the middle and favored classes. Children and youth rushed to the schools as their parents had rushed to the frontier; and the more gifted or fortunate among them went on to college or university, as the more daring or shrewd among their fathers had acquired the more profitable land, forest and mineral resources of the country. In America, to a peculiar degree, the road to honor and privilege lay through the acquisition of wealth. As Secretary Ickes stated in the address already quoted, "the material things of life have always been the most appealing to us. It has been our theory that wealth covered a multitude of sins."

[30] The New York *Times*, July 7, 1933.

Under the regime of the individualistic economy that spread over the country in the early nineteenth century, this devotion of the school to helping the individual to succeed in a material way was supported by the logic of the age. But today, as evidence presented in every chapter of this volume proves, the situation is fundamentally altered. The American people now find themselves in an economy that is becoming increasingly co-operative and collectivist in nature. As a consequence the magnificent school enterprise, with all of its worship of efficiency and quantitative methods, is harnessed to social purposes that are out of harmony with the facts of the epoch. The more than 5,000,000 boys and girls now attending the high schools of the country, all looking forward to economic preferment, reveal the bankruptcy of the inherited educational philosophy. The school, along with industry and agriculture and medicine and the family and the remaining social institutions, faces a period of fundamental reconstruction. Through the instrumentalities of organized education American children are being inducted into a society that has passed away.

CHAPTER VI

RECREATION

The emergence of recreation during the past century and a half as a fairly distinct social interest administered increasingly by a trained and specialized personnel may be compared with the growth of organized education. In the world of the eighteenth century in America professional entertainers and amusement mongers were extremely rare. In the sphere of recreation, as in the domain of economy, the household was relatively self-contained. Moreover, the separation of recreation from activities associated with occupation, religion, government, and family and community life was almost unheard of. And the thought of buying entertainment would have seemed peculiarly incongruous, except perhaps in the case of the most favored classes. The average individual obtained his recreation in pursuing the ordinary round of activities called forth by the diversity of interests and the march of the seasons.

In recent decades this development of recreation as a special interest has been profoundly affected by the growth of invention and technology. The increasing productivity of human labor has greatly extended the hours of leisure. "During the last fifty years," . . . conclude Wolman and Peck, "it is probable that the normal work week in American industry has decreased by 20 hours."[1] Although leisure, like the other good things of life, falls unevenly on the different occupations and classes, men and women and children all have more free time than formerly. And, if the testimony of the engineers is to be trusted, the future will witness a continuation and even an

---

[1] Leo Wolman and Gustav Peck, "Labor Groups in the Social Structure," Chapter XVI in The President's Research Committee on Social Trends, *Recent Social Trends in the United States* (New York, 1933), II, 828.

acceleration of all of these tendencies. The air is full of reports of new methods, processes, and machines that will displace or at least greatly conserve human energy, and of rumors about a six- or five- or four-hour working-day and a five- or four-day working-week. Certainly, if the modern productive mechanism can be made to run efficiently and to serve the masses of the people, leisure will become a distinctive feature of the society of the future and the appropriate employment of free time the controlling factor in the enrichment of life. Since historically the American people have been peculiarly absorbed in occupational interests, a cultural revolution may well be under way.

HISTORIC PATTERNS

The present forms of recreational and leisure-time activities in the United States reflect the peculiar history of the American people. Their mode of settling the new continent has given to their culture a certain rootless quality. As a rule they came to America as individuals and families, and not as organic self-contained social groups; they precipitated themselves into a strange natural environment to which their institutions were not closely adapted; they moved with incredible speed across a vast territory and thus broke again and again the continuity of the generations; they passed in rapid succession from a primitive pioneering existence to a settled agrarian life and then to a highly industrialized economy. At no time in their history, with the possible exception of the first century and a half, which embraced the settlement of the eastern seacoast, were they permitted to develop a mature and coherent cultural pattern. Almost before they had sent their roots beneath the surface in any given setting, they were forced to shift to new soil. As a consequence, that rich folk life, composed of song and dance and ceremony and festival, which forms an integral part of any fully ripened culture, and which meets the recreational needs of a people, has been largely absent in America.

The Rural Heritage.[2] From the time of the coming of the first settlers to the close of the march across the continent, life for the masses of the people was hard and narrow. Whatever may have been the lot of the aristocracy—north, south, east, or west—for the great majority of the population physical labor was arduous and prolonged. There was little time for recreation. Cities were few and the means of transportation and communication primitive. Recreational opportunities for the most part therefore were limited by the resources of the family and the small farming community. The home was the center of the more common amusements; the church undoubtedly served to fill a great void in the life of the people; and in time the district school became a center of numerous social activities.

The recreations of colonial days, though varying from place to place, were derived largely from England. But with the settlement of the Northwest Territory, beginning in the later years of the eighteenth century, great changes occurred. The old community life was destroyed. Hunting and fishing and trapping, and even Indian fighting, though not recreational in purpose, added to the interest in life. Because of the isolation, the visit of a chance traveler was made an occasion of social significance. For the same reason the building of a cabin or the harvesting of a crop was often converted into a crude festival. A social outlet for the emotions was provided at intervals by community gatherings, camp meetings, fights, circuses, traveling lecturers, hypnotists, and mountebanks, as well as by new cults, religions, and divers mass enthusiasms. Men gloried in the exercise of their muscles, loved wrestling matches, and engaged in innumerable kinds of physical competition. And as the frontier moved west across the plains, over the mountains, and on to the coast, it developed new forms of recreation. One

[2] See especially Charles A. Beard and Mary R. Beard, *The Rise of American Civilization* (New York, 1927); and James Mickel Williams, *Our Rural Heritage* (New York, 1925).

need only mention the cattle range with its interest in horsemanship and the use of firearms, and the gold rush with its shootings, prostitutes, drinking bouts, and vigilance committees.

With the passing of the frontier social life took on a more settled character. The situation in rural New York has been described by Mr. Williams.[3] Here the neighborhood was the center of a kind of informal recreation. There was much interest in outdoor sports, such as fights, rough games, and wrestling matches, "pulling stick," corn-husking, and pole-setting contests, and various forms of crude horse-play. Raisings, bees, and socials were popular, as well as parties at which, after a heavy meal, the young played blind man's buff and the old "visited" or propounded conundrums. At the weekly singing school volume, rather than melody or harmony, seems to have been the object. On General Training Day, following the parade and exercises, all took part in a general "jollification," with roast pig at the taverns and a masquerade ball in the evening. Recreation was of the simple, active, physically exuberant type. As a consequence of long acquaintance, economic independence, and a sense of equality, there was everywhere a feeling of good fellowship and a constant exchange of jests and jokes. Among the children at play, whether during the school recess or in the neighborhood, the same spirit and pattern prevailed. But whatever may have been the quality of the recreations, the community was practically self-sufficient.

The Rise of Industrial Civilization. The rise of industrial civilization, which proceeded with ever-increasing momentum during the nineteenth century, rapidly undermined the economic foundations of the simple recreational life of the farming community. Great numbers of men moved into the cities and industrial centers; and those who remained on the farm and in the agricultural villages found themselves being drawn swiftly into the orbit of urban influences. For the former, the

3 James Mickel Williams, *op. cit.,* 6, 111–121.

recreational activities of the past were impossible; for the latter, they had lost their savor. Thus a great vacuum was created in the cultural life of the people.

Among the bourgeoisie, a class that grew rapidly in numbers and wealth with the advance of the new dispensation, idleness, display, and conspicuous consumption became the order of the day. Those who could afford it, and many who could not, interested themselves in fine horses and attended horse shows; acquired pretentious city houses and filled them with color, glitter, and pomp; bought their way into "the four hundred" and then turned to Europe for the purpose of forming alliances with the aristocracy of the old world. Also from the civilizations beyond the Atlantic they purchased art treasures, not always as objects of beauty, but often as tokens of wealth. In an effort to surpass one another in expenditure they prepared lavish feasts and indulged in the most luxurious forms of entertainment.

In the rural districts the added wealth led to similar forms of rivalry. First appeared showy harness and equipment of carriages for display on the highways; then came the improvement of the roads, the development of fast driving and horse racing, and the organization of driving-park associations. Large and highly ornate houses were built; the piano took the place of the organ; the consumption of liquor and tobacco increased; and hostesses vied with each other in the extravagance of their hospitality.

The life of the great masses of the people was also being forced into unfamiliar molds. In the congested areas of growing cities the poor multiplied their numbers, dwelling in quarters inadequate for decent living and in neighborhoods without provision for the play of children. To satisfy the cravings for amusement of the laboring and middle classes, including persons engaged in mercantile, clerical, and professional pursuits, various forms of commercialized recreation appeared—prize fights, organized sports, circuses, dime museums, dance halls, cheap vaudeville and burlesque performances.[4] Barnum met stupendous success with a circus on the grand scale. Wild west shows became the rage. Also the people no doubt found much release in camp meetings, religious controversies, and political contests.

With the building of railroads and the coming of new modes of transportation professional singers, elocutionists, magicians, and dramatic companies began to tour the small towns and rural districts. Since the churches, which had formerly housed social gatherings of all kinds, often closed their doors to these performers, public halls and "opera houses" were erected. During the period of prosperity covering the years from 1879 to 1884, social pleasures outside the church received their first great impetus in many a rural community. While the old amusements of hunting, fishing, and wrestling continued, others, such as baseball, archery, trap shooting, polo, bicycling, and roller skating, rose to prominence. Here and there public roller skating rinks and bowling alleys appeared.

More and more, passive participation and vicarious interest in the show or the game took the place of the active expression of earlier times. In recent years the automobile, the movie, and the radio have accentuated this tendency. Also formal organization played a larger and larger rôle in many types of social activity. Women got together in clubs to entertain, to inform, and to improve themselves. The founding of the General Federation of Women's Clubs in 1889 led to the formation of other groups and the enrichment of programs. In the small towns and open country the organization of numerous clubs and societies was stimulated by the traditional rivalries of factions and population centers. Secret societies grew in number and strength. Both personal prestige and business success often depended on belonging to the more socially desirable fraternal orders.

A composite and graphic picture of recreational changes tak-

4 Rollin Lynde Hartt, *The People at Play* (Boston, 1909), Chapter I.

ing place during the last generation in a representative midwestern community is to be found in Middletown.[5] Among the more important of these changes are the reduction of the length of the working day and the inauguration of the Saturday half holiday; the decline of hiking and fishing; increased emphasis on leisure-time activities engaged in with others, such as talking, riding, and card playing; transference of the library from church to school; growth of bridge at the expense of reading; increased interest in imaginary narratives; less group singing and more listening to music; greater passive appreciation of art; the development of new forms of behavior around the automobile; the spread of the vacation habit; the growth of the cinema; the passing of the hostile attitude toward the theater; the development of the radio; the decline of the church and the neighborhood as the basis of association; the increase in the number and the variety of clubs; the shift in clubs from literary to civic concerns; the loss of vitality on the part of fraternal orders; the growth of interest in parties; the reduction of entertainment in the home; the introduction of class differences in card playing—pedro for the workers, bridge for the bourgeoisie; the advance in both the formality and the cost of club, fraternity, and sorority dances; the decline of the age-long institution of the chaperone; and the general extension and weakening of the bonds that hold people together.

The listing of these specific changes, however, fails to tell the whole story. The social foundations of recreation have been much affected. The aggregation of people in great population centers has created "friction of space" in city development and simply crowded out traditional forms of play. There is no longer enough room to do many of the things done by earlier generations.[6] At the same time the growth of transportation has led to the centralization of recreational agencies and the

[5] Robert S. Lynd and Helen M. Lynd, *Middletown* (New York, 1929), Chapters XVIII–XIX.
[6] Niles Carpenter, *The Sociology of City Life* (New York, 1931), 249–254.

decay of the socializing influences of certain basic institutions.[7] Loyalty to the home, the church, and the neighborhood have declined[8] and the old intimate life of the community has been weakened.[9] Even certain modes of expression, such as spontaneous singing and whistling on the part of children, seem to have been suppressed by the noise and hurry of the streets.[10] On the other hand new forms of recreation have appeared that could not be provided within the narrow boundaries of the family or the farming community.

THE PRESENT SITUATION

As the foregoing pages indicate, recent generations have witnessed great changes in the recreational habits of the American people. In moving from a simple agrarian to a complex industrial society they have been compelled to abandon many of the practices of their ancestors and to fashion new forms of play suited to the changed conditions. The result has been the growth of a vast program of recreation which was largely unknown two generations ago. For the years 1928, 1929, and 1930 J. F. Steiner has estimated the total annual cost of recreation in the United States at more than $10,000,000,000 or approximately one-eighth of the national income.[11] This enormous sum gives some measure of the impact of industrial civilization on the recreational life of the American people.

[7] Frederick M. Thrasher, *The Gang* (Chicago, 1927), 3–25; Clifford Shaw, *Social Factors in Juvenile Delinquency*. National Commission on Law Observance and Enforcement, Volume II of Report on the Causes of Crime, 1931 (Washington, 1931), Chapters I–V.

[8] Joseph K. Hart, *Community Organization* (New York, 1920), 47–49, 130, 137; Arthur Evans Wood, *Community Problems* (New York, 1928), Chapter I; J. F. Steiner, *Community Organization* (New York, 1925), Chapter III.

[9] Charles Horton Cooley, *Social Organization* (New York, 1915), Chapter XXX; Robert A. Woods, *The Neighborhood in Nation Building* (Boston, 1923), 2, 121.

[10] Harvey C. Lehman and Paul A. Witty, *The Psychology of Play Activities* (New York, 1927), 131 ff.

[11] J. F. Steiner, "Recreation and Leisure Time Activities," Chapter XVIII in *Recent Social Trends in the United States*, II, 949.

Forms of Recreation. From the standpoint of expenditures, by far the most important division of recreation in the United States embraces the activities of travel and mobility. According to Mr. Steiner, the American people spend almost six and one-half billion dollars annually on vacation travel at home, vacation travel abroad, and pleasure-use of cars, motor boats, motor cycles, and bicycles.[12] They spend $3,200,000,000 on automobile touring alone and $1,246,000,000 on other pleasure-uses of the automobile. It has been "estimated that 45,000,000 people took vacation motor tours in this country during 1929."[13] The automobile has thus become the dominant factor in those forms of recreation that require expenditure of money.

Next in order come the so-called commercial amusements, including the moving picture, the radio, commercialized sport, cabarets, and night clubs, which account for almost $2,250,-000,000 annually.[14] In January 1931 the motion picture industry employed 325,000 persons, had an investment estimated at $2,000,000,000, and maintained 22,731 theaters with a seating capacity of 11,300,000 and a total weekly attendance conservatively estimated at 100,000,000.[15] Radio broadcasting, which dates from 1920, now reaches into 40 per cent of the homes of the nation and sends out over the air a continuous and varied program of music, sermons, talks, speeches, stories, and advertising.[16] Although professional baseball seems to be suffering from competition with other forms of amusement, "more than 10,000,000 people attended the games of the two major leagues during the season of 1930."[17]

On games, sports, outdoor life, and related modes of recreation the American people spend annually approximately $880,000,000.[18] The largest item of expenditure here is on

---

[12] *Ibid.*, 949.   [13] *Ibid.*, 922.   [14] *Ibid.*, 949.
[15] *Ibid.*, 940. According to the findings of the Motion Picture Research Council, this figure should be reduced to 77,000,000. See Henry James Forman, *Our Movie Made Children* (New York, 1933), 3.
[16] *Ibid.*, 941–942.   [17] *Ibid.*, 931.   [18] *Ibid.*, 949.

sporting and athletic goods and amounts to $500,000,000. There are also included toys, games, and playground equipment, phonographs and accessories, resort hotels, commercial and other camps, college football, playing cards, pool, billiards, and bowling equipment, hunting and fishing licenses, and fireworks. Interest in various sports, from the standpoint of active participation, seems to be on the increase. Apparently this is particularly true of golf and tennis—sports, however, that are largely limited to members of the more favored economic classes. The number of golf courses grew from 743 in 1916 to 5856 in 1930.[19] And it has been estimated that there are 1,200,000 public park tennis players in the country.[20]

The annual expenditures on leisure-time associations amount to more than $380,000,000.[21] Here are included social and athletic clubs, luncheon clubs, lodges, and youth service organizations. Practically every important athletic interest has its national society. Then there are innumerable informal social, bridge, and dancing clubs. Although the fraternal societies were primarily a product of the nineteenth century, their total membership in 1930 has been estimated at 35,000,000.[22] The luncheon club movement, which dates from 1910, probably enrolls about 500,000 persons. In 1926 the General Federation of Women's Clubs claimed a membership of 3,000,000 women.

Governmental expenditures for recreation, embracing municipal, county, state, and federal outlays, constitute the smallest item in the recreational budget of the American people. They total but little more than $190,000,000.[23] Within this division are included municipal parks, children's playgrounds, public school recreational facilities, state and national parks and forests.

An examination of these forms of recreation shows how completely the isolation of the past has been destroyed and

---

[19] *Ibid.*, 926.   [20] *Ibid.*, 928.   [21] *Ibid.*, 949.
[22] *Ibid.*, 936.   [23] *Ibid.*, 949.

how thoroughly the nation has become integrated. In the field of sport, the radio, and the movie the names of star performers are household words from one end of the country to the other. Changes in the playing rules of bridge, baseball, or tennis spread quickly from coast to coast. And a new stroke in golf is discussed simultaneously in San Francisco, Chicago, and New York. Moreover, the line between town and country has all but disappeared. The radio recognizes no geographical barriers; and the automobile pays small heed to political boundaries. The farmer goes to the village, the villager to the small town, and the resident of the small town to the city, each in search of amusement. Also the process may be reversed. The limiting factor is no longer place of residence, but rather the nature of one's interest and the size of one's purse.

The Organization of Recreation. Prior to the rise of industrial civilization recreation was almost completely a function of the family and the neighborhood. It was informal in character and inexpensive. Men, women, and children provided their own recreation. But with the appearance of the new order the problem presented many novel aspects. The family lost its self-sufficiency, the neighborhood often disintegrated, strange forms of recreation appeared, and the population found itself drawn into a pecuniary economy. In the sphere of leisure-time activities, moreover, the American people pursued for the most part a policy of *laissez-faire.* As a consequence, the vast and varied program of games and sports and amusements that has appeared in response to changed conditions has grown up under the most diverse auspices. The individual, the family, the church, and various non-profit seeking groups and agencies continue the older tradition. Business enterprise, which was quick to grasp the opportunity for material gain presented by the breakdown of the inherited modes of recreation, occupies a central position in the picture. Finally, government, though arriving relatively late on the field, is playing an ever-increasing rôle. The scope of each of these three organizing forces—individual and group initiative, business enterprise, and government—will be briefly examined.

Individual and group initiative. Much of the recreation of the American people is still conducted, at least in part, under the auspices of the family. This is even true of that dominant form of leisure activity centering in the use of the automobile. Yet the fact is patent that the growing opportunities for recreation outside the home, for children as well as older persons, has set in motion certain centrifugal forces which tend to weaken the rôle of the family circle in this sphere. Although the tendency has been combatted with some success by various religious, recreational, and educational groups, the home today is less the scene of associated activities for all members of the family than in previous generations. Other agencies, lying outside the domains of business and governmental enterprise, such as churches and co-operative groups, have become interested in the organization of recreation.

The church has evinced an increasing interest in recreation. The more adaptable of the churches have recognized that an abundant life and a rich personality require the full and free expression of the play impulses. Since the days of the prohibition of "stage plays" by the Puritans and the outright condemnation of all play by official Methodist and other Protestant denominations, a revolution has taken place. Today in villages and small towns the church is not infrequently the leading recreational center. For the past twenty-five years the movement to introduce play activities into religious programs has been growing. While originally the major motive may have been the enlistment of members, broader purposes are beginning to rule, recreation often being utilized in moral and religious instruction. Among Catholics, Jews, and Protestants organized efforts are being made to associate with religious concepts the ideals that develop in children at play. Also in growing numbers churches are maintaining community halls to serve the social needs of their members; and latterly under the category of religious education recreational programs for children have been provided. Week-day religious schools and summer church schools in Protestant churches alone number over 11,000.[24]

The countless clubs and societies in America furnish an enormous amount of recreation. The parent-teacher associations, though organized ostensibly for the purpose of co-ordinating home and school, are held together chiefly by the interest on the part of mothers in entertainment and association. Private golf clubs and athletic societies have appeared everywhere. Mention has already been made of the growth of fraternal orders, women's organizations, and luncheon clubs for business and professional men. And labor unions and employers' organizations both undoubtedly serve the recreational as well as the economic needs of their members.

The so-called "character building agencies" have taken the lead in furnishing recreation for boys and girls, young men and young women. In 1931 the total membership of the Y. M. C. A. alone aggregated over 1,000,000. The services of the boys' department of this organization, the Boys' Club Federation, the Boy Scouts of America, the 4-H Clubs, and the Order of De Molay together reach 14 per cent of all boys twelve to twenty-one years of age in the eastern and Pacific states, 12 per cent in the central and western, and 8 per cent in the southern states.[25] Somewhat less impressive is the work of the agencies ministering to the needs of girls and young women.

Business enterprise. Under the reign of *laissez-faire* business enterprise has come to play a major rôle in furnishing recreation for the American people. According to the survey

[24] The Cleveland Foundation Committee, Cleveland Recreation Survey, Volume IV, *The Sphere of Private Agencies,* prepared by Mrs. Katherine Vassault (Cleveland, 1920), 52–64; LeRoy E. Bowman, "Community Recreation" in *Christianity and Social Adventuring,* Jerome Davis, Editor (New York, 1927); Norman E. Richardson, *The Church at Play* (New York, 1922).

[25] Leeds Gulick, *Programs for Boys and Young Men* (Chicago, 1931).

in Cleveland, in the case of recreation pursued outside the home, public agencies claimed three-fourths of the hours of children of school age, co-operative agencies one-half of the hours of adults, and commercial agencies three-fourths of the hours of young folks from sixteen to twenty-five years of age. Among the great agencies that are exploited for private gain should be mentioned organized sport, the cinema, the radio, and the theater. There are of course many others. And almost every form of recreation has a commercial aspect.

During the past generation the organization of sports for commercial purposes has grown to enormous dimensions. Professional baseball, with its many leagues, its high-salaried players, and its millions of patrons, is illustrative. The World Series, consisting usually of about half a dozen games, has in each of five different years brought in gate receipts of more than $1,000,000. At these games nothing happens, except that one or the other side wins. While this may be regarded as a harmless form of amusement, by enlisting the time, the enthusiasm, the loyalty of multitudes, it tends to divert attention from matters of more serious consequence. Through the newspapers, urged on by the desire to build up circulation, a wholly fictitious value is placed upon the fortunes of teams and individual players. Besides strengthening the sedentary quality of life in industrial society through the development of the spectator, it introduces the pattern of business enterprise into the field of sport. The commercial spirit has even invaded the domain of college athletics.

In the case of the cinema the domination of the profit motive seems to have been complete from the first. Since the establishment of the industry (as it is very appropriately called) in 1907, its every development has been governed by the efforts of producers, distributors, and exhibitors to get larger and larger shares of ever-increasing box-office receipts. The result has been a record of extraordinary technical triumph and enormous physical expansion. Truly here is one of the most powerful cultural instruments that technology has given to mankind.

The great physical and technical advance has no parallel in the improvement of the content of the film. In spite of twenty-five years of experience the product of the "industry" remains for the most part in a state of infancy. This condition, however, is not due to a lack of interest on the side of the public in the problem. Women's clubs and religious organizations the country over have passed resolutions demanding better movies; the Motion Picture Producers and Distributors of America have established a public relations department, ostensibly to co-operate with civic groups; the National Board of Review, designed to propagate good pictures and to oppose censorship, places its stamp of approval on every entertainment film after it has been passed upon by a group of laymen; and a number of states and cities have adopted censorhip laws and ordinances. Actually, very little has been accomplished to increase the æsthetic and cultural quality of the films. Although a few pictures of genuine artistic, literary, and dramatic merit have been produced, the overwhelming majority are characterized by pretentiousness combined with immaturity in both conception and execution. Through a perennial appeal to sex and melodrama the cinema provides for the masses an escape from reality and for business enterprise a possible road to riches.

The most common expression of concern has to do with the effect of the movie on children. It is well known that through this agency, as well as through the radio and the newspaper, boys and girls are admitted to the adult world, with an unnatural emphasis on sex, sadism, crime, and generally a life of idle luxury and ostentatious display. According to the findings of a series of studies conducted under the auspices of the Motion Picture Research Council, the weekly attendance of minors at movies is approximately 28,000,000 and of children under fourteen 11,000,000.[26] An analysis of the contents of 1500 pictures composed of 500 produced in each of the three years 1920, 1925, and 1930 and including all feature pictures produced by the leading companies in those years, lends vigorous support to the conclusion derived from common observation. The investigator found "that out of 500 pictures in 1920, 82 per cent dealt with the three major themes of crime, sex and love; in 1925, 79 per cent were preoccupied with these themes, and in 1930, 72 per cent. In that year, however, mystery and war pictures, which often included crime, or, at all events, violence, rose from small figures to 9 per cent, which goes to swell the above totals. In other words, somewhere between 75 and 80 per cent of all pictures dealt with love, sex, crime or mystery films."[27] In concluding his discussion of the content of the movie, and after pointing out that a really good picture is occasionally produced, Mr. Forman makes the following summary statement: "The chances are more than even that they (the children) will encounter upon the screen an unsavory sex picture, a crime picture poorly and superficially contrived, or something bristling with vulgarity and innuendo, abounding in shoddy characters with tawdry goals in life, of questionable morals or occupations, or wholly immoral."[28]

Studies of the retention on the part of children of movie experience, and of the effects of the experience on sleep, on physical and mental states, and on conduct and delinquency, have led W. W. Charters, Chairman of the Committee on Educational Research of the Payne Fund, under whose general direction the inquiry was conducted, to the conclusion that "the motion picture is powerful to an unexpected degree in affecting the information, attitudes, emotional experiences, and conduct patterns of children."[29] To meet this situation various proposals have been made. The sub-committee on the cinema

[26] Henry James Forman, *op. cit.*, 18.
[28] *Ibid.*, 53.
[27] *Ibid.*, 29–30.
[29] *Ibid.*, viii.

of the White House Conference in 1930 recommended more "family programs," better and more uniform legislation, an extension and improvement of the work of film committees, and the encouragement of amateur dramatics by schools, recreation agencies, and churches.[30] But the development of the motion picture into the fine cultural instrument that it is capable of becoming would seem to depend on the appearance of a more critical and intelligent public and the removal of the domination of the commercial spirit.

The latest and, with the automobile and the motion picture, one of the most universal forms of amusement and recreation is the radio. By 1930, according to the Census, this agency, though scarcely known a decade before, was reaching 12,078,345 homes. Since 1920 innumerable improvements and inventions have been made and huge sums have been invested in more than 600 broadcasting stations. As in the cinema, where the great costs of equipment and production can be met only by reaching a large audience, so in the case of the radio the dependence on advertising makes a wide appeal imperative. In both instances the result is a general low level of entertainment, although the position of the radio is somewhat superior, because of the great variety of stations and of programs. Yet even the finest performances which are sent out over the air are commonly marred by the accompanying appeal of the salesman. Moreover, there is no integration of stations and no general planning of programs to serve the cultural needs of the people.

With the development of the cinema and other competing forms of entertainment the theater has been having a difficult time. While the number of first-class playhouses in New York City multiplied four times from 1900 to 1928, the theater was rapidly disappearing in the rest of the country. This tendency was checked somewhat by the little theater movement which resulted in the use by local groups of remodelled barns, aban-

[30] James Edward Rogers, *The Child and Play* (New York, 1932), 111.

doned chapels, school buildings, and actual theaters in the production of plays. Also the extension departments of universities have sent to hundreds of groups package libraries dealing with pageantry, dramatics, and stage management.[31] Nevertheless, the theater does not face a particularly bright future. Under the pressure of commercial exploitation it tends to follow in the footsteps of the movies and to deal superficially with the problems of American life. Indeed, as a general rule, it provides a way of escape from that life and a compensation for its inadequacies.

As a background for organized sport, the cinema, the radio, and the theater, commercial enterprise has provided for the American people a bewildering variety of cheap forms of amusement: dance halls, houses of prostitution, speakeasies, pool and billiard rooms, vaudeville performances, burlesque shows, amusement parks, and many others. In fact business has overlooked few opportunities for making profit out of the leisure time resulting from the growth of technology and the craving for excitement generated by the monotony of industrial occupations. And as the appetites of the population become jaded, thrill is added to thrill and sensation to sensation. That the consequent program of recreation was unsuited to the deeper cultural and spiritual needs of the people became clearly apparent in the second half of the nineteenth century.

Government. With the passage of the years a reaction against this condition set in and government became interested in the problem of recreation. Thus the playground movement, originating in the eighties in the charitable efforts of Boston women to provide younger children with sand boxes and space for play, has spread from coast to coast. As a consequence there has grown up a sense of community responsibility for parks, playgrounds, bathing beaches, and other forms of recreational facilities. At the turn of the century, interest in the development of public parks, not as scenic places but as play

31 Kenneth MacGowan, *Footlights Across America* (New York, 1929).

areas, gained great momentum. In the ten-year period from 1892 to 1902 the number of cities possessing parks grew from 100 to 800. And by 1926 this figure had reached 1680. From 1925 to 1930 the park areas of 534 cities increased by one-third.[32] In these parks often may be found facilities for children's play, for boating, bathing, and skating, and for playing tennis, baseball, horseshoes, basketball, football, and croquet. Less often provision is made for golf, polo, sailing, coasting, and a number of other pastimes. Many parks contain buildings suitable for educational and social purposes, especially club houses, field houses, and museums. In recent years counties and states have followed the lead of cities. Near large urban centers in particular have extensive parks been created in which provision is made for almost every outdoor activity. Then there is the national park system which now embraces twenty-two parks with a total of 8,027,216 acres. In the last fifteen years, partly because of the expenditure of large sums on roads, lodges, and camp sites, visitors to these parks have increased enormously.[33] The national forests, organized in the first instance for conservation purposes, in 1931 covered 185,251,582 acres. And the year before they were visited by 31,905,000 persons.[34]

The Playground and Recreation Association of America, which was founded in 1906, early adopted the policy of fostering the organization of a playground or recreation commission as a separate department of municipal government. Other leaders have contended that the school should accept full responsibility for the play of all children. The rapid growth of physical education has lent support to this view. During the decade succeeding 1900, the school developed an intense interest in athletics, but in athletics for the few, in the wining team. From 1910 to 1920 "many teams in many sports"

[32] *Park Recreation Areas in the United States,* Bulletin No. 565, U. S. Bureau of Labor Statistics (Washington, 1932).
[33] Annual Reports of the National Park Service, Department of the Interior.
[34] Annual Reports of the Forest Service, Department of Agriculture.

became the slogan. Then health education gradually assumed a central position in the sphere of physical training. According to the statistics of the Association, 1000 cities report paid leadership in recreation, double the number of ten years ago. Outdoor playgrounds, recreation buildings, athletic fields, golf courses, bathing beaches, swimming pools, tennis courts, skating rinks have increased in proportion. Playgrounds also have grown rapidly, having doubled from 1910 to 1920 and increased by nearly two-thirds in the next decade. The trend, moreover, is toward evening and all-year use, as well as toward the diversification of activities and the employment of trained directors.[35] The play of children is coming to be regarded as an essential part of education; and in the last few years great numbers of schools have added to their play facilities. Many states have passed laws requiring play space for schools.[36] For indoor recreation school buildings are less well-equipped: in 1926–27 fewer than one-third had gymnasiums and fewer than one-half either gymnasiums or play rooms. Also less than one-fourth of the cities studied could boast one or more public schools with swimming pools.[37]

Although governmental expenditures constitute but the smallest fraction of all sums spent on recreation by the American people, the growing interest of government is one of the major trends of the age in the sphere of recreation.[38] The number of persons taking advantage of facilities provided at public expense amounts for the season to 5,000,000 for golf, 6,000,-000 for tennis, 8,000,000 for ice-skating and field athletics, 11,000,000 for baseball, 15,000,000 for pool swimming, and 38,000,000 for beach bathing. In 1931 2,000,000 campers and 4,000,000 picnickers used the national forests. Even real estate agents are commencing to include playgrounds in

35 Yearbooks of The National Recreational Association, New York City.

36 Marie M. Ready, *School Playgrounds* (Washington, 1930), 4–9.

37 Marie M. Ready, *Physical Education in City Public Schools* (Washington, 1929).

38 J. F. Steiner, *op. cit.,* 954.

their development plans. Also railroads and hotels occasionally provide play opportunities for children. In recent years community centers, operated in connection with the public schools, have tended increasingly to organize recreational programs.[39] Finally, city planning is making methodical provision for the leisure-time needs of urban dwellers.[40]

The Quality of Recreation. On the purely quantitative side the achievements of the American people have been stupendous. Attention has been directed to the enormous expenditures of time and money on recreation, to the mounting list of inventions that serve the leisure needs of the people, and to the amazing variety of activities in which men and women and children engage during their free hours. The land literally teems with organizations and institutions that are dedicated to the interest of play. Indeed the demands of the innumerable recreational agencies have become so insistent, the stimuli so continuous and ubiquitous, that the ordinary citizen must long to escape and enjoy the solitude of field and forest and stream. In particular has commercial enterprise endeavored to break down every barrier that protects the individual from the world. Clearly, the present recreational offering cannot be criticised on the grounds of its quantitative inadequacy.

On the qualitative side the situation has called forth much unfavorable comment. Two major criticisms have been made by many students of the question. It has been charged, in the first place, that modern recreation emphasizes too exclusively passive and vicarious forms of participation; and, in the second, that it is crude and primitive and superficial in its cultural appeal. The bases of these two criticisms will be briefly examined.

In pre-industrial society the individual as a rule participated

[39] Eleanor T. Glueck, *The Community Use of Schools* (Baltimore, 1927), Chapters V, VI.

[40] *Regional Survey of New York and Its Environs,* Volume V, "Public Recreation" (New York, 1928); Volume VII, "Neighborhood and Community Planning" (New York, 1929), 45–76; *Regional Plan of New York and Its Environs,* Volume I, "The Graphic Regional Plan" (New York, 1929), 336–394.

actively in practically all forms of recreation. In the games and sports, the dances and festivals of that society there was a place for everybody who was not disqualified by reason of age or sex or special disability. The amateur ruled the recreational arts; the professional performer was rare. With the rise of industrial civilization the ordinary citizen has tended to become a mere spectator in the realms of music, drama, and even sport. He listens to and watches the performance of experts, and would commonly become embarrassed if asked to perform himself. Mention need be made only of college football, professional baseball, prize fighting, the cinema, the radio, and the theater. In field after field, where in former times active participation was the rule, recreation has been reduced to the enjoyment of a spectacle. Whether this is due primarily to the "friction of space" created by the growth of cities, to the urge for profits on the part of business enterprise, or to a native human reluctance to expend energy needlessly, the fact remains that recreation has thus been robbed of certain of its historic qualities. It has lost some of its value as a builder of character.

A necessary corollary of this development of the passive forms of recreation is an increase in costs. The recreations of the American citizen, particularly those that reflect the rise of industrial society, are expensive—in many cases very expensive. The services of experts, of star performers whose fortunes are entrusted to shrewd business managers, are not given away. Also wherever commercial enterprise operates, whether in the sphere of sports or music or drama, there is often an effort to attract patrons merely by lavish expenditure. Moreover, automobiles, even the least pretentious makes, are relatively costly and place a heavy financial burden on families in both poor and moderate circumstances. Bathing and outing trips commonly involve outlays for travel, for clothes, and sometimes for lodging. Under a regime of business, by stimulating competition in display, artificial wants may be sedulously cultivated. Thus fishing, hunting, golf, tennis, baseball, football, hockey, skating, and swimming each has its special garb and equipment. And in order to keep the wheels of industry turning the fashion is changed from season to season. If these facts are projected upon the background of the gross inequalities in the distribution of wealth which characterize capitalistic society, it is apparent that great masses of the American people are recreationally impoverished. In the last analysis the richness and the variety of leisure-time activities must depend in large measure on individual and family income.

The second basic charge against the current forms of recreation is that their cultural appeal is crude and primitive and superficial. Certainly few would deny that the leisure-time activities in which the masses engage contain too little of refinement, beauty, and elevation of spirit. In general they are marked by shallowness and sterility; they impart no deep and lasting satisfactions; they provide but an escape from the boredom and purposelessness of life. Consider the vast spectacles of commercialized sport, the vapid sentimentality of the movies, the stupidities of the comic strips, the sensationalism of the daily press, the banalities of the radio, and the devotion to the commonplace in the theater. In no sphere of interest are the contradictions so characteristic of American life more plainly visible. One of the most disconcerting facts about contemporary society is the broad chasm that separates technical from cultural achievement. The most superb instruments are put to the most trivial uses. Indeed they may be employed to debase the taste of the people. In this indictment practically all informed persons concur.

The reason for this condition is complex. The very rapidity of social change that has marked the present epoch has doubtless been an important factor. When everything is moving, when institutions are being uprooted, when life in its various aspects is being shifted to new foundations, recreational forms must of necessity exhibit a primitive and elementary quality.

The fact should not be forgotten that industrial civilization is still in its earliest infancy. The traits of maturity consequently can scarcely be expected to manifest themselves in any department of life. The most that can be hoped for is some show of promise.

The factor of social change, however, does not operate alone in accounting for the low plane on which so many leisure-time activities are pursued. Of equal importance is the domination of commercial enterprise. With the breakdown of folk recreation business men proceeded to exploit the popular thirst for amusement. And since profits tended to vary directly as the number of patrons, particularly in a competitive world, programs were organized with a view to making the widest possible appeal. This has meant the degradation of standards to the lowest common denominator—to emphasis on sex, melodrama, mystery, adventure, sentimentality, and triviality. Moreover, from the standpoint of revenue, a simple appeal to untutored impulses can be substituted effectually for artistic quality.

Finally, groups dominating the economic and political life may have felt some fear of recreation and art forms that deal realistically and honestly with contemporary society. The rulers of ancient Rome understood fully the rôle of the circus in the government of a people. But the circus of antiquity was a feeble instrument in comparison with the press, the cinema, the radio, the automobile, and professional baseball.

THE PROBLEM OF RECREATION

The changes in recreational habits and institutions that have swept over the country during the last two or three generations are not the product of any reasoned conception of the good life. Nor do they represent a progressive and systematic development. Rather have they come from the unregulated play of blind and conflicting forces. The American people have formulated no adequate theory of recreation; they have given little consideration to the function of play in the evolution of a culture; they have generally assumed that the problem is merely one of providing amusement for the population, of filling the vacant hours with pleasant diversion. To be sure, by the enactment of blue laws, the imposing of censorship, and the prohibition of recreation practices that run counter to traditional standards of right and wrong, they have given expression from time to time to the Puritan strain running through their mores. But such measures make no contribution to a positive and intelligent attack upon the problem.

An adequate program of recreation may be asked to recognize and meet five basic issues: first, the organization of industry in the interests of general well-being, comfort, and beauty; second, the transmuting of economic into cultural gains; third, the conduct of recreation as an educational and cultural force; fourth, the development of folk art and new forms of creative expression; and fifth, the fostering of a sense of public responsibility with respect to the entire question of recreation.

Perhaps the most basic question of all is the management of industry in the interests of the people and the subordination of the economic to humane considerations. Heretofore American society has revolved about the economic interest: work has been the ruling passion: the tradition has even been fostered that men should play in order to fit themselves for work rather than that they should work in order to lay the material foundations for a richer spiritual life. The correction of this tradition would mean the frank recognition of the instrumental character of economic institutions, the placing of human rights above property rights everywhere, the organization of production in the interests of the wholesome utilization of human energy, the reduction of fatigue, of excessive strain, and of over-specialization. In a word, economic activity would be forced to take its proper place in a well-integrated social life.

The task of transmuting economic into cultural gains is another aspect of this first basic problem. The conquests in the economic field and the diminishing need for man-power in production should find expression in an increasing amount of leisure time for the masses of the people. That there have been great gains along these lines in the immediate past cannot be questioned. And yet, because of the instability of the economic order, they have been neither systematic nor secure. In the absence of economic security the conditions essential to the spirit of play cannot be procured and enforced leisure becomes a demoralizing rather than a recreating force in the life of the individual. Increased leisure, if it is to bear cultural fruit, should be accompanied by increased family incomes or by an extension of the public services. At present in normal times three-fourths of the families in the United States are unable to provide adequate play opportunities for their members. The evidence is conclusive that expenditures on recreation must always wait upon the satisfaction of the fundamental needs of subsistence. The problem seems to resolve itself into larger provision of leisure for all, a more generous and equitable distribution of income, a reduction in the cost of particular forms of recreation, and a further development of community concern in playgrounds, gymnasiums, parks, bathing beaches, and social centers, in music, dancing, drama, cinema, and radio. Particularly should attention be directed toward the needs of rural districts and the smaller communities.

In the third place, recreation should be regarded and conducted as an educational and cultural force. This of course is merely saying that it should be recognized for what it really is. The character of the American people and of their civilization will no doubt depend as much on recreation as on education. The line between the two interests cannot be clearly drawn. Recreation meets a great spiritual need in the individual, and in meeting it helps to build and mold his tastes and interests. The development and direction of the play activities of a people should consequently be looked upon as an educational task, broadly and generously conceived. Workers in this sphere should no longer be regarded as entertainers and purveyors of amusement, but rather as persons on whom society has placed certain of its most vital cultural responsibilities. This does not mean that recreations would be taken solemnly. To pursue such a course would be to destroy them. But it does mean that the recreational life would receive the thoughtful consideration that it deserves.

In the fourth place, the development of folk art and new forms of creative expression should be encouraged. Recreation, like every other activity engaged in by civilized man—the building of a factory, the planning of a city, the construction of a highway, the preparation of food, or the conduct of government—must always carry an æsthetic quality. And in the case of play the relationship with art is peculiarly intimate, because of the condition of freedom and spontaneity which presumably characterizes both. One of the great needs of industrial society is the development of a rich folk life comparable from the standpoint of function to the folk life of the earlier agrarian civilization. An aspect of this problem is the fostering of new forms of creative expression. The advance of technology has made such a course imperative. Whether the hours away from work will eventually assume the dimensions that the engineers now confidently predict may be a debatable question; but certainly leisure time will increase as economic forces are mastered. Under such conditions, to leave the field to entertainment and amusement, which cultivate a passive mentality on the part of the patron, would be to court cultural disaster. Avocations of deep spiritual significance, through which the individual could express himself, would seem to be necessary for the full growth and flowering of human personality. Moreover, it would probably be necessary on the economic side to provide a proper balance to the growth of mechanized industry.

Finally, public responsibility for meeting the recreational needs of the people should be much further developed. Already the principles of *laissez-faire* have been greatly weakened in this field. The domination of the profit motive in the realm of cultural interests is beginning to seem incongruous. The necessity for the formulation of a general social policy regarding the play activities of the population is becoming increasingly apparent. While much can be done by the voluntary action of private groups, such groups lack the authority and the expert knowledge necessary to deal with the problem as a whole and on the scale made necessary by the growth of industrial society. This should not be construed as meaning the regimentation of the individual, but rather as involving the construction of a social framework within which individual initiative may be expected to flower. Only through community action, sometimes involving the entire nation, can the more serious deficiencies of the present program be corrected: the inequalities between the social classes, the poverty of backward sections of the country, the concentration of opportunities in a relatively small number of favored areas, the failure to make full use of the natural beauties of the land, and the condition of cultural and æsthetic bankruptcy that prevails generally in the radio, the cinema, and the theater. In any program of social planning, whether city, county, state, or national, the problem of recreation should be given a central position.

Chapter VII

SCIENCE

Prior to the nineteenth century science played a very minor rôle in the life of the masses of the American people. Although the discovery and settlement of the new world had their roots in scientific advance, although thought and institutions were already being greatly modified by this great creative force, and although the Revolutionary period included such brilliant names as Benjamin Franklin and Benjamin Thompson, science was still confined to the intellectual elite and retained the character of an interest of the naturally curious. Beyond the daily routine of living the minds of ordinary men were occupied with politics and theology. Society, moreover, made practically no provision for the prosecution of any form of scientific inquiry. The influence that was destined to place its characteristic stamp on the modern age and to destroy the foundations of the existing order had scarcely been isolated as a social function.[1]

THE NATURE OF SCIENCE

Science, to be sure, is not wholly the child of the modern age. Its origins can be traced far back into the past, beyond the civilizations of antiquity and even to the magical practices of primitive peoples. Wherever men have added to their knowledge of life and environment, there the spirit of science may be found. But the science that is today transforming the world is the science whose foundations were laid by Copernicus,

[1] The emphasis in this chapter will be placed on scientific inquiry as a social function rather than on the accumulation and organization of scientific knowledge. Also, though science is an extremely broad category and embraces every field in which its methods are applied, including the spheres of mental and social phenomena, it will be confined here to the physical and biological realms.

Galileo, Descartes, and Newton, and whose superstructure has been erected by a long line of distinguished investigators. Not only have these men sought knowledge with diligence and honesty and understanding; they have also perfected methods and canons of inquiry that in themselves have come to constitute a great tradition and are now capable of deliberate and systematic application to ever wider fields of experience.

As a creative and active force in the world, science presents two aspects. On the one hand, it is purely intellectual and disinterested—the fruit of man's simple desire to know, of his curiosity about the universe of stars and storms and seasons, of his craving to look beneath the event and to explore the region beyond the horizon, of his effort to fathom the mysteries of life and to push back the veil of ignorance. And now in the course of a few centuries an incredibly small number of men and women of genius, responding to this primal intellectual urge and employing the methods and instruments of science, tools of their own devising, have measured the heavens and recorded the birth of stars, penetrated to the innermost citadel of matter and unlocked the secrets of the atom, examined the strata of the earth and reconstructed the history of living things, studied the laws of heredity, collected the relics of the human past, dug into the ruins of buried cities, perused the documents of recorded history, mastered the symbols of forgotten languages, and painted an increasingly trustworthy picture of man's adventure on the earth. The story of this disinterested quest for knowledge and scrupulous rejection of error is one of the most glorious chapters in the history of the race.

On the other hand, science is practical and utilitarian: the most terrible of all the weapons that man has devised for the subduing of his enemies: the most powerful of all the tools that man has invented for the mastery of his environment. Science may be the fruit of man's disinterested love of truth; it is also the most ruthless and effective of all roads to power.[2] In its

2 See Bertrand Russell, *The Scientific Outlook* (New York, 1931).

applied form it is technology. It is this second conception that is uppermost in the mind of the average citizen when he grows eloquent about the "wonders of science." To him science is a dependable form of magic, a worker of miracles, a veritable Aladdin's lamp. And who, as he contemplates the triumphs of science, can take serious issue with this popular view? Allied in recent times with the genius of invention, which can be traced back to the chipping of flints and the taming of fire, science has harnessed numerous forms of energy, multiplied the productivity of nature, created strange forms of plants and animals, fabricated new substances and materials, annihilated both space and time, devised useful machines without number, and made possible the immeasurable easing of the physical burdens of mankind.

The point should be emphasized that these two aspects of science are closely interdependent. The advance of disinterested knowledge has ofttimes been promoted by the pursuit of purely practical ends. Of far more significance is the dependence of applied science and technology on the fruits of fundamental research that is indifferent to the questions of direct and immediate utility. The applications of any new principle of science are rarely apparent at once. In fact generations may have to pass before the practical importance of such a pinciple is understood. Thus the computation of the ephemerides by Regiomontanus made possible the discovery of America by Columbus, the work of Faraday the founding of the modern electro-motive industry, the researches of Maxwell and Hertz the development of the radio, and the experiments of Mendel great advances in plant and animal breeding. In the field of science, as in many other spheres of human endeavor, a narrow practicality tends toward sterility.

SOCIAL CONSEQUENCES OF SCIENCE

The influence of the advance of science on human life and institutions, as the foregoing passages suggest, is deep and far-reaching. "Of all the elements of modern culture," says Preserved Smith, "as of all the forces moulding modern life, science has been the greatest. It can be shown that all other changes in society are largely dependent upon this. Thought, philosophy, religion, art, education, laws, morals, economic institutions, are to a great extent dependent upon the progress of science. Not only does science alter the technique in the production of wealth, but it alters man's view of the world in which he lives. The world-view is perhaps the decisive factor in moulding life and civilization."[3] There is, however, no intention here of suggesting that science is an independent force operating beyond the reach of social influences and relationships, of the struggle of groups and classes, of the shifting currents of thought and aspiration. On the contrary, it is strongly conditioned by the social milieu and the total cultural apparatus.

The mere increase of the stock of impractical knowledge about the world may lead to profound social changes and disturbances. This is due to the organic character of culture. New knowledge commonly challenges established theories, arouses conflicts in the popular mind, and imperils powerful interests that may be vested in ancient error. So it was in the sixteenth century when Copernicus, Tycho Brahe, and others undermined the foundations of the prevailing geocentric theory of the universe; and again three hundred years later when Darwin and his fellow workers assaulted the accepted views regarding the process of creation and the position of man in nature. Today the researches of the physicists are having their influence on theology, philosophy, and even social theory.

While the advance of science has dispelled many groundless fears, made man secure against time-honored dangers, and immeasurably increased his power over nature, it has at the same time introduced an element of grave instability into his world. In dispelling fears it has crushed the hopes with which the fears

[3] Preserved Smith, *A History of Modern Culture* (New York, 1930), I, 17.

were joined; in removing dangers it has destroyed the faiths that made life significant; in increasing power it has brought into question the purposes toward which power might be directed. To the scientific mind nothing is certain, nothing is final, nothing is sacred: all things are in flux, all conclusions are tentative, all values are functions of time and circumstance. Even the most firmly established truths may be repudiated tomorrow. Under the rule of science therefore no solid rock of belief can remain to which man may cling in time of either fortune or adversity, unless it be the method of science itself. On its practical side, moreover, science is adding to man's spiritual unrest by perpetually altering the physical conditions of life. In fact it is today engaged in drawing the outlines of a civilization that is radically unlike the great historic civilizations from which men have received their major institutions, ideals, and philosophies—a civilization that undergoes rapid and continuous change, that puts its faith in progress rather than stability, that is always characterized by a condition of extreme uncertainty, and yet that does remove many of the insecurities of the past. The practical triumphs of science, the changes that follow in the wake of the test-tube and the calculus, are related elsewhere in this volume.[4]

The consequences of scientific and technological advance are of course by no means to be regarded as necessarily and inevitably beneficent. Innumerable instances to the contrary might be cited. Science has made war so frightful and deadly that a conflict on a world scale today might literally destroy great nations and cause civilization to decay or sink back through the centuries. Even in the sphere of economic affairs, where only desirable results might reasonably be expected, the advance of science may bring misery rather than happiness. The expression "technological unemployment" has recently been coined to designate the displacement of men by machines in the making of goods. During the eight-year period from

[4] See above Part One, Chapter III, "Technology."

1919 to 1927 the number of productive workers in the fields of agriculture, mining, manufacturing, and transportation decreased by 1,894,000. Also the growth of the power to produce, because of technical improvements, seems to be partly responsible, under the existing economic system, for those great convulsions which periodically shake the economic structure of the world, throw millions of men out of work, and bring suffering to vast populations. Finally, the charge has been made that the spread of science and the scientific mind from one area to another leads inevitably to the standardization, mechanization, and de-humanization of life. Some students therefore have predicted that science, if unchecked or uncontrolled by higher ethical purposes, will bring grief and disaster to mankind.

Whether such gloomy prophecies are to be fulfilled probably depends on the desires of men. From one standpoint science is just a great new force let loose in the world: like the rays of the sun or the tides of the sea it is neither good nor bad: it stands ready to serve any master; it merely awaits the harness. With the help of science man may by pressing a button start a conflagration that will consume the world; or in similar fashion he may inaugurate a series of changes that will give substance to the highest conceptions of security, justice, and beauty. As a consequence, the question of the place of science in society —how it is organized, supported, and controlled—has become a crucial issue of modern times. To this question, as it pertains to the United States, the remainder of the chapter will be devoted.

RESEARCH FACILITIES

The magnitude of the present program of scientific research is revealed by the material support which it receives. How extensive the support may be, however, is a question that cannot be answered with precision because of the vast range of institutions and agencies involved. The absence of any comprehensive and inclusive program, the lack of a generally acceptable definition of the nature of scientific work, and strangely enough, the failure of a society that proudly claims to be founded on science to make a study of science itself as a social manifestation. A commonly accepted estimate for the period immediately preceding the depression beginning in 1929, however, places the total expenditure in the United States for this purpose at $200,000,000 a year. While this is not a large sum in a country that spends its billions on liquor, tobacco, and automobiles, it represents a development almost exclusively of the last two generations. Also, according to estimates, scientific inquiry engages the services of more than 35,000 investigators.

The work of research is carried on for the most part by four different agencies or sets of agencies: the federal government, the colleges and universities, the great foundations, and private industry. A brief account of the activities conducted under each of these four auspices will give a fairly clear picture of the growth and organization of scientific research in the United States.

The Federal Government. In the course of the years the federal government has interested itself more and more in the promotion of research. At present approximately one-third of the $200,000,000 devoted annually to scientific investigation is provided by the government at Washington. While this constitutes only the smallest portion of the national budget, it represents a comparatively large contribution to the advancement of knowledge. It also bespeaks the multifarious interests of the government in research. Practically every federal department or bureau carries on some line of inquiry that might be labelled scientific. Although much of this work is no doubt of little permanent worth and most of it is devoted to rather narrowly practical ends, some research of great value to the nation and to the cause of science is being done.

A consideration of the interest of the federal government in the promotion and utilization of science may well begin with the Smithsonian Institution. Although this agency is only quasi-public in character and does not represent the earliest concern of the nation in science, the conditions attending its establishment have given it a peculiar significance. According to William Howard Taft,[5] it should be regarded as the parent of American science. Also it has a long record of public service that might well be emulated by all governmental agencies.

The Smithsonian Institution was founded by a bequest of James Smithson, a direct descendant on his mother's side of King Henry VII and an English chemist and mineralogist of repute. Although he never visited the United States and lived in an age when Englishmen of his social rank prophesied the inevitable collapse of democratic institutions, at his death in 1829 he left his entire fortune of $515,169 "to the United States of America, to found at Washington under the name of Smithsonian Institution, an establishment for the increase and diffusion of knowledge among men." After extended discussion and controversy the Institution was chartered by act of Congress in 1846.[6]

In terms of present-day resources this original endowment, even with the additions made immediately by the government which brought the total to $1,000,000, seems extremely modest. Yet with this sum, which under careful management and through the receipt of several relatively small gifts amounted to about $1,300,000 in 1924, the Institution has left a deep impress on American life and thought. In one capacity or another it has received the services of many illustrious scientists—men like Joseph Henry, Spencer Fullerton Baird, Louis Agassiz, Asa Gray, and Ales Hrdlicka. Also it has given grants to Morley to determine the relative atomic weights of oxygen and hydrogen; to Michelson to measure the standard meter in wave-lengths of light; to Schuman to study the ultra-violet

[5] William Howard Taft, "Smithsonian Institution—Parent of American Science," *Science* (February 25, 1927), LXV, 191–194.
[6] Carl Russell Fish, *The Rise of the Common Man* (New York, 1927), 239.

rays; to Goddard to perfect the high-flying rocket; and to other distinguished investigators. The activities of the Institution range from fur-seal investigation in the North Pacific, geological research in the Altai Mountains of Siberia and Mongolia, and studies of the flora of Latin America, to extensive co-operative work with the Bureau of Plant Industry, the Biological Survey, the Forestry Bureau, the Fish Commission, the Geological Survey, and numerous other branches of the United States government. So generally has it won the public confidence that for many years the National Museum, the National Art Gallery, the National Zoological Park, the Bureau of American Ethnology, the International Exchange Service, the Astrophysical Observatory, and the Regional Bureau of the International Catalogue of Scientific Literature have all been entrusted to its administration. In many other ways the influence of the Smithsonian Institution has extended far beyond the use of its own funds.[7]

The largest single appropriation of the federal government for research goes to the Department of Agriculture which was established by act of Congress on May 15, 1862, "to acquire and diffuse among the people of the United States useful information on subjects concerned with agriculture in the most general and comprehensive sense of the word.'" For the fiscal year ending June 30, 1931, more than $17,000,000, or approximately 26 per cent of the departmental budget, was assigned to research. The uses to which this sum was put may be indicated by listing the more important divisions of the department. The major units through which it discharges its numerous functions are the Weather Bureau, the Bureau of Animal Industry, the Bureau of Dairy Industry, the Bureau of Plant Industry, the Forest Service, the Bureau of Chemistry and Soils, the Bureau of Entomology, the Bureau of Biological Survey, the Bureau of Public Roads, the Bureau of Agricultural

[7] See C. G. Abbott, "The Smithsonian Institution at Work," *Review of Reviews* (June, 1924), LXIX, 635–641.

Economics, the Bureau of Home Economics, the Plant Quarantine and Control Administration, the Grain Futures Administration, and the Food, Drug, and Insecticide Administration. The department also maintains an information and library service, co-operates with the forty-eight states in the co-ordination of research and the organization of agricultural extension, and conducts experimental stations and laboratories at many points in the United States and in Alaska, Hawaii, Porto Rico, Guam, and the Virgin Islands. In spite of many shortcomings the department has undoubtedly contributed greatly to the advancement and diffusion of knowledge in the fields of agricultural production, forestry, food chemistry and bacteriology, road building, rural engineering, and meteorology.

A second major division of the federal government, which has been interested in research on a large scale, is the Department of Commerce. Organized as an independnt department by act of Congress approved on March 4, 1913, its one concern has been the promotion of American business at home and abroad. Since business is the most powerful political force in the country, the work of this department assumes especial significance. For the fiscal year ending June 30, 1931, its expenditures amounted to $61,477,117.63.[8] Of this sum almost eight and one-half millions were devoted to activities that may be classified as research. Although the department includes such important sections as the Bureau of Census, the Patent Office, the Coast and Geodetic Survey, the Bureau of Mines, the Bureau of Fisheries, and eight other branches of service, attention will be directed altogether to the work of the Bureau of Standards, from the standpoint of research the most important of the thirteen divisions of the department and certainly one of the most significant developments in the whole sphere of government.[9]

[8] *Annual Report of the Secretary of the Treasury on the State of Finances for the Fiscal Year Ended June 30, 1913* (Washington, 1931), 574.

[9] Under the administration of Franklin D. Roosevelt the work of the Department of Commerce has been considerably curtailed. Whether this marks a permanent change of policy remains to be seen.

The Bureau of Standards[10] was established by act of Congress on March 3, 1901. First associated with the Treasury Department, in 1903 it was transferred to the Department of Commerce and Labor and ten years later to the newly created Department of Commerce. In essence it is a great scientific and technical laboratory designed to serve the various departments of the government and the industries of the country. It is housed in ten major and seventeen minor buildings, owns a highly specialized scientific library of 31,000 volumes, subscribes to some 730 technical periodicals, receives an annual appropriation of more than $3,000,000, and employs a staff of 1066 persons (June, 1931), of whom about one-half are scientists trained in physics, chemistry, and engineering. It works in the closest possible co-operation with industry and places its findings at the disposal of industry. One of its most interesting functions is a broad program of testing that embraces practically every conceivable type of commodity to be found on the retail or wholesale market, except food and drugs and a few products covered by other bureaus. In the course of a single year the bureau makes more than 170,000 tests; and on the basis of its findings specifications are drawn and federal purchases made. The resulting savings to the government have been estimated at $100,000,000 per annum.

A third great agency through which the federal government conducts important research is the Public Health Service. In the fiscal year of 1931 this branch of the federal administration, which operates under the jurisdiction of the Secretary of the Treasury, expended more than $12,000,000[11] on scientific inquiry. Clearly the American government, in its support of research, is but reflecting the temper of the age. And the fact that this interest is for the most part a development of the last

[10] *National Bureau of Standards: Its Functions and Activities,* Circular of the Bureau of Standards, No. 1 (Washington, 1925), 14–15.

[11] *Annual Report of the Secretary of the Treasury on the State of Finances for the Fiscal Year, Ended June 30, 1931* (Washington, 1931), 272.

generation would seem to indicate the beginning of an important social trend.

Colleges and Universities. What proportion of the 677 four-year colleges and universities of the country are engaging in scientific research of a serious character is a difficult question to answer. The fact that they all have aspirations in this direction, that they commonly rate themselves according to the number of faculty members holding a research degree of the higher rank, and that many of them publish annually extended lists of studies and researches completed by the staff during the year, suggests a very general devotion to science. But the immaturity of the student mind, the heavy teaching schedule, and other arduous duties associated with the conduct of the higher learning in America make sustained thought and research all but impossible in the great majority of colleges and universities.

A special difficulty to be encountered in any effort to appraise the resources and activities of the academic world in the United States is the tradition of institutional autonomy which has taken deep root in American education.[12] The colleges and universities of the country follow no comprehensive and co-ordinated program of scientific investigation. Ordinarily each school goes its own way without much regard for what its sister institutions are doing, except to enter into competition with them for students, faculty, and funds. Here the doctrines of *laissez-faire* reign almost undisturbed. Under such circumstances any precise statement of what the colleges and universities are doing in the sphere of research lies outside the realm of possibility.

Some things, however, may be said. The great colleges, technical schools, and universities, of which there are more than a score, are the most important centers of scientific endeavor in the country. Although they are often hampered by tradition, by the limitations of the academic mind, and by the inhibitions

12 See above, Part Two, Chapter V, "Education."

placed upon them by powerful social forces operating through legislative bodies, boards of trustees, and the thirst for rich endowments, they are on the whole far more disinterested and farsighted in their outlook than any other agency of scientific inquiry in the nation. These institutions, moreover, are not only the major dependence of the country for the training of scientists; they are also the chief centers for the prosecution of research in the fundamental sciences. It has been estimated that of the 5500 or 6000 persons working in these fields approximately 5000 are to be found in the universities. Although this is a relatively small number in comparison with the 30,000 devoting their energies to the more practical aspects of science, they are conducting the researches from which the applications of the future will be derived. These institutions, moreover, are contributing directly to the advance of applied science. In 1928 at least 190 college laboratories were engaged to a considerable extent in industrial research and commercial testing.[13]

In a recent study[14] of the funds available in the United States for support and encouragement of research in science and its technologies, the National Research Council lists a total of 235 organizations. In conducting the inquiry the council canvassed every organization mentioned in the Handbook of Scientific and Technical Societies in the United States; every university or college reporting research funds to the American Council on Education; every foundation with scientific interest listed in the Russell Sage Foundation's pamphlet on American Foundations; and all miscellaneous organizations reported in magazines or newspapers as having research funds. No accurate statement, however, of the amount of money spent annually for scientific research in the United States is possible on the basis of the study. This is due to the fact that many organizations declined

[13] W. A. Hamor, "Industrial Research," *Encyclopædia Britannica*, 14th edition (New York, 1929), XIX, 206.
[14] *Funds Available in the United States for the Support and Encouragement of Research in Science and Its Technologies*, Bulletin of the National Research Council, No. 66 (Washington, 1928).

to state the amount of their resources; that many were unable to separate the part used for research from that used for administration; and that others reported the amount of the principal but not the annual expenditure. Nevertheless the inquiry shows a deep and widespread interest on the part of colleges and universities in the promotion of research in both the sciences and the technologies.

Private Foundations. That the private foundation, characteristic product of American capitalism, should manifest interest in the promotion of scientific inquiry is entirely natural, because this institution is as varied in its purposes as the tastes of captains of industry. As Frederick P. Keppel has said, "American foundations range . . . in purpose from some objective of more than parochial narrowness, as, for example, to provide the services of a brass band upon the anniversary of the donor's death, all the way to the promotion of 'the well-being of mankind throughout the world.' "[15] The interest in science, however, is a major one. An investigation[16] of the work of 122 foundations in the United States in 1930 controlling capital funds amounting to approximately $950,000,000 shows the physical sciences occupying third place, being surpassed by only medicine and education. In the year of the inquiry these sciences received 9.2 per cent of the total appropriations of the foundations, or almost $5,000,000.

In the promotion of research the foundations have followed two major policies. On the one hand, they have founded special institutes, each with its own permanent staff, to prosecute inquiry along certain lines; on the other, they have subsidized for longer or shorter periods particular projects or lent their support to existing institutions. Perhaps the best examples of the first of these policies are the Rockefeller Institute for Medical Research in New York City and the Carnegie Institution

---

[15] Frederick P. Keppel, *The Foundation* (New York, 1930), 7.
[16] The Twentieth Century Fund, *American Foundations and Their Fields* (New York, 1931).

of Washington. In agencies of this kind approximately 500 scientists are engaged in fundamental research. Owing to the fact that the second of the two institutions mentioned is dominated by the broader purpose, it will be briefly examined as illustrative of the type. Thereafter something will be said about the second method of promoting research.

The Carnegie Institution of Washington was founded by Andrew Carnegie on January 28, 1902, and provided with an endowment of $10,000,000. To this amount $2,000,000 was added in 1907 and $10,000,000 in 1910. At various times and under diverse conditions other funds have been received until the total endowment is now estimated at $30,000,000. The purpose of the institution, as set forth in the articles of incorporation, is "to encourage, in the broadest and most liberal manner, investigation, research, and discovery, and the application of knowledge to the improvement of mankind."[17] Under this broad mandate research of a fundamental character is being conducted in the following major fields: embryology, genetics and eugenics, nutrition and vitamin chemistry, plant biology, marine biology, geophysics, seismology, terrestrial magnetism, and astronomy. The institution has its grounds, buildings, laboratories, libraries, equipment, and permanent staff. In addition to supporting its own staff it gives aid to selected investigators working in their own libraries and laboratories.

The second method which the foundations have employed in the promotion of research, that of subsidizing projects and institutions, has been followed very extensively. In fact the great part of the funds which these agencies devote to the advancement of their varied interests is first distributed to other agencies or persons. Of the 122 foundations studied by the Twentieth Century Fund, 94 employed this method, whereas only 47 engaged in the direct operation of services. While no record is available to show precisely how the $5,000,000 assigned

---

[17] *Carnegie Institution of Washington,* Year Book No. 19, 1920 (Washington, 1921), x.

in 1930 to the physical sciences was distributed, most of it undoubtedly went to the great universities and research institutes. It is known that, aside from a heavy subsidy of the physical sciences in general, biology received most generous support. There followed in descending order physics, astronomy, chemistry, zoology, botany, and geology. Although the type of control over research exercised by foundations established by men of great wealth may be subject to serious question, that much excellent work in the physical sciences has been done under the auspices of these institutions is undoubtedly true.

Business and Industry. During the past generation industrial research, as carried on by private enterprise, has developed at a phenomenal rate. According to Maurice Holland, scientific research in industry in the United States was "almost an unknown thing in 1900."[18] Today the country is literally dotted with industrial research laboratories, most of which are maintained under private auspices. At the beginning of the Great War there were probably about 375 such laboratories in the United States. By 1927 the number had increased to 1000 and by 1931 to 1620. The majority of these agencies are the property of individual companies; many others, perhaps three or four hundred, are commercial consulting laboratories used by firms that do not have research facilities of their own. Then, as already noted, extensive co-operation between private enterprise and government departments and bureaus has been developed. The Bureau of Standards, the Bureau of Chemistry and Soils, the Bureau of Mines, and the Public Health Service particularly have fostered the growth of this relationship. Also the colleges and universities have been drawn rapidly into the field. Private industry has established increasingly close connections with these institutions. In the chemical industry alone some seventy individual companies are making research grants

[18] Maurice Holland, *Industrial Explorers* (New York, 1928), 24.

to the higher schools of the country. In addition, numerous trade associations promote research of some kind by co-operating with governmental agencies, sending investigators to special institutes, supporting fellowships and scholarships in colleges and universities, making use of commercial laboratories, and founding laboratories of their own.[19]

The scale on which American industry is organizing and becoming dependent on research may be illustrated by reference to the Bell Telephone laboratories and the laboratories of the Eastman Kodak Company. The former represent the most extensive research program undertaken by any private enterprise in the United States. Their history, moreover, is the history of the growth of industrial research in the country. In 1875, before the invention of the telephone, Alexander Graham Bell was investigating the problems of electrical communication in a corner of a Boston workshop. Thus were founded the laboratories which bear his name and which have been maintained continuously ever since. They were operated as a department of the American Telephone and Telegraph Company of Boston until 1907 when for practical purposes they were transferred to the Western Electric Company, the manufacturing unit of the Bell System. In January 1925 they were incorporated under the joint ownership of the American Telephone and Telegraph Company and the Western Electric Company. From a corner in a workshop in Boston they have expanded into a group of buildings in the vicinity of 463 West Street, New York City, with a floor space of more than 1,000,000 square feet. Also in numerous scattered and distant locations, specialized laboratory units are operated to take advantage of differing geographical and weather conditions. In the present spacious quarters the most elaborate equipment is housed and 4600 physicists, chemists, metallurgists, engineers, and experts in various fields of technical endeavor work together to disclose the secrets underlying the progress of telephony. In 1930

[19] W. A. Hamor, *op. cit.,* 206–207.

this vast research project was being supported at the rate of $19,000,000 a year.[20]

The laboratories of the Eastman Kodak Company also hold a significant place among the industrial laboratories of the country. They date from 1886 when George Eastman employed a young chemist to devote his time entirely to experimentation. According to the records, this young man was the first trained chemist to be engaged by an American manufacturer to devote himself wholly to research with no time limits on his efforts. The result was a discovery in 1889 that laid the foundations of the modern film industry—the use of camphor in a nitro-cellulose solution to produce a transparent flexible film on which the emulsion could be coated. In 1913 the research laboratories proper were established with a building containing 19,000 square feet of floor space and a staff of twenty persons. By 1922 three additional adjacent buildings had been taken over, making a total of 40,000 square feet, and the staff had grown to 120. In 1931 a new seven-story building was erected with 273 rooms and 93,000 square feet of floor space. In that year the staff numbered more than 200 chemists, physicists, and photographic technologists, of whom approximately 100 held university degrees. As a result of the development of about forty-five years the Eastman Kodak Company now has a group of trained scientists working on the theory of photography, the development of new photographic apparatus, materials, and processes, the study of the physical and chemical properties of gelatine and cellulose, and the production of synthetic organic chemicals.[21]

It would be interesting to follow the development of other great research laboratories, maintained by private industry, particularly the General Electric Company's research laboratory with its staff of approximately 450 investigators, the Gen-

20 See *Bell Telephone Laboratories,* Bureau of Publications, Bell Telephone Laboratories (New York, December, 1930).

21 Walter Clark, "Eastman Chemical Research," *The Chemist* (January, 1932), IX, 14.

eral Motors research laboratories with their 384 employees grouped into twelve sections and three departments, the B. S. Goodrich Company's laboratories with their staff of over 300 chemists, engineers, and assistants, and the Goodyear Tire and Rubber Company's laboratories with a force of more than 500 persons. But the two great systems of laboratories already examined will suffice to give some idea of the nature and scope of an important form of scientific research which has developed almost entirely in a single generation.

Within the field of industrial research, however, there is one institution which merits description because of its influence and unique character. Reference is made to the Mellon Institute, founded at the University of Pittsburgh in 1911 and permanently organized in 1913 when Andrew and Richard Mellon gave something more than a half million dollars for the establishment of an institution designed to bring about a more intimate alliance between science and industry. One-half of the gift was used to erect a building in honor of the donors; the balance went to form a permanent endowment fund. In the autumn of 1930 work was started on a new building which will cover practically a whole city block and provide "eight working floors." The institute is now sufficiently endowed to bear all expenses associated with its conduct, except the salaries of investigators or fellows, who come to its laboratories as the representatives or employees of various manufacturers. Thus through a system of so-called fellowships the unsurpassed research equipment of the institute is placed at the service of private industry. During the period from 1911 to 1930 approximately 3500 companies have benefited directly, either as individuals or as members of industrial associations, by work carried out under this system. Without doubt the institute has been a most effective agency in the promotion of industrial research of the more practical type in the United States.[22]

[22] Harry Knowles, "Blazing a Trail for the Industries," *Scientific American* (September 2, 1916), CXV, 206. Also Lawrence W. Bass, "Research at the Mellon Institute during 1929–30," *Science* (May 30, 1930), LXXI, 561–562.

THE PROGRAM OF RESEARCH

The rapid growth of scientific inquiry during the past generation, the large sums of money devoted to the prosecution of research, and the large number of persons, institutions, and agencies engaged in the advancement of knowledge all suggest a great and growing interest on the part of the American people in this fundamental division of human endeavor. The situation, however, cannot be fully presented in these terms. Of more importance for society than the extent of research facilities is the question of the purposes toward which the research is directed and the further question of the efficiency with which the facilities are made to function. Both of these questions will be examined.

Dominant Purposes.[23]   It is well known that when science serves American business it serves first of all the purposes for which business is commonly conducted in the United States. The central and controlling purpose of business, in whatever phrases it may be clothed, is the pursuit of private gain. This means that when science is brought into the pay of business, it becomes immediately devoted, not to the disinterested search for truth nor to the promotion of the common good, but rather to the discovery of knowledge that will be commercially valuable and that will be to the pecuniary advantage of the owners of industry. That this is inevitable under the present organization of the economic life would seem to be fairly obvious. To be sure, in the degree that the interests of society and of private enterprise are in harmony, no hurtful consequences should flow from the control of research by industry. But a condition of even relatively close harmony does not and cannot exist. On the contrary, the conflicts are deep-seated and abiding.

One of the first consequences of placing the conduct of scientific research in the hands of private industry is the practice of

[23] For the data on which this section is based we are indebted to a very large degree to Mr. F. J. Schlink, Director of Consumers' Research, who permitted us to use his own personal files, as well as those of the organization.

secrecy—a practice that is hostile to the whole spirit of science. In an address at the Congress of Technology, held at the Massachusetts Institute of Technology on April 10th and 11th, 1911, to celebrate the fiftieth anniversary of the founding of the institute, Professor William H. Walker outlined the situation. He pointed to the tendency on the part of captains of industry to revive the spirit of alchemy. In part his statement reads as follows:

"They [captains of industry] still strive to transmute the base materials of the earth into gold. But where the alchemist was satisfied only with seeing the noble metal glittering in his alembic, the modern business man is content in obtaining from his still a treasury certificate. . . . Wherein have modern methods of alchemy changed from those of that eminent scholar who bore the name Phillipus Aureolus Theophrastus Bombastus von Hohenheim? . . . The great and insurmountable obstacle to progress was nothing more than the jealous secrecy engendered by selfish competition. Both confidence and cooperation were entirely wanting. Each one feared that his neighbor might profit by his experience were it to become known, never realizing that he must in the end get much more in return than he gave. . . . In applied chemical research the spirit of alchemy tends to creep in. The builder keeps his materials of construction, and his designs, a secret, and so boards up his bridge that those who cross over it cannot see how it was built, nor profit by his experience. The moment a thing becomes useful we become jealous of its possession; we become narrow in our horizon; we sell our scientific birthright for a mess of pottage; we become alchemists."[24]

Although this statement was made some twenty years ago, it is still substantially true. The captains of industry, however, are not to be accused of selfishness. They are merely playing

[24] William H. Walker, "The Spirit of Alchemy in Modern Industry," *Science* (June 16, 1911), XXXIII, 913–918.

the game according to the rules laid down by the inherited economic order—an order that makes survival dependent on as-
siduous devotion to one's own private interests. Consider the
case of the Mellon Institute, which probably represents the
finest development of research in industry. Here is an institution with magnificent equipment and laboratories, founded
by American philanthropy, yet the research conducted within
its walls must serve the interests of private enterprise. Since
each fellow, as the investigator is called, is in the pay of a particular manufacturer or group of manufacturers, all discoveries
which he makes during the period of his fellowship are the
property of the concern or concerns providing his salary. In its
official publication the institute is very emphatic and unequivocal on this point:

"The Institute furnishes laboratory, library, and consulta-
tive facilities, the use of its permanent research equipment, direction to the progress of the work, and an environment that
stimulates productive investigation. All results obtained by
the Industrial Fellowship are the property of its donor.

"Each Industrial Fellowship is a case of trust and is operated
in strict accordance with the terms of the agreement governing
its operation. . . . Information pertaining to its subject matter
and progress is not released to the public unless the donor so
desires. Further, the knowledge gained by one Industrial Fellow along one investigational line becomes available to another
man, *provided such co-operation does not violate a trust.*

"The Institute has a tried system of reporting, and all records,
reports and correspondence are given secure guardianship.

"Reports on progress made and difficulties encountered are
submitted weekly from each Industrial Fellowship to the executive staff. These private reports are considered for purposes
of advice and guidance and serve to record all research observations and results. Confidential monthly reports are transmitted to the donors, and yearly summary reports are prepared
and placed in the archives of the Institute, to be released for

publication at such times as will not injure the interests of the donors. The Institute has definite instructions governing the preparation of all types of reports. Scientific or technical papers are not prepared for publication without the consent and approval of the donor concerned. Moreover, the donor decides as to whether patent protection shall be sought for new processes or products that are developed."[25]

An enthusiastic observer, in reporting the practice of the institute, has unwittingly revealed the extent to which the spirit of science may be violated when science is made to serve private interests: "Industrialists are naturally jealous of their trade secrets; whatever they impart to the chemists must never be disclosed, lest irreparable injury result. So it is a rigid rule at the institute that no fellow shall ever inquire what his associates are doing, though they may weigh chemicals on the same balances, work at the same table, and even take advantage of one another's specialized knowledge by consultation about perplexing matters. Since the institute has been in operation there has never been occasion to question the adherence of any member to this standard of honor."[26] Scientists of course know nothing of any such "standard of honor"; neither do they have experience of "irreparable injury" resulting from the disclosing of information. On the contrary, science thrives on the freest exchange of ideas and publication of findings. Yet under the present regime of industry the Mellon Institute is constrained by the necessities of the case to pursue its present course. If it were to follow the established traditions of science, it would find itself without investigators.

This guarding of private property interests through secrecy sometimes takes the extreme form of deliberate suppression of knowledge or invention. If the results of scientific inquiry are put to use, the practice of secrecy, while still hampering the

[25] Mellon Institute of Industrial Research, *Industrial Fellowships* (Pittsburgh, 1924), 8–9.
[26] Harry Knowles, *op. cit.*, 206.

development of technology, would merely make possible the maintenance of monopoly prices. The suppression of knowledge, however, has far more serious consequences. The efficiency of an industry may be kept at a lower level than is necessary over a considerable period of time. "There are countless numbers of patents," says Chief Clerk Woolard of the United States Patent Office, "which, if in operation, would much cheapen the articles they could produce, but they are intentionally shelved to prevent competition. Concerns operating under old inventions for which they have expended great sums to erect plants, buy up these new and cheaper methods to prevent competitors from getting hold of them. They then tuck them away in their safes, never to be used."[27] The temptation to suppression seems to be particularly strong in the case of discoveries which may greatly lengthen the life of a commodity and thus restrict the market. According to the testimony of competent students, fabrics, common tools, and even automobiles might be made of far more durable materials than those that are employed at the present time. Indeed the ingenuity and extended training of investigators may be taxed to devise the formulæ of substances that make an excellent first impression but deteriorate rapidly.[28]

The most extreme case of the violation of the free spirit of inquiry through the operation of the profit motive is probably found in the sphere of advertising. Here practices abound that can only be described in terms of the degradation of science.[29] Instances without number can be found in newspapers and magazines and on the billboards that mar the natural beauties of the public highways. In the New York *Times* of Thursday, July 7, 1932, there appears a great half-page advertisement, entitled: SCIENCE PICKS BEST CIGARETTE; OLD GOLD WINS FROM ALL RIVALS. In the center of the advertisement is the reproduc-

---

[27] Quoted in Stuart Chase, *The Tragedy of Waste* (New York, 1925), 204.
[28] The razor blade is a case in point.
[29] See T. Swan Harding, *The Degradation of Science* (New York, 1931).

tion of a photograph of a laboratory in which five "scientists" are presumably guiding and following the results of an experiment. The expression which the photographers have caught on the faces of these men intimates that the future of science, and even of civilization, hangs in the balance. Indeed, the suggestion conveyed is that one of the most momentous discoveries of the ages is about to be disclosed. Also, without giving names, the advertisement states that "the scientists of two leading universities have checked these tests."[30] Such prostitution of a great and noble tradition, a tradition honored with the names of Aristotle, Lucretius, Bacon, Galileo, Harvey, Newton, Lavoisier, Faraday, and Darwin, is possible only in a society that is thoroughly saturated with the spirit of commercialism. Perhaps the climax was reached recently when American firms dealing in disinfectants, toilet waters, haberdashery, musical instruments, clothing, and other products, offered large sums of money to Albert Einstein on his visit to the United States, if he would only consent to sign his name to statements that he had used the articles and found them satisfactory. His comment[31] on this effort to make profit out of an illustrious name reveals the breadth of the chasm that separates science from the counting house: "Is it not a sad commentary upon the commercialism and, I must add, the corruption of our time that business firms make these offers with no thought of wanting to insult me?"

In somewhat less overt fashion science also tends to serve business through the departments and bureaus of the federal government.[32] At any rate it refuses to be single-minded in its devotion to the broader and more inclusive social interests.[33]

[30] If this is true, it constitutes an interesting commentary on the scientific integrity of the universities involved.

[31] The New York *Times,* November 23, 1930.

[32] See F. J. Schlink, "Government Bureaus for Private Profit," *Nation* (November 11, 1931), CXXXIII, 508–511.

[33] Following the change of federal administrations in March, 1933, some steps have been taken which suggest that the interests of the consumer may receive more consideration than in the past.

By legislative enactment[34] the scientific and technical research facilities of various governmental organs have been put at the disposal of American industry for the past thirty-five years under the Research Associate Plan. The Bureau of Chemistry and Soils and the Forest Products Laboratory of the Department of Agriculture and the Bureau of Mines of the Department of Commerce conduct research on behalf of private firms. The research laboratory of the American Society of Heating and Ventilating Engineers, heavily dominated by business interests, is located in the Pittsburgh station of the Bureau of Mines. In 1929 the American Gas Association and twenty-eight companies representing the electrical, mining, and metallurgical industries were supporting jointly ten research studies in mining and metallurgy at the Carnegie Institute of Technology in co-operation with this same governmental division. There are also research associates in the Public Health Service of the Department of the Treasury. But probably the most intimate connection between government and industry is maintained by the Bureau of Standards. According to the report of the Director,[35] ninety-seven research associates representing thirty-eight industrial associations and individual firms were stationed in the various laboratories of the bureau in 1931. Under this plan of co-operation, which is rightly regarded as aiding American business,[36] a manufacturer or an association of manufacturers places at the bureau a graduate physicist, chemist, or engineer to conduct an investigation along some particular line. Upon appointment the research associate, as he is called, is assigned to the appropriate division and assumes the status of an employee of the bureau, except that his salary is derived from private sources. He is also given access in the bureau

34 W. A. Hamor, *op. cit.*, 206–207.

35 *Annual Report of the Director of the Bureau of Standards to the Secretary of Commerce for the Fiscal Year ended June 30, 1931*, Miscellaneous Publication, No. 131 (Washington, 1931).

36 G. K. Burgess, "What the Bureau of Standards is Doing for American Industry," *Industrial Management* (November, 1925), LXX, 257–263.

to information that is denied the consumer. The results of his investigations are immediately made available to the supporting firm or firms. They may or may not be reported to the general industry through the official channels of the bureau.

All of this may seem entirely pointless. Yet it is axiomatic that any organ of government will inevitably fall under the influence and will accept the point of view of the interests with which it is in perpetual association. This is clearly reflected in the policies of the Bureau of Standards. Although innumerable brands and makes of goods found on the retail market are tested in the laboratories of the bureau, this vast store of useful information is not available to the general public. When a certain private citizen in his capacity as a consumer wrote to the bureau in July of 1931 asking about the relative merits of particular makes of fire extinguishers, he received the following reply from a member of the staff: "I regret that I cannot give you a recommendation as to particular makes of fire extinguishers to be preferred for certain services, since it is contrary to the policy of the Bureau of Standards for its employees to give out such information either officially or privately." Indeed a distinguished investigator in the employ of the bureau wrote in a private letter on November 16, 1926: "Now, I cannot, as you know, commit the bureau to any opinion on how the buyer is to be informed. We would last a week or less if we published the results of tests." In making its own purchases the government endeavors to protect itself against the misrepresentations of the market place, but it refuses to render this service to the public.[37] Such a policy is of course easily intelligible. American industry, having become dependent on high-pressure salesmanship and advertising, would find itself completely demoralized and forced to seek new foundations, if the objective light of science or even of disinterested informed judgment were permitted to play upon

[37] See Stuart Chase and F. J. Schlink, *Your Money's Worth* (New York, 1927), Chapter XI.

its products. At no point in the entire economy does the rationality of technology expose more clearly the irrationality of inherited economic practice and thought.

This same tender regard for business enterprise may be found in the Bureau of Agricultural Economics, which would seem to have been founded primarily to guard the interests of the masses of the people. In the early part of 1932 a professor of home economics in a large state university suggested that the canned goods marketed in the country be labelled so as to give to the consumer dependable knowledge regarding grades of foods. The following excerpt from a long letter written by a representative of the bureau in reply to the suggestion outlines the position of the government in the matter:

"Consider that one inevitable effect of a general advocacy by the Department of labeling canned goods in accordance with the U. S. grades would be the exposure of the fact that almost all nationally advertised brands of canned fruits and vegetables must of necessity have been somewhat below the U. S. 'A' Grade, or 'Fancy,' and must usually be nothing more than 'Standard' or U. S. 'C' Grade, or a mixture of 'Standards' with 'Extra Standards.' . . . I think it will be obvious to you that a change in our policy with a view to bringing about the situation which you suggest, namely the placing of the grades on the labels, would be met with the most determined opposition on the part of the most powerful canning interests in the nation—those who have expended fortunes in advertising their trademarks and brands. It is of course not obvious that such opposition would have much effect on the smaller canners or those who have been unable to finance national advertising, but it is conceivable that the opposition might be so bitter that certain handlers of or brokers in canned goods might find themselves compelled to choose between handling U. S. graded goods on the one hand and nationally advertised goods on the other; and you will realize that few dealers will wish to be deprived of the privilege of handling the goods which enjoy the benefit of national advertising."[38]

The curious conflict of economic interests which prevails in the United States and the relative strength of the contending parties is also well illustrated in an incident which occurred in 1931. It seems that the Public Health Service had cautioned the people by radio against overeating in hot weather and particularly against eating too much meat. Immediately meat packers and large stock associations registered vigorous protests with the Secretary of the Treasury, who has jurisdiction over the Public Health Service, on the ground that a governmental agency has no right to interfere with business. In taking issue with the counsel of the scientists the Institute of Meat Packers addressed a letter[39] to Secretary Mellon revealing the profitable uses of cultural anthropology. "During the Arctic summers," so this memorandum read, "the Eskimo is exposed to extremely hot and disagreeable weather, but he does not change his eating habits. He continues to eat meat." As a consequence of such cogent argument and probably the use of more effective modes of persuasion, the medical men were badly worsted and ordered thereafter to submit their public utterances to the Treasury Department for censorship.[40]

Even the universities, in spite of their long tradition as champions of the spirit of science, have by no means been free from the taint of commercialism. That they should reflect the points of view and the interests of the dominant forces of the age is of course to be expected. The very fact that the controlling boards of these institutions are composed for the most part of business men would naturally tend in this direction. But the primary concern here is not with such a general and all-pervading influence. In many and subtle ways private enter-

---

[38] This letter was dated from Washington, March 4, 1932.
[39] The New York *Times*, June 7, 1931.
[40] Cf. *Editor and Publisher The Fourth Estate* (June 27, 1931), LXIV, 50.

prise strives to persuade universities and university professors, the representatives of science in the public mind, to place their stamp of approval on its products and methods. Although innumerable illustrations of this practice might be given, attention will be confined to a single instance.

Perhaps the boldest and most systematic effort ever made in American history to corrupt the educational institutions of the country was the attempt on the part of power companies during the nineteen-twenties to bring the schools and colleges of the country to the support of their program.[41] In their effort to reach teachers, professors, and superintendents of school systems they did not hesitate to use any method that promised success—flattery, coercion, entertainment, or dollars. E. R. A. Seligman, writing on behalf of the American Association of University Professors, has thus described the campaign of the power interests: "Large sums of money have been given to universities, colleges, and research institutions; grants ranging from insignificant travelling expenses to considerable annual stipends and to as much as five or ten thousand dollars for single studies have been paid to individuals; research projects have been subsidized; arrangements have been made for courses and individual lectures; advice has been given in the writing or revision of textbooks; and in various other ways there has been a close connection between public utilities and the academic profession." Although the universities as a whole came out rather well in the investigation conducted by the Federal Trade Commission, many individual instances of corrupt influence were brought to light.[42]

On the dome of the building of the National Academy of Science and National Research Council in Washington may be seen the following inscription: "To science, pilot of industry, conqueror of disease, multiplier of the harvest, explorer of the

[41] See above, Part Two, Chapter III, "Communication."
[42] For a complete account of the investigation see Ernest Gruening, *The Public Pays* (New York, 1931); Jack Levin, *Power Ethics* (New York, 1931); and Carl D. Thompson, *Confessions of the Power Trust* (New York, 1932).

universe, revealer of nature's laws, eternal guide to truth." Such an ideal, however acceptable in the abstract, can hardly be said to motivate a large part of the work which is conducted in the name of science in American industry today. In its applied phases in particular science is too often made to serve, not the high ideal here proclaimed, but the pecuniary interests of private persons and enterprises. It may even be and often is employed in the obscuring of truth, the dissemination of falsehood, and the general exploitation of the people. This condition is due to the deep-lying conflicts between public and private interests which characterize American society.

Efficiency of Research Facilities. The narrowness of purpose, the conflicts of interest are clearly reflected in the absence of any comprehensive plan of research conducted in the name of society as a whole—in the chaos, the inco-ordination, the lack of balance, the duplication of effort in the program of inquiry. In accordance with the doctrine of *laissez-faire* scientific work is carried on by thousands of different agencies each of which regards itself as more or less sovereign and in the great majority of cases pursues some special or limited end. To be sure, these weaknesses are moderated somewhat by the nature of science itself, by the tradition of free exchange of ideas, by the deliberations of numerous voluntary organizations of scientists and technologists, and by the appearance of certain practices and institutions which point toward co-ordination and co-operation. Nevertheless the contrary forces are so powerful that this charge of inefficiency is substantially true today.

One of the most characteristic features of the program of research is the disproportionate emphasis on the immediately practical and commercially profitable. Thus, of the $200,000,000 devoted annually to scientific work in the United States only about one-tenth is allocated to those forms of research that are fundamental in character and have regard for the more far-reaching interests of society. The result is a badly distorted program of investigation. As American industry skims the

cream from natural resources without thought of the morrow,
so it exploits the broad scientific principles evolved by the
scientists of the past and of other lands. While this may be due
in part to the practical temper of the people, it is certainly due
primarily to an economic regime driven by the motive of private gain. Under such a regime a particular enterprise will of
necessity invest its funds almost exclusively in research projects that will be profitable to itself and as a general rule, because
of the severity of the competition, immediately profitable.

Owing to the severe dislocation of social institutions and
modes of life occasioned by the growth of physical science and
technology, the suggestion has come from several quarters that
a moratorium be declared on scientific inquiry and invention.
The tragedy of such a suggestion lies in the fact that under the
present social organization the progress of science can be
neither halted nor utilized in the interests of the whole nation.
The American people today are confronted with the strange
anomaly of a society uniquely dependent on science and yet
lacking organization or machinery designed to develop and
control this powerful force. Until such organization or machinery is created men may fittingly debate the question as to
whether science may not have brought more of evil than of
good into the world. Today a large fraction of the population
must live in continual dread lest some new invention destroy
their means of livelihood; and the whole world trembles at
the thought of a vast international conflict waged with the
latest products of the laboratory.

The only alternative to the present policy of drift is an attempt to organize a comprehensive and balanced program of
research in the interests of society as a whole. To such a proposal the common answer is that, while it may seem desirable,
it is practically impossible. According to this view the scientific
or inventive spirit thrives only under conditions of complete
freedom. As "the wind bloweth where it listeth," so the investigator must be permitted to range freely over the universe and

explore the regions that suit his fancy. In this contention there is undoubtedly much of truth; the creative mind cannot do its best work under coercion. And yet so varied are the talents of the race and so easily are interests molded by circumstance or opportunity that a broad program of research, conceived in terms of the long-run needs of the nation, should release rather than regiment the powers of individual scientists. And it should not be forgotten that at present the abilities of vast numbers of persons are undoubtedly cramped by the narrowness and poverty and downright dishonesty of much that is done under the ægis of science. In a country as large as the United States provision could be made, within the limits of an organized program of inquiry, for the utilization of practically any really superior gift.

The recent history of invention and technology throws some light on this question. Since the establishment of the United States Patent Office by act of Congress of July 4, 1836, the status of the inventor has undergone a profound change. During the early decades of the industrial revolution and down almost to the close of the nineteenth century in America the relation between science and invention was extremely tenuous. The inventor was usually a practical man with little or no scientific training—a sort of inspired tinker, someone has called him. His method was that of trial and error, and he made small use of records. He stumbled on his discoveries or depended upon an occasional flash of insight. He developed no technique that he could pass on to his successors. Burbank in the realm of plant breeding and Edison in the field of electricity were perhaps among the last of a long and illustrious line reaching back through such men as Watt and Stephenson to the primitive artisan.

Although the old tradition that invention defies organization and must wait upon the mood of the inventor continues to prevail in the popular mind, the weight of experience is inclining overwhelmingly in the other direction. In the second half of the nineteenth century Germany demonstrated for all time the decisive superiority of organized and systematic research over the ancient and hallowed union of inspiration and rule-of-thumb. While the first aniline dye was discovered by an English chemist in 1856, the coal-tar chemical industry became German before 1890. Through the careful and thorough organization of research, for which Germany is now famous throughout the world, hundreds of coal-tar products were developed. As a consequence, "German chemical companies, soon merged into a powerful trust, exacted tribute from every textile dyer, hospital, physician, invalid, food manufacturer, baker, confectioner, and printer in the world."[43] The example set by Germany is now being assiduously followed by private enterprise in the other great industrial nations. According to Henry D. Hubbard of the Bureau of Standards, "inventions are planned and made to order with aims and methods just as definite as the planning and building of a house."

In yet another sense the history of industrial research is significant in this connection. Within the limits of a single enterprise investigation is rapidly assuming a co-operative or collective character. In a word the individual scientist seldom, if ever, works alone. On the contrary, he commonly functions as a member of a group and according to some definitely conceived plan of investigation. Problems are divided and subdivided, and their elements assigned to individuals or small groups. Everywhere in industry today therefore may be seen chemists, metallurgists, physicists, and engineers uniting in an attack upon some stubborn problem. And few indeed are the difficulties that fail to respond to such an organized offensive. The result has been systematic and steady progress in applying science to the achievement of practical ends. If this method of

[43] Waldemar Kaempffert, "Invention as a Social Manifestation," Chapter II in *A Century of Progress*, edited by Charles A. Beard (New York, 1933), 63.

planned and co-operative inquiry can be employed successfully to enhance the profits of private industry, it can be employed on a yet larger scale to promote the general well-being of the entire commonwealth.

American society, moreover, has already taken some steps in the direction of a more efficient organization of scientific research. Seventy years ago, in 1863, the National Academy of Science was granted a charter by act of Congress and the approval of President Lincoln. According to the provisions of this charter "the Academy shall, whenever called upon by any Department of the Government, investigate, examine, experiment, and report upon any subject of science or art."[44] In 1916, at the request of President Wilson, the Academy "created the National Research Council as the active agent of the Academy to assist the Government in organizing the scientific resources of the country for its need at that time."[45] A widespread conviction that the Council, though founded to meet war conditions, might also be useful in times of peace, led the President to issue an executive order on May 11, 1918, asking the Academy to perpetuate the Council and to assign the following duties, among others, to it:

"1. In general, to stimulate research in the mathematical, physical, and biological sciences, and in the application of these sciences to engineering, agriculture, medicine, and other useful arts, with the object of increasing knowledge, of strengthening the national defense, and of contributing in other ways to the public welfare.

"2. To survey the larger possibilities of science, to formulate comprehensive projects of research, and to develop effective means of utilizing the scientific and technical resources of the country for dealing with these projects.

[44] *National Research Council: Organization and Members* (Washington, 1931), 5.
[45] *Ibid.*, 6.

"3. To promote co-operation in research, at home and abroad, in order to secure concentration of effort, minimize duplication, and stimulate progress."[46]

What science might achieve in the improvement of the human lot is only vaguely suggested by its past and present accomplishments. This is particularly true in a country like the United States, where nature has concentrated so much of her wealth. But if science is to be utilized to the full, definite and deliberate provision will have to be made for the attainment of that end. Today, in spite of the many changes which science has wrought in the social order, its power is poorly directed and imperfectly used. Its inner logic, which is rational, integrated, and universal in character, is profoundly out of harmony with the present social order with its emphasis on competition, secrecy, and personal gain.

[46] *Ibid.*, 6.

Chapter VIII

ART

The trends in art in the United States must be sketched on the background of changing institutions and modes of life and in terms of the more powerful forces that have molded and conditioned American culture—the migrations to the new world, the settlement of the Atlantic seaboard, the severing of political ties with the mother country, the westward sweep of population, the spread of democratic ideas and habits, the propagation of the doctrines of *laissez-faire,* the rise of machine industry and technology, and the growth of social and economic planning. Particularly must the development of art be related to the movement from the self-contained household economy of the colonial era to the highly differentiated and closely integrated economy of today.

Such a broad social approach is necessary because art is commensurate with life. However common may be the view that art is an esoteric interest pursued by strangely gifted persons, the fact remains that it cannot be considered apart from the ordinary concerns of ordinary men and women. Every human activity possesses an artistic quality. The use of the voice, the carriage of the body, the preparation and serving of food, the making of tools and weapons, the fabrication of garments, the construction of houses, the building of roads and cities, the performance of religious rites, the conduct of government, the employment of leisure hours, and the general ordering of personal and social affairs, as well as painting and sculpture and music and poetry, each has its æsthetic side. Indeed the entire life of a people may be judged according to canons of art, according to standards of grace and charm and beauty. To confine æsthetics within limits less catholic in scope would narrow the concept unduly and condemn the artistic impulses to a measure of sterility.

FUNDAMENTAL HANDICAPS

America was long considered the Caliban of nations by both native and foreign æsthetes. The character of her people and her institutions, the very course of her history, has seemed to many to be hostile to the growth of an artistic tradition. Most of the cultural achievements of the American people have appeared immature, or imitative, or both. On the whole, their taste, when not merely slavish, has seemed crude. For generations poets, painters, and novelists were driven abroad, or remained at home to be frustrated, insulted, neglected. Henry James and Whistler went into permanent exile. Melville fell almost entirely silent before he was thirty-five. Emily Dickinson did not publish her verses. Mark Twain is said to have kept his most serious thoughts to himself. And while painting and sculpture remained undistinguished throughout the greater part of the nineteenth century, architecture and the objects of daily use sank to the very depths of bad taste between 1860 and 1880.

"We're the disinherited of art!" cried the exiled painter in Henry James' *A Madonna of the Future*. "We're condemned to be superficial! We're exiled from the magic circle! The soil of American perception is a poor little barren deposit. Yes, we're wedded to imperfection! An American, to excel, has just ten times as much to learn as a European! We lack the deeper sense. We have neither taste nor force. How should we have them? Our crude and garish climate, our silent past, our deafening present, the constant pressure about us of unlovely conditions, are as void of all that nourishes and prompts and inspires artists as my sad heart is in saying so! We poor aspirants must live in perpetual exile . . ."

This lament of a half century ago has been repeated many

times since. Although it has no doubt often been made by persons steeped in the values of a foreign culture and yearning after the patronage of a settled aristocracy, it has contained much of honesty. From the standpoint of artistic development the American people have suffered from a number of peculiar handicaps. Mention will be made of the demands of the virgin continent, the character of the settlers, the spread of democracy, and the interruption of the artistic tradition. A high development of art, say Keppel and Duffus, "demands an economic surplus, over and above the necessities of life. It also demands, or reflects, a certain stage of culture—perhaps it is not inaccurate to say a cultural surplus."[1] These surpluses were largely absent in pioneering America.

The Demands of the Virgin Continent. During his prolonged peace mission in Paris after the Revolution, John Adams wrote wistfully to his wife: "I must study politics and war that my sons may have the liberty to study mathematics and philosophy." And in order that his great grandson, he might have added, should have the opportunity of visiting the Cathedrals of France and of writing *Mont Saint Michel and Chartres,* one of the great books of æsthetic appreciation. No doubt in those earlier days many a sensitive spirit, like John Adams, was tempted to the luxury of artistic creation or philosophic speculation, and then turned back to more pressing duties. Toward the close of the eighteenth century Thomas Jefferson, in recommending the study of architecture to American youth, remarked that painting and sculpture were "too expensive for the state of wealth among us. They are worth seeing but not studying." Not until the frontier was closed and the continent more or less settled could Americans be expected to devote themselves to the refinement of life.

Meanwhile the bare necessities of living had to be won, a strange land explored, savages conquered, forests felled.

[1] Frederick P. Keppel and R. L. Duffus, *The Arts in American Life* (New York, 1933), 25.

Houses had to be built and government established. The pioneer who did not begin with severe Spartan ideals soon had them forced upon him. "He had forever to be 'up and doing,'" writes Waldo Frank. "He had no leisure to digest what he had done. By the same token, he abhorred that vicarious experience which is art. To read of the voyage of Ulysses meant to stop voyaging himself. To dwell upon the terrible loveliness of life meant first to settle down. These occupations, therefore, became temptations of the Devil. The pioneer, in order to save himself from the sheer threat of being overwhelmed by his surrounding world, needed to combat it—its loveliness and passion."[2]

Although this may be an extreme statement of the case, the frontier was undoubtedly a powerful molding force in American history. Its influence is clearly revealed in the development of art and letters, as well as in the realm of economics and politics. The first pioneers of course cleared the ground, pushed back the Indians, and established the earliest settlements; but "in their wake followed pioneers of ideas and special competence, quite as brave and worthy." Dixon Ryan Fox has indicated the stages in the evolution of professional competence: "first, when foreign practitioners of the specialty are received by the pioneer community; second, when the native youth go to the old country to attend upon instruction; third, when institutions of the special learning are established in the new land, though still dependent on the metropolis for the equipment of their teachers; fourth, when the institutions have sufficiently developed to maintain themselves."[3] It has been suggested that in great music the American people are still largely in the first stage; in painting and sculpture they are passing rapidly from the second to the third and even to the fourth stage; and in university scholarship they reached the fourth stage only at

2 Waldo Frank, *Our America* (New York, 1919), 21.
3 Dixon Ryan Fox, "Civilization in Transit," *American Historical Review* (July, 1927), XXXII, 753–754.

the end of the last century. Thus does a new country slowly attain maturity. Not until the physical basis is well established can art and letters be expected to flourish.

The Character of the Settlers. It was the English mainly who settled the United States. Not the French, the Italians, the Spanish, or the Germans, with their rich traditions in the various arts, but the English whose æsthetic genius expressed itself chiefly in literature and only to a limited degree in painting, sculpture, architecture and music. Moreover, on the whole, the English immigrants to America came from the various Protestant dissenting sects recruited from the lower social ranks. And they sought in the new land economic opportunity, as well as religious liberty. They championed a stern, industrious morality, and abhorred the idleness and luxuries of the aristocracy. On the refinements of life, as cultivated by the Anglicans or Roman Catholics, they looked with suspicion; art they considered sinful and worldly, tending to divert man from God and duty. These sober people of the English lower middle class fixed the color of American life for generations. Suzanne LaFollette has thus described their attitude to certain forms of art:

"The Colonial Puritans were blood brothers of those image breakers who desecrated the churches of England under Cromwell with such thoroughness that nothing is rarer in England today than an example of mediæval religious art. There were no images to destroy in America, but the Puritans could at least see to it that none was fashioned in those sections where their influence was paramount. They went farther, indeed. Any attempt to please the eye, they were inclined to regard as a diversion from the one purpose which they considered valid: the attempt to please God."[4]

The Puritans, however, cannot be held entirely responsible for all that is harsh, austere, and life-denying in American

[4] Suzanne LaFollette, *Art in America* (New York, 1929), 4.

culture. According to Thomas Cuming Hall, they constituted only a small minority of the original colonists and, moreover, were less "puritanical" then they have been painted. The true Puritans sprang from the more prosperous levels of society and were not uncritically opposed to art and letters. John Milton, though by no means typical, shared their general views. Strictly speaking, it was not the Puritans but the dissenting sects deriving from Wyclif that restrained the early artistic development. "Until America had given the dissenting masses money and possession," says Mr. Hall, "literature and art had little place in their rather starved imaginations. This was not the fault of either Puritanism or of America, but of the long and bitter struggle with a Normanized upper class in England, separated by both religious tradition and the possession of political power from the great body of the plain people."[5]

In spite of the passage of generations and of vast changes in mode of life, this ascetic tradition persists. If art is not to be avoided entirely, it is a residual interest—something to be taken up after "really important matters" have been cared for. It is not a common necessity but a function of galleries and auditoriums, a concern of effeminate men and old ladies. As a result of this attitude, a large part of American art has been timid and superficial, avoiding the darker, the more tragic aspects of existence. And for the same reason, the figure of the censor has always loomed over the artist to cramp his style and to enforce the traditional mores. The development of American sculpture during the nineteenth century was doubtless retarded because the use of nude models, when not forbidden, was discouraged.

The original English heritage alone might in time have created a noble literature. It would probably have done little else. Fortunately, the new country early began to welcome

[5] Thomas Cuming Hall, *The Religious Background of American Culture* (Boston, 1930), 119.

immigrants from all parts of Europe. Theodore Thomas, who
gave the first impetus to the appreciation of fine music, was a
German immigrant; Sousa, "the march king," had a Portuguese father and a Bavarian mother; Victor Herbert was an
Irishman. And today it is the Jews, from Irving Berlin to
George Gershwin, who dominate the musical stage. The rise
of the other fine arts in America owes much to non-English
stock.[6]

The Spread of Democracy. When the presidential power
passed from John Quincy Adams to Andrew Jackson, the aristocratic dignity and discrimination of New England gave way
to the boisterous and swaggering democracy of the west.
The people stormed the citadels of government. There followed the three busy decades of Jacksonian Democracy which
carried the country into the Civil War. This was "the Golden
Day" of American literature, the day of Emerson and Thoreau,
of Hawthorne and Poe, of Melville and Whitman; it was also
the day of incongruous Greek temples, some quite beautiful,
scattered indiscriminately about the country. But there was
reason to believe that the arts would suffer sorely in a country
which had no leisure class to patronize the artist and no richly
traditioned peasantry.

De Tocqueville, with his usual penetration, sensed and
gauged the forces at work. While conceding that "the example
of the Americans does not prove that a democratic people can
have no aptitude and no taste for science, literature, or art,"
he contended that a democracy does prefer the useful and the
comfortable to the true and the beautiful and that it inevitably
encourages the artisan to produce a large quantity of imperfect
commodities at a low price rather than a few fine objects at a
high price. "In the confusion of all ranks," he said, "every one
hopes to appear what he is not, and makes great exertions to
succeed in this object. . . . The hypocrisy of virtue is of every

[6] See Allen H. Eaton, *Immigrant Gifts to American Life* (New York, 1932).

age, but the hypocrisy of luxury belongs more particularly to the ages of democracy."[7]

De Tocqueville's comments on the specific arts are also worth re-reading after a hundred years. He noted the great quantity of mediocre paintings and the flimsy statues modelled in plaster. He was astonished by a number of small palaces of white marble which proved to be of whitewashed brick with columns of painted wood. The only authors whom he acknowledged as American were the journalists. "They indeed are not great writers but they speak the language of their countrymen and make themselves heard by them." He believed that the principle of equality had dried up most of the traditional springs of poetry—gods, kings and nature. Yet he found a new inspiration in the onward sweep of men toward the Pacific:

"I readily admit that the Americans have no poets; I cannot allow that they have no poetic ideas. In Europe, people talk a great deal of the wilds of America, but the Americans themselves never think about them: they are insensible to the wonders of inanimate nature, and they may be said not to perceive the mighty forests which surround them till they fall beneath the hatchet. Their eyes are fixed upon another sight: the American people views its own march across these wilds—drying swamps, turning the course of rivers, peopling solitudes, and subduing nature. This magnificent image of themselves does not meet the gaze of the Americans at intervals only; it may be said to haunt every one of them in his least as well as in his most important actions, and to be always flitting before his mind."[8]

The Interruption of the Artistic Tradition. But in time the virgin continent would be occupied, the settlers of lower middle

[7] Alexis de Tocqueville, *Democracy in America* (New York, 1898), Vol. II, 59–60.
[8] *Ibid.,* Vol. II, 90.

class origins would improve their lot, and the spirit of democracy would spend itself or seek an appropriate artistic expression. There remains a fourth factor that has followed the footsteps of the immigrants to America and their descendants from the day the first colonists embarked for Jamestown down to the present moment in their history. The evolution of their institutions has been attended by a succession of interruptions. This has given to their culture a comparatively superficial and rootless quality.

In the first place, as pointed out in an earlier chapter, the migration to America must have disturbed greatly the process of cultural growth. Since a culture in its very nature represents the delicate adjustment of a given people to a given geographical setting, many of its more subtle elements simply cannot be transported to radically different surroundings. Then in the settlement of North America, it must be remembered, there was no movement of completely organized social groups. On the contrary, the new land was peopled by individuals and families, bound together in no coherently integrated social pattern. On the average, the less successful, the less skilled in the practical as well as the humanistic arts crossed the Atlantic. Certainly few gifted artists came to the colonies. Even skilled artisans were rare, the great majority of the early settlers being yeomen and laborers. "It seems probable," Mr. and Mrs. Beard write, "that at least one-half the immigrants into America before the Revolution, certainly outside New England, were either indentured servants or Negro slaves."[9] Moreover, as the decades and generations passed, the stream of immigration became increasingly polyglot in character. All of this means that the American people, at the very beginning of their history, were forced to break many connections with the past and to develop their artistic talents amid strange surroundings.

[9] Charles A. Beard and Mary R. Beard, *The Rise of American Civilization* (New York, 1927), Vol. I, 103.

For a considerable period, after the founding of the first settlements, the colonists endeavored with a considerable measure of success to re-establish the social and cultural patterns of the old world. Well-ordered communities, based for the most part on agriculture, and sheltered by the long ridges of the Appalachians, gradually matured along the coast. Here the artistic impulses of the population found an ever finer expression in the building of homes and churches and in the making of garments, furniture, and utensils. But before this civilization, derived from farming and handicrafts, could fully establish itself, its development was interrupted. Towards the close of the eighteenth century the American people broke over the Alleghanies and within a hundred years occupied all the lands to the west. At approximately the same time they began to invent machines, build factories, and move into cities in ever-growing numbers. Consequently, except for the brief interlude of colonial times, when the tempo of life was relatively moderate, they have been perpetually on the move. They have changed not only their dwellings but also their modes of living. Not once, moreover, have they been permitted to develop a ripe civilization on any foundation. From the standpoint of artistic achievement, since great art is always the mature fruit of a long tradition, the result has been disastrous. The most heroic efforts of individuals cannot take the place of the cumulative power of the generations.

THE GROWTH OF AN ARTISTIC TRADITION

In spite of these fundamental handicaps, however, the American people did develop, slowly but steadily, a fine artistic tradition during their first two hundred years on the new continent. This tradition was securely rooted in that relatively self-contained family economy which was the dominant social fact in colonial and pioneering life; it flowered in the handicrafts which grew out of the household industries as the community took form and made specialization possible. It evolved from the vital and vigorous folk art of the period. The great master craftsmen who appeared in the eighteenth century in many fields were merely those persons who by reason of special aptitude, interest, and training "did the folk things pre-eminently better than their fellows."

The difficulties attending the creation of this tradition were enormous. Attention has already been directed to the practical demands of a virgin continent, the æsthetic prejudices and aversions of the settlers, and the interruption of the process of cultural development involved in the migration to America. The colonies, moreover, encountered great difficulties in persuading skilled craftsmen to cross the Atlantic and endure the hardships of the pioneer in a strange country at a time when they enjoyed special privileges at home. As a consequence, the colonial artisan was commonly treated with great consideration and even exempted from certain obligations. As late as 1680 in Virginia, according to Philip Alexander Bruce, "a handi-craftsman was regarded by the planters with the highest esteem and courted with their utmost art."[10] As a result of all of these unfavorable conditions the tools, the utensils, the furnishings, and the houses of the early colonial period were generally crude and primitive. "So far as information is to be derived from records," writes Mr. Bruce regarding Virginia, "there was no residence in the Colony in the seventeenth century which could make any pretension to beauty of design. The homes even of the most prominent planters were simple and plain."[11] Elsewhere apparently the situation was not greatly different. Under the harsh conditions associated with the struggle for survival the principle of simple and un-adorned utility governed the practical arts. Yet, says Suzanne LaFollette, the houses had a certain charm because they were

[10] Philip Alexander Bruce, *Economic History of Virginia in the Seventeenth Century* (New York, 1896), Vol. II, 410.
[11] *Ibid.*, 134.

built "in terms of the life that was to be lived in them."[12] Harold D. Eberlein and Abbot McClure have thus appraised the work of the period:

"If work was primitive, and it often was, it was, however, honest and possessed of strong individuality, and generally showed a striving to realise, albeit blindly and imperfectly at times, the inherently sound principle of ubiquitous grace, so dear to and so consistently practiced by the Greeks, who deemed the meanest pots and pans not unworthy of comely shape and fitting ornament. Many of the articles were product of *home manufacture,* and so it would not be fair to contrast them with the work of skilled artisans. And yet, if we do contrast them with much of the cheaper present-day merchandise it would often be to the advantage of the home-made; for, while frankly amateurish and primitive, few examples of this home-made work were downright *ugly,* as are the hideous carpets, pieces of furniture, and the like sold by some of the cheaper establishments of to-day."[13]

As the settlers established themselves in the new environment, as they transferred craft skills and knowledges from mother country to colony, as they became familiar with American materials and conditions, as they accumulated a material surplus, as they acquired a modicum of leisure, as the severity of the economic struggle moderated, as they mastered the art of life in America, power of execution grew, taste improved, and an artistic tradition took form and gathered momentum. Although there resulted no great painting, or music, or poetry, there did evolve ever finer patterns of the things of common use. The current craze for antiques, though explained in part by the interest of the bourgeoisie in ostentation, is a genuine tribute to the art of the pre-machine age.

[12] *Op. cit.,* 13.
[13] Harold Donaldson Eberlein and Abbot McClure, *The Practical Book of Early American Arts and Crafts* (Philadelphia, 1916), 13.

This artistic development assumed both a private and a public aspect, although the distinction cannot be clearly drawn. On the one hand, it expressed itself in dwellings and in personal and family possessions; on the other, it assumed the form of churches, public buildings, and village and town design.

Colonial dwellings, like tools and clothing and furniture, were dominated by the twin conceptions of utility and permanence. There were no real estate booms or developments in those days; there was no building for a market. Although the style of construction varied in response to local conditions and historical heritage so that four more or less distinct types of architecture appeared in New York, New England, the Middle Colonies, and the South, everywhere men built for themselves and their children or for their neighbors. A jerry-built house was consequently a gross incongruity—an exercise in self-deception or in the cheating of one's friends. Today those colonial homes, dotting the landscape from the Carolinas to Massachusetts, stand as silent monuments to the integrity, the skill, and the versatility of the craftsman of a hundred and fifty or two hundred years ago. "The vital quality of the early and truly Colonial architecture," says Harold D. Eberlein, "has not been exhausted and after nearly three hundred years we turn to it to find it still rich in adaptability to many of our present requirements."[14]

In the making of the objects of ordinary use the colonial artisan entered almost every field. Throughout the colonies women pursued the arts associated with the textile industry— the spinning and weaving of linen, the making of homespun garments, the weaving of woolen coverlets, the piercing, patching and quilting of bedspreads, the working of samplers, the embroidering of pictures and wearing apparel, the making of dyes, and the dyeing of threads and fabrics. Similarly men everywhere engaged in cabinet making, in painting furni-

[14] Harold Donaldson Eberlein, *The Architecture of Colonial America* (Boston, 1915), 10.

ture, glass, tin and other substances, in carving wood and stone, and in the simpler forms of metal working for domestic and architectural use.[15]

Other arts such as glass making, pottery making, sign-painting, allegorical painting, portraiture, pen-and-brush illumination, handblock printing on fabrics and paper, and the more complex forms of metal working developed in local areas and particularly in the cities. "It is plain to be seen," conclude Eberlein and McClure, "that every part of our country settled before the third decade of the nineteenth century has some share in early craft development, some point of interest, some cause for proper local pride."[16] The heights attained by these eighteenth-century craftsmen are suggested by the following tribute paid to the workers in metal by Suzanne LaFollette:

"Silver, pewter, wrought iron, and brass followed the prevailing fashions. Not again have metals been wrought into such beautiful forms as in the silver tea services, chafing-dishes, porringers, candlesticks, ladles, and other objects of this century; the brass warming-pans, sconces, andirons, candlesticks, furniture mounts; the wrought-iron gates and railings, hinges, knockers, and utensils. It was the heyday of the craftsman, his final glorious period of achievement, before the triumphant invasion of his province by the industrial revolution."[17]

But colonial art was not purely private and personal. It also served the community. And of this form of art the church was by far the most important and universal expression. Everywhere, north and south, the church building was to be seen, usually an impressive structure representing the dominant public interest of the age. Into the building of these edifices the people put their finest work. Of secular public buildings there were comparatively few. Yet certain of these were of unusual excellence. Mention need be made only of Independence Hall

15 Harold Donaldson Eberlein and Abbot McClure, *op. cit.*, 16–17.
16 *Ibid.*, 17.   17 *Op. cit.*, 32.

in Philadelphia and Faneuil Hall in Boston. Finally the colonial community, and particularly the New England town, was laid out and developed with some regard for æsthetic considerations. At any rate it was not looked upon as a field for real estate speculation and in many instances it retains today a large measure of beauty and quiet charm.

THE BLIGHTING OF TASTE

The first half of the nineteenth century recorded the dissolution of the colonial culture. The leisurely development of the sheltered life along the Atlantic was interrupted: the nation marched west—over the Alleghanies, across the basin of the Mississippi, and on to the Golden Gate. Under the impact of new forces the household economy melted away, the community lost its integrity, the machine destroyed the craftsman, a predatory individualism rose to economic dominance, men became devoted to money-making, and a new ruling class, product of the commercial spirit, displaced the colonial aristocracy. Increasingly men produced, not for use, but for the market, for profit. Thus the foundations of the artistic tradition, which had taken form during two centuries, were demolished.

When Henry Adams returned to America in 1868 he was astounded by the changes that had occurred within a brief decade. He was astounded by the brutality and depravity of the men who governed the country. Yet he saw quite clearly what had happened; he saw that strange forces had risen to power; he saw that an agrarian society was being submerged by the rise of industrialism. "The generation between 1865 and 1895 was already mortgaged to the railways and no one knew it better than the generation itself."

The Civil War established the rule of coal, iron, and steam; it brought the planters and farmers to the feet of industrialists and bankers. It produced an aftermath of general moral corruption not unlike that following the World War. Also the Homestead Act of 1862 released millions of acres of public land, from Iowa to California, to settlement. As a result, while land-hungry hordes started westward, great numbers of speculators remained in the east to gamble on the stock market. The entire country was caught up in a vast orgy—"the great barbecue," in Parrington's phrase—and the amenities were forgotten. The effect on the arts has been outlined by T. F. Hamlin:

"Land speculation in new or growing cities—and all the cities East and West were growing with continually increasing speed—was inevitable, and brought the ideal of cheapness into building as it never had been brought before. Cheap materials, cheap construction, speed, speed, speed, quick turnover and large profits—such an ideal leads to no great art. It breaks down the very foundations of creative design; it struck also the deathblow of the Greek Revival, and there was nothing to take its place. There began under this influence a decline of all artistic conscience—in strange consonance with a decline of financial and political conscience in the years following the Civil War, the results of which are, unfortunately, still all too apparent."[18]

In this struggle for wealth and power precipitated by the opening of the public lands and the rise of machine production a new type of man made his appearance. This type is well represented in Wingfield-Stratford's description of those self-made English capitalists whose triumph was registered by the First Reform Bill and whose outlook on life has left its stamp on capitalistic society in America, as well as in Britain:

"The great millowners and ironmasters of the late eighteenth and early nineteenth centuries were a hard-headed and

[18] T. F. Hamlin, *The American Spirit in Architecture* (New Haven, 1926), Vol. 13 in *The Pageant of America,* 140.

usually hard-hearted breed of men, who had fought their way
to fortunes by sheer cut-throat competition, and with the prospect of bankruptcy never very remote. Of education they had
little, of culture none at all. In the Greek quality of mag-
nificence, that had so conspicuously shone in the merchant
princes, the Canynges and Jacques Coeurs of the early Renaissance, they had no part. On the other hand they were
just as free from the splendid vices of that time as they were
from the snobbishness which was destined to transform the
Victorian middle class. They were eminently respectable, conspicuously independent. Such vices as they had were rather of
the negative order, lack of sympathy, lack of imagination, all
that is implied in Ricardo's conception of an economic man.
Their ethics were those of the Black Hole, 'every man for himself and the weakest to the wall.' "[19]

These words apply with almost equal force to the self-made
American capitalists from Jay Cook and Jay Gould to John D.
Rockefeller and Henry Ford. And the picture is not altered
greatly by the fact that some of them or their successors bought
fine pictures and founded institutions of learning. They were
of the type of Cecil Rhodes, "the first man of a new age,"
according to Spengler, whose frank motto was "expansion is
everything."[20]

Carlyle seems to have been the first to use the phrase, "captains of industry," but he meant leaders of imagination and
chivalry, who might have saved England from the economic
chaos and inhumanities of ninety years ago. He did not mean
gamblers who were to pile fortune upon fortune without
regard for either the present or the future of society. But
these dominant types, thrown up by the forces of the new age,
were effects as well as causes. They were made possible by

[19] Esmé Wingfield-Stratford, *The History of British Civilization* (New
York, 1930), 940–941.
[20] Ralph Borsodi, *This Ugly Civilization* (New York, 1929), 230–240.

the system of machine and power production that came into being over-night. While neither science nor capitalism is new, the whirring machines which produced industrial society emerged with a rush and a roar less than two centuries ago and threw the whole scheme of things out of order. A backward look on these two centuries reveals, not the course of a stream, but the path of a storm. The rate of change has been too rapid to permit the maturing of a cultured pattern. In spite of all talk about comfort and progress, the prevailing mood has been one of frenzy and hectic excitement.

With ironmasters and millowners completely in power, the ideal and the envy of the mass of people, with the economic interest openly dominant, the other major values, and especially the æsthetic, were certain to suffer. It was a question whether the traditional arts would disappear, be prostituted to the spirit of the times, or escape to some uncorrupted empyrean. In any event a tremendous strain was to be placed on man's devotion to beauty. The æsthetic consequences of the substitution of machine for hand production proved to be revolutionary in scope and substance.[21]

Coal, iron, and steam changed the complexion of life, literally as well as metaphorically. Cities and countrysides were recklessly defaced; new towns, completely lacking in æsthetic quality, were quickly put together. The natural beauty of the country, no less than its material resources, was subordinated to the acquisition of wealth. Under the reign of *laissez-faire* grand art, which had always been the special concern of the state or the community, practically disappeared; and commodity art, which had hitherto been under the guardianship of the craftsman, was forced to surrender to the drive for private gain. With government reduced to the rôle of policeman, commercial enterprise had a free field everywhere. As a result of the wholesale sacrifice of the environment to "business," the simple, visual taste of the population must have atrophied

[21] See Lewis Mumford, *Technics and Civilization* (New York, 1934).

seriously. "Coketown," as pictured by Dickens in *Hard Times,*
was the great cathedral of the Ricardian religion:

"It was a town of red brick, or of brick that would have been
red if the smoke and ashes had allowed it; but as matters stood
it was a town of unnatural red and black like the painted face
of a savage. It was a town of machinery and tall chimneys,
out of which interminable serpents of smoke trailed themselves
for ever and ever, and never got uncoiled. It had a black
canal in it, and a river that ran purple with ill-smelling dye,
and vast piles of building full of windows where there was a
rattling and a trembling all day long, and where the piston of
the steam-engine worked monotonously up and down like the
head of an elephant in a state of melancholy madness. It contained several large streets all very like one another, and many
small streets still more like one another, inhabited by people
equally like one another, who all went in and out at the same
hours, with the same sound upon the same pavements, to do the
same work, and to whom every day was the same as yesterday
and to-morrow, and every year the counterpart of the last and
the next."[22]

The picture is still all too familiar. Coketown began in England but reached its greatest height in America. The darker
spiritual implications of such an environment are expressed in
James Thomson's *City of Dreadful Night* or the more recent
Waste Land of T. S. Eliot. Carlyle, Ruskin and William Morris foresaw all the moral, æsthetic and hygienic problems that
men are now trying so desperately to solve. Today Ralph
Borsodi carries on the attack with the cold reasoning of a certi-
fied public accountant. As symbols of "this ugly civilization"
he selects the smoke of Pittsburgh, the smells of Chicago, and
the noise of New York.[23]

It is cause for no surprise that architecture, the most funda-

[22] Charles Dickens, *Hard Times* (London, 1924), 28.   [23] *Op. cit.,* 2.

mental of human arts, went to pieces during the nineteenth century, in Europe as well as in America. Under the drive for "progress" there was no time to explore and understand the possibilities of the machine or of the new materials it provided; there was no time to assimilate the vast store of ideas that archælogists and historians of art were accumulating. Consequently there was a ceaseless and indiscriminate imitation of earlier styles, with little effort at creative originality and little consideration of appropriateness to a highly different civilization. Bastard versions of Greek, Roman, Romanesque, Gothic, and oriental architecture spread over the country. Monstrous curlicues of wood and iron appeared on chimney, gable, and façade. "Nothing," says Suzanne LaFollette, "better reflects the helplessness of a people whose whole life was undergoing an unprecedented dissolution and readjustment than the attempt to borrow from a dead past a means of expression which its own spiritual chaos rendered it incapable of creating for itself."[24]

The blighting influence of industrialism, however, was not confined to architecture. There was no branch of industrial art, according to Miss LaFollette, "which did not deteriorate."[25] "If architecture fared badly in the mass," writes Lewis Mumford, "it did even worse in the more intimate forms of decoration and furniture. In these departments a practised handicraft was eliminated by the steady introduction of labor-saving machinery—the lathe, the scroll-saw, the planing machine, the power loom; and this process was accompanied by a positive loss in design."[26] The consequent "monstrosities of rosewood and black walnut with machine-turned legs and scroll-sawed backs" can still be remembered.

The first reaction of sensitive souls to the situation was an impulse to stop the march of the machine and to revive the

[24] *Op. cit.*, 112.   [25] *Ibid.*, 113.
[26] Lewis Mumford, "The Arts," Chapter XII in *Whither Mankind*, edited by Charles A. Beard (New York, 1928), 290.

handicrafts. William Morris and others labored heroically and desperately to this end, but without success. The solution clearly lay in another direction. The advance of technology could not be halted. On the other hand, to ask machines to imitate handicraft designs, or to test their products by handicraft standards, was a grotesque mistake. They simply could not express "the endearing irregularities" of the individual craftsman. Why should there not be designs appropriate to the work of the machines? Why should the new mechanical processes and new materials not lead to entirely new forms and types of art? Such questions the twentieth century is trying to answer.

The issues were complicated in the United States by the peculiar history of the country. As already noted, the swift march of the population across the continent and the rapid growth of cities gave American civilization a uniquely rootless character. Both of these movements, moreover, manifested a strong speculative quality. "Boom-towns sprang up like mushrooms and disappeared as quickly. Land constantly changed hands as the influx of population sent values soaring . . . the diaspora gave for decades a character of restlessness and impermanence to American life."[27] In such a shifting environment the arts could not flourish. Also there was no established leisured class to protect the artist, as there had been in Europe for many centuries. After the Civil War, however, the *nouveaux riches* began to patronize the arts in a grand manner, and pillaged Europe with an efficiency that has brought to America some of the finest collections in the world. In their minds the problem of æsthetic backwardness was simple. It was a matter of gaining possession of the objects of art.

Stanford White was perfectly frank about this. He is said to have supported many of the chief art dealers of Europe. It was not sufficient for him to imitate or buy a Florentine ceiling or mantelpiece; he brought over the entire room! "Once

[27] Suzanne LaFollette, *op. cit.*, 110.

when reproached for despoiling the old world, he defended himself by saying that Rome had plundered Greece, that every Renaissance had its beginnings in the past."[28] Such a conception of a Renaissance, however, while bringing some wonderful artistic creations to America and improving the popular taste, perhaps at the same time retarded the development of creative talent.

While the distinguished firm of McKim, Mead and White in New York City looked to the past, certain architects in Chicago were beginning to look to the future. John Wellborn Root, Daniel Burnham, and Louis H. Sullivan realized clearly that modern life, especially modern American life, demanded something more than warmed-over Greek or Gothic styles. They were inspired by the splendid Romanesque adaptations of Richardson; they had steel columns and the elevator to work with; they saw the first timid, awkward skyscraper go up. Here were great issues and they met them squarely in several notable public buildings, but their work was deluged under the classic revival of the World's Fair of 1893.

In the meantime their dreams had been realized in a bridge spanning the East River in New York. The Roeblings, though regarding themselves not as artists but as engineers, identified the problems of appearance with the problems of structure and function. The result was a masterpiece more satisfying perhaps than any modern building. But at the time this was not suspected.

In Europe music and painting were able to survive the onrush of industrialism, as Mr. Mumford points out, simply by withdrawing from the main current of affairs. From Beethoven to Richard Strauss, German music proceeded on its course throughout the nineteenth century insensitive to the changes that were sweeping through society. From Delacroix to Cezanne and Renoir the French painters continued their great experiments. But it was not through any wide public interest

28 Charles C. Baldwin, *Stanford White* (New York, 1931), 2.

that these masters lived; most of them had independent incomes or passed their days in dire poverty—to be appreciated after death.

In America two excellent painters appeared during the nineteenth century, although it has remained for a later generation to discover them. Thomas Eakins was too honest and austere in his art to win the patronage of the wealthy or the sentimental appreciation of the masses. Albert Pinkham Ryder, "the greatest of American painters," according to Thomas Craven, was a recluse from economic necessity, as well as temperament; and he hardly tried to make himself known. Yet his eerie dramas and misty seascapes make him the Melville of painting and a great figure in the whole romantic tradition.

In the sphere of music these early years of industrialism witnessed little achievement of first rank in America. In *The Rosary* and the *Water Scenes* Nevin attained a very limited perfection. Although Edward McDowell has been placed on a secure plane with Grieg, some have suspected that he weakened himself by endeavoring to keep his own style pure and by cutting himself off from the great traditional reservoirs of the composer. It remained for a visiting Bohemian, Dvorák, to give American musicians a proper understanding of the possibilities of negro folk music. Whether or not he "intended to use actual negro tunes, or merely to catch their spirit," in his *New World Symphony*, he initiated, thirty-five years ago, the most important tendency of American musical composition.

THE RECOVERY OF TASTE

The reaction to the blighting effects of industrialism appeared early among the more sensitive-minded. Certainly since the days of Emerson an increasing volume of protest has been raised. Wealth has accumulated, educational opportunities have been extended, leisure has been increased, restrictions have been placed upon the practice of *laissez-faire,* the community has tended to reassert itself in many areas, and men have begun to come to terms with the machine. According to Keppel and Duffus, "the long time curves of leisure, income and interest in the arts, in present day United States, follow parallel trends."[29] And again these authors point out that in contemporary America "there is an æsthetic unrest, just as there is an economic and social unrest."[30] The changes under way will be illustrated by reference to the changing fortunes of architecture, painting, sculpture, and music and to the rise of social planning as an æsthetic conception. Then in a separate section certain new forces will be examined.

Architecture. Since the opening of the twentieth century American architecture has been coming of age. There were notable beginnings in Chicago, as already suggested, fifty years ago, which were largely submerged by the classical revival after the World's Fair of 1893. The severe stripped lines of the Monadnock Building expressed their work and realm, as did the Auditorium Building and the Transportation Building at the Fair. But John Wellborn Root died in his early prime and Louis H. Sullivan went into obscurity before he was fifty—a prophet, far ahead of his time, to be remembered not so much for any specific structures as for his ardent crusade for a new architecture suitable to a new age.

Sullivan's constant insistence was that the form of a building should express its function—that *form follows function.* A grain elevator, an office building, a railroad station, a church, or a theater, each demands its own peculiar design. Moreover, the form of the building must frankly reveal its materials and mode of construction rather than seek to disguise them. Is not the candor of a great bridge the very essence of its beauty? Here in America are new resources, possibilities and ideals, and all these, cried Sullivan with the prophetic voice of a

[29] *Op. cit.,* 5.   [30] *Ibid.,* 207.

Whitman, must be embodied in an indigenous architecture that is not merely an imitation of European antiquity. Sullivan was a wayward, arrogant genius and he did not always carry out his principles, but he stated them nobly in *The Autobiography of an Idea* which he finished shortly before his death in 1923.

There was a young draftsman in Sullivan's Chicago office who understood the vision of *Der Meister* and pursued it with even greater intelligence and imagination. He was Frank Lloyd Wright whose *Autobiography* is the record, not of a pathetic frustration, but of a long and arduous series of triumphs—one of the most profound and illuminating books of the time and invaluable for the student of art and æsthetics. Here are the ideas of Sullivan matured and completed. Here is the philosophy of one who was thinking in terms of straight lines, "streamlines," and flat surfaces before cubism appeared or the airplane was invented. Far from scorning the machine and crying for the lost days of the handicrafts, Wright decided early in his career to take full advantage of the machine and all of its works. His ideal of an "organic architecture" grows within the mind of the reader as he describes homes built in the so-called "prairie style," or the Midway Gardens in Chicago, or the Imperial Hotel in Tokio, thoroughly modern and yet suited to its Japanese setting, or St. Mark's Tower (as yet only a dream) aflame in metal and glass!

In developing an architecture that will "make our machine power and our millions democratically beneficent," Wright starts with one fundamental principle, "one great new integrity—a sense of the within as reality." In other words, he starts with the doctrine of his teacher that form follows function. "Architecture, as modern," he says, "now becomes the expression of the liveable interior space of the room itself. The *room-space itself must 'come through!'* The 'room' must be seen as architecture, or we have none. No longer do we have outside as outside. Or inside as inside seen as two separate things. Now the outside may come inside, and the inside may go outside. They are *of* each other."[31] And then he adds that "it is in the nature of the modern building to grow from its site, come out of the ground into the light—the ground seen as component part of the building itself—and we have primarily a new ideal of building as organic: 'dignified as a tree in the midst of nature.' "[32]

In realizing the new ideal which, according to Wright, should serve "our general culture" as well as architecture, the architect has at his disposal "four limitless new resources." The first is glass—a super-material, "because it holds new means for awakened sensibilities. . . . If known in ancient times, glass would have abolished ancient architecture completely. This super-material—GLASS—as we now have it, is a miracle. Air in air to keep air out or keep it in. Light itself in light, to diffuse or reflect or refract light. By means of glass . . . open reaches of the ground may enter as the building and the building interior may reach out and associate with the ground . . . More and more we will desire the sun. . . . Before long, by way of glass, the garden will be the building as much as the building is the garden. . . . Walls themselves will become as windows, and windows as we know them will be seen no more. Ceilings will become as window-walls, too, often enough. The textile may now be used as a beautiful robe for space, an attribute of architecture instead of the decorator's camouflage."[33]

The second new resource is "a new standard of means," plasticity, continuity, tenuity—achieved through the use of metals and particularly steel. Plasticity eliminates "all the separate identities of the post and beam architecture." Continuity "economizes material, labor and space in a more developed sense and gives to the structure the significant outlines of remarkable stability. Instead of false masonry-mass comes

[31] Frank Lloyd Wright, *An Autobiography* (New York, 1932), 352.
[32] *Ibid.*, 352–353.   [33] *Ibid.*, 353, 354.

significant outline and the pattern of structure." The "tensile strength of a strand of steel" has liberated new forces. "So this tremendous new resource of *tenuity*—this quality of *pull* in a building—see it ushering in our new era in John Roebling's Brooklyn Bridge—was lacking in all ancient architecture."[34]

The third new resource is "a new sense of the nature of materials." Technology has placed in the hands of the architect and builder a vast variety of materials. And each material must be permitted to express its own character: "A stone building will no more *be* nor *look* like a steel building. A pottery, or terra cotta building, will not be or look like a stone building. A wood building will look like none other, or it will glorify the stick. A steel and glass building could not possibly look like anything but itself. It will glorify steel and glass. And so on all the way down the long list of available riches in materials: Stone, Wood, Concrete, Metals, Glass, Textiles, Pulp, and Pigment; riches so great that no comparison with Ancient Architecture is at all sensible or in any way essential to Modern Architecture."[35]

The fourth new resource is the conception of "pattern as natural." Conscious striving after ornamentation or imitation of the ornamental forms of the past violates the principle of integrity. "Ornament," says Wright, should be as *integral as poetry* and should mean "not only *surface qualified by human imagination,* but imagination giving *natural pattern* to structure itself." By this fourth and crowning resource "we may give greater structural entity and human significance to the expression of the whole building."[36] "It (architecture) looks and sees the aeroplane fly overhead, emancipated from make-believe, free to be itself and true to itself. Architecture looks and sees the steamship ride the seas, triumphant as the superb thing it is, for what it is; sees the motor-car becoming more the machine it should be, daily less like a coach, gradually acquiring the freedom to be itself for what it is. In all modern

[34] *Ibid.,* 354–356. [35] *Ibid.,* 356. [36] *Ibid.,* 358.

mobilizations or utensils whatsoever, architecture, awakening, sees the Machine Age more and more freely declaring for Freedom to express the simple facts of structure and be itself. And the purpose of its own being is but crudely seen in these true mechanical forms of its utensils."[37] Thus technology and engineering extend their sway into the realm of æsthetics.

These are the bare elements of Wright's theory. They are not the irresponsible suggestions of a drawingboard architect, but the tested convictions of an architect-engineer who has made his major dreams come true. But Wright is only one of a number of American architects who have been designing factories, warehouses, office buildings, and homes in the spirit of their times and their environment. There are independent developments, not only in New York City and in the Middle West but in New Mexico and California as well. Listen to the words of Theodore Sizer:

"The cultivated and inquisitive European is vastly more interested in our recent skyscrapers, our new methods of construction, and functional use of materials and ornament, than in our occasional sculpture and acres of paint . . . The tide is beginning to turn. It is Europe which is now turning to us for inspiration, as yet only in architecture, usually the forerunner in any new artistic movement. After three hundred years we have commenced to contribute something new, something distinctly American, to the art of the world."[38]

Painting.[39] Recent "acres of paint" show a great advance over the nineteenth century and a genuine, creative independence. But perhaps most significant of all is the trend towards an alliance between painting and architecture. "Wall painting on the grand scale—a sweeping social commentary

[37] *Ibid.*, 361.
[38] Theodore Sizer, "The Development of American Art," in *Aspects of the Social History of America* (Chapel Hill, 1931), 21–22.
[39] See Frederick P. Keppel and R. L. Duffus, *op. cit.*, 116 ff.

taxing the organizing ability of the artist to the utmost—has received its first modern impetus in the murals of two powerful and energetic Mexicans, Rivera and Orozco," says Thomas Craven. The one has decorated the walls of the San Francisco Stock Exchange, the Detroit Museum of Fine Arts and several buildings in New York; the other has worked by himself in a hall of Pomona College, California, and with Thomas Benton on the walls of the New School for Social Research in New York City. Then there are other important signs of a development of mural painting, including an exhibit by the Museum of Modern Art in the winter of 1931, to which many easel artists contributed.[40]

Sculpture. Similarly, American sculpture, which has always been extremely backward, may be vitalized by an alliance with architecture. At least there is the fine example of Lee Lawrie, who worked hand in hand with Bertram Goodhue on the Nebraska State Capitol and the Los Angeles Public Library, possibly the most beautiful building recently constructed in America. "Goodhue's early conferences in the west left the impression that he was almost more zealous to impress upon his patrons that the capitol would be monumental only with Lawrie's aid than to assure himself of their comprehension of the structural thought which he himself had conceived and which it should express. His attitude was, at heart, an eager recognition of the intimate, the inherent interdependence of the two shaping arts."[41] And the result was that Lawrie's heroic figures, such as those of Lincoln and Hammurabi, as well as his symbolic groups and smaller ornaments of Indian corn and bison head, became an integral, necessary part of the total structure, "being employed only where an accent is needed to arrest the eye or where a contour calls for softening."

Music. In the realm of music the advance is recorded not

[40] Thomas Craven, *Men of Art* (New York, 1931), 510–11; *The Hound and Horn,* July–September, 1932.

[41] H. B. Alexander, "The Sculpture of Lee Lawrie," *The Architectural Forum* (May, 1931), LIV, 596.

in the fine music being written, but rather in the tremendous quantities of fine music being listened to, directly from the concert stage, as well as indirectly from the phonograph and radio. In spite of the prevalence of jazz, the taste of the entire nation seems to be rapidly improving.[42] To be sure, the extreme modernist will say that jazz itself is putting new life into music and that George Gershwin is already a master to be classed with the immortals. Pitts Sanborn replies that "jazz is not a new form of music, but rather a new and more mechanized manner of playing." And again he writes:

"We have witnessed in America one of the greatest phenomena of expansion and construction the world has ever known. We are in the midst of an intensely emotional period, such as invariably leads to great and genuine expressions of art—but that only when calm is restored. Nor will it be what we are having now: not jazz, not the wild essays of 'modernism.' Thus it was generations after the flaming outbursts of Protestantism that Bach gave the world his colossal masterpieces of religious art. Some excellent work has already been done. Perhaps the finest orchestral music by a native American is 'The Pleasure Dome of Kubla Khan' of the late Charles Tomlinson Griffes, whose art songs are also outstanding. Nor are our older masters, McDowell and Nevin, to be sneered at. But the Machine Age has wrought a great panoply ready for the hand of our future geniuses. The demand is here. The facilities are here. Undoubtedly our geniuses will be forthcoming. Musically, the great things doubtless lie just around the turn of the road."[43]

Social Planning. The youngest of the arts, but greatest in the possibilities for the æsthetic enhancement of human life, is *planning* or *designing*—not utensils, or dresses, or paintings, or even buildings—but towns, cities, regions, and finally, perhaps,

---

42 See Frederick P. Keppel and R. L. Duffus, *op. cit.*, 174.
43 Fred J. Ringel, *America as Americans See It* (New York, 1932), 278.

entire countries! Here indeed is the supreme art, since it must embrace in its conception and execution all of the other arts and create the conditions for their expression. The first faltering steps toward planning were taken in the latter part of the last century when cities turned to the laying out of large public parks, chiefly for hygienic reasons.[44] The art or science was definitely established with the publication of Sir Ebenezer Howard's *Garden Cities of Tomorrow* in 1902. In the meantime, and particularly during the past ten or fifteen years, popular interest in planning, legislation with respect to planning, and actual practice in planning have increased rapidly. In certain of its forms it has been recognized by the Supreme Court of the United States.[45] The Tennessee Valley project of the Roosevelt Administration represents an effort to apply the idea of planning to a great region.

The range of possibilities inherent in social planning may be suggested by notable instances already to be seen in the United States. There are various model towns such as Radburn, New Jersey, "with an internal park system completely out of the range of traffic." Westchester County, New York, has lavished millions on splendid parkways and permanently anticipated the horrors of overcrowding. Partly through real estate accidents and partly through foresight, Los Angeles is becoming rapidly decentralized, a series of fine spacious towns stretching toward the sea, instead of a single straggling city. Recently have appeared the twelve massive volumes of the New York Regional Plan which cannot be carried to completion in less than thirty or forty years. Whatever may be said as to the details of this plan, it indicates a growing concern for the future.

Any comprehensive program of social planning will of course involve the making of weighty decisions. This may be illustrated by present differences of opinion regarding concen-

[44] Theodora Kimball Hubbard and Henry Vincent Hubbard, *Our Cities To-day and To-morrow* (Cambridge, 1929), 5.
[45] *Ibid.*, 10.

tration and distribution of population. One group insists that the movement toward the city, *urbanization,* must inevitably increase and consequently envisages yet loftier buildings and more intricate problems of traffic. Another maintains that there is, and certainly should be, a tendency away from the vast city, toward *ruralization,* and foresees one vast park-like country lightly populated, "enjoying the greater freedom, the ability to spread out without inconvenience, the most valuable gift brought by the undreamed of power of these new servants—electrical intercommunication, the automobile, the telephone, the airship, the radio, and the press."

SOME NEW FORCES

The advance of industrial civilization has not only shifted ancient arts to new economic foundations and vastly altered the conditions under which all the arts are practised. It has also released new forces, produced new instruments, promoted new interests, and greatly increased the leisure of men. These developments and their implications cannot of course be treated at length here: they will merely be illustrated by reference to the automobile, the cinema, the radio, and sport.

The Automobile. As soon as the automobile ceased to be a horseless carriage, as soon as it struck out for itself, it was on its way to becoming a work of art. It is perhaps the first product of the machine age to reach a kind of maturity. In it form and function—the dream of the modern architect—are remarkably combined; grace, speed, and power take on a single meaning. The variety of automobiles and their constant modifications have schooled the eye to line and color, have forced the people to standards and distinctions, to habits of vision that would have been acquired in no other way. Unintentionally the automobile designers have provided classes in art appreciation for the whole world. Even Henry Ford, under pressure from the Chevrolet, was forced to yield to æsthetic considerations. The man who had once proclaimed that he would not "give five cents for all the art the world had produced" declared in an advertisement of his new model in 1927: "The new Ford has exceptional beauty of line and color because beauty of line and color has come to be considered, and I think rightly, a necessity in a motor car today."[46]

So man's æsthetic interests are being furthered in many untraditional ways, shocking and painful as it may seem to the conservative æsthete. As the fine arts have become more practical the practical arts have become finer. There is good reason to believe that more creative energy and talent of a high grade are now going into the practical than into the fine arts. Nevertheless it must be admitted that there is much of fad, fancy and fashion in all this, and that the larger part of commercial art is superficial, garish, cheap and meaningless. The heritage of *laissez-faire* economics and of the domination of the market has by no means been liquidated.

The artistic advance represented by the automobile, however, is genuine and is reflected in other products of the machine age. Thus the æsthetic evolution of the airplane has been even more impressive than that of the automobile. *"Structural daring,"* says Frankl, *"always becomes in the end æsthetically most satisfactory."*[47] The beautiful clipper ships, the finest contributions of Yankee genius, were pushed off the sea by grotesque steam vessels, but the magnificent ocean liner has been the result. Or again consider the development of the locomotive, or the Pullman car, from the crude pretense of the first models to the suave luxury of the latest. In fact the Pullman company has put out a most illuminating series of pamphlets tracing this story, which show the final elimination of those acres of imitation wood. And the improvement of the Pullman cars is but a symbol of the general advance in interior decorating, from wall surfaces and furniture to toilet and

46 Frederick P. Keppel and R. L. Duffus, *op. cit.,* 133.
47 Paul T. Frankl, *Machine-Made Leisure* (New York, 1932), 50.

kitchen utensils. It is often pointed out that, from the stand-point of beauty as well as economy, the kitchen and the bathroom are the most satisfactory rooms in the contemporary house.

The æsthetic influence of the automobile, however, extends far beyond its own composition. It has powerfully accelerated the building of great highways, the widening of streets and roads, and the extension of state and national parks. Although the old country lane had its peculiar charm, the curving beauty of the Lincoln Highway or of the road to the Yosemite Valley is adding something to the artistic inheritance. Such improvements continue, while the unsightliness of the present gasoline stations, hot dog stands and sign boards will tend to disappear —in fact, are disappearing at the demands of the motorist himself. And the time may come when landscaping will be regarded as an essential part of highway construction. Social planning would seem to be moving in this direction.

The automobile is placing at the service of the population the rich natural beauties of the country. Since Americans spend so much of their time on the roads and so little in picture galleries, it is essential that they learn to look at nature in something more than a literary, or sentimental, or historical way. Not only should the size of mountains or the width of rivers or the variety of colors be noticed—these things, certainly, but much besides. The more distinctly æsthetic values are waiting to be observed quite as patiently as in an inaccessible and stuffy art gallery. Unfortunately, the art critics have confined themselves almost exclusively to "still life" or "dead life" and have not condescended to examine the external world. Thomas Munro has recently written a series of articles on the "Æsthetic Appreciation of Nature" which should help to meet the need in this field of human delight.[48]

The Cinema. Since the moving picture, which is now shaping the folkways of the world to an incredible degree, is less

[48] *The American Magazine of Art* (April, June, August, 1932).

than thirty years old, in its talking form less than ten, comparisons with arts and institutions that go back thousands of years should be undertaken only with great hesitation. Such comparisons are apt to be unilluminating, as well as invidious. Men are only beginning to appreciate the function and possibilities of the cinema; they are only beginning to develop appropriate æsthetic principles. Moreover, in view of the mechanical difficulties and the human obstacles involved, it is perhaps surprising that so much has been accomplished to date. After seeing a few scenes of a talking picture taken, amid all the infinite complexity of directors, actors, scenery, lights, cameras, and sound instruments, one is amazed that a "talkie" ever actually reaches the theater. In spite of these temporal allowances, however, the point must be conceded that countless cheap and vulgar things have been done in the name of the moving picture art. Yet the fact should not be overlooked that this art was conceived as a form of business enterprise, was largely controlled in its origins by ex-clothing manufacturers, and has been run from the beginning for private gain. The fabrication of ready-made garments, which began on a large scale during the Civil War, could scarcely be expected adequately to prepare these magnates to be æsthetic pioneers, arbiters of taste, or the founders of a new art. It was inevitable that their taste should often or generally prove to be crude, florid, grotesque, sentimental; it was inevitable that they should sacrifice depth and delicacy to sheer mass and glitter. With a few rare exceptions, they chose directors after their own kind. The result has been on a level with the "true story" and "confession" magazines. Until the industry was well established, the forceful, conspicuous exhibitionist, who was guiltless of finer qualities, had the best chance of winning the megaphone. Only in recent years has richer talent, often from Europe, been welcomed in Hollywood.

As for the early performers themselves, they fell far below the average of the stage. The sheer novelty of the film was so great that a pretty, or handsome, or grotesque face was far more important than acting ability. As there were no lines to be spoken, neither voice nor a meagre gift of memory was required in the first generations of cinema "artists." Although the talking film may have ruined the peculiar pantomimic contribution of the silent picture, which has never been deeply exploited, it has raised incomparably the quality of the acting personnel. Literacy is now expected in both stars and directors. But there is another side to the story:

"The low cultural level of the cinema is not to be blamed upon the stupidity of those who create it, but upon their complete and not unreasonable contempt for their patrons, the fans, the dreary millions to whom so much reference has been made. 'What's the use of trying to be artistic?' the film folk justifiably enquire. 'If we give them anything really good, they don't understand it. The only thing that isn't over their heads is Sex.' "[49]

And so R. E. Sherwood, the author of *Reunion in Vienna,* presents the lords of Hollywood as martyrs, "shackled by the consciousness of the world market. They have been servants not only of 120,000,000 U. S. citizens, but of the entire human race . . . whatever they say, or whatever their masses of statistics may prove, they know that the very universality of the cinema has been the principal obstacle to its progress. Hollywood has discovered again and again that all the races, and even all the parishes, have patriotic sensibilities which must not be offended."[50]

The question may be asked, however: Who forced the world markets on Hollywood? Who forced the "industry" to administer to the lowest common denominator of mankind? If "the low cultural level of the cinema is not to be blamed upon

49 R. E. Sherwood, "Hollywood: The Blessed and the Cursed" in *America as Americans See It,* edited by Fred J. Ringel (New York, 1932), 72.
50 *Ibid.,* 67–68.

the stupidity of those who create it," it must be recognized as the fruit of their struggle for personal gain. In their passion for profits, they have been extravagant without being genuinely experimental. They have been playing safe when pretending to be bold. The artist has been made to serve the purposes and wishes of the counting house.

Many works of art have had what may be called a universal appeal. They have appealed to generation after generation down through the ages. But no artist of renown ever had an international and timeless audience in view. He has always created for his own contemporaries, for a specific people at a specified time. And the deeper his song pierces their hearts, the wider and larger it reverberates through the world. So, if the moving picture is to make any further profound advance, if it is to win a place beside the great traditional arts, it must be relieved of the obligation to please all humanity at once, it must be relieved of "the consciousness of a world market," it must be relieved of its tenderness for the box office. Let one director at least create for his own people; let him do a picture for a definite section or class. He may not make millions for his corporation, but he will have a chance of making an immortal masterpiece. With many technical problems already solved and with the gross economic problems susceptible of solution the movie should be on the road to becoming the great synthetic art of industrial society.

The Radio. The radio is a third mechanical product of the age that is already exerting a profound influence on the æsthetic life of the nation. In general use only about a decade, its infinite possibilities are only beginning to be suspected. The more intelligent directors and performers are confessedly ignorant and eager to learn. For the most part, however, its achievements, except on the technical side, lie in the future.

Up to the present the radio in the United States has been largely a tool of business enterprise. Its cultural functions have consequently been subjected to much abuse. Yet in spite of the torrents of crude advertising and cheap amusement sent out over the air, the radio has already contributed much of delight and something of education.[51] "There may be," H. G. Wells suggests, "a very great rehabilitation of poetry and fine prose composition under the influence of radio. For two or three generations we have read our poetry in books; we may return again to hearing it."[52] Or it may be that out of the present little skits on the radio a new form of drama, undisturbed by vision, will arise. Wagner's music dramas were made perhaps for the human voice, but not for the human figure.

Sport. In the sphere of sport industrial society has revived and developed a very ancient interest of mankind. The Greeks, moreover, at least the Athenians of the classic period, recognized the æsthetic aspect of athletics. Here unquestionably is an important department of art. And here in striking fashion form follows function. The most remarkable athlete is the most pleasing to watch; a great runner cannot be an awkward runner. Æsthetes may gossip endlessly about the relation of form and function, but in the realm of physical skill, form and function are literally identical. "Good form is simply the technique by which an athlete acquires the maximum degree of efficiency." "Significant" or "plastic" form is therefore to be envisaged on the track or playing field as well as in the picture gallery.

The typical athlete or coach has little interest in the fine arts or the philosophy of Roger Fry! The artist or intellectual is apt to be indifferent to physical skill, if not definitely scornful of it; he will gaily indulge in awkward, ugly and stupid movements on the tennis court or golf links, whereas he would shudder to be considered insensitive or illiterate. But with a little practice, one will learn to find some of the æsthetic satisfaction from watching a Nurmi or a Venzke that is custom-

[51] See Frederick P. Keppel and R. L. Duffus, *op. cit.*, 165–167.
[52] H. G. Wells, *The Work, Wealth and Happiness of Mankind* (New York, 1931), 784.

arily sought in the contemplation of fine sculpture or painting.

It is tempting to present a gallery of pictures—to recall the versatility of Tilden with his racquet, the slashing drives of William Johnston, the perfectly timed strokes of Bobby Jones, the sustained power of William Arthur Carr, the effortless flowing stride of Nurmi, the flashing speed and delicacy of movement of "Red" Grange, the quick grace of Ty Cobb stealing a base, the powerful swing of Babe Ruth driving the ball into the deep outfield, the serpent like feint of Sharkey, or the tireless pedalling of the veteran rider MacNamara who seems to be a part of his bicycle. But to pile up illustrations is unnecessary. Clearly there is a genuine æsthetic element in athletics, which rivals the visual delights to be found in galleries of pictures and statues. Instead of talking about the healthy Athenians and admiring plaster copies of the ancient discus thrower, the lover of beauty might go occasionally to a good track meet or even learn to pitch horseshoes with skill.

THE FINE ARTS VERSUS THE PRACTICAL ARTS

The separation of the fine and practical arts is a recent phenomenon in human history—the product of a peculiar set of circumstances that may well pass away as quickly as they arose. "Let us recognize," writes Paul T. Frankl, "that our period—the Machine Age—is practically the only one in the long history of humanity, during which there has been so sharp and distinct a division between the 'Industrial Arts' and the so-called 'Fine Arts.' This division has worked to the detriment of the full and satisfying maturing of the creative spirit. Turn again to the Renaissance, that epoch which best exemplifies the flowering of the creative impulse in literature and painting. The great painters of that period were not primarily painters; they were goldsmiths, medallion-makers, engineers, and, sometimes, bad architects."[53] Almost until the opening of

[53] *Op. cit.,* 48–49.

the last century, "it would have been inconceivable that the painter should be divorced from his crafts."

Certainly there is no sharp distinction in primitive society between the fine and the practical arts. There is no sharp antagonism between beauty and use. Music and dancing have a practical value. The labors of the tribe are the rites of the tribe. Pictures are painted on tents and caves. Tools and clothing are decorated with elaborate care. Similarly, in the handicraft culture of Mexico today artistry may be found to coincide with utility. And so it was in the industries of colonial America.

In Periclean Athens the artists and craftsmen co-operated to build a city; in the Middle Ages they co-operated to build cathedrals; in the Renaissance they co-operated enthusiastically to rebuild the world. Supreme geniuses, but also symbolic, were Cellini and Leonardo: the one jeweler as well as sculptor and cut-throat; the other primarily inventor and engineer. In these three periods the so-called fine arts were bound up with the practical arts, and so imbedded in life. The artists themselves were, on the whole, vigorous, practical men of the world, not hypersensitive exiles obsessed with their own achievements. For art these were the healthy times when sculpture and painting were related to architecture—not the prizes of museums and millionaires.

It was only in the last one hundred and fifty years that the fine arts were dissociated from the rest of life and raised to virginal heights—objects of "immaculate perception." It was only in the last one hundred and fifty years that the "fine" artist could look with lofty scorn on all the essential activities of man. An unprecedented situation: the author of a little sonnet, the composer of a trivial sonata, considering himself infinitely superior to the designer of beautiful plate, the creator of excellent furniture, the builder of a magnificent bridge, or the planner of a majestic city!

This fundamental cleavage has been almost fatal to western humanity. It has made an unnatural and brutal separation be-

tween the means and the ends of life—between what Dewey
has called instrumental and final goods, as if a useful thing
could not possibly be beautiful and a beautiful thing could not
possibly be of use. The division has widened in society between
the wage earners, who produce the means of existence, and
the members of a favored class, who enjoy the luxuries and
make collections of paintings and antiques. At the same time
the masses of workers are forced to live amid unsightly surroundings, use cheap and vulgar goods, and find compensation
in the sensations of the tabloid press and the moving picture.
The possession of works of art becomes one of the chief badges
of great wealth—supreme examples of conspicuous waste in a
pecuniary society.[54]

There is much evidence, however, that this cleavage between
the fine and the practical arts is being narrowed or bridged.
The demand for the social control of economy is growing;
interest in social planning is spreading; and the domination of
life by the market-place is being challenged. Much of the best
talent, moreover, is going into the practical arts—into advertising, designing and interior decorating. "Design" has become
a primary consideration—often ridiculously or superficially emphasized—in all walks of life. On purely æsthetic grounds, the
airplane and the automobile are perhaps the most distinguished, tasteful products of the age. There are signs that
sculpture and painting are returning to enrich architecture.
The gap between Beauty and Use is also being closed. The
trend seems to be towards a society in which the artistic talent
of the race, working through the powerful instruments created
by technology, will devote itself, not to the embellishment of
the homes of the rich and the filling of museums and galleries,
but rather to the æsthetic improvement of the objects of common use and the conditions amid which the masses of people
live.

[54] See Thorstein Veblen, *The Theory of the Leisure Class* (New York,
1899).

CHAPTER IX

JUSTICE

The administration of justice has been profoundly affected by the growth of industrial civilization. Indeed few aspects of social life have been more deeply influenced by the impact of technology. While the ideal in its more abstract form has perhaps changed but little, its meaning in concrete social situations and the conditions of its realization have been radically altered. Also the task of administering justice has assumed the proportions of a major social function. Like medicine, education, recreation, scientific research, and artistic creation of the highest order, it has become a clearly differentiated interest of society and a concern of specialists. For the adjudication of a great mass of civil disputes and the apprehension, trial, and punishment of criminal offenders, an extensive and complicated system of police, courts, and prisons has come into being. The nature of these changes and of the problems generated may best be revealed by first noting the conditions prevailing in agrarian society.

JUSTICE IN AGRARIAN SOCIETY

In the pre-industrial age in America the administration of justice manifested few complications. As a function of the state it entered but rarely into the life of the ordinary individual. Crimes were few in both kind and number, being confined for the most part to crimes of passion and of mental aberration. In the farming community of this period property was extremely safe. Locks and keys were little used. Policemen were unknown. Owing to the sparseness of population social contacts outside the family were comparatively limited. The people of a particular neighborhood, moreover, were fairly homogeneous with respect to nationality, social position, and world outlook. They believed in their institutions and usually held in common deep religious and moral convictions. The corrosive sweep of ideas, so characteristic of a society of high mobility and cultural intermingling, was still in the future. Social control was achieved very largely through the molding influence of home, church, and local community.

In a society of this type serious disputes were not common. Differences of course arose from time to time, but as a general rule they were settled out of court. The very idea of going to the law was often looked upon as a violation of the mores and perhaps as a sign of weakness. There were other and less costly ways of achieving justice. Because of the breadth of family function, the great majority of disputes arose in the home and were settled before the family council. Quarrels between neighbors were of not infrequent occurrence and sometimes resulted in bitter feuds, but very commonly the parties to the quarrel composed their differences under the pressure of community opinion and the healing power of the years. The settlement of minor disputes by physical encounter was widely practised and doubtless added variety to a life that always inclined toward monotony. For a man to refuse to resort to trial by strength and skill of body was often regarded as cowardly, at least in those regions near the frontier. Occasionally the pioneering community took the law into its own hands, organized vigilance committees, conducted lynching parties, and engaged in various forms of extra-legal procedure.

The few cases that did reach the courts of agrarian society were in a very genuine sense tried by and before the neighborhood. The judge probably knew personally the parties to the dispute and was acquainted with the more relevant circumstances. Also the trial was attended in force by the community, providing one of the major spectacles or amusements of rural

America. "Before the days of the automobile, the movie, and the radio," writes Dean Roscoe Pound, "before urban amusements were available to every farmer every day, along with politics, the criminal trials at the court house were the staple diversion. During 'court week' the wagons of the farmers were tied up about the court house square and an appreciative audience watched the fine points of the trial-game as an urban audience might watch the fine points of a professional baseball game."[1] The following account of the functioning of the county court in colonial Virginia reveals a similar situation:

"Court-day was a holiday for all the country-side, especially in the fall and spring. From all directions came in the people on horseback, in wagons, and afoot. On the court-house green assembled, in indiscriminate confusion, people of all classes, the hunter from the backwoods, the owner of a few acres, the grand proprietor, and the grinning, needless negro. Old debts were settled, and new ones made; there were auctions, transfers of property, and, if election times were near, stump-speaking."[2]

It was to meet such conditions that American legal institutions were devised. Throughout the colonial period English practices and ideas were being transported across the Atlantic and adapted to life in the new world. Yet "for most practical purposes," according to Dean Pound, "our legal history may be said to begin after the Revolution." Until the middle of the eighteenth century "justice was administered by lay magistrates, by soldiers, clergymen, or administrative officers, and by legislative assemblies, rather than by courts in a modern sense." There were no law reports until the end of that century. With the launching of the nation a new era opened. Consequently, "the last quarter of the eighteenth century and the first quarter of the nineteenth century is the formative period of Ameri-

[1] Roscoe Pound, *Criminal Justice in America* (New York, 1930), 163.
[2] Oliver Perry Chitwood, *Justice in Colonial Virginia* (Baltimore, 1905), 94–95.

can law as it stands today; it is the period in which the English legal materials were received and made over by a body of men learned in the law, sitting on the bench, making law in the legislatures, or lecturing and writing as law teachers."[3] The administration of justice in twentieth century America is thus entrusted to institutions that antedate the age of coal and iron and gasoline—that took form at a time when the doctrines of individualism in economy and of absenteeism in government were sweeping over the country and were in fairly close harmony with the facts of social life.

Nothing said here, however, should be interpreted to mean that justice was administered equally and efficiently throughout the population in pre-industrial society. The contrary was certainly the case. During the colonial period the inequalities in economic and social status, which abounded both north and south, were clearly reflected in the laws and the courts. In Massachusetts "a true gentleman" could not be sentenced to the whipping post—a punishment reserved for "common, vulgar fellows"; and the scales of justice were definitely weighted in favor of those who bore the title of "Mister." Well down into the nineteenth century debtors had few rights and could be clapped into prison. In the south the Negro labored under the disabilities of chattel slavery and the "poor whites" were subjected to conditions of material and spiritual degradation. Even on the frontier the influence of wealth and position early became manifest: real estate speculators gambled with other people's money, a creditor class captured the citadels of economic power, and in hard times the poor were forced off their lands by the law and compelled to move on into the west there to repeat the harsh and bitter experience of the pioneer. All of this, and more, is true. Yet the fact remains that in agrarian America the problem of the administration of justice was far less complex than it is today.

[3] Roscoe Pound, *op. cit.*, 117–118.

JUSTICE IN INDUSTRIAL SOCIETY

With the coming of industrial society the problem of the administration of justice assumed a radically different character. The number of social contacts and of occasions of friction multiplied immeasurably, the population grew more and more heterogeneous, the power of the family, the church and the neighborhood weakened, the faith of men in the inherited ideas and institutions declined, the detection and apprehension of offenders became ever more difficult, and the triumph of profit-seeking enterprise in a pecuniary economy raised the acquisition of wealth to the level of a public virtue and undermined the ethical foundations of the law. The present situation may best be understood if attention is directed first to certain trends in the administration of justice attending the spread of industrialism and then to the facts regarding the attainment of the ideal of freedom and equality of justice in the United States.

Trends in the Administration of Justice. The nineteenth century witnessed the appearance of many new problems in the administration of justice. The growth of cities, of large-scale enterprise, of a closely-knit society placed a wholly new set of responsibilities upon the law and the courts—questions of employment, of living conditions, of housing standards, of food and water supply, of traffic regulation, of industrial, tenement, automobile, and transit accidents. The withdrawal of manufacturing from the home led to laws regarding child labor and compulsory schooling, hours of work for women and various forms of insurance. In a word, burdens of ever increasing magnitude respecting justice were transferred from the family and the unorganized community to the state. Indeed toward the close of the nineteenth century the family iteslf began to show signs of disorganization. Juvenile and domestic relations courts were the result.

That this period should be marked by an enormous expansion in judicial and legal activity was inevitable. The expansion of commerce and industry and the rapid growth of population stimulated a great increase in litigation. Thus, "where a century ago a volume of the reports of the Supreme Court of the United States covered a period of fourteen months, during which time eighty-four causes were decided, a single volume of the reports of that court covers the single day of June 16, 1913, in which decisions were rendered in sixty causes."[4] The annual increase of the rulings of courts, of which there are now 1,500,000 available as judicial precedents, covers "170,000 printed pages."[5] Legislative chambers also have been busy grinding out laws at a rapid rate. "According to a reported count," declare Clark and Douglas, "the five years prior to 1914 show a total of over 62,000 statutes passed and included in the printed volumes of laws in the United States."[6]

For the enforcement and interpretation of this growing body of statute and common law there has been a corresponding development of the machinery of justice. The first occupational census, taken in 1850, reports 2119 watchmen, but no policemen. The word *policemen* did not appear in the census until 1870; and a police force, as now understood, was a product of the latter half of the nineteenth century in the United States.[7] In 1930 there were in the country 41,823 marshals, sheriffs, and detectives, 131,687 policemen, and 148,115 guards, watchmen, and doorkeepers.

In the case of the profession of law growth has proceeded but little faster than the population, or from 23,939 "lawyers" in 1850 to 160,605 "lawyers, judges, and justices" in 1930. The training of the lawyer, however, has experienced radical change

[4] Charles W. Eliot, Moorfield Story, Louis D. Brandeis, Adolph J. Rodenbeck, and Roscoe Pound, *Efficiency in the Administration of Justice* (Preliminary report for The National Economic League, Boston), 8.

[5] Charles E. Clark and William O. Douglas, "Law and Legal Institutions," Chapter XXVIII in the President's Research Committee on Social Trends, *Recent Social Trends in the United States* (New York, 1933), II, 1430.

[6] *Ibid.*   [7] Roscoe Pound, *op. cit.*, 148.

during this period. In 1850 the great majority of the members of the profession were trained in law offices by a kind of apprenticeship; today they are being trained in law schools of various grades. In form of service rendered the bar has reflected the movement of ideas and interests in American history. Prior to the Civil War leadership went to the trial lawyer, in the second half of the century, to the defender of the railroads, while today it "seems to have passed to the client-caretaker." Law, therefore, like so many other activities, has become absorbed by business enterprise. As President Harding once remarked, "the business of America is Business." The consequence for the administration of justice is fairly obvious:

"The office of a leader of the bar is a huge business organization. Its function is to advise, to organize, to reorganize, and direct business enterprises, to point out dangers and mark safe channels and chart reefs for the business adventurer, and in our older communities to act, as one might say, as a steward for the absentee owners of our industries. The actual administration of justice in the courts interests him only as it discloses reefs or bars or currents to be avoided by the pilot of business men. Thus the leaders of the bar in the cities are coming to be divorced not only from the administration of criminal justice, but from the whole work of the courts, and the most effective check upon judicial administration of justice is ceasing to be operative."[8]

The various changes in legal institutions seem not to have kept pace with the course of events. Since the law, ever-respectful of precedent, is essentially conservative, the adaptations thus far achieved are superficial in character. The localism, suited to a land of great distances and of primitive means of communication, has persisted down to the present. "While the country was in process of economic unification," writes Dean Pound, "it was increasingly provincial in its law. Attempts to improve

[8] Roscoe Pound and Felix Frankfurter, editors, *Criminal Justice in Cleveland* (Cleveland, 1922), 603.

the criminal law were met not merely with indifference; they encountered positive resistance from lawyers convinced that the local law and practice, as they had learned them, were a precious local possession."[9] There is also an overlapping and a conflict of jurisdictions that can only be explained in terms of the rural heritage. The same author has thus described the condition in the realm of criminal justice:

"Each state, each county, each municipality, each court, each prosecutor, each police organization—and often more than one is operating in the same territory—is likely to go its independent course, with little or no regard for what the other is doing. It may even happen that state and federal prosecuting agencies or judicial officers may cross each other's paths and interfere with each other's operations. The well known case of Dodge, wanted in New York for perjury and fled to Texas, is an extreme but characteristic example. Before he could be taken back to New York, there were four writs of habeas corpus, there was a conflict of jurisdiction between state and federal officials, there were four extradition warrants, one injunction, one appeal, and one contempt proceeding. Even then it was necessary for a masterful detective to take the bull by the horns and put the fugitive into the hands of justice by an extra-legal coup. Nothing could illustrate better the extreme decentralization, the want of organization or coöperation, the overgrowth of checks and hindrances, and the hypertrophy of procedure which embarrass the administration of criminal justice in the economically unified land of today."[10]

The actual functioning, in industrial society, of the ideas and institutions inherited from pioneering and agrarian times will now be examined. Following a statement of the American ideal of freedom and equality of justice, the administration of justice to the poor, to racial and cultural minorities, and to

[9] Roscoe Pound, *op. cit.*, 146.   [10] *Ibid.*, 175.

political non-conformists, will be briefly reviewed. Here will be found the measure of the efficiency of the system, the fact being fully recognized that in many cases final responsibility rests, not upon the courts, but upon the social and economic order.

Freedom and Equality of Justice. "To no one will we sell, to no one will we refuse or delay, right or justice." This ideal, expressed in the Great Charter wrested from King John at Runnymede more than seven centuries ago, can be traced far back through the history of the Anglo-Saxon peoples. It crossed the Atlantic with the first colonists and took root in the culture of the new world. It was embodied in the Declaration of Rights of the Massachusetts Constitution adopted in 1780:

"Every subject of the Commonwealth ought to find a certain remedy, by having recourse to the laws, for all injuries or wrongs which he may receive in his person, property or character. He ought to obtain right and justice freely, and without being obliged to purchase it; completely, and without any denial; promptly, and without delay; conformably to the laws."

In commenting on this ancient ideal and particularly on this provision of the Massachusetts Constitution, Reginald Heber Smith thus summarizes the situation in the United States:

"Freedom and equality of justice are twin fundamental conceptions of American jurisprudence. Together they form the basic principle on which our entire plan for the administration of justice is built. They are so deep-rooted in the body and spirit of our laws that the very meaning which we ascribe to the word justice embraces them. A system which created class distinctions, having one law for the rich and another for the poor, which was a respecter of persons, granting its protection to one citizen and denying it to his fellow, we would unhesitatingly condemn as unjust, as devoid of those essentials without which there can be no justice . . .

"As state after state has been added to the Union, its people, in constitutional assembly, have written the same declaration (as Massachusetts) into their fundamental law. In New York the declaration is contained in a statute, but this is exceptional. To-day, the constitution of nearly every state, by express provision of the Bill of Rights, guarantees the freedom and equality of justice. The Fourteenth Amendment to the Constitution of the United States adds to the state guaranty the authority of the supreme law of the land.

"As a matter of law, the right stands inviolable. It is recognized and established by the highest possible authority. But that is not all. Its incorporation into the Bills of Rights transformed the principle from merely a legal or juristic conception to a political consideration of supreme importance. Not only was the right to freedom and equality of justice set apart with those other cardinal rights of liberty and of conscience which were deemed sacred and inalienable, but it was made the most important of all because on it all the other rights, even the rights to life, liberty, and the pursuit of happiness, were made to depend. In a word, it became the cornerstone of the Republic."[11]

Justice and the Poor. After a careful study of the entire question, Mr. Smith concludes that "the administration of American justice is not impartial, the rich and the poor do not stand on an equality before the law, the traditional method of providing justice has operated to close the doors of the courts to the poor, and has caused a gross denial of justice in all parts of the country to millions of persons."[12] That this is the condition, in spite of the ideal treasured through the centuries, seems to be the universal testimony of competent scholars. "The rich have many law books written to protect their privileges," writes Edward A. Parry, an English jurist, "but the poor who are the

[11] Reginald Heber Smith, *Justice and the Poor,* The Carnegie Foundation for the Advancement of Teaching (New York, 1919), 3–4.
[12] *Ibid.,* 8.

greater nation have but few."[13] In an address before the Virginia Bar Association, William Howard Taft spoke as follows:

"Of all the questions which are before the American people, I regard no one more important than the improvement of the administration of justice. We must make it so that the poor man will have as nearly as possible an equal opportunity in litigating as the rich man, and under present conditions, ashamed as we may be of it, this is not the fact."[14]

The Manly Report of the United States Commission on Industrial Relations in 1915 found "denial of justice in the creation, in the adjudication and in the administration of law,"[15] one of the major sources of industrial unrest. In a bulletin issued the same year the American Judicature Society states the case in unqualified language: "If there is one sad anomaly that should stand out in our present days of conscientious self-searching, it is the harsh fact that, with all our prating about justice, we deliberately withhold it from the thousands who are too poor to pay for it."[16] *The San Francisco Recorder* of November 6, 1916, is equally emphatic:

"The equal administration of the laws is a right guaranteed by the fundamental law of the land; and yet no person will deny that this privilege is more honored in the breach than in the observance; for there are very many people in every American community who, through ignorance of their rights or their inability to pay the imposts levied by the state as a condition precedent to the pursuit of justice in the courts, are constantly being denied that equal administration of the laws and the justice that is supposed, logically, to follow it."[17]

The causes of denial of justice to the poor have already been suggested in part. Like most other things, justice in the United

---

[13] Edward A. Parry, *The Law and the Poor* (New York, 1914), 1.
[14] Quoted in Reginald Heber Smith, *op. cit.*, 6.   [15] *Ibid.*, 8.
[16] *American Judicature Society* (Chicago, April, 1915), Bulletin VIII, 24.
[17] Quoted in Reginald Heber Smith, *op. cit.*, 8.

States costs time and money. There are consequently millions who cannot afford to purchase it. More fundamentally the situation has been complicated by great historic changes. Although the poor have been the victims of severe discrimination in every society, even in the American pioneering community of a century ago, their lot has been made peculiarly difficult by the rise of industrial civilization. Dean Pound has clearly outlined the significance of these changes:

"Our judicial organization and the great body of our American common law are the work of the last quarter of the eighteenth century and the first half of the nineteenth century. On the other hand our great cities and the legal and social problems to which they give rise are of the last half of the nineteenth century, and indeed the pressing problems do not become acute until the last quarter of that century.

"One of these problems was 'to make adequate provision for petty litigation in communities where there is a huge volume of such litigation which must be dealt with adequately on pain of grievous denial of justice; to provide for disposing quickly, inexpensively, and justly of the litigation of the poor, for the collection of debts in a shifting population, and for the great volume of small controversies which a busy, crowded population, diversified in race and language, necessarily engenders.' "[18]

The point should be observed that the fault lies not in the substantive law. Here one may find no corresponding "taint of partiality." It is in the process of administration that the greater inequalities enter the picture—justice is denied through delay, through court costs and fees, and through expense of counsel.

The complications attending the administration of justice in American courts make possible, if they do not definitely encourage, delay after delay in the adjudication of both civil

[18] Quoted in *ibid.,* 7.

and criminal cases. The way in which this circumstance affects the poor man accused of crime has been set forth by Justin Miller:

"One of the greatest disadvantages of the poor, innocent man in his contacts with the law in the earlier steps of his case, is delay. The guilty man may, and often does, actually court delay. The innocent man who can afford to employ attorneys and detectives and who is at large on bail may also gain by delay. But the one man who stands to lose by reason of it is the poor and innocent one. Delay for him means, first, the loss of his job; second, reduction of his chances of getting another job, by reason of the unsavory reputation which incarceration gives him; third, loss of his family and his home, because absence of the breadwinner means in many cases inability to pay the rent and installments on the furniture, delinquency of wife and children and a break-up of the family; and, worst of all, loss of his own self-respect and respect for the government under which he lives. We have not far to look for one of the main reasons for disrespect of law and government, when we permit such conditions to obtain. Of course the same results of delay may happen in the case of the guilty man, but in his case we regard incarceration as necessary and the length of time spent in jail is, comparatively speaking, unimportant. Of course, even in the case of the guilty man, if his offense is only a minor one, he may be unduly punished by reason of such delay.

"The man who knows the ropes, who is able to make the proper intercessions and supplications, who is willing to plead guilty to a lesser charge, or who is able to make effective promises of better future conduct, may go free easily. The man who is represented by counsel, or better still by influential political friends, can frequently secure speedy release. The man who is out on bail does not care how long the case drags on. But the poor, innocent man, unacquainted with the ways of the inferior courts, unrepresented by counsel or friends, and especially such a man who loudly asserts his innocence, demands a jury trial and rejects with scorn a proffered light sentence or fine in return for a plea of guilty, is very apt to be returned to custody to 'stew in his own juice' until the 'proper' time has arrived for jury trials. This is especially apt to be true in the case of the man who was originally imprisoned to work out a grudge of some one close to the organization."[19]

The thwarting of civil justice by delays is revealed in a case tried in the Philadelphia courts and described by Mr. Smith as "typical of a condition which has existed in every large city":

"A wage-earner had a claim for ten dollars, which represented a week's work. On January 19, 1911, the Legal Aid Society tried his case in the Magistrate's Court and secured judgment. On February 8, 1911, the defendant appealed to the Court of Common Pleas, which gave him the right to have the entire case tried all over again. On March 11, 1911, the plaintiff's claim was filed in the Court of Common Pleas and the case marked for the trial list. Owing to congested dockets the case did not actually appear on a trial list until February 7, 1912.

"Here entered a rule of procedure which would be incredible if it did not exist. A case marked for trial Monday must be tried Monday or Tuesday or else go off the list entirely. That is, if any prior case or cases marked on Monday's calendar should occupy the time of the court during Monday and Tuesday, then all other cases assigned on that list are cancelled and the parties must begin at the bottom again, re-marking the case for trial and awaiting the assignment. While this is going on in one session, another session of the same court may have no cases and so be obliged to suspend, for, under the legal procedure, it was forbidden to do the common-sense

[19] Justin Miller, "The Difficulties of the Poor Man Accused of Crime," *The Annals* (March, 1926), CXXIV, 66–67.

thing of transferring cases from a congested to an empty session of court.

"The wage-earner's case, assigned for February 7, 1912, was not reached on that day or the next, and so went off the list. It was re-marked and assigned for April 3, 1912. Not being reached on April 3 or 4, it again went off and did not reappear until October 10, 1912. Fortunately, it was reached and tried on October 11, 1912, and judgment entered for the plaintiff. It took one year and nine months, and required eleven days in court for both attorney and client, to collect the original ten dollars."[20]

Court costs and fees constitute a second cause of denial of justice to the poor. These charges vary enormously from city to city and from state to state. And according to Mr. Smith, there seems to be no principle by which they are "determined and regulated." The system has simply grown up through the centuries; and if it "were brought forward de novo, it would be ridiculed as absurd."[21] The costs may include such items as writ of summons fee, service of process fee, entry fee, calendar fee, trial fee, entry of judgment fee, issuance of execution fee, appellate fees, and fees for witnesses, briefs, and transcripts. Also the plaintiff in a civil suit "must, on motion, furnish a bond to guarantee that the defendant, if successful, shall not be out of pocket. . . . The net result is that a poor person who is unable to give or secure such a bond may be thrown out of court altogether."[22] And a little further on in his argument, Mr. Smith declares: "The result is no different than it would be if our bills of rights read,—'Every subject who can furnish a bond of fifteen or seventy-five dollars ought to obtain justice freely, completely, and without delay; to all others the courts are closed.' "[23]

20 Reginald Heber Smith, *op. cit.*, 18.
21 *Ibid.*, 23.   22 *Ibid.*, 29.   23 *Ibid.*

In a somewhat more recent study, John MacArthur Maguire found a similar state of affairs:

"It is known that in the single city of Boston during a period of about six years almost four hundred claimants were unable to start actions because they could not pay court fees. Small as these fees were, statutory insistence upon their advance collection caused as blunt a denial of justice as if the legislature had posted on the court-house door a sign: 'No plaintiffs admitted except those who have at least five or ten dollars in their pockets.'

"Turning . . . to the existing statutes, we find them unsatisfactory for a variety of reasons. Lack of administrative provisions . . . also a glaring lack of breadth and uniformity. Some statutes help plaintiffs but not defendants. Some aid residents but not non-residents. Some extend solely to citizens and exclude aliens. Some apply only to inferior courts, leaving poor suitors helpless on appeal. These distinctions are inimical to the maintenance of close commercial and social relations which our federalized organization demands. They are at war with any practical spirit of fairness. What American state would think of saying in terms that its courts or some of its courts were inaccessible to a poor man because he was on one side of a case rather than the other, because he was a non-resident or an alien, or just because he *was* poor? Yet many states are tolerating laws which say one or more of these things by necessary implication."[24]

In a yet more recent study, Kenneth Dayton passes the following judgment on court fees:

"The poor man, suing to recover $50 in wages, pays three-quarters of the expense of the court maintained for his benefit; the wealthier litigant in the higher courts pays roughly a tenth. But of course the real discrepancy is much greater than

[24] John MacArthur Maguire, "The Model Poor Litigants' Statute," *The Annals* (March, 1926), CXXIV, 86–87.

this, because the poor man pays precisely the same fees in the Municipal Court for a $50 claim as a corporation for a $1000 claim, and with no distinction whether the claim is disposed of in fifteen minutes or two days. Hence, proportionately, the poorest litigant probably pays substantially over 100 per cent of the cost of handling his case, though he is least able to bear the expense."[25]

Finally, there is the question of the expense of counsel. In the administration of justice in the United States the "lawyer is indispensable." And since his charges must of necessity be considerable, the mere "simplification of procedure and reorganization of courts," as important as such reforms are, will by no means make justice free and equal. As Mr. Smith contends, "the problem of the attorney will still remain the great stumbling-block."[26] This investigator, after making an analysis of the costs of counsel and of the distribution of income in the country, comes to the following conclusion:

"From this calculation it appears that there are in the United States over 35,000,000 men, women, and children whose financial condition renders them unable to pay any appreciable sum for attorneys' services. It is true that in country districts and in the smaller towns such people generally are able to secure assistance from lawyers as a matter of kindness or charity; consequently it is primarily in the larger cities that inability to pay fees results in a denial of justice. Even if we were to eliminate however, the 78 per cent of our population living in cities and towns containing less than 100,000 inhabitants, there would still remain nearly 8,000,000 persons who do not know where to turn for legal advice and assistance when the need arises. These figures are only approximations. Cut them in two and it is still perfectly apparent that a thoroughgoing, equal administra-

[25] Kenneth Dayton, "Costs, Fees, and Expenses in Litigation," *The Annals* (May, 1933), CLXVII, 41.
[26] *Op. cit.,* 31.

tion of justice must take cognizance of, and provide for, a class of citizens, numbering millions, who cannot secure for themselves the legal services without which the machinery of justice is unworkable."[27]

The general contrast between the rich and the poor in the administration of justice has been drawn by Mr. Miller:

"The first contact with the law comes with arrest. If a complaint is made against a particular person, a wide discretion exists in the police officers as to when and under what circumstances an arrest may be made. If the person complained of is one of standing in the community, who is personally acquainted with the officers, it is entirely possible that no arrest in the formal sense will ever be made at all. He may be called on the telephone or he may be visited by an officer who will notify him of the complaint and advise him to make an appearance before the judge at a particular time when bail can be fixed and his release secured pending further disposition of the case. In some cases it is not even necessary for the accused person to make a personal appearance in court. A bail bond is prepared by some person whose business it is to do so, which is presented to the court and an entry made releasing the accused person from a custody which in reality never existed. In some notorious cases of bail-bond abuse, it appears that the bail-bond broker merely calls the judge on the phone, informs him that he will provide a bond, and the order is made without further delay. In such cases it also appears that many times nothing further happens. The case of the accused person is never called in court, or if it is called, he does not appear, the bail bond is declared forfeited, but no steps are ever taken to collect it, and the matter ends there.

"Contrast with this procedure that which takes place when the accused person is a poor man unacquainted with the methods of manipulation suggested above, who has no acquaintance

[27] *Ibid.*, 33.

with the police, or with those persons, shyster lawyers, bail-bond brokers, runners, *et al,* who regularly grease the wheels of justice for their own particular purposes. Such persons are arrested at such time and place as suits the convenience of the arresting officers, regardless of the time of day or night, and regardless of age, sex or present condition. They are hauled off to places of detention and sometimes kept there for indefinite periods of time, awaiting the slow turning of the wheels of the judicial machine. At this point the right to give bail is entirely overlooked unless the accused person knows enough to demand and to exercise that right. The right to immediate service of counsel is overlooked unless the accused person knows enough to demand his right in this connection.

"Of course if he is a poor man, he is not in a very advantageous position for exercising either one of the rights mentioned. Instead of either one of the rights being an advantage to him, it may very well be used for his exploitation. There are usually about jails, members of the police force, stool pigeons, men under sentence, or professional shysters, who make it a business to find out whether a newly arrested person has any money in his possession, or if he has relatives or friends from whom he can procure money. If he has neither money nor friends, he is left in jail to await whatever may happen to him. If, as the evidence is developed, it turns out that the case against him is a poor one, he may be soon discharged, and whatever damages he may have suffered by reason of loss of employment or loss of social standing are for him to bear. If on the other hand it is found that he has money or friends from whom money can be secured, then he is at once solicited to employ a lawyer whose fee is determined largely by how much he can get from the accused person. Or he is solicited to purchase a bail bond from a broker of the type mentioned above, who charges him as a premium an exorbitant fee of approximately 25 per cent of the total amount of the bond. If he has money enough to put up cash bail and does so, the chances are very good that when the bail is finally discharged, the cash will never come back to him, but will find its way into the hands of the shysters above mentioned. . . .

"After verdict, the poor man may be again under very serious handicaps. His right to counsel at the expense of the state usually does not extend beyond the trial. If he wishes to appeal, he must find the money to pay for it. That requires a substantial sum, frequently beyond his reach. As a consequence, conviction in the trial court is usually the end of the poor man's day in court, though for men who can afford it, appeals are frequently successful."[28]

In a study of lawlessness in law enforcement a federal commission appointed by President Hoover to investigate the condition of law observance and enforcement in the United States found the poor peculiarly subject to various forms of illegal coercion. "That the third degree is especially used against the poor and uninfluential," observed this commission, "is asserted by several writers, and confirmed by official informants and judicial decisions. The likelihood of abuse is less when the prisoner is in contact with an attorney. The poor and uninfluential are less apt to be represented."[29]

To remedy these evils and to extend equal justice to the poor, various reform movements have been promoted by public-spirited citizens during the past half century. Legal aid for the unfortunate, which was first considered in 1875, has grown to large proportions and reveals the development of a definite social conscience regarding this matter. Other reforms have embraced small claims courts, conciliation, arbitration, domestic relations courts, industrial accident commissions, administrative tribunals, administrative officials, assigned counsel, and the defender in civil cases.[30] The appearance of the public defender

[28] *Op. cit.,* 64–65, 69.
[29] National Commission on Law Observance and Enforcement, *Report on Lawlessness in Law Enforcement* (Washington, June 25, 1931), No. 11, 159.
[30] For a detailed account of each of these reforms, including legal aid work, see Reginald Heber Smith, *op. cit.,* Parts II and III.

is particularly noteworthy. According to Sutherland and Gehlke, in 33 states the court provides the indigent defendant with a defender at public expense, "although 23 of these states provide compensation only in capital cases." While these students observe that the poor man is "not always well served by such a defense, since no expenses are allowed the defender for travel, investigation and the cost of witnesses," they conclude that "the experiences of those states and cities in which the defender has been made a part of the public machinery for justice are universally favorable."[31]

These many reforms, however, though contributing much to the alleviation of the lot of the poor, "do not obviate the need of a comprehensive solution."[32] They fail to penetrate to the heart of the problem. If the state gives justice to some and sells it to others, genuine equality before the law is not achieved. The fundamental difficulty therefore is not to be found in the law and the courts; rather does it reside in an economic system that permits poverty and riches, that generates the great inequalities in wealth and income characteristic of American society under the regime of private capitalism, and that fails to provide the material resources for the equal administration of the law.

Justice and Racial and Cultural Minorities. In general, racial and cultural minorities receive something less than fair treatment at the hands of the police and in the courts of the United States. Indians, though made citizens by special act of Congress, are actually denied many rights guaranteed by the fundamental law of the land; Orientals, including Chinese, Japanese, Filipinos, and Hindus, feel the weight of racial prejudice; and immigrants, particularly those coming from the south and east of Europe, are subject to more or less unfavorable discrimination. When such origins are associated with poverty and cul-

---

[31] Edwin H. Sutherland and C. E. Gehlke, "Crime and Punishment," Chapter XXII in *Recent Social Trends in the United States*, II, 1151–1152.

[32] John MacArthur Maguire, *op. cit.*, 87.

tural backwardness—a common condition—representatives of minorities are especially likely to be the victims of injustice. Owing to limitations of space attention will be confined here to the most severely underprivileged group in the country—the American Negro.

In most parts of the United States the possession of a black skin or even of a trace of Negro blood, provided the fact is known, is the occasion of many and diverse social disabilities. This is a generally admitted fact. As yet the democratic ideal has not been applied to persons of African descent. In ten states of the Union the Negro is denied the right to vote. In his case the "unequivocal guarantees of the federal constitution" are violated in fact, if not in strict legal terms.[33]

More than the members of any other race or group, the Negro is the victim of mob violence and extra-legal action. This fact is perhaps most fully exemplified in the history of lynching. From 1882 to 1933, the period covered by the records, 3604 Negroes met death by lynching in the United States. During the year 1933, in spite of decades of agitation against the practice, the number was 24. Lynching, however, is only the extreme form of mob violence. According to Johnson and Seligman, "in many parts of the South, up to the present, when a Negro has been accused of a major crime against a white person, or even has been a party in civil litigation, that Negro has had no rights, legal or otherwise, which the white community feels bound to respect."[34]

The Negro is more subject to arrest than his white brother. This is apparently due partly to the fact of racial prejudice; but it may also be traced to his relatively defenseless position in the social order. He is usually poor; he is denied certain political rights; and generally he has few resources and little influ-

[33] See pamphlet *Black Justice* (New York, May, 1931), American Civil Liberties Union.

[34] James Weldon Johnson and Herbert J. Seligman, "Legal Aspects of the Negro Problem," *The Annals* (November, 1928), CXXXX, 90.

ence. Policemen find that "it is unquestionably safer 'to pick up and mug' a Negro than a white person, because there is less fear of an unpleasant 'comeback.' "[35] Steiner and Brown even found economic forces influencing the arrest of Negroes in North Carolina:

"When a county has once adopted the plan of convict road work, it becomes necessary to maintain a convict road force sufficient in number to justify the overhead charges for equipment and supervision. Under such circumstances the local criminal courts tend to be looked upon as feeders for the chain gang, and there is evidence in some instances that the mill of criminal justice grinds more industriously when the convict road force needs more recruits."[36]

When the Negro reaches the court the discrimination continues. He will be tried before a white judge; and in the southern states, with only very rare exceptions, he will face a panel of white jurors.[37] According to Judge Scanlan of Chicago, "juries will convict a colored man with less hesitation than they will convict a white man on the same kind of evidence."[38] Regarding the impartiality of the trial judge, the Chicago Commission has this to say: "While judges in most courts treated Negro defendants as considerately as they did whites, conditions in other courts were quite different. One judge frequently assumed an attitude of facetiousness while hearing Negro cases. The hearings were characterized by levity and lack of dignity. In one instance the judge was shaking dice during the hearing of the case."[39] The discrimination against the Negro

35 The Chicago Commission on Race Relations, *The Negro in Chicago* (Chicago, 1922), 335.

36 Jesse F. Steiner and Roy M. Brown, *The North Carolina Chain Gang* (Chapel Hill, 1927), 6.

37 Morris L. Ernst, Lewis Gannett, and James Weldon Johnson, quoted in American Civil Liberties Union pamphlet, *Black Justice*, 21.

38 Quoted in Chicago Commission on Race Relations, *op. cit.*, 353.

39 *Ibid.*, 333.

in the courts, even in northern cities, is thus summarized by
Herman C. Adler:

"Repeatedly colored men have been convicted on evidence
which I know perfectly well would not have been satisfactory
in white cases. I know that was so in the case of the East St.
Louis riot where a colored man was sent down to the Southern
Illinois Penitentiary for participating in the riots on the charge
of murder. Even the prosecuting officer, on reviewing the facts,
a year later, admitted he did not believe the evidence sufficient.
If that had been a white man the chances are that he would not
have been convicted upon that evidence.

"We had the same thing here in Chicago: a colored man sent
to the penitentiary on a charge of attempted rape where the
identification was made by a child of six or eight years who
picked him out of a crowd under suspicion. No such evidence
ought to be accepted. We know there is prejudice, and when
there is prejudice we know the person against whom the prejudice is directed has a hard time."[40]

Discrimination, however, appears not to terminate with the
verdict of guilty. After conviction, often on inadequate or
faulty testimony, the Negro is likely to receive a more severe
sentence than the white man for the same offense. "The punishment meted out to Negro offenders," writes Edward B.
Reuter, "is characteristically more severe than that of white
offenders. They are committed to prison more frequently and
receive longer sentences for similar offenses."[41]

Justice and Political Non-Conformists. The struggle for the
right to express unconventional ideas and opinions is perhaps
as old as human history. And the struggle to deny this right
is no doubt equally ancient. The fathers of the republic, recognizing the value of freedom of expression to the individual
and society, endeavored to safeguard it through a provision em-

[40] *Ibid.*, 352.
[41] Edward B. Reuter, *The American Race Problem* (New York, 1927), 351.

bodied in the supreme law of the land. "Congress shall make no law," reads the First Amendment to the Constitution of the United States, "respecting an establishment of religion, or prohibiting the free exercise thereof; or abridging the freedom of speech, or of the press; or the right of the people peaceably to assemble, and to petition the government for a redress of grievances." The so-called free speech clause is included in the constitutions of all the states.

There is no space in these pages to tell the history of the fortunes and hazards of political dissent in the United States. The major facts are well known. In every period of national crisis, from the days of the Alien and Sedition Laws of 1798 down to the Espionage Acts of 1917 and 1918, personal rights guaranteed by the Constitution have, as a matter of course, been abrogated. In days of insecurity, particularly in times of war, the individual in any society may expect to be sacrificed for what the group regards as its welfare. Also movements aiming at fundamental social reform have commonly been subjected to more or less severe persecution at the hands of the majority and of vested interests. Thus organized labor, especially when it has advocated radical changes in the economic order, has often felt the discrimination of the police and the courts. This story follows the course of the industrial revolution in America, beginning perhaps with Frances Wright in the first quarter of the nineteenth century but scarcely growing acute until after the Civil War. It embraces such places, personalities, incidents, and organizations as the Molly Maguires, the riots of 1877, the Knights of Labor, the Haymarket tragedy, the American Federation of Labor, the Homestead strike, Coxey's Army, "The Debs Rebellion," the Industrial Workers of the World, "Big Bill" Haywood, the socialist movement, the dynamiting of *The Los Angeles Times* building, the Mooney-Billings trial, the United States v. Abrams, the great steel strike of 1919, the Communist Party, the Centralia affair, the Sacco-Vanzetti case, Harlan County, Kentucky, and the Toledo riots of 1934. These references merely mark high points in a bitter struggle that has been going on for generations. And in this struggle the spokesmen of change and of the laboring classes have commonly been denied free and equal justice in the American courts. This conclusion may be illustrated by three world-famous cases of the last seventeen years—the Mooney-Billings case of California, the Abrams case of New York, and the Sacco-Vanzetti case of Massachusetts.

On the twenty-second of July, 1916, a huge preparedness parade was held in the city of San Francisco. At six minutes past two, when the celebration was approaching its climax, a dynamite bomb was exploded at a central point in the line of march. Six persons were killed instantly, forty were injured, and four of the latter died within a few days. The cry arose at once that "The radicals did it"; and a number of labor leaders were arrested and charged with the crime. Prominent among these were Warren K. Billings and Tom Mooney. Both were convicted at the trial, the former being sentenced to life imprisonment and the latter to death by hanging. Under pressure from various sources, including the President of the United States, Mooney's sentence was commuted to life imprisonment. This case has attracted attention throughout the civilized world; but in spite of continuous agitation and petitions the two men remain in prison today.

Among the most extraordinary incidents in the history of the case was the effort to suppress a report of an inquiry of the trial conducted by competent investigators appointed by the National Commission on Law Observance and Enforcement. The Commission itself refusing to make the findings public, the report was published independently by the investigators. According to this report,[42] "the prosecution in its investigation was unfair to the defendants,"[43] the district attorney "showed a lack

[42] *The Mooney-Billings Report*—Suppressed by the Wickersham Commission (New York, 1932).
[43] *Ibid.*, 34–35.

of appreciation of the quasi-judicial nature of the prosecutor's office,"[44] the proceedings "had their origin in arrests that were unlawful,"[45] and neither the police nor the district attorney respected the "right of counsel."[46] The character of the witnesses, whose testimony has kept two men in prison for eighteen years, is described as follows:

"McDonald, a syphilitic, and 'psychopathic liar'; Crowley, a syphilitic whose testimony, when defending himself unsuccessfully against prosecution, was condemned by the judge that tried his case; Oxman, who testified falsely, and who signed letters whose clear effect was to induce another to do the same thing; Mrs. Edeau, who was a victim of hallucinations, and whose testimony was demonstrably false; Sadie Edeau, whose testimony followed her mother's, and falls with it; Estelle Smith, a prostitute with a police record."[47]

After reviewing the case from beginning to end and "considering the record as a whole," the investigators arrived at the following nine conclusions:

"(1) There was never any scientific attempt made by either the police or the prosecution to discover the perpetrators of the crime. The investigation was in reality turned over to a private detective, who used his position to cause the arrest of the defendants. The police investigation was reduced to a hunt for evidence to convict the arrested defendants.

"(2) There were flagrant violations of the statutory laws of California by both the police and the prosecution in the manner in which the defendants were arrested and held incommunicado, and in the subsequent searches of their homes to procure evidence against them.

"(3) After the arrest of the defendants, witnesses were brought to the jails to 'identify' them, and their 'identifications'

<table>
<tr><td>[44] Ibid., 50.</td><td>[45] Ibid., 58.</td></tr>
<tr><td>[46] Ibid., 59.</td><td>[47] Ibid., 185.</td></tr>
</table>

were accepted by the police and the prosecution, despite the fact that these witnesses were never required to pick the defendants out of a line-up, or to demonstrate their accuracy by any other test.

"(4) Immediately after the arrests of the defendants there commenced a deliberate attempt to arouse public prejudice against them, by a series of almost daily interviews given to the press by prosecuting officials.

"(5) Witnesses were produced at the trials with information in the hands of the prosecution that seriously challenged the credibility of the witnesses, but this information was deliberately concealed.

"(6) Witnesses were permitted to testify at the trials, despite such knowledge in the possession of the prosecution of prior contradictory stories told by these witnesses, as to make their mere production a vouching for perjured testimony.

"(7) Witnesses were coached in their testimony to a degree that approximated subornation of perjury. There is a strong inference that some of this coaching was done by prosecuting officials, and other evidence points to knowledge by the prosecuting officials that such coaching was being practiced on other witnesses.

"(8) The prejudice against the defendants, stimulated by newspaper publicity, was further appealed to at the trials by unfair and intemperate arguments to the jury in the opening and closing statements of the prosecuting attorneys.

"(9) After the trials, the disclosures casting doubt on the justice of the convictions were minimized, and every attempt made to defeat the liberation of the defendants, by a campaign of misrepresentation and propaganda carried on by the officials who had prosecuted them."[48]

The second case will be reviewed more briefly. It seems that on the morning of August 23, 1918, several thousand copies of

[48] *Ibid.*, 242–243.

two pamphlets were thrown from an upper story window at the intersection of two streets in New York City. The pamphlets, one in English and the other in Yiddish, attacked the United States government for despatching troops to Russia. Investigation by the military police led to the arrest of the authors and distributors of the tracts—Jacob Abrams, a young man of twenty-nine years, and five younger associates. The prisoners, with the exception of a certain Schwartz who died before trial, were brought before the district court on October 10, 1918, charged with violating four clauses of the Espionage Act of 1918. They were all found guilty and sentenced: one to three years in prison, one to fifteen years and $500 fine, and three to "twenty years and $1000 on each count."

After careful study Zechariah Chafee has reviewed the handling of the case in the following terms:

"The systematic arrest of civilians by soldiers on the streets of New York City was unprecedented, the seizure of papers was illegal, and the charges of brutality at Police Headquarters are very sinister. The trial judge ignored the fundamental issues of fact, took charge of the cross-examination of the prisoners, and allowed the jury to convict them for their Russian sympathies and their anarchistic views. The maximum sentence available against a formidable pro-German plot was meted out by him to the silly futile circulars of five obscure and isolated young aliens, misguided by their loyalty to their endangered country and ideals, who hatched their wild scheme in a garret, and carried it out in a cellar."[49]

Justice Holmes of the Supreme Court of the United States in a dissenting opinion rendered an even more severe judgment:

"In this case sentences of twenty years imprisonment have been imposed for the publishing of two leaflets that I believe

[49] Zechariah Chafee, *Freedom of Speech* (New York, 1920), 159.

the defendents had as much right to publish as the Government has to publish the Constitution of the United States now vainly invoked by them."[50]

The final case to be considered here has already sent its reverberations around the world. It begins at three o'clock in the afternoon of April 15, 1920, when in South Braintree, Massachusetts, two armed men killed the paymaster of a local shoe factory and his guard, and robbed them of approximately $15,000. On May 5, Nicola Sacco and Bartolomeo Vanzetti, two Italian workmen, the one a shoe-cutter and the other a fish-peddler and both known for their radical activities, were arrested and charged with the crime. The trial began on May 31, 1921, more than one year after the arrest. Approximately seven weeks later, on July 14, 1921, the two men were found guilty of murder in the first degree. Thereafter, because of the discovery of new evidence and the wide interest in the case, their fate hung in the balance until April 9, 1927, when the sentence of death was imposed upon them. They were executed just after midnight on August 22, of the same year.

The trial was conducted in a prejudicial atmosphere which the judge apparently made no effort to dispel. Felix Frankfurter has emphasized this fact:

"By systematic exploitation of the defendants' alien blood, their imperfect knowledge of English, their unpopular social views, and their opposition to the war, the District Attorney invoked against them a riot of political passion and patriotic sentiment; and the trial judge connived at—one had almost written, co-operated in—the process."[51]

Mr. Frankfurter even declares that Sacco and Vanzetti were the victims of an understanding between the local authorities and federal agents and that they were deliberately sent to the

[50] *Ibid.*, 120.
[51] Felix Frankfurter, *The Case of Sacco and Vanzetti* (Boston, 1927), 59.

electric chair, not for murder and robbery, as charged, but for their ideas:

"Hitherto the prejudicial methods pursued by the prosecution, which explain the the convictions, rested on inferences, however compelling. But recently facts have been disclosed, and not denied by the prosecution, to show that the case against Sacco and Vanzetti for murder was part of a collusive effort between the District Attorney and agents of the Department of Justice to rid the country of these Italians because of their Red activities. In proof of this we have the affidavits of two former officers of the Government, one of whom served as post-office inspector for twenty-five years, and both of whom are now in honorable civil employment."[52]

In reviewing the evidence brought to light after the trial which indicated that the crime had been committed by a criminal gang, well known to the police, Mr. Frankfurter thus puts the case:

"Can the situation be put more conservatively than this? Every reasonable probability points away from Sacco and Vanzetti; every reasonable probability points toward the Morelli gang."[53]

A new trial was denied. Passion, pride of opinion, and legal technicalities barred the way. The account may be closed with the words of Vanzetti uttered on the day sentence was pronounced, April 9, 1927:

"If it had not been for these thing, I might have live out my life, talking at street corners to scorning men. I might have die, unmarked, unknown, a failure. Now we are not a failure. This is our career and our triumph. Never in our full life could we hope to do such work for tolerance, for joostice, for man's onderstanding of man as now we do by accident.

52 *Ibid.*, 67–69.   53 *Ibid.*, 101.

Our words—our lives—lives of a good shoemaker and a poor
fish-peddler—all! That last moment belongs to us—that agony
is our triumph."[54]

Perhaps the most disturbing instance of the denial of justice
to political dissenters and non-conformists in the history of the
nation occurred in the years immediately following the World
War. In those years the officials of the United States Department of Justice, in a nationwide effort to root out radical activity and thought, engaged in the wholesale violation of the
Consitution that they had sworn to uphold. The denial of justice became so flagrant that a distinguished group of jurists,
headed by Roscoe Pound, Dean of the Harvard Law School,
conducted an investigation of the activities of the Department.
The findings of these jurists are thus summarized in the first
two paragraphs of their report to the American people which
was given to the press in May, 1920:

"For more than six months we, the undersigned lawyers,
whose sworn duty it is to uphold the Constitution and Laws of
the United States, have seen with growing apprehension the
continued violation of that Constitution and breaking of those
Laws by the Department of Justice of the United States government.

"Under the guise of a campaign for the suppression of radical
activities, the office of the Attorney General, acting by its local
agents throughout the country, and giving express instructions
from Washington, has committed continual illegal acts. Wholesale arrests both of aliens and citizens have been made without warrant or any process of law; men and women have been
jailed and held *incommunicado* without access of friends or
counsel; homes have been entered without search-warrant and
property seized and removed; other property has been wan-
tonly destroyed; workingmen and workingwomen suspected
of radical views have been shamefully abused and maltreated.

[54] Osmond K. Fraenkel, *The Sacco-Vanzetti Case* (New York, 1931), 21.

Agents of the Department of Justice have been introduced into radical organizations for the purpose of informing upon their members or inciting them to activities; these agents have even been instructed from Washington to arrange meetings upon certain dates for the express object of facilitating wholesale raids and arrests. In support of these illegal acts, and to create sentiment in its favor, the Department of Justice has also constituted itself a propaganda bureau, and has sent to newspapers and magazines of this country quantities of material designed to excite public opinion against radicals, all at the expense of the government and outside the scope of the Attorney General's duties."[55]

The foregoing pages show that the ideal of the Great Charter remains to be realized; that freedom and equality before the law are denied to a large proportion of the population; that the poor are unable to pay for the price of justice; that inequalities of wealth and income are reflected in the courts; that racial and cultural minorities are subject to unfavorable discrimination; and that holders of unpopular opinions often experience the abrogation of constitutional guarantees. Aside from weaknesses in human nature, which tend to show themselves in every age and social system, the major difficulty seems to lie in the rapid change from an agrarian to an industrial society; in the development of private capitalism; and in the severe struggle for wealth and position in a highly competitive, but closely integrated, economy. Judicial institutions have not kept pace with social change; nor is the populace prepared to tolerate the expression of the diverse points of view that jostle one another in the complex world of the present. In many of their ideas and loyalties the American people are still living in the age of Andrew Jackson.

[55] *Report Upon the Illegal Practices of the United States Department of Justice,* National Popular Government League, Washington (May, 1920), 3.

Chapter X

GOVERNMENT

Since the founding of the Republic the whole structure of American society has been transformed. That government should escape the impact of the forces released by technology was of course impossible. As a matter of fact, while political institutions have resisted change with great tenacity, the very conception of government has experienced a revolution during the past one hundred and fifty years. Beginning their national existence with the theory that economics and politics are fairly distinct departments of social life, the American people, without really being aware of their shift of position and even while continuing to employ the language of their fathers, are well on their way to the opposite arc of the cycle. The line between economy and government is becoming increasingly difficult to discern. Here certainly is one of the most profound trends in the history of the United States. In the present chapter an effort will be made to bring out its more essential elements.

THE DIVORCE OF POLITICS AND ECONOMICS

During the latter part of the eighteenth century the thought of the western world was turning to the emancipation of the individual from feudal and monarchical restraints and the establishment of a system of individual liberty, including both personal and property rights. In the regime under attack, which had come down from the Middle Ages, emphasis was laid on the duties of the lower classes to their feudal superiors and on the control of industry by guilds and government, with increasing activity on the part of the latter. Prices, wages, quality of goods, selling and marketing, and foreign trade were all regulated and controlled by the one or the other, or by both. The right of the individual to do as he pleased with his labor and property was everywhere denied; and the status of the individual was fixed by birth under law and custom. Although there were many exceptions to the rule, speaking generally, the social order was fixed and each person had a fixed place in it.

But by the end of the eighteenth century feudal society was breaking up in Europe. While some countries, such as England and France, were more advanced on that road than others, the system was destined to crumble everywhere, even in backward Russia. Attempts on a large scale to transfer feudalism to the English colonies failed, mainly on account of the abundance of cheap land and raw materials. Despite the institution of slavery and an occasional great estate, and despite a marked community life along the seaboard, for the most part, and particularly on the frontier, the single farmstead and a strong individualism held the center of economy. At the same time in England mechanical industry and capitalist enterprise were breaking down the old guilds and attacking restraints on trade. It was more than a coincidence that Adam Smith published his great treatise on economic individualism, *The Wealth of Nations,* in 1776, the very year of the proclamation of the Declaration of Independence.

In substance Smith's work was a defense of economic individualism or *laissez-faire,* and a protest against guild, community, and government interference with the right of every man to do as he pleased with his person and property. He contended that the individual knows his own interest better than any guild or government officer and, if let alone, will employ his labor and capital to the best advantage to himself. Smith then went on to argue that where each individual is free and follows his own interest, the result is beneficial to the country as a whole. It is a strange thing, he admitted, that the general good should result from selfish action on the part of everyone; and he could account for the fact only by reference to some inexplicable divine mystery. Yet he held that such is the nature of society. Turning to foreign trade, Smith argued that the same freedom from restraint should prevail there: individuals in each country should be allowed to exchange goods freely with individuals in foreign countries and thus introduce benefits all around. In short, government was to be confined to keeping order at home and defending the country against foreign foes; and the individual was to be free to do as he liked in the realm of economy. Under this scheme wealth would be "naturally" distributed and each would receive that portion to which he was entitled by his talents, enterprise, and labor. If some rose to affluence and others sank into misery, such results were the rewards of virtue and of idleness justly apportioned.

While this conception of government was making headway in England, it was spreading widely in the United States, especially among the Jeffersonian Republicans who represented particularly the individualistic farmers of the back country. "The less government the better" was the prevailing slogan. "Let the government keep order and refrain from interfering with economy and the distribution of wealth and the people will do the rest," was another way of phrasing the idea. Like all schemes, however, it was not universally accepted. The Federalists and their successors, the Whigs and Lincoln Republicans, rejected it in part. They insisted that the government should protect and promote business enterprise by tariff discriminations, subsidies, bounties, and other forms of intervention. Thus, while farmers and laborers were to be treated as individualists and were to receive no favors from government, business men were to be protected against foreign competition and assisted in developing their enterprises. On this account the system of individualism was never carried to its logical conclusion in the United States. Yet for a long time, subject to the exceptions mentioned, it was the dominant conception of government in the country. Under that system the frontier was carried to the Pacific and natural resources were exploited with marvelous results in output of wealth. And in the course of a century and a half the doctrines of individualism were so deeply imbedded in the mind of the American people that in 1928 a former president of the United States Chamber of Commerce could declare, amid the applause of his confreres, that "the best public servant is the worst one. . . . A thoroughly first-rate man in public service is corrosive. He eats holes in our liberties. The better he is and the longer he stays, the greater is the danger."

GOVERNMENT INTERVENTION IN ECONOMY

As the railways were built (frequently with government aid on a large scale), the continent rounded out, huge industrial cities established, and more than one-half the people drawn into urban centers, changes appeared in the practice of government and the whole system of individual liberty was attacked. With the passage of time business concerns showed a marked tendency to concentrate in the hands of immense corporations in which individual enterprise played a small rôle. On the other side, it was evident that poverty, misery, and slums accompanied the system of liberty and that the system had not in fact brought about the general welfare which had been promised in its name. From year to year the functions of governments—municipal, state, and federal—multiplied, indicating an abandonment of *laissez-faire* in practice. Although the doctrine continued to be passionately defended in theory, even by those who benefitted from each concrete repudiation of its provisions, before the twentieth century was far advanced, the system of individualism was riddled in many places by innumerable laws and administrative practices.

The Growth of Government Functions. The steady development of government intervention in all departments of economy and cultural life and the gradual substitution of collective action and responsibility for individual enterprise and initiative are known to every citizen. This sweeping tendency of the age is evident in the growth of public expenditures, the multiplication of civil servants, and the expansion of governmental activities. Efforts have been made to check it, but those who have opposed it in one field have usually advocated it in another.

From 1913 to 1930, according to the President's Research Committee on Social Trends, the proportion of the national income devoted to the maintenance of governmental functions was almost doubled.[1] Also, "governments in general," says the Committee, "have been increasing in size and power. The only other great social organizations to compare with them in rates of growth are our economic institutions. This growth seems to have occurred despite conflicting views as to what the functions of government should be."[2] The new rôle of the federal government has been described by Charles A. and William Beard:

"Under the pressure of these new forces, government itself has become an economic and technical business on a large scale. It comes into daily contact with all industries, sciences, and arts. As a purchaser of goods in a bewildering variety for its normal needs, government must deal with such involved matters as chemical composition, physical properties, and durability. An operator of battleships, dirigibles, canals, and wireless stations, it faces technical questions of the highest complication. A regulator of railways, telegraph lines, and other means of transportation and communication, it must command, for effective work, abilities equal to those of corporation managers, certainly greater than those of stockholding owners. A promoter of shipping, industry, and aviation, through direct or indirect subventions, it inevitably deals with the mechanics of these enterprises, unless forsooth it is to subsidize obsolescence and

[1] *Recent Social Trends in the United States* (New York, 1933), I, lxiii.
[2] *Ibid,.* lx.

426 SOCIAL FOUNDATIONS OF EDUCATION

inefficiency at public expense. Even in taxing—that ancient function—it must classify, analyze, and evaluate thousands of products flowing from machines, upon which it imposes duties and excises. As an employer of agents to carry on its intricate activities, government draws into its service representatives of all the professions, sciences, and arts known to technology."[3]

In the sphere of state government, according to Finla Goff Crawford, a revolution has occurred during the past forty years:

"A new conception of the state has arisen (from 1890 to 1920). It is now looked upon as an agency for the promotion of the well-being of its citizens. This position is in contrast with the old idea of the state which had for its chief function police activities. The rugged individualism of the middle nineteenth century has been checked and restricted by the socialized state . . . the authority of the state more and more has been invoked to protect the individual against the hardships resulting from the social and economic circumstances of modern life."[4]

In the city, which is peculiarly the product of the age of industrialism, the advance of government has been especially rapid and comprehensive. The distance traveled in a century may be gauged by noting the limited functions granted by the legislature of Illinois to the incorporated town of Chicago in 1835:

"To the nascent city of Chicago were granted no substantial property rights in land, no special business privileges or monopolies, no right to control the composition of its own membership, no power to acquire land beyond its boundaries except for cemeteries, no authority to maintain a meetinghouse, no common pasture, the right to license but not to own and oper-

[3] Charles A. Beard and William Beard, *The American Leviathan* (New York, 1930), 7.
[4] Finla Goff Crawford, *State Government* (New York, 1931), 498.

ate ferries, no royalties, no power to grant hunting and fishing licenses, and no power to provide a local court. The only trading functions conferred at this time upon Chicago were 'to lease the wharfing privilege of said town' but not to operate wharves directly, and 'to build market houses; (and to) establish and regulate markets,' which may have included the power to operate them."[5]

The actual growth of the functions of the city of Detroit from 1824 to 1921 has been studied by Lent D. Upson.[6] The findings of this inquiry have been summarized by William Anderson as follows:

"Detroit began its municipal history in 1809 and became a city in 1824. It then had eleven elementary functions, branches, or officers upon which it expended money, namely, elections, a legislative body, an executive, legal advice, taxation, a treasurer, police, a municipal court, a fire department, an elementary school, and street grading. Of these, it will be observed, only the last five really rendered services directly to the people. The other six may be classed as 'overhead' or 'staff' functions, necessary and useful indeed, but not themselves the ends for which a city exists.

"From 1824 down to the beginning of the Civil War only ten new functions were added, namely, poor relief, street paving, sewers, sewer cleaning, water supply, school census, controller, street lighting, high school, and prison, making in all twenty-one functions or objects of expenditure in 1861. In the next twenty years Detroit grew to be a city of 116,000 people, yet it added only fourteen new functions, of which the most important were a public library (1864), parks and publc buldings (1871), and an evening elementary school (1875). In 1880 the total number of separate functions was thirty-five, of which ten really gave important services directly to the people, while

5 William Anderson, *American City Government* (New York, 1925), 397.
6 Lent D. Upson, *The Growth of a City Government* (Detroit, 1931).

the others were overhead functions or were mere subdivisions of some one or other of the ten major services.

"In the first fifty-seven years of its municipal history (1824–80), the Detroit city government seems merely to have been laying foundations for future activities. The next forty years (1881–1920) saw the city's functions increase more than 400 per cent, from 35 to a total of 184. In the same period, of course, the city grew tremendously, reaching 993,000 population in 1920."[7]

This same author has described the conditions which led to the rapid growth of the functions of city government after 1880:

"From 1880 on the growth of cities was phenomenal. Every decade thereafter in the United States has shown a larger growth in urban than in rural population. The rush into the cities has accelerated instead of abated; but as it was big with promise for the industrial future of the country so it was also bristling with problems which could not be solved by the individualistic formula of 'let alone.' Health and police, local transportation and lighting, housing and city planning, imperatively demanded the action of the local government. Unrestricted private competition in some fields, such as gas and street railways, led first to ruin for some of the competitors and then to the destruction of competition itself through the combination of the forces of those who remained. Unregulated private building made cities hideous, unsafe, and insanitary. Railroads and factories ruined the waterfront, or obscured in smoke and drowned in noise fair districts which should have been set aside for homes."[8]

The Character of Government Functions. Although many efforts have been made to classify those functions of government which represent intervention in the realm of economic affairs, no single classification has been universally accepted.

[7] *Op. cit.*, 401–402.   [8] *Ibid.*, 399.

The arrangement employed here therefore, which should be regarded as illustrative rather than systematic and exhaustive, has been adopted merely for purposes of convenience. From the standpoint of the assault on the doctrines of individualism in economy, there are at least nine spheres of activity in which government has intervened: control of banking and credit, erection of tariff barriers, conservation of natural resources, service to business, assistance to agriculture, protection of urban workers, regulation of corporate enterprise, performance of various economic functions, and levying of taxes. In the account of government participation in each of these spheres of activity attention will be confined to the period ending with the Hoover administration. Reference to that series of measures launched by the federal government following the inauguration of Franklin D. Roosevelt as President of the United States on March 4, 1933, which would seem to mark the culmination of a long trend, will be reserved to the end of the chapter.

Control of banking and credit. One of the earliest checks on *laissez-faire* took place in the sphere of banking and credit. Even in the days of the agrarian and commercial economy banks collected individual savings and lent them to persons proposing to engage in productive enterprise. With the growth of industry this service expanded greatly, since it was found possible to make loans many times in excess of cash holdings. For years by far the greater part of the financing of manufacturing and commercial undertakings was managed by the banks. The great convenience of the credit-economy thus established was manifest from the beginning. As brokers for the country's investments, bankers early revealed the importance of their rôle; they decided what men or lines of endeavor should be given licenses to produce.[9] They became arbiters of the economic destiny of the nation. Where loans were

[9] "Credit is in effect a license or a permit from society to a syndicate, to an individual, or to the management of a corporation to tap the earth's energy supply and create goods and services. At present society has delegated the issuance

freely granted, the rapid development of an industry was possible; where they were withheld, the pace was retarded. For the making of these crucial decisions the banking business soon developed its own rules. Departure from the received canons of safety, which was chronic in many areas, meant frequent bank failure, stoppage of all credit, and consequent widespread disorganization. The permission given to many banks of feeble or corrupt management to issue notes, which might circulate as paper currency, threatened the stability of the monetary structure and even of the whole price-system.

In the minds of the propertied classes throughout the nineteenth century this situation naturally called for drastic action on the part of the state. The result was a long struggle of the commercial and industrial east against the agrarian and pioneer south and west in favor of a stable system of money and credit. In this struggle the east was finally victorious and succeeded in establishing the National Banking System during the Civil War period and the Federal Reserve System under the Wilson administration. Both of these measures, supported by legislation requiring regular inspection of all banks under the Federal Reserve System and rigid enforcement of stringent rules for the safety of trust funds, went far towards substituting central control for simple competition in the formulation and regulation of banking policy. Though control was still far from complete at the time Franklin D. Roosevelt entered the White House, more than 4000 banks having failed in the United States during a three-year period beginning near the close of 1929, it nevertheless represented the most severe limitations on the free play of economic forces attempted by the government down to 1933.

of such permits to persons who control banking houses, insurance companies, underwriting houses, and stock-exchange houses. Even the stock exchange is an indirect instrument for manufacturing credit, as the rise in value of listed stocks provides the owners with additional collateral or bank loans and also facilitates the issue of new stocks." Harper Leech, *The Paradox of Plenty* (New York, 1932), 98–99.

Erection of tariff barriers. Through tariff discriminations, subsidies, bounties, reciprocity treaties, aid in the extension of foreign trade, and other forms of interference with what was once called "the natural course" of industry and commerce the state has placed a second powerful check on *laissez-faire*. By successive stages the rates have been extended and raised until now almost all manufactured goods, except a few luxuries, some agricultural products, and certain important raw materials and minerals, are practically excluded from entry at American ports. Such a tendency points toward the abandonment of the automatic regulation of world price levels and also of the international currency system based upon gold; offers irresistible temptations to domestic producers to seek gratuities through prices supported by tariff barriers; and bears the imprint of the substitution of deliberate national policy for the competition of the market place. Moreover, since the protective system offers the advantages of a quasi-monopoly to any group of producers capable of finding shelter under its provisions, it holds out a powerful inducement to forsake competition in favor of collusion. Thus does the motive of personal gain tend to destroy the economic order that sanctified its operation.

As this form of behavior has manifested itself in various countries, the idea of complete free trade in the field of international exchange has been universally abandoned, if practice is any criterion of judgment. Despite long discourses in certain quarters on the necessity of removing "trade barriers in the way of the natural course of commerce," the nations of the earth are moving rapidly in the direction of "controlled trade." Although academicians have heaped much abuse on the heads of statesmen for lending encouragement to this "economic nationalism," there is discernible a noteworthy drift of opinion among both economists and publicists in the direction of what the Germans call "Autarkie," that is, the control of exports and imports with reference to the development of the largest possible self-sufficiency and security in domestic economy—a self-sufficiency and security as little subject as possible to the wars and other vicissitudes which periodically disrupt international commerce. In the realm of theory, some economists hope for "a return to free trade"—a state of affairs which never existed; others champion temporary adjustments designed to modify present trade restrictions; and still others are considering the nature and possibilities of "controlled trade," based upon a positive conception of domestic economy.

Conservation of natural resources. The failure of competitive business to show sufficient regard for the future in the exploitation of the land, the animal life, the timber, the minerals, and the water power of the nation[10] has led both state and federal authorities to place restrictions on the free use of these resources. The Bureau of Fisheries has assumed important responsibilities for the conservation of the fish of the country; the Bureau of Biological Survey has been charged with corresponding duties with respect to animal life; national policies for the guarding of the remaining public lands are in process of formation; the Forest Service has been given the task of administering the national timberlands; the Federal Oil Conservation Board has negotiated a series of inter-state treaties designed to diminish the wastes of competitive production of petroleum; and numerous other measures have been taken in this field, in the name of the public welfare, to check and regulate the action of private enterprise. "With the idea of safeguarding the heritage of the country," write the Beards, "the Government has undertaken extensive scientific research into the best methods of extracting energy from coal or oil. . . . All in all, the influence which Washington now exerts upon the handling of natural resources in the United States is indeed extensive."[11]

Service to business. Besides the erection of tariff barriers to protect different branches of industry and the performance of

10 See above, Part Two, Chapter II, "Economy."
11 Charles A. Beard and William Beard, *op. cit.,* 549.

various economic functions for the general benefit of the people, from time to time government has rendered many services to American business. Thus in the commercial activity of the country the state is constantly in evidence. The Consular Service exists mainly to promote American business abroad; and the Department of Commerce, besides assisting, seeks to some extent to co-ordinate, the business life of the nation. In order to encourage foreign trade, individuals and firms desiring to form non-competitive export corporations have been given special exemption from the anti-trust laws. And during the years covered by the Harding, Coolidge and Hoover administrations the federal government became increasingly an agency for serving and promoting American commercial enterprise throughout the world.

The great depression beginning in 1929 forced the government to interfere on an heroic scale in both industry and commerce. Even President Hoover, ardent champion of the doctrines of "rugged individualism," found himself forced to advocate measures totally contrary to his avowed philosophy. Thus through the Reconstruction Finance Corporation banks, railroads, insurance companies, building and loan associations, and other forms of business, all received heavy loans guaranteed by the government. The first quarterly report[12] of the Corporation made on April 1, 1932, showed that the Corporation had advanced $192,350,000 on 974 loans distributed among 935 institutions as follows:

To 858	banks and trust companies	$158,182,242
" 30	building and loan associations	4,879,750
" 18	insurance companies	7,080,000
" 2	joint stock land banks	775,000
" 1	live stock credit association	496,990
" 2	agricultural credit corporations	21,200
" 8	mortgage loan companies	6,517,000
" 16	railroads	60,787,757

[12] *Commercial and Financial Chronicle* (April 9, 1932), Vol. 134, 2646.

Assistance to agriculture. In order to advance the interests of American agriculture the federal government has engaged in a vast range of activities. The Department of Agriculture, with its many bureaus and services, was established for this purpose. On the one hand, by scientific research and the dissemination of information, by the establishment of government land banks for supplying credit, by irrigation works, by waging war on plant and animal diseases, and by lending financial aid in the organization and operation of co-operative marketing, government has engaged in a vigorous program for the improvement and enlargement of production. It has furnished money to help farmers obtain seeds, stock, and implements. Its agents give advice and counsel on all branches of agricultural economy. And tariff discriminations protect farm products against foreign competition. On the other hand, through various instrumentalities and measures, such as the Federal Farm Loan Board, the Federal Farm Board, and the Agricultural Marketing Act, government has engaged in an almost frantic effort to curtail production, to raise the prices of farm produce, to control marketing operations, to lift farmers out of debts incurred largely under governmental encouragement, and otherwise to assist them in escaping from the poverty and uncertainty into which they have fallen under the system of individual liberty. Incidentally, the construction of highways at public expense, the establishment of rural free delivery, and state and federal support for local schools have been undertaken in part at least with a view to raising, through collective effort, the standard of life in rural regions.[13]

Protection of Urban Workers. In the field of labor relations the inadequacy of the doctrine of *laissez-faire* early became manifest. In the face of the great aggregations of capital that appeared with the growth of industrialism, the individual workman was helpless. As a consequence, the principle or dogma of freedom of contract in particular has been subjected

13 See Charles A. Beard and William Beard, *op. cit.,* 513–545.

to assault after assault at the hands of the government. In all important industrial areas state legislation has limited the working day to ten hours or less and has placed severe restrictions on the employment of children. Also prohibition of night work for women is characteristic of advanced industrial states. Where labor is organized, and in many enterprises where it is not, individual bargaining over the employment contract is more or less a thing of the past. Public interference with respect to the conditions of work has advanced step by step with the progress of industrialization.

Also the state has extended various forms of assistance to urban workers. Among them should be mentioned safety and sanitary legislation for factories, mines, and railways; workmen's compensation laws and administration; widows' pensions; mothers' pensions; old age pensions; minimum wage legislation; tentative beginnings in unemployment insurance (Wisconsin and Ohio); free education; park, playground, tenement, and housing legislation; establishment of prevailing rates of wages for public works; health, hospital, and free-clinic services; legislation permitting the organization and restricted functioning of trade unions; limitation of hours of work on interstate railways, in mines, and in other dangerous employments.[14]

Regulation of corporate enterprise. Although in fact no sharp distinction can be made between private enterprises "affected with public interest," and those that are "strictly private," such a distinction is made in the law. The former include railways, gas and electric plants, street car lines, and similar undertakings which hold charters from governments and are usually monopolistic or semi-monopolistic in nature. These so-called public utilities have gradually been subjected to government regulation with respect to rates, charges, earnings, and services. In general theory they are not profit-making enterprises at all, but public service institutions entitled to earn

14 See Charles A. Beard and William Beard, *op. cit.*, 484–512, and 578–614.

merely a fair return on prudent investment. While the practice of course often deviates widely from the theory, such is the controlling principle which is supposed to be applied or toward which public policy seems to be moving. Thus the Interstate Commerce Commission has gradually shorn the railroads of most of their character as independent enterprises and is now bringing about their consolidation into a few great regional units. The competitors of the locomotive on road, river, and canal will doubtless soon be co-ordinated and fashioned into a regulated national transport system. The maintenance of the government barge lines of the Mississippi Valley, the financing and supervision of the Panama Canal and inland waterways, and the lavish subsidies of ocean and coastal shipping and of river and harbor improvement have already made water-transport partially dependent on the federal government. Aviation has its own subsidy from the Post-Office Department.[15] The Federal Power Commission has established a feeble hold on certain power sites and probably awaits expansion into a body for the general regulation of the hydro-electric industry.

Other corporate enterprises, not regarded as public utilities, have also been brought within the range of government intervention. For many years the state has been attempting, by means of anti-trust legislation, to prevent the growth of corporate enterprise and to maintain the tradition of free competition.[16] These efforts, however, as indicated elsewhere, have not been successful. They have not checked the formation of gigantic corporations and the concentration of large portions of industrial wealth, apart from banking, in the hands of 200 such undertakings. More recently public opinion, if not government practice, has been veering in the direction of the acceptance of the corporate trend and governmental regulation

[15] For summary record of federal legislation called forth by the development of transportation see Leonard D. White, "Public Administration," Chapter XXVII in *Recent Social Trends in the United States*, II, 1394.
[16] See Charles A. Beard and William Beard, *op. cit.*, 447–483.

in the public interest; and to all appearances the Government of the United States today stands on the verge of significant and undisguised collective action in the general supervision of corporate undertakings with respect to financing, earnings, and services.

Performance of various economic functions. In addition to regulating and supervising and promoting and safeguarding, government has gradually invaded the field of economy and taken over one function after another. Although this tendency is revealed in much that has already been reported, it is of sufficient significance to merit special mention. Many generations ago the state proceeded to remove the school from the domain of private enterprise. The postal service likewise has long been regarded as a function of government. In recent decades this development has gained great momentum because of the advance of modern science and technology. Illustrative of this trend are the protection of the public against infections and contagions in accordance with the discoveries of bacteriology and medicine; the requirement and regulation of safety appliances and control over the use of explosives, gases, and other dangerous commodities; provisions for safety at sea; regulation of the use of the radio to prevent interference and confusion in broadcasting; public education in matters of health and safety; city and regional planning to mitigate the evils of congestion in living conditions, traffic, industry and commercial activities. Lent D. Upson has summarized the impact of the growth of medical knowledge on the functions of municipal government:

"Modern scientific progress . . . has played no small part in the increase of municipal activities and costs. For example, in medicine the discovery of the germ basis of contagious disease has made possible its effective control. Following this, the public has realized that disease prevention is more important than efforts at cure. Consequently, public health activities have been expanded with great rapidity. The citizen of the new city pays for and enjoys the benefits of quarantine enforcement, food inspection, visiting nurses, tuberculosis treatment, medical examination of school children, purification of water supply, disposal of sewage and other wastes, and kindred efforts for the reduction of morbidity and mortality."[17]

Levying of taxes. Besides assuming the functions listed above, all of which "interfere with the natural course of economic affairs," American governments—local, state, and federal—intervene directly, through specific taxation, in "the natural distribution of wealth." Until the opening of the twentieth century, the Government of the United States derived nearly all its revenues, save in exceptional times, from customs duties and internal excises, that is, from indirect taxes falling on the consumers of goods. At the same time the local and state governments relied principally on general property taxes. In the main, efforts to transfer a part of the burden to the recipients of large incomes and inheritances had been defeated by legislative opposition and judicial interpretation. In 1913 an amendment authorizing the taxation of incomes was incorporated in the federal Constitution and an effort was made to shift a part of the burden of taxation to incomes of corporations and individuals and to inheritances. About the same time a similar trend occurred in many of the states. Such legislation, in the eyes of its leading sponsors, was designed to effect "a more equitable distribution of wealth" and to afford "greater equality of opportunity." At all events it constituted a drastic government interference with what was once generally regarded by respectable citizens as "the natural and just distribution of wealth," and marked a significant departure from the system of individualism that prevailed in the nineteenth century.

17 Lent D. Upson, *Practice of Municipal Administration* (New York, 1926), 5.

THE IMPACT OF TECHNOLOGY

In the main the growth of government functions and the intervention of the state in the domain of economy have followed the extension of technology throughout the economic order.[18] The advance of engineering from one sphere of activity to another has fundamentally altered the structure of the mechanism for the production and distribution of goods and services. It has also introduced into the field of practical endeavor new conceptions and principles which tend to undermine the localism and individualism of the pre-industrial age. This question of the impact of technology on government may be further developed under the headings of centralization, differentiation, efficiency, and rationality.

Centralization. Under the regime of technology, as already observed, there occurs an intense and minute specialization in agriculture, industry, and commerce and a correlative linkage of enterprises by means of new forms of transportation and communication. All of these tendencies cut across local and state boundaries and accelerate the movement toward centralization. Following the disappearance of the self-sufficing homestead came the disappearance of the self-sufficing village, county, town, and state. Old jurisdictional boundaries, appropriate to the age of agriculture and handicraft, of stage coach and sailing vessel, lost their original significance; they were cut and slashed in every direction by channels of economic interconnection. Units of government established within these geographical boundaries, with powers adapted to their respective jurisdictions, cannot control activities which are tied into the economy of the entire American Union—highways, railroads, sanitation, banking, radio broadcasting, and specialized

[18] See above, Part Two, Chapter III, "Technology"; also William Beard, *Government and Technology* (New York, 1934).

production in industry and agriculture. The result throughout the nation has thus been described by Leonard D. White:

"A definite shift in the balance of power as between the federal government and the states, and as between the states and local governments, has been quietly but steadily taking place during the last thirty years. This tendency is the continuation of a movement already established at the turn of the century and has proceeded with relatively great rapidity in the regulation of transportation and utilities, in education, in public health and the construction of highways. It has proceeded very slowly in the supervision of police and fire services, in parks and public recreation, and in the control of elections. It has proceeded rapidly in some states in the control and audit of local expenditures, in the supervision of personnel policies and welfare activities, but in other states there has been substantially no change."[19]

The Beards have drawn a sharp contrast between the society of today and that of 1787:

"Hence it follows that a searching treatise on American government must reckon with the technological revolution wrought by science and machinery since the federal Constitution was drawn up more than a century ago. For the old congeries of provincial societies, founded principally on agriculture and local commerce, which made up the United States in 1787, machine industry and the various means of rapid communication have substituted a Great Society, based on national and international markets. Railways, telegraph lines, airplanes, and the radio override historic political boundaries, weld this country into a single economic organism, and steadily weave it into the web of world civilization. To speak of

---

[19] Leonard D. White, "Public Administration," Chapter XXVII in *Recent Social Trends in the United States,* II, 1402. See also *ibid.,* 1393–1394; Finla Goff Crawford, *op. cit.,* 16, 504; Arthur W. Bromage, *American County Government* (New York, 1933), 3–35.

government merely in the political language of the eighteenth century is like talking of travel in the terms of gigs and schooners."[20]

Charles E. Merriam has pointed to the appearance of new units for the discharge of governmental and quasi-governmental functions:

"Broadly speaking, industrial and social relations overflowed the banks of the states and swept out over the nation in a flood too great to be controlled by any one state, as in the case of corporations transacting business in many different commonwealths. Industry, education, the United States government, began to recognize various 'regions' as important units in their activity. The Federal Reserve Board operated through 12 districts, for example, while large numbers of groups were organized as New England, Southern, Mississippi Valley, Western, Northwestern, Pacific Coast, associations, societies, conferences and congresses."[21]

Perhaps the great municipalities furnish the most striking instances of the over-riding of old political boundaries. These communities are "usually composed of a large number of independent, and sometimes overlapping political organizations of varying size and description." New York contains 145 political subdivisions; Philadelphia, 119; Pittsburgh, 127; and Chicago, 90. New York, Chicago, Philadelphia, St. Louis, Cincinnati, Washington, Kansas City, Louisville and Portland each lies in two or more states. New York lies in or embraces 14 counties; Philadelphia, 8; San Francisco, 5; Boston, 5; and St. Louis, 4. "This extraordinary political complexity of the typical metropolitan area," according to a committee of the National Municipal League, "is attributable, in part, to a plan of governmental organization long antedating the present era of urbanization

[20] Charles A. Beard and William Beard, *op. cit.*, 5.
[21] Charles E. Merriam, "Government and Society," Chapter XXIX in *Recent Social Trends in the United States*, II, 1494.

and devised to meet wholly different conditions. It arises from a lack of any comprehensive design in the development of urban growth, and the absence of statesmanlike leadership in overcoming inertia."[22]

With respect to the situation in the Chicago area, Mr. Merriam makes an even more arresting statement:

"In the Chicago region . . . which we construe as fifty miles from State and Madison streets, there are not less than 1800 independent governing agencies undertaking to carry on the governmental functions incidental to the life of a community of something over 4,000,000 people. Metropolitan Chicago extends into four different states, Illinois, Wisconsin, Indiana, and a corner of Michigan; it includes fifteen counties and an innumerable array of cities, villages, towns, townships, school districts, park districts, drainage districts."[23]

This over-riding of inherited political boundaries is not wholly due, however, to the development of a complex and closely integrated society. It is also to be traced in part to the fact that technological enterprises themselves, being related to physical geography—rivers, forests, and minerals—must often spread over many local and state jurisdictions. In the distribution of her resources nature has not respected county and state, or even national lines. The protection of water-sheds, the conservation of forests, the development of flood control, the building of hydro-electric stations, and the rationalization of mineral exploitation, commonly call for government action that transcends the jurisdiction of a single state. Examples lie on every hand: the Boulder Dam project on the Colorado River, efforts to check disastrous floods on the Mississippi River, the Muscle Shoals enterprise on the Tennessee River, the adminis-

22 National Municipal League, Committee on Metropolitan Government, *The Government of Metropolitan Areas* (New York, 1930), 27–28.
23 Charles E. Merriam, *The Written Constitution and the Unwritten Attitude* (New York, 1931), 42–43.

tration of the Port of New York, Appalachian reforestation, elimination of waste in the exploitation of oil, plans for reviving the paralysed coal industry, and co-ordination of public and private timber developments.

All such vast undertakings, conceived by technology, require an extension of federal functions and accelerate the tendency to centralize authority and responsibility at Washington. As this trend has grown more powerful from year to year, it has raised the question of a fundamental readjusment of the constitutional system, especially with reference to the distribution of powers between the Federal Union and the states. If this is not done, it is evident that the Constitution will have to be construed with extreme liberality. Otherwise it will not permit the rationalization of industry in accordance with the requirements of the inherent logic of technology. Mr. Merriam has even gone so far as to say "that it is necessary to face in the near future the reorganization of state boundaries in such manner as to bring the lines of social and economic interest and power more nearly to those of formal government."[24] The movement toward centralization is indisputable; the new problems are pressing: the challenge is already here.

Differentiation. The trend toward centralization in government has been attended, as pointed out elsewhere in this volume, by the two-fold process of differentiation and integration in economy. As a result the comparative simplicity of the pattern of political forces characteristic of agrarian America has been practically destroyed. In the struggle for power geographical sections have given way in considerable measure to powerful economic groups that span the nation. Functions that were discharged by the colonial household are now performed by great industries reaching from ocean to ocean and even beyond the seas. "One of the most interesting phenomena of modern times," writes Mr. Merriam, "is the development of various forms of highly organized groups, bringing pressure to

[24] *Ibid.,* 60–61.

444   SOCIAL FOUNDATIONS OF EDUCATION

bear upon governmental officials and in particular upon legislators . . . Washington has in part become a center of competing groups, with their propagandas, their lobbies, their impressive headquarters, all becoming an integral part of the
government of the land."[25] The Beards have contrasted the
present situation with that faced by the fathers at the time
of the framing of the Federal Constitution:

"In bringing about this amazing differentiation among citizens, the technical revolution has at the same time created new
and bewildering forms of property, which find sharp repercussions in the governing process. James Madison, the father of the
Constitution, spoke of a landed interest, a manufacturing interest, a commercial interest, and the few minor interests which
operated in politics in his era; to them have since been added
railway, oil, public utility, sugar, rubber, and a hundred other
powerful interests represented by active and highly paid agents
in Washington."[26]

The might of these battling groups, which disregard the
political boundaries laid down in another age, has grown with
great rapidity. Under the reign of the doctrines of individualism in economy, coupled with the rise of the corporation,
wealth and economic power have become so concentrated that
not infrequently private interests have been able to challenge
successfully the authority of government or at least to bend
government to their will. The strength of certain of these interests may be revealed by a few comparisons. Data for the
years 1929–1930 show the annual gross revenues of the United
States Steel Corporation to be twice those of New York City,
four times those of New York State, and almost sixty-seven

---

[25] *Ibid.*, 69–70. See also by the same author, *Government and Society*,
Chapter XXIX in *Recent Social Trends in the United States*, II, 1512–1513; H.
S. Childs, *Labor and Capital in National Politics;* Marcus Duffield, *King Legion*
(New York, 1931); E. P. Herring, *Group Representation Before Congress*
(New York, 1929); and Peter Odegard, *Pressure Politics* (New York, 1928).
[26] Charles A. Beard and William Beard, *op. cit.,* 6.

times those of Maine.[27] And yet in 1815 no private agency in the United States except a few banks could command funds to the amount of $1,000,000.

The power of these interests, as political forces, has been greatly increased by certain inventions. Through the telegraph, the rotary press, the telephone, the radio, the cinema, and other mechanical contrivances, technology has placed in their hands effective instruments for the spread of propaganda and the molding of public opinion.[28] It is not surprising therefore that in the game of wresting favors and privileges of all kinds from legislators, executives, and courts, government tends everywhere to become corrupted. As Lincoln Steffens points out in his autobiography and as innumerable Congressional investigations prove, the corrupt politician is the tool of the respectable business man who, in obedience to the maxim of classical economics, sedulously, intelligently, and effectually strives after material gain. More significant for the future of politics, however, than subversive tendencies, which are part and parcel of the inherited economic tradition, is the swift organization of society into great functional groups which may be expected to contribute the framework of the industrial state of the future. The National Industrial Recovery Act, to be examined later, seems to be hastening this process of rebuilding the social pattern. As technology annihilates distance and surmounts natural barriers, geographical considerations must play a decreasing rôle in the organization and conduct of government.

Efficiency. One of the most revolutionary conceptions of technology is that of efficiency. In the sphere of economy this idea has already worked miracles and destroyed ancient institutions and practices; in the domain of government it is beginning to exert pressure; in both it challenges the tradition of

[27] Charles E. Merriam, "Government and Society," Chapter XXIX in *Recent Social Trends in the United States*, II, 1512.
[28] See above Chapter III on "Communication."

laissez-faire. With growing insistence engineering journals apply the concept to the development and exploitation of water, timber, mineral, and other resources and point out the wastes and the violations of the permanent interests of society which inevitably flow from the traditional methods involving reliance upon almost unrestricted private initiative. Unless business enterprises can combine on a national scale and thus control exploitation and development in accordance with the requirements of efficiency, the Federal Government will be compelled to extend its intervention to the borders of the industries affected. But if such enterprises should so combine, they would become so gigantic and so powerful as to call for regulation and control by the Federal Government with respect to methods, practices, rates, and services. In either case the powers and responsibilities of government would increase and the process of collectivization already under way would be intensified.

Indeed, as previously indicated in various connections, an enormous centralization of basic industries in the hands of two hundred corporations has actually occurred. The idea of breaking them up into competing units has been almost universally abandoned. The Government of the United States, therefore, seems to have no choice between allowing economic affairs to drift, perhaps into chaos, and encouraging additional consolidations with respect to the rational use of resources. The former appears to be unthinkable and the latter imperative. At all events any positive effort on the part of the government to promote the development of resources in the light of engineering efficiency will augment centralization and add new and perplexing functions to those already assumed. In other words, the social drive on individual enterprise carried on by gigantic private corporations, combined with the pressure of technology upon wasteful methods of using all resources, is manifested in the sphere of government by extension of functions, by centralization, and by increasing collectivism.

Moreover, the scientific method, which is the method of

efficiency, is certain to penetrate farther and farther into the processes of government. "Though undoubtedly limited in its application," say the Beards, it "promises to work a revolution in politics no less significant than that wrought in society at large by mechanics. It punctures classical oratory—conservative as well as radical—and offers to explore worlds unknown to politicians of the archaic school."[29] Also, according to these authors, in their discussion of the age-long controversy over the comparative merits of mass and aristocratic rule, it brings into the sphere of government as never before the concept of trained intelligence:

"In reality such thinking does not go to the heart of the matter at all, for the simple reason that an ever larger area of government, as well as industry, is being occupied by machinery and science; the operations of public administration become increasingly technical in character, involving a knowledge of chemistry, physics, and higher mathematics in their several branches. Hence the problems they present cannot be solved by intelligence, no matter how superior, unless it is factually informed. Power to deal with such realistic issues is proportioned to technical competence, not merely to degrees of natural understanding.

"In the presence of an intricate question respecting the hydraulics of river improvement, the physics of hull design and the water resistance of ships, or tide prediction, the most sagacious and highly educated lawyer or editor in America is about as helpless as the most ignorant laborer. Jefferson's plowman and professor stand on the same footing. Hamilton's rich and well-born and his despised mass of the people are in the same boat."[30]

Rationality. Back of the concept of efficiency is the concept of rationality. And rationality involves foresight, design, and planning. Although as a rule the new functions of govern-

[29] Charles A. Beard and William Beard, *op. cit.,* 8.   [30] *Ibid.,* 12–13.

ment, enumerated in preceding pages, were assumed one at a time, with little reference to large social policy, it was soon discovered that they were more or less closely related to one another, in complementary or antagonistic fashion. In cities for example, housing, parks, playgrounds, and industries are vitally connected with ways and means of rapid transportation. Indeed it has slowly dawned on the consciousness of the American people that no important branch of government and economy stands on an entirely independent basis and operates separately without reference to the whole. Consequently, as the state multiplied its functions, the necessity of making adjustments among them became apparent, even to superficial observers. Inevitably efforts to make such adjustments led to the conception of large-scale planning. Near the opening of the twentieth century the idea rose to prominence in municipal affairs; in 1910 the first national conference on city planning was held; the organization of an association to promote the idea followed; and all over the country cities began to plan and zone in an effort to introduce into their physical arrangements a measure of rationality. From modest beginnings a philosophy of planning, which included all features of urban life, was gradually evolved. In due course, regional, state, and national planning appeared in discussions of public affairs and leaders everywhere recognized the imperative need of planning—coordinating, adjusting, and extending the functions of government.

In this way the conception of planning had entered American social thought before it was dramatized by Soviet Russia. It was inherent in the rationality of technology; it accompanied the expansion of private corporate enterprise; it cut into all theories, policies, and practices of government. The question bequeathed to the present generation therefore is not: Shall there be planning? That question is already answered. The only relevant question pertains to degree, methods, and purposes. The issue cannot be avoided. It involves first principles of government and economy, and means the application of collectivist methods to a social complex which has become increasingly collectivist in nature. The task has been visualized by Sir Arthur Salter in the closing paragraph of his discussion of the framework of an ordered society:

"Man has accomplished half his task; he has wrested enough of Nature's secrets from her to give the material basis of a high civilisation to every country in the world; to provide not only the necessities but the comforts of life to the whole of the world's teeming population. The other—and the more difficult —half remains; that of controlling his own human relationships, and directing his own activities so that they are not mutually destructive."[31]

That this task is one of great difficulty is suggested by the conservatism of political institutions. Although government has responded in many ways to the advance of industrial civilization, as these pages plainly show, government is still divided from the reality by a deep chasm. The persistence of political boundaries that obstruct the efficient performance of innumerable social functions illustrates the point. Moreover, as the Beards say, "nearly all the fundamental ideas and institutions of modern politics—universal suffrage, representative government, courts, executives, cabinets, and taxation, for instance—originated in the age of stage coaches, tallow candles, and wooden sailing vessels."[32] The spoils system persists in many states; and the government of the country is conducted for the most part by "an army of over 750,000 elected officials." In the words of Charles E. Merriam, "the danger in American government at the present time is not *lack of stability, but lack of mobility,* failure to make prompt adjustments to the new era in industry and science. Government is at many points a generation behind

[31] Sir Arthur Salter, *The Framework of an Ordered Society* (New York, 1933), 59–60.
[32] Charles A. Beard and William Beard, *op. cit.,* 4.

the development of social and economic life and the urgent problem is that of bridging the gap."[33] In reviewing the findings of the President's Research Committee on Social Trends, Mr. Merriam has thus summarized the situation:

"Notwithstanding many important exceptions and counter trends, the prevailing attitude has been non-theoretical and intolerant toward other systems than our own, and non-experimental in the field of governmental structure, especially if constitutional change were involved. In business and in mechanical enterprise the general attitude has been that of free and welcome experiment, but the opposite has been true in governmental affairs, where the weight of tradition has been more heavily felt and where proposals for change have been identified with treason to the state. The Lusk Committee declared: 'No person who is not eager to combat the theories of social change should be entrusted with the task of fitting the young and old of the States for responsibilities of citizenship.' This is not merely the result of preoccupation with expansive interests, or of a special American type of mentality, but grows largely out of the identification of the present industrial situation with the preservation of the status quo in constitutional arrangements, and the fear that change might jeopardize existing property interests."[34]

THE REUNION OF POLITICS AND ECONOMICS

The trend toward the reunion of politics and economics came to a head in the great crisis which opened in 1929. For two generations the extension of government into the field of economy had been a marked feature of American life. Under the stresses and strains generated by the depression this movement expanded swiftly in every direction. Although public expenditures were subjected to much hostile criticism and curtailments were made in many departments, no fundamental

[33] Charles E. Merriam, *The Written Constitution and the Unwritten Attitude* (New York, 1931), 25.
[34] Charles E. Merriam, *op. cit.*, 1534.

functions were abandoned. Indeed all classes of the population —bankers, railway owners, farmers, insurance companies, and millions of unemployed and suffering working people in town and country—turned to the state for assistance. Agriculture and business enterprise in themselves were apparently powerless to start the engines of production. Every significant effort to prevent the collapse of society and to stimulate the productive processes involved government initiative or action or both.

In the first years of the depression the federal government, while protesting its faith in the doctrines of individualism, organized the Reconstruction Finance Corporation and loaned money by the hundred million to banks, railways, building and loan associations, farmers' organizations, and various economic institutions in a gigantic effort to stave off bankruptcy and ruin. Yet the decline in purchasing power, the lowering of production, and the growth of unemployment continued. Apparently the climax was reached on March 4, 1933, when the new administration, immediately following the inauguration ceremonies, assumed dictatorial power over the banking facilities of the country and proceeded to carry through a program of legislation without precedent in American history. So impressive were the more important measures passed by the Seventy-Third Congress that they should be briefly catalogued. Though the logical fruit of the developments of more than half a century, they came so quickly that they may well prove to mark a turning point in the evolution of government in the United States. They represent the avowed reunion on a nation-wide scale of politics and economics.

This legislation, though not revolutionary, constituted a fairly comprehensive attack upon the depression and embraced the subjects of banking and finance, unemployment relief, agricultural readjustment, home mortgage relief, public works, railroad reorganization, and industrial control. The Emergency Banking Act, passed on March 9, confirmed the regulations already proclaimed by the administration and, among other things, conferred on the President the power to "investigate, regulate or prohibit . . . any transactions in foreign exchange, transfers of credit between or payments by banking institutions, as defined by the President, and export, hoarding, melting or earmarking of gold or silver coin or bullion or currency, by any person within the United States or any place subject to the jurisdiction thereof." Just before adjourning on June 13, Congress passed the Banking Act of 1933 which increased the power of government over the banks of the country. An amendment to the Agricultural Relief Act, passed on May 12, empowered the President to reduce the weight of the gold dollar by as much as 50 per cent and to establish a suitable ratio between the gold and silver dollar. The Securities Act of May 27 requires the registration of securities with the Federal Trade Commission twenty days before they are offered to the public. On May 12, Congress passed legislation directing the Reconstruction Finance Corporation to provide $500,000,000 for state and local relief in addition to $300,000,000 authorized under the Emergency Relief and Construction Act of 1932. On June 6, a law was passed to establish a national system of public employment offices. An act for the relief of agriculture, passed on May 12, was designed to establish and maintain, by a complicated process, a "balance between the production and consumption of cotton, wheat, corn, hogs, dairy products, tobacco, rice and beet and cane sugar and to re-establish the relation existing during 1909–1914 between prices received by farmers and prices paid by them for manufactured articles." On June 13, the Federal Farm Loan Bank Act was amended to provide relief to home owners. An act passed on March 31 was expected to put 250,000 to 275,000 unemployed at work to carry on a program of forestation and to prevent forest fires, floods, soil erosion, and plant pests. Legislation of May 18 provided for the development of the vast Tennessee Valley project, involving flood control, reforestation, operation of the Muscle Shoals hydro-electric station, and the general industrial development of the valley. On June 16, a law was passed calling for radical reorganization of the railways of the nation and the creation of a Federal Co-ordinator of Transportation. Finally, there was the National Industrial Recovery Act passed on June 16, and designed "to provide for the general welfare by promoting the organization of industry for the purpose of co-operative action among trade groups, to induce and maintain united action of labor and management under adequate governmental action and supervision, to eliminate unfair competitive practices, to promote the fullest possible utilization of the present productive capacity of industries, to avoid undue restriction of production (except as may be temporarily required), to increase the consumption of industrial and agricultural products by increasing purchasing power, to reduce and relieve unemployment, to improve standards of labor, and otherwise to rehabilitate industry and to conserve natural resources." The Act thus calls for the general co-ordination, under governmental auspices, of the industries of the country. Also it carries an appropriation of $3,300,000,000 to prosecute an elaborate program of public works.[35] The following statement, issued by President Roosevelt at the time of the signing of the Act, shows how it was conceived by its author:

"History probably will record the National Industrial Act as the most important and far-reaching legislation ever enacted by the American Congress. It represents a supreme effort to stabilize for all time the many factors which make for the prosperity of the nation and the preservation of American standards.

"Its goal is the assurance of a reasonable profit to industry and living wages for labor, with the elimination of the piratical methods and practices which have not only harassed honest business but also contributed to the ills of labor.

[35] The data of this paragraph are taken for the most part from *Information Service*, Vol. XII, No. 26 (June 30, 1932). Also see Benjamin S. Kirsh, *The National Industrial Recovery Act* (New York, 1933).

"While we are engaged in establishing new foundations for business which ultimately should open a return to work for large numbers of men, it is our hope through the so-called public works section of the law to speedily initiate a program of public construction that should early reemploy additional hundreds of thousands of men.

"Obviously, if this project is to succeed, it demands the wholehearted co-operation of industry, labor and every citizen of the nation."[36]

THE NATION

Reflection upon the great social changes of the past one hundred and fifty years in America suggests the thought that the family has given way to the nation. At any rate the rôle of the family has been greatly reduced and many of the functions performed in the household of the eighteenth century— economic, medical, educational, and cultural—have been removed from the home. The family can no longer minister to the diverse needs of the individual; it cannot even give him assurance of material security. It can neither maintain an independent economic existence nor keep its cultural unity from generation to generation. Consequently any attempt at the rational ordering of life must transcend the boundaries of the family circle and be made reasonably commensurate with the scope of the forces to be controlled and the functions to be co-ordinated. The growth of governmental activities and the trend toward central planning, outlined in the present chapter, which run contrary to the historic individualism of the nineteenth century and to deep-seated prejudices of the American people, indicate the emergence of a new integration involving the entire nation. This of course merely means the twentieth century is striving to do on a vastly enlarged scale what the eighteenth did in a small way in the family and neighborhood.

36 The New York *Times* (June 17, 1933).

This rise of the national unity in economy, however, does not mean that character, enterprise, and a high sense of responsibility in individuals and families and communities has ceased to be a fundamental requisite in the ordering, the advancement, and the enrichment of life in America. On the contrary, unless the social base in field, factory, workshop, homestead, and neighborhood is sound and the functions of individual and household are faithfully and intelligently discharged, no amount of central planning and direction can be effective. This fact cannot be too strongly emphasized, or too often repeated. Yet it is evident that, with the development of collective machinery in government and economy, the right of the individual to do as he pleases with his person and property comes under severe and exacting restraints. To maintain the balance between the constricting effect of collective control and operation and the living powers of the individual, family, and community will require all the resources of understanding and virtue that the nation can command. As the prolix legislation of the later Roman Empire demonstrates, centralization of power does not in itself guarantee the perdurance of society. Individual, family, and community vitality must accompany the process of socialization if the great society is to continue and to make possible the enlargement and refinement of life.

Chapter XI

WORLD RELATIONS

The American people do not inhabit the world alone. Nor is their land isolated from Europe and Asia as it once was. The integrating forces released by technology, which in a century and a half have destroyed the self-sufficiency of household and farming community, have refused to halt before the boundaries of the nation. The United States has moved out into the world and become increasingly dependent on the fortunes of the other peoples of the earth. And today she is an integral part of a social and economic complex that embraces all but the most backward and inaccessible districts of the globe. A drought, a good season, a natural catastrophe, a new invention, a novel idea, a powerful personality, a financial disaster, a war, or a revolution in any part of this increasingly closely integrated world complex sends reverberations through the entire structure. For good or for ill the destinies of the various branches of the human race have become closely interwoven.

THE TREND TOWARD WORLD INTEGRATION

At the time of his inauguration as first president of the United States on April 30, 1789, Washington looked out upon a country of comparative insignificance living on the periphery of western civilization. By the side of the great states of Europe the infant republic was extremely feeble. In population it ranked not far above "such little states as the Netherlands, Portugal, or Sweden"; and its "whole settled area, comprising a strip along the Atlantic Coast, and the mere beginnings of settlement beyond the Appalachian Mountains, was less than the area of the present state of Texas."[1] In economic, political, and military power the country was undeveloped; and the American people were protected from foreign aggression and from the quarrels of the old world by the barrier of the North Atlantic. During the colonial period "at best three months were required for sending a dispatch from London to America and procuring a return."

During the past one hundred and fifty years the nation has not only vastly extended its borders in America and become a closely integrated society:[2] it has also been drawn steadily, but irresistibly and ever more swiftly, into a great world complex. This trend may be illustrated by reference to the growth of transportation and communication, the growth of foreign commerce, the growth of cultural contacts with other countries, and the growth of political commitments beyond the national borders.

"Of all inventions, the alphabet and the printing press alone excepted," said Macaulay, "those inventions which abridge distance have done most for the civilization of our species." Certainly the advances in transportation and communication lie at the root of the increasing integration of the world. A few facts will show how the distances which once isolated the American people have been abridged. In 1492 the sailing vessel *Santa Maria,* of one hundred tons register and commanded by Christopher Columbus, crossed the Atlantic from Spain to San Salvador in seventy days. More than a century later the *Mayflower* sighted land after a voyage of sixty-one days from Plymouth, England. In 1819 the first steamship, the *Savannah,* with side paddle wheels and a full complement of sails, crossed from Savannah to Liverpool in twenty-five days. Twenty years later the English steamer *Great Western* cut the time to thir-

[1] Clive Day, *A History of Commerce* (New York, 1922, revised edition), 469.
[2] See above Chapter III on "Communication."

teen. Finally, in August, 1933, the giant Italian liner *Rex,* with a total passenger capacity of 2032 persons, displacing 51,000 tons and burning 1100 tons of oil a day at peak performance, maintained an average speed of 28.92 knots for a distance of 3181 miles and crossed the Atlantic from Gibraltar to New York in the record-breaking time of four days, thirteen hours, and fifty-eight minutes.

With the coming of air transport the expanse of the Atlantic and of all oceans and continents is being further and radically contracted. In May, 1919, the American hydroplane, *N.C.-4,* flew from Trepassy, Newfoundland, to Lisbon, Portugal, in twenty-six hours and forty-seven minutes of flying time. In June of the same year a British biplane crossed from St. John's, Newfoundland, to Clifden, Ireland, in sixteen hours and twelve minutes. But the most impressive demonstration of the abridgment of distance through technological advance is seen in the performance of Wiley Post in July, 1933. In a solo flight he encircled the earth, from New York to New York, in seven days, eighteen hours, forty-seven minutes, and twenty seconds. Four centuries earlier, on September 20, 1519, Fernando Magellan, a Portuguese navigator, set sail from San Lucar de Barrameda, Spain, with a fleet of five vessels to circumnavigate the globe. Almost three years later, on September 9, 1522, after a voyage of incredible hazard and hardship involving the death of the commander and the loss of four vessels, one lone ship dropped anchor in Seville Roads bearing the distinction of having made the first trip around the world. The contrast between the sixteenth and the twentieth century requires no comment. It merely remains to add that an Italian aviator has attained the flying speed of 426 miles an hour.

In the sphere of point to point communication distance has not merely been abridged: it has been annihilated. In 1866 the laying of the first successful trans-Atlantic cable was completed; in 1901 the letter "S" was transmitted from Europe to

America by wireless telegraph; in 1927 men sitting in Washington and London conversed by wireless telephone; beginning in the early 1920s great broadcasting stations were established in all industrially advanced countries; and the perfection and wide utilization of television would seem to be only a matter of a few years. In 1927 companies incorporated in the United States operated 105,893 nautical miles of ocean cable. Thus, through various instrumentalities, the three months required by colonial America to communicate with Europe have been reduced to seconds.

The development of these new forms of transportation has been attended by an enormous expansion of international commerce. This is reflected in the growth of shipping. The gross tonnage of the United States merchant marine engaged in foreign trade increased from 124,000 tons in 1789 to 6,296,000 in 1930. In the forty years from 1890 to 1930 the gross tonnage of the merchant fleets of the world grew from approximately 21,000,000 tons to almost 70,000,000. Also freight rates are now only the smallest fraction of what they were in the days of sailing vessels.

In 1790 the total value of the foreign trade of the republic amounted to less than $45,000,000. In 1929, the last year of the post-war prosperity, it was in excess of nine and one-half billions. The per capita value of exports and imports combined rose during this period from $10.99 to $76.91. This advance, however, did not proceed steadily throughout the history of the nation. A rapid increase at the opening of the nineteenth century was followed by a marked decline. For several decades the growth of foreign commerce did not keep pace with the growth of population. "While the share of the average inhabitant in foreign trade was over $30 in 1800," writes Clive Day, "it was little over $20 in 1860, and ranged between $10 and $15 through much of the intervening period."[3] The great development consequently took place after the Civil War. It was at

[3] *Op. cit.,* 514.

this time that the United States began to engage in earnest in the struggle for the markets of the world.

The trend toward the incorporation of America into the international economy is revealed in changing trade relations, as well as in the increase in the volume of foreign commerce. In 1790, according to Mr. Day, "the United States sent to the two great continents of Africa and Asia less than one-third of a million of dollars of exports,"[4] or less than one-sixtieth of its total exports. At that time foreign trade was confined almost entirely to western Europe and the West Indies—to Great Britain, France, Spain, the Netherlands, and Portugal and to the American dominions of these countries. Commerce with Germany, the Baltic peoples, and eastern Europe scarcely existed. In 1929 more than one-third of the foreign trade of the United States went to Asia, South America, Oceania, and Africa. The routes between North America and Europe have been supplemented by innumerable connections with other parts of the world.

The growth of cultural contacts has accompanied the advance of foreign trade. This is revealed in the development of the United States postal service. The value of international money orders has grown from $1,965,000 in 1875 to $76,113,000 in 1930. Between 1910 and 1930 the volume of foreign mails dispatched by sea increased markedly—letters from 3,142,000 pounds to 7,103,000 and other articles from 17,832,000 to 83,-377,000. Travel abroad has assumed large proportions. In the early days of the republic few citizens crossed the Atlantic to visit foreign lands. In 1930 477,260 citizens arrived from abroad and 462,023 departed. The corresponding figures for aliens, who were neither immigrants nor emigrants, were 204,514 and 221,764. Thus there is a perpetual intermingling of Americans with other peoples both at home and abroad. In the arts and the sciences national boundaries no longer exist. Dis-

4 Ibid., 491.

coveries, inventions, ideas, and thought are increasingly the common achievements and possessions of the various branches of the human race. Even sports are becoming international in character. And in the United States, as well as in other countries, despite the recrudescence of extreme nationalism in many quarters, scores of organizations and societies are engaged in promoting international understanding.

Finally, on the political side the American people have surged over their national boundaries. In 1867 they acquired Alaska from Russia. Then at the turn of the century they moved into the West Indies, took possession of Puerto Rico, established a protectorate over Cuba, seized the Panama Canal Zone, and generally assumed a position of dominance in the whole Caribbean basin. At the same time they pushed out across the Pacific, acquiring in rapid succession Hawaii, Guam, the Philippine Islands, and American Samoa. Through a comprehensive consular service, reaching into all important regions of the world, the national government turned its attention to the promotion of American business enterprise throughout the earth.[5]

So in the course of a century and a half the position of the United States in the world suffered radical change. With the closing of the frontier, the occupation of land and resources at home, the growth of manufacturing, the increase of wealth and power, and the advance of transportation and communication, the country was forced to look abroad. Like other industrial nations the American people pursued the ways of imperialism, laid the foundations of a colonial empire, and proceeded to build a powerful navy to protect their interests in distant waters. Simultaneously, in spite of their own boundless resources and the unexampled richness of the domestic market, they turned their attention increasingly to foreign trade, not

[5] See Louis M. Hacker and Benjamin B. Kendrick, *The United States Since 1865* (New York, 1932), 668–682.

only for the export of raw materials but also for the sale of manufactured goods abroad. By the close of the nineteenth century they were sending their soldiers into the Orient; and in 1917–18 they transported more than 2,000,000 men across the Atlantic to participate in the wars of the Old World. By the time the conflict was over they were a creditor nation for the first time in history and exporting capital at the rate of approximately a billion a year. The age of isolation was over. A few settlements along the Atlantic coast, far removed from the centers of civilization, had grown into a continental nation and become closely woven into the fabric of world relations.

THE INSTITUTION OF WAR

This trend toward world integration, however, has not proceeded at an even pace in all realms of activity. In the sphere of technological advance and in the exchange of goods it has gone farthest; in the field of political relationships, except for the appearance of such new instrumentalities as the World Court and the League of Nations, which at least for a time have passed into eclipse, it has scored few solid victories. The world is still divided into independent and sovereign nations much as it was before the day of the railroad, the steamship, the automobile, the airplane, the telegraph, and the radio. This absence of political integration expresses itself from time to time in the most terrible of all human institutions—war.

The fact should be recognized, however, that war is not a new institution. As James T. Shotwell has put the case:

"From the dim beginnings of society, and beyond, down to this very hour, war has been used without question and almost without interval; and upon the vicarious sacrifice of its countless victims rests the structure of our peace. . . . Blood and iron have been not only the historical instruments of every state for the assertion of its will among its neighbors, but they have been as well the instruments within the state by which political

institutions have come into life and maintained themselves
throughout the centuries."[6]

War, or at least some form of struggle for survival, has
inhered in the very nature of things. In a world in which every
living organism tends to multiply far more rapidly than the
means of subsistence, deadly strife would seem to be inevitable.
While the position of man, because of his powers of invention,
is somewhat different from that of the lower animals, the
ancient law of the jungle has marked every period of human
history. With the rise of modern nations war has become
more terrifying than ever before, even though certain savage
and cruel practices have been abandoned. To the national state
the right to declare war has been regarded perhaps as its most
precious right. Indeed it has been looked upon as "proof and
token of sovereignty itself."[7]

The Growing Tension Among the Nations. The causes of
war seem to have become somewhat aggravated by the rise of
industrial society. So long as the new modes of production were
confined mainly to one country, as they were down to the
middle of the nineteenth century, free commerce among the
nations tended to promote the interests of all, as those interests
were conceived by ruling groups and classes. But as nation after
nation, particularly in western Europe and America, followed
England along the paths of industrialism, the foundations of
exchange were transformed. Since under the institutions of
capitalism, with its inequalities in the distribution of income,
the trend is always toward a surplus of both consumer and
capital goods, there is a perpetual demand for growing markets.
And since the raw materials essential to industrial civilization
are very unevenly distributed over the earth, there arises a
similar demand for concessions in the more backward and defenseless parts of the globe. These facts have led the industrial

[6] James T. Shotwell, *War as an Instrument of National Policy* (New York,
1929), 8-9.
[7] *Ibid.*, 14.

nations into an ever more severe competition for markets, colonies, and spheres of influence. The result in the second half
of the nineteenth century was a tendency toward the abandonment of *laissez-faire* in the international field, the union of
business and government, the growth of imperialism, the race
for armaments, and war. The course of events has thus been
summarized by Parker T. Moon:

"An anti-imperialist, free-trade Europe was converted to
imperialism, rather suddenly in the seventies and eighties,
when England began to feel the competition of other industrial
rivals, when manufacturing nations began to raise protective
tariff walls around their own markets and to compete bitterly
for foreign markets, when steamships and railways provided
facilities for world commerce and conquest, when greedy factories and hungry factory towns called out for raw materials
and foodstuffs, when surplus capital, rapidly accumulating,
sought investments in backward countries, when the doctrine
of economic nationalism triumphed over the old individualistic liberalism."[8]

The scope of the imperialist operations which formed the
background of the first World War and which continue to
disturb the peace of nations is incompletely grasped by the
ordinary American citizen. The following passage from Mr.
Moon reveals the far-reaching ramifications of modern imperialism:

"Of ancient imperialism, of the empires of Alexander, of
Cyrus, of Cæsar, we have heard much and of Napoleon's
spectacular exploits every schoolboy has read. But the realms
conquered by military emperors of past ages were baubles,
trifles compared with the far-flung dominions which have

8 Parker Thomas Moon, *Imperialism and World Politics* (New York, 1926),
56–57. For a thorough account of the part played by economic forces in shaping
American foreign policy see Charles A. Beard, *The Idea of National Interest*
(New York, 1934).

been won, more often with the pen than by the sword, in our own supposedly prosaic generation. . . . More than half of the world's land surface, and more than a billion human beings, are included in the colonies and 'backward countries' dominated by a few imperialist nations. Every man, woman and child in Great Britain has ten colonial subjects, black, brown and yellow. For every acre in France there are twenty in the French colonies and protectorates. Italy is one-sixth as large as her colonies; Portugal, one twenty-third; Belgium, one-eightieth. The nations of western Europe are dwarfs beside their colonial possessions."[9]

The Increasing Cost of War. The rise of industrial civilization has not only aggravated the causes of war and created a condition of severe tension throughout the world. It has also increased the costs of war. This aspect of the question will be elaborated under the captions of financial cost, human cost, and general destructiveness. While all three categories are inter-related, it will be helpful to treat them separately.

Financial cost. During the past century the financial cost of war has grown to enormous proportions. This is clearly revealed in the available data on armaments, pensions, war debts, and general property damage attending the conduct of war. The combined weight of these several sources of cost may be revealed by an examination of the federal budget of the United States and of the estimated total cost of the World War and other wars.

The maintenance of modern armies and navies is an extremely expensive business. No longer is it primarily a question of feeding and clothing soldiers and sailors and equipping them with musket and cutlass. War today is waged with battleships, submarines, airplanes, tanks, artillery, and numerous products of the chemical laboratory. To provide these weap-

[9] *Ibid.,* 1. See also Carlton J. H. Hayes, *The Historic Evolution of Modern Nationalism* (New York, 1931), 282–285.

ons in quantity requires the services of a most advanced technology and a high degree of industrial organization. The expenditures of the federal government for this purpose increased from an appropriation of $80,602,375 in 1895 to a budget allotment of $694,805,800 in 1933. This meant an advance during a thirty-eight year period from $1.15 to $5.73 per person.[10] In 1930, according to the League of Nations Armaments Year Book, the United States led the nations of the world in military and naval expenditures.

Pensions constitute a second cost of war. Something of the nature of this burden is revealed in the outlays for veterans of the Spanish-American War of 1898, the Philippine Insurrection of 1899–1902, and the Boxer Rebellion of 1900. From 1899 to June, 1933, the total expenditure amounted to approximately $800,000,000 or two-thirds of the cost of these three wars or campaigns.[11] Moreover, the number of pensioners, including veterans, widows, minor children, and nurses, grew from 299 in 1899 to 233,875 in 1932, or to more than two-thirds of the number of men engaged.

In the course of a war a nation piles up debts that must be paid by coming generations. These debts may be either international or domestic in character. In the one case, they add new complications to the relations of nations; in the other, they place an unwonted strain on the internal economy. The federal budget for 1933 included an item of $1,138,803,400 to amortize and pay the interest on the public debt bequeathed to the nation by past wars.[12] This was almost seven times the estimated cost of the Revolutionary War.

The total economic cost of war, however, is not to be measured in terms of armaments, pensions, and war debts. The indirect damage to property and trade is of necessity very

10 Christian Social Action Movement, *Leaders' Handbook* (Chicago, 1932), 72–73.
11 "How Pensions Have Grown: The Record of the Spanish War," special article in the New York *Times,* Sunday, March 26, 1933.
12 Christian Social Action Movement, *op. cit.,* 72–73.

large. Entire cities may be destroyed, and commerce is always interrupted. Also millions of soldiers in times of both war and peace are maintained in an unproductive state—unproductive, that is, from the standpoint of the administration of the national economy. Then human life itself, particularly when represented by vigorous youth, has economic value. The direct costs of the World War have been estimated at $186,000,000,000; the indirect costs at approximately $152,000,-000,000. Ernest L. Bogart has compiled the following table in which the total costs are distributed:

Total direct costs, net....................		$186,333,637,097
Indirect costs:		
Capitalized value of human life:		
Soldiers	$33,551,276,280	
Civilians	33,551,276,280	
Property losses:		
On land	29,960,000,000	
Shipping and cargo....	6,800,000,000	
Loss of production.......	45,000,000,000	
War relief	1,000,000,000	
Loss to neutrals..........	1,750,000,000	
	$151,612,552,560	
Total indirect costs.................		$151,612,552,560
Grand total		$337,946,189,657[13]

An examination of the federal budget reveals the magnitude of the burden which the institution of war has placed upon the American taxpayer. Senator Wesley L. Jones, Chairman of the Senate Committee on Appropriations, has recently shown that "during the year ending July 3, 1930, the total expenditures of the United States for preparations for war and payments arising out of past wars were $2,800,000,000. This was 70

[13] Ernest L. Bogart, *Direct and Indirect Costs of the Great World War*, Carnegie Endowment for International Peace, Division of Economics and History, Preliminary Economic Studies of the War, No. 24 (New York, 1919), 299.

per cent of the total federal expenditures for the year, exclusive of post-office expenses."[14] Thus before the launching of the domestic program of the Roosevelt administration, war absorbed more than two-thirds of the national budget. Only thirty cents of the federal dollar went to the promotion of peaceful services—to agriculture, to commerce, to forestry, to public works, to unemployment relief, to health and education, and the arts and sciences.

The increasing economic burden of war can be best indicated perhaps by a comparison of the World War with previous wars. Will Irwin states that the direct cost of all wars from 1793 to 1910 amounted to only $23,000,000,000, as contrasted with $186,000,000,000 for the World War.[15] In the case of the United States the World War cost almost four times as much as the other five wars in which the country engaged since the founding of the republic, including the Revolutionary War. The figures are $22,625,000,000 and $5,842,000,000 respectively.[16] The struggle that gave birth to the nation cost but $170,000,-000; and the Civil War that rocked the foundations of the republic for four years cost only $3,478,000,000. And it should be recalled that the country had scarcely mobilized its resources for the struggle of 1917–1918 before the armistice was signed.

Victor L. Berger has endeavored to put meaning into the astronomical figures employed in estimating the cost of the World War by translating them into goods and services with which all are familiar. Although his estimate is somewhat higher than others and although any attempt of this kind commits certain economic fallacies, the statement itself is illuminating:

" . . . According to the best statistics obtainable, the World War cost . . . $400,000,000,000 in property. In order to give some idea of what this means, just let me illustrate it in the following: With that amount we could have built a $2500 house and furnished this house with $1000 worth of furniture and placed it on five acres of land worth $100 an acre, and given all this to each and every family in the United States of America, Canada, Australia, England, Wales, Ireland, Scotland, France, Belgium, Germany and Russia. After doing this there would be enough money left to give each city of 200,000 inhabitants and over in all the countries named a $5,000,000 library, a $5,000,000 hospital and a $10,000,000 university. And then, out of the balance we could still have sufficient money to set aside a sum at 5 per cent interest which would pay for all time to come a $1000 yearly salary for each of an army of 125,-000 teachers, and, in addition to this, to pay the same salary to each of an army of 125,000 nurses. And, after having done all this, we could still have enough left out of our $400,000,000,-000 to buy up all France and Belgium and everything of value that France and Belgium possess; that is, every French and Belgian farm, home, factory, church, railroad, street car—in fact, everything of value in these two countries in 1914. For it must be remembered that the total valuation of France in 1914, according to French official figures, was $62,000,000,000. The total of Belgium, according to Belgian official figures, was in the neighborhood of $12,000,000,000. This means a total valuation of the two countries in 1914 of less than $75,000,000,000. In other words, the price which the leaders and statesmen of the Entente, including the 'statesmen' of the United States, made the people of the world pay for the victory over Germany was equal to the value of five countries like France, plus five countries like Belgium."[17]

Human cost. There is of course no quantitative measure of the human cost of war. Who can gauge the misery, the suffering, the horror, the relapse into barbarism and savagery occasioned by the death struggle of armies and whole nations and

[17] Victor L. Berger, "A Leading American Socialist's View of the Peace Problem," *Current History* (January, 1928), XXVII, 471–472.

marked by the use of modern engines of war! The English language scarcely contains the words necessary for an adequate and accurate description. At least such a task is beyond the powers of the social scientist. It must be left to the poet and the dramatist.[18]

Moreover, economic costs cannot be separated from human costs. Life in army or navy may unfit men for the ordinary occupations; the ravaging of fields destroys homes and drives families into poverty; the destruction of cities spreads disease, starvation, and death; and the imposition of taxes bows the back of labor and deprives children of educational opportunities. Economic cost always carries with it a human cost, because in the last analysis wealth is created by the travail of men. The war placed intolerable material burdens on the masses of the people in many countries. That they were intolerable is proved by the fact that whole populations have revolted. There are, however, certain data available which are not predominantly economic in character and which provide another measure of war.

Among such data are the facts reporting loss of human life. In comparison with the past, modern warfare is deadly beyond comprehension. Mr. Bogart finds that the total "loss of life resulting from the important wars of the nineteenth century," beginning with the Napoleonic Wars of 1790–1815 and ending with the Balkan Wars of 1912–13, amounted to only 4,449,300.[19] The corresponding figure for the World War was somewhere between eight and nine millions. But the death toll of a war should not be confined to the casualties among the combatants. When the non-combatants are included, this authority estimates the total deaths of the war at 26,000,000. Then to this figure must be added 20,000,000 wounded, 9,000,000 war

[18] See Maxwell Anderson, *What Price Glory* (New York, 1927); Henri Barbusse, *Under Fire* (New York, 1928); and Erich Maria Remarque, *All Quiet on the Western Front* (New York, 1930). Also see Lawrence Stallings, *The First World War* (New York, 1933), a pictorial account.

[19] *Op. cit.,* 270.

orphans, 5,000,000 war widows, and 10,000,000 war refugees.
Even this is not all. There should also be included "the indirect losses from revolution, famine, and pestilence, the increased
death rate and the total losses due to the war. According to the
Swedish Society for the Study of Social Consequences of
the War, the total loss must be put down at 40,000,000 lives."[20]
What these bare figures mean in lost genius, crippled bodies,
deranged minds, blasted hopes, and charged memories is not
recorded on the pages of history.

Another human cost of war, which can only be mentioned
here, is the legacy of hate which it leaves behind. One might
expect the vanquished to be embittered, as indeed they are;
but the victors also quarrel over the spoils and sow the seeds
for future conflict. Today, fifteen years after the Treaty of
Versailles, minor wars are being waged in various parts of
the world and the great nations tremble again on the brink
of international conflict. Hatreds and injustices bred by the
last war are preparing the way for the next. With the exception of those disarmed by the peace treaty, the powers are
more heavily armed in 1934 than they were in 1914. These
facts would suggest the futility of engaging in "a war to end
war."

General destructiveness. All that has been said in the foregoing pages makes it abundantly clear that the last one hundred
and fifty years have witnessed an appalling increase in the
destructiveness of war. Certain aspects of this question merit
additional and special attention. Also a word should be said
about trends in perfecting the instruments of war during the
period since 1918. The nature of the next world war, if it is
ever waged, may well be contemplated by the coming generation.

One of the most obvious characteristics of war in the twentieth century is the tendency to erase the line dividing combat-

[20] Sherwood Eddy and Kirby Page, *The Abolition of War* (New York, 1924),
49–50.

ants from non-combatants. In previous ages, at least since the appearance of complex societies, conflict was confined for the most part to the point where contending armies or fleets met in battle. Today all this is changed. The workman in a munitions factory, the farmer raising foodstuffs, or anybody engaged in rendering some service necessary, either directly or indirectly, to the successful waging of war may be quite as valuable as the man at the front. Indeed the propagandist, skilled in the molding of public opinion at home and abroad, may be as effective as a whole army. A modern war therefore, if it is to be successful, must be carried on by a highly disciplined and closely united people: the whole nation—men, women, and even children—girds itself for the conflict. This makes the destruction of cities and the undermining of the morale of the civil population equal in importance to the defeat of battalions and the sinking of warships. And with the new forms of transportation, communication, and radio-control the fight can be carried to the very heart of an enemy country.

Since the World War, if occasional reports may be trusted, human ingenuity, as never before, has been set the task of creating new and ever more terrible and powerful agents of death.[21] Advances have been made in the perfecting of various mechanical devices such as the submarine, the airplane, and the tank. The following dispatch to the New York *Times* from a London correspondent published in the issue of October 19, 1930, lifts the curtain for a moment on the holocaust that technology is preparing for mankind:

"Visions of the next war were unfolded before the empire's Prime Ministers today when the War Office revealed its newest monsters of destruction at Aldershot. A new giant tank, like a steel crab on wheels, rumbled across the shellholes amid the swirl of dust, the roar of engines and the crackle of guns. Old-

[21] For a general account of the situation see *What Would Be the Character of a New War?* by Eighteen of the World's Greatest Experts (New York, 1933).

fashioned caterpillar tanks controlled by wireless fought a
battle before the Prime Ministers' eyes like portents of a war
which would be fought not by men but by machines. New
machine gun devices were brought into action to reveal new
refinements and destructiveness. The most hair-raising of the
day's monsters was the tank which moved like a crab. It had
been designed to solve every problem of a shell-torn battle area
and wriggle over obstacles which during the World War had
put caterpillar tanks out of action. When it came to gaping
craters it simply lifted its wheels in the air one at a time and
crawled to the other side. Like the claws of a nightmare the
tank's wheels stretched from shellhole to shellhole, each wheel
with its own driving power and each with its own grip on the
surface. . . . There was neither color nor glory in today's picture of war. Drab gray ironclads swarmed over the countryside,
often hiding behind smoke screens. Only occasionally a
glimpse of infantry betrayed the fact that men were engaged.
. . . As a last surprise a 'dark horse' tank made its appearance
—a mammoth sixteen-ton contrivance, which will supersede the
type now used by the British Army. The capacities of this tank
are still a jealously guarded secret, but it won the race around
the Aldershot drill ground today with the greatest ease."[22]

A few quotations will reveal how comparatively backward
was the knowledge of poison gases during the World War.
And there is little reason for believing that in a major conflict
these instruments would not be used. When passion is running
high and nations are engaged in a life and death struggle,
short shrift will be made of humane sentiments; men will use
any weapon that may be at hand; the more deadly it is, the
more quickly are they likely to turn to it. Mr. Duff Cooper,
former British Under-Secretary of War, was probably correct
when he declared that "no nation, having once taken the
ghastly decision to go to war, is justified in abstaining from

[22] From the New York *Times*, October 19, 1930.

any step which will bring that war to the swiftest possible conclusion. . . . So long as we have weapons of war let them be cheap and nasty."[23]

Doctor Hilton Ira Jones, Director of Scientific Research of the Redpath Bureau, has described the military possibilities of a new lethal gas:

"It is a deadly poison and would destroy armies as a man might snuff out a candle. I do not believe the nations of the world would want to use it for warfare, simply because it always kills. War, if it comes again and is to be deadly, will never again be fought with shot and shell. It can't be, for it is so much cheaper to destroy life wholesale with this new gas. It may be manufactured at the rate of thousands of tons a day and it costs much less than powder and cannon, yet it will destroy armies more thoroughly, more effectively, more quickly."[24]

Brigadier General William Mitchell of the United States Army, when pleading before the House Committee on Appropriations for more defensive airplanes, stated that "a few planes could visit New York as the central point of a territory 100 miles square every eight days and drop enough gas to keep the entire area inundated . . . 200 tons of phosgene gas could be laid every eight days and would be enough to kill every inhabitant."[25] Captain D. B. Bradner, when Chief of Research of the Chemical Warfare Service, spoke in similar vein at a Congressional hearing:

"One plane carrying two tons of the liquid (a certain gas-generating compound) could cover an area of 100 feet wide and 7 miles long, and could deposit enough material to kill every man in that area by action on his skin. It would be entirely possible for this country to manufacture several thousand tons

23 *Army, Navy and Air Force Gazette* (July 25, 1929), 627.
24 Quoted by Elvira K. Fradkin, *Chemical Warfare—Its Possibilities and Probabilities* (pamphlet, published by the Carnegie Endowment for International Peace, New York, 1924), 140.
25 Will Irwin, *op. cit.*, 46.

a day, provided the necessary plants had been built. If Germany had had 4000 tons of this material and 300 or 400 planes equipped in this way for its distribution, the entire first American army would have been annihilated in 10 or 12 hours."[26]

Brevet Colonel J. F. C. Fuller of the British Army in an essay on the warfare of the future spoke as follows concerning the general possibilities of gas warfare:

"It is quite conceivable that many gases may be discovered which will penetrate all known gas armor. As there is no reason why one man should not be able to release one hundred cylinders simultaneously, there is no reason why he should not release several million; in fact, these might be released in England today electrically by a one-armed cripple sitting in Kamchatka directly his indicator denoted a favorable wind."[27]

Corroborative testimony came from Major-General E. D. Swinton of the British Army:

"It has been rather our tendency up to the present to look upon warfare from the retail point of view—of killing men by fifties or hundreds or thousands. But when you speak of gas . . . you must remember that you are discussing a weapon which must be considered from the wholesale point of view and if you use it—and I do not know of any reason why you should not—you may kill hundreds of thousands of men, or at any rate disable them."[28]

This same authority foresees the use of yet more deadly weapons as physical and biological science advances:

"I imagine from the progress that has been made in the past that in the future we will not have recourse to gas alone, but will employ every force of nature that we can; and there is a tendency at present for progress in the development of the

[26] *Ibid.*, 46–47.   [27] *Ibid.*, 47.   [28] *Ibid.*, 47–48.

different forms of rays that can be turned to lethal purposes. We have X-rays, we have light rays, we have heat rays. . . . We may not be so very far from the development of some kinds of lethal ray which will shrivel up or paralyze or poison human beings. . . . The final form of human strife, as I regard it, is germ warfare. I think it will come to that; and so far as I can see there is no reason why it should not, if you mean to fight . . . prepare now . . . we must envisage these new forms of warfare, and as far as possible expend energy, time and money in encouraging our inventors and scientists to study the waging of war on a wholesale scale instead of . . . thinking so much about methods which will kill a few individuals only at a time."[29]

In the light of recent developments in technology various attempts have been made to depict the character of the "next war." While many of these forecasts are doubtless highly fantastic, if nations do resort to trial by force again, it is certainly safe to predict that a second world conflict will be far more deadly than the first. A writer in *The Journal of the United States Cavalry Association* thus paints the picture:

"We may imagine what may be expected of the air force in another war. Bombers capable of carrying great loads of high explosives and capable of flying high and fast will be able to penetrate to centres of production and create tremendous damage, provided sufficient fighting planes are available to destroy the enemy fighters and thus enable these bombers to carry on."[30]

Brigadier General Lord Thomson, Air Minister in the British Government, employs even more realistic language:

"The next war will be fought in the air, it will consist of aeroplane raids above the great cities, and the primary attack

29 *Ibid.*. 49-50.   30 Elvira K. Fradkin, *op. cit.,* 131.

will be against civilians, including women and children. Against these, incendiary, explosive and poison gas bombs will be used. No defense that has yet been devised will prevent the death of thousands of persons in any city thus attacked, and the organized life of any great metropolitan center would be brought to a standstill for days or weeks."[31]

THE TREND TOWARD WORLD ORGANIZATION

The increasing interdependence of nations in the economic and cultural realms has already been noted. In these spheres the world is rapidly becoming one vast social complex, even though various areas and peoples may endeavor to maintain a certain measure of independence. While no developments of equal magnitude in the field of political organization have appeared, certain steps have been taken, however feeble they may be, that suggest the beginnings of world organization. At any rate the time has passed when any nation can live wholly by itself. The World War demonstrated the strength of the forces that bind the peoples of the earth together.

The trend toward international co-operation may be traced back to the middle of the last century.[32] The International Telegraph Union, involving today some sixty countries, was established in 1868; and the Universal Stamp Union, now embracing practically the whole world, was founded in 1875. Other efforts, of a quasi-political character, pointing toward the creation of a world organization include the inauguration of the International Union of Weights and Measures in 1875, an international union for the protection of industrial property in 1878, an international union for the protection of literary property in 1883, an international union for the co-operative publication of customs tariffs in 1890, an international union of railway freight transportation in 1890, an International Insti-

[31] *Ibid.*, 130.
[32] Manly O. Hudson, *Progress in International Organization* (Stanford University, California, 1932), 7.

tute of Agriculture in 1905, and an International Institute of Public Health in 1907.[33]

In the more strictly political field a number of developments occurred before the World War. In 1889 conferences were held which led in time to the formation of the Pan-American Union; in 1899 the first peace conference assembled at The Hague; and eight years later the second of these conferences was convened. Out of these conferences, in addition to their educational influence on the peoples of the world, came the Permanent Court of Arbitration. While such efforts proved utterly incapable of settling major disputes and preventing the greatest war of history, they marked a trend which in subsequent years has gained considerable momentum.

Out of the war and the peace, besides various voluntary bodies and movements and an immense amount of agitation for the achievement of permanent peace through some kind of world organization, came the League of Nations. Though associated with the Treaty of Versailles and dominated by the victors in the war, this new instrument of government represents the most articulate expression of the trend toward the political union of the nations which has yet appeared. The purpose of the League is thus enunciated in the preamble to the Covenant:

"The High Contracting Parties,

"In order to promote international cooperation and to achieve international peace and security

    by the acceptance of obligations not to resort to war,

    by the prescription of open, just and honourable relations between nations,

    by the firm establishment of the understandings of international law as the actual rule of conduct among Governments,

    and by the maintenance of justice and a scrupulous re-

[33] *Ibid.*, 9–12.

spect for all treaty obligations in the dealings of organised peoples with one another,
"Agree to this Covenant of the League of Nations."[34]

Since the World War a number of other steps toward world organization and the abolition of war as an instrument of national policy have been taken. The International Labor Organization, created by the peace treaties, provides for the periodical calling of an international conference to consider the conditions of labor in the various countries; and the Permanent Court of International Justice, founded by the League of Nations in 1920, places at the disposal of nations machinery for the peaceful settlement of disputes. Mention should also be made of the Pact of Paris, signed in 1928 by fifteen governments and later by most of the remaining governments of the world, which proposed to complete the diplomatic revolution begun in the Covenant of the League of Nations "by severing the historical dependence of diplomacy on war."[35]

How successful these first attempts to translate the implications of modern technology into political conventions will prove to be, is of course a question that must be left to history. In these pages only the great trend itself may be noted.

And yet in conclusion a word should be said regarding the difficulties of the tasks that lie ahead. The world continues to present the aspect of an armed camp, with wars and rumors of war filling the air. The basic conditions out of which military struggles emerge have by no means been removed. The same conflicts of interest may be observed today that lay at the root of the conflagration beginning in 1914. Indeed these conflicts may have been sharpened by a number of changes that have appeared since the war—the spread of industrialism to backward and agrarian countries, the growing restlessness of the colored races under the domination of the white man, the challenge which communism throws out to capitalistic

[34] *Ibid.*, 123. [35] James T. Shotwell, *op. cit.*, 180.

institutions, and the rise of extreme forms of nationalism under the ægis of fascism. The industrial nations compete ever more keenly for the markets of the world; and natural resources, raw materials, and human populations are still very unevenly distributed over the earth. The merest glance about the globe in the spring of 1934 suggests that the great powers, in both the east and the west, are moving rapidly and inexorably toward the repetition, on a greatly enlarged and far more deadly scale, of the horrors of 1914–1918.

The increasing cost of weapons of offense and defense has added to the difficulties of keeping the peace. On the one hand, it stimulates rival nations to engage in a race of armaments and to watch the actions of one another with jealous and suspicious eyes. This inevitably increases the strain between peoples and breeds the psychology of war. On the other hand, under the institutions of private capitalism, since vast fortunes can be and have been made from the manufacture and sale of arms to belligerent nations, the makers of munitions develop a vested interest in war. The dangers inherent in this situation have been set forth by Nicholas Murray Butler, for many years President of the Carnegie Endowment for International Peace:

"The profit-making motive is expressing itself in the manufacture and shipment of arms as never before in times of ostensible peace. Those profit-making undertakings which are interested in the manufacture and shipment of arms are steadily reaching out to influence the policy of governments as well as the approach to public opinion through the press. . . . It is becoming increasingly clear that one of the greatest obstacles to farther progress toward international cooperation to establish and maintain the peace of the world is to be found in the activities and influences of those important and powerful groups in various countries whose interests lie in the manufacture and sale of instruments and munitions of war for private profit. The growing movement to make the manufacture of munitions of war a government monopoly will be greatly strengthened as public opinion comes to recognize the dangers of permitting the continuance of conditions under which zeal for private profit is free vigorously to oppose the highest public interests of the people of the world."[36]

The situation has been further complicated by the appearance of divided counsel among persons honestly devoted to the abolition of war and the peaceful settlement of international disputes. On the one side are those who believe that the cause of peace will best be served by a complete return to the doctrines of free trade as developed by the British classical economists at a time when England was the "workshop of the world" and private capitalism was in the earlier stages of its development. They would remove all governmental barriers to international commerce and place their trust in the world-wide competition of private enterprise. On the other side are those who contend that the World War itself was a product of this philosophy, modified as the severity of the competition increased and powerful private interests captured the governments of their respective countries. They point out, moreover, that as the practice of *laissez-faire* disappears within the national borders and gives way to economic planning, it will also be driven out of the international field. The planning of the domestic economy, so they argue, implies of necessity the control of foreign trade. They therefore look ultimately, not to the abolition or even to the weakening of the nation as an economic integer, but rather to a world order founded on closely and efficiently organized national groups.

[36] Nicholas Murray Butler, *Annual Report of the Director for the Year 1932,* Division of Intercourse and Education, Carnegie Endowment for International Peace (New York, 1932), 8. For a comprehensive and well documented account of the relations of war and munition making see H. C. Engelbrecht and F. C. Hanighen, *Merchants of Death* (New York, 1934).

World planning, which may be regarded as the distant goal of such a policy, would thus grow out of and be an expression of the planning of individual nations or regions. At present the United States would seem to be moving in the latter direction.

PART THREE

PHILOSOPHY AND PROGRAM

CHAPTER I

THE TREND OF THE AGE

The way has now been cleared for the preparation of a plan of action in the field of education. The natural and cultural landscape, amid which the American people live, has been briefly surveyed. The findings of the social sciences regarding the basic elements in the material and spiritual heritage, the functioning of existing institutions, and the major social trends and tensions of the age have been passed in rapid review. There remains the task of formulating an educational philosophy and an educational program that are in harmony with objective fact and that at the same time point toward the refinement and fulfillment of the accepted ideals of the American people. To this task the rest of the volume will be devoted. The observation should be made, moreover, that educational philosophies and programs are but aspects or expressions of comprehensive social philosophies and programs. The more inclusive problem therefore cannot be ignored in the present undertaking.

At this point the relation between objective findings and practical endeavor should be made abundantly clear. Such findings do not compel a particular course of action. Indeed they compel no action whatsoever. Yet in the making of choices they can be disregarded only at the peril of inviting failure to attend the course of enterprise. They set the limits within which success may be achieved and provide indispensable tools with which the social practitioner must work. Thus, while the data of the social sciences do not furnish the statesman or the educator with categorical imperatives, they do tell him which purposes among many are feasible and indicate by what means chosen purposes may be achieved. The imperatives of the social sciences are always conditional and contingent. The question of values, except as realities to be described and measured, lies beyond the realm of impersonal inquiry. Nevertheless a commission of social scientists, asked to prescribe their own disciplines for the schools, must go beyond their inert data and adopt for the time the rôle of the practical man. If they refuse to do this, they assume the office without accepting the responsibilities of the educator. The first of these responsibilities is to select from the welter of social trends and movements those which are most fundamental from the standpoint of human welfare and relationships.

A PERIOD OF TRANSITION

The facts assembled in the foregoing chapters prove beyond question that American culture today is passing through an epoch of profound transition. The term "today," however, must not be taken literally. It does not mean the present twenty-four hours, or this month, or this year, or the period of the great depression, or even of that interval in world history beginning in August, 1914, and marked by the most devastating of wars between the nations and by a succession of social convulsions and revolutions throughout the earth. Rather is the term used to designate an age that for America reaches well back into the eighteen-hundreds and may be expected to extend far into the twentieth century—an age that is striving to come to terms with the products, the implications, and all the conditioning influences of science and technology.

To say that the present is an age of transition may seem to repeat a commonplace. It would appear that in a rapidly changing world every age is an age of transition. In a superficial sense this is true, but only in the sense that any age, being the child of the past and the parent of the future, is transitional between what has gone before and what is to come after; it is false in the sense that it assumes change to be purely quantitative and unidirectional. Change, even rapid change, may proceed for a period without seriously disturbing the bases of social life. Thus within the limits of a hunting economy numerous inventions and refinements may be introduced which merely tend to individualize, elaborate, and perfect the traditional modes of living. But there may come a time, as the historical record proves again and again, when changes appear that herald the coming of a radically new order—an order based upon agriculture, animal-breeding, and settled life. A society in which changes of this second type are dominant is obviously in a period of transition. The American people are living today in such a society. The very foundations of the social order are being transformed and long-cherished doctrines are being frankly questioned or repudiated.

The age of individualism in economy—the age that nurtured the young republic—is patently drawing to a close. The age of corporate, social, or collective action in economy is opening. Here is the great trend of the present epoch, a trend that is affecting every institution and placing its stamp on every department of life, a trend that must be taken into account by every statesman or educator who pretends to deal with reality. The significance of this trend may best be revealed by an examination of the development and decay of the individualistic tradition in American economy.

THE INDIVIDUALISTIC TRADITION

The individualistic tradition in economy is by no means as old as many believe. The first English settlers on the North American continent were certainly not committed to it. They were still under the influence of the closely regulated and highly socialized economy of feudal society in which the rights of individual enterprise were severely circumscribed. The Vir-

ginia Company in founding the colony at Jamestown ordered
the common sharing of land and food; and Captain John
Smith endeavored to rule the settlement according to the socialist doctrine that "he who does not work shall not eat." In
an early record of the colony the evils of private trading are
excoriated. The complaint is made in referring to the operations of persons who today would be classified as business
men, that "there was ten times more care to maintain their
damnable and private trade, than to provide for the Colony
things that were necessary."[1] And in colonial Massachusetts,
under the rule of the Puritan theocracy, there was little in-
clination to encourage the free play of personal initiative. The
charter granted to the city of Albany in 1686 by Governor
Dongan on behalf of James II conferred upon the municipal
authorities the powers "to establish, appoint, order and direct
the establishing, making, laying out, ordering, amending and
repairing of all streets, lanes, alleys, highways and bridges,
water-courses and ferries, in and throughout the city, or leading
to the same." The city was also granted extensive property
rights and extensive business privileges. It was given "all the
waste, vacant, unpatented and unappropriated land lying and
being within the said city, . . . together with all rivers, rivu-
lets, coves, creeks, ponds, water-courses, . . . and also the royalties of fishing, fowling, hunting, hawking, mines, minerals
and other royalties and privileges belonging or appertaining
to the city of Albany, gold and silver mines only excepted."[2]
In further summarizing the contents of this charter, which
presumably reflected the temper of the age, Mr. Anderson
writes as follows:

"As if these grants were not enough, the royal governor
conferred also upon the city corporation the fishing privilege
in the Hudson throughout Albany County, the right to cut

[1] John Gardiner Tyler, *Narratives of Early Virginia* (New York, 1907), 158.
[2] Quoted in William Anderson, *American City Government* (New York, 1925), 393-394.

firewood and timber for building and fencing purposes in the neighboring manor of Rensselaerwyck for twenty-one years, the right to take all stray animals found within the city, the power to license tavern-keepers, victualers, and all retailers of liquor, and the right to hold a market twice a week forever, on Wednesdays and Saturdays. The monopoly of the Indian trade throughout an extensive area was also granted to the corporation for the benefit of its freemen."[3]

This tradition of collective and community responsibility seems to have prevailed down to the middle of the eighteenth century. A heritage from mediæval England, it was doubtless re-enforced for a period by the conditions of life in the new world. Until the colonists had firmly established themselves along the Atlantic coast, learned the art of Indian warfare, and overcome the initial difficulties of living in a strange land, group and community solidarity of a high order was necessary for survival. But before the issuing of the Declaration of Independence powerful disintegrating forces had made their appearance. The "strong winds of individualistic doctrine" were sweeping over the country, and men sought freedom from the exactions and restraints of the state. Among the major influences leading to the overthrow of the collective tradition were two essentially contrary tendencies—the westward movement of population and the rise to power of the enterprising middle class.

The settlement of North America, from the founding of the first colonies down to the coming of the last immigrant, was for the most part an achievement of individual enterprise. The country was peopled very largely by men and women seeking to improve their own lot in this world, and not by the representatives or members of any organized society. Moreover, the crossing of the Atlantic, itself an exercise of personal initiative of no mean proportions, involved the break-

[3] *Ibid.*, 394.

ing of innumerable ties with the past and a kind of emancipation of the individual from the accustomed social restraints. Also, as already intimated, after the settlers had mastered the more elementary problems of sustaining life in the new environment, the power of the community or of any ruling caste to coerce the individual was greatly weakened. If the demands of society became irksome, he could move to the frontier and there find an abundance of free or cheap land on which he might proclaim the independence of himself and family. The pioneer, moreover, moving ahead of government, came naturally to regard the state as an alien and even hostile influence.

The wealth and extent of the country, combined with the relative sparsity of the population, contributed largely to the development of a peculiar type of social pattern founded on individual and household. As soon as the military power of the European settlers became sufficient to guarantee a measure of safety from Indian attack, the major force making for compact community organization disappeared. Men then dared, as individuals and as families, to strike out for themselves in the struggle to possess the rich lands of the Mississippi and the west. This tendency, which had its beginnings in the colonial era, was confirmed and strengthened by the Preemption Act of 1841 and the Homestead Act of 1862 of the Federal Congress. As a result the American economy took the form, not of the village, which was characteristic of the old world from the Strait of Gibraltar to the Bering Sea, but of a land dotted with homesteads and occasional trading centers. The comparatively large farms and great distances fostered the isolation of the family and bred in the people a strong individualism and independence in economy. It was these conditions that produced the "independent farmer" of hallowed tradition who in the words of the British traveler, John Melish, could "stand erect on the middle of his farm, and say, 'This ground is mine; from the highest canopy of heaven, down to the lowest depths, I can claim all that I can get possession of within these bounds; fowls of the air, fish of the seas, and all that pass through the same.' . . . None dare encroach upon him; he can sit under his own vine, and under his own fig tree, and none to make him afraid."[4]

The fact should be noted, however, that this was in reality familism rather than individualism. As a rule the family, and not the individual, was the unit. Owing to the low level of technology, the reliance upon human energy, and the primitive character of the productive process, the household could be fairly self-contained on a low level of consumption. A single cash crop would provide the family with all the money required for the purchase of articles of trade; and within the home there were social solidarity, division of labor, and a rational sharing of goods and services. The great age of individualism in American history therefore was marked by integration on the scale demanded by the status of the practical arts and the general conditions attending the gaining of a livelihood.[5] That fine independence of spirit, therefore, which is one of the most precious spiritual possessions of the American people, was made possible by the economic security provided by the family. For a time, after the passing of the self-sufficient household, the domestic and world demand for the produce of the farmer, combined with the appreciation of land values attending the growth of population, also guaranteed to the farmer a large measure of economic security. Thus, since, prior to the middle of the last century, the great majority of the people were engaged primarily in agriculture, if government would only insure the safety of life and property and protect the individual or family in the right to the fruits of labor, all would go well and essential justice would be done.

A second powerful factor contributing to the development

[4] For full quotation see above, p. 17. John Melish, a textile manufacturer of Glasgow, visited the United States in the years 1806 and 1807, and 1809, 1810, and 1811.

[5] See above, Part Two, Chapter I, "Family."

of the individualistic tradition, but which provided quite a different emphasis, was the rise of the so-called middle classes. The age of the discovery and settlement of America was an age of profound change and unrest throughout the western world. Among other things the epoch witnessed the rapid disintegration of the collective economy of feudal society and the liberation of the individual from many restraints in the sphere of commerce and industry. The assault upon the traditional order was led by merchants and tradesmen who had established themselves in the mediæval towns and whose power resided in property accumulation. These elements in the population, demanding freedom for economic enterprise, whether in the realm of manufacture, commerce, or finance, gradually overcame the feudal aristocracy, assumed control of the state, and formulated a social philosophy congenial to their temper and aspirations. John Locke, their ablest spokesman in the seventeenth century, contended that "the great and chief end, therefore, of men uniting into commonwealths and putting themselves under government, is the preservation of their property." To them the essential functions of the state were to protect private property, maintain the sanctity of contracts, and thus set the stage for the free play of economic forces. The natural laws supposed to govern the operation of these forces were expounded by Adam Smith in the *Wealth of Nations,* the classic of economic thought during the era of private capitalism.[6] It was the rising middle classes, moreover, that dominated the early settlement of America, led the country in the Revolutionary War, wrote the federal Constitution, and, except for the brief period of dominance by the Western farmers and the Southern planters, set the tone of economic and political thought in the United States during the nineteenth century.

These two roots of the individualistic tradition in American history must of course be clearly distinguished, even though

[6] See above, Part Two, Chapters II and X on "Economy" and "Government."

they have often re-enforced and tempered each other. The individualism of the independent freeholder of Jeffersonian democracy is not to be confused with the individualism of business enterprise in a complex industrial society. The one is essentially self-contained, while the other is essentially predatory in its social outlook. There is something splendid in the individualism of the pioneering farmer who with wife and children strikes out into wilderness and single-handed, except for the occasional assistance of neighbors, wages battle with the raw forces of nature, asking no favors from organized society and engaging in no attempt to exploit his fellow men.

The individualism of business enterprise is of a quite different order. Its celebrated maxim of *caveat emptor* reveals its innermost spirit and reflects an attitude of indifference and irresponsibility toward general welfare. The individualistic farmer asserted his independence of society; the individualistic merchant made society the scene of his operations. To be sure, the social and craft morality of the pre-industrial era, built up through thousands of years of racial experience, held this doctrine of calculated selfishness in check and doubtless softened its expression. Yet in the course of time the earlier ethics was greatly weakened, the artisan tended to become content with shabby, if profitable, work, employed labor resorted to sabotage and malingering, the spirit of the racketeer spread through the economy, and private business itself repudiated the underlying principles of individualism, sought escape from the rigors of competition through various forms of combination and collusion, and turned to government for franchises, tariffs, subventions, and innumerable special privileges.

The authenticity of the individualistic tradition in American economy is easily and abundantly documented. As already indicated in this volume, it has left its imprint on practically every phase of life and thought. The great masses of the people have been reared on its precepts; political and intellectual leaders have preached its doctrines. Its power over the mind of the American people may be illustrated by brief reference to its expression in treatises on economic theory, in the conquest of the continent, in great state documents, and in the conduct of public education.

An account of the influence of the works of Adam Smith and his successors on the thought of the American people need not be repeated here. The fact will merely be recorded that these writers, in an effort to describe and make intelligible the economic life and tendencies of the late eighteenth and early nineteenth centuries, outlined an economic theory that survives today, even though its social bases have been largely destroyed by the onward march of events. This theory assumed that "the pecuniary self-interest of each individual, if given free play, would lead to the optimum satisfaction of human wants." The concepts and institutions through which self-interest was to be given free play were private property, private enterprise, individual initiative, the profit motive, wealth, and competition.[7] Thus was conceived the idea of a self-regulating social mechanism that could be counted upon to lift mankind to ever higher levels of economic achievement and well-being. For man in his collective capacity to interfere in the operation of this mechanism would, according to the theory, result in inefficiency and even disaster.[8] With few exceptions, wherever economics has been taught in the schools and colleges of the United States, these doctrines have been authoritatively presented.

Far more significant, however, than all the theoretic instruction of the schools and the press is the fact that the American people in crossing the continent *lived* the doctrines of economic individualism for three or four generations. And

[7] Adolph A. Berle and Gardiner C. Means, *The Modern Corporation and Private Property* (New York, 1932), 345.
[8] See above, Part Two, Chapter II, "Economy."

they, or at least the more dominant elements among them, lived those doctrines with a large measure of material success. Almost within the space of a single century, from 1790 to 1890, they broke over the Allegheny Mountains, occupied the Mississippi Valley, pushed across the great plains, traversed the ranges and plateaus of the western mountains, and established their settlements along the Pacific coast from San Diego to Puget Sound. In their course they felled immense forests, brought vast areas of virgin soil under cultivation, constructed a comprehensive network of highways, railroads, and other agencies of transportation and communication, covered the land with houses, factories, shops, villages, towns, and cities, and attained the most remarkable record of wealth production and accumulation that the world has ever seen. In this vast achievement, moreover, government played a relatively insignificant rôle. Private enterprise marched well in advance of organized society and placed its clear stamp on American character and institutions.

That this struggle to possess a continent under the ægis of individual initiative had its harsher features is recognized by all students of American history. "The thirst of a tiger for blood," wrote John Quincy Adams to a friend in 1838, "is the fittest emblem of the rapacity with which the members of all the new states fly at the public lands. The constituents upon whom they depend are all settlers, or tame and careless spectators of the pillage. They are themselves enormous speculators and land-jobbers. It were a vain attempt to resist them here."[9]

The Oklahoma Run, the last of the great rushes for nature's goods staged within the borders of the United States, gives in epitome perhaps the history of this long battle on the part of individual men and women to gain title to the material re-

[9] Henry Adams, *The Degradation of the Democratic Dogma* (New York, 1920), 31.

sources of the country. It was in 1889, and the territory of Oklahoma was being opened for settlement. On the appointed day "twenty thousand settlers crowded at the boundaries, like straining athletes," awaiting the signal that would start them across the line.[10] But let Miss Edna Ferber take up the narrative. In her novel *Cimarron,* one of the characters, a man who had taken part in the Run, paints the following realistic and interpretative picture of the event:

"Twelve o'clock. There went up a roar that drowned the crack of the soldiers' musketry as they fired in the air as the signal of noon and the start of the Run. You could see the puffs of smoke from their guns, but you couldn't hear a sound. The thousands surged over the Line. It was like water going over a broken dam. The rush had started, and it was devil take the hindmost. We swept across the prairie in a cloud of black and red dust that covered our faces and hands in a minute, so that we looked like black demons from hell. Off we went, down the old freight trail that was two wheel ruts, a foot wide each, worn into the prairie soil. The old man on his pony kept in one rut, the girl on her thoroughbred in the other, and I on my Whitefoot on the raised place in the middle. That first half mile was almost a neck-and-neck race. The old fellow was yelling and waving one arm and hanging on somehow. He was beating his pony with the flask on his flanks. Then he began to drop behind. Next thing I heard a terrible scream and a great shouting behind me. I threw a quick glance over my shoulder. The old plainsman's pony had stumbled and fallen. His bottle smashed into bits, his six-shooter flew in another direction, and he lay sprawling full length in the rut of the trail. The next instant he was hidden in a welter of pounding hoofs and flying dirt and cinders and wagon wheels . . . he was trampled to death

10 Frederick J. Turner, *The Frontier in American History* (New York, 1920), 278.

in the mad mob that charged over him. Crazy. They couldn't stop for a one-legged old whiskers with a quart flask."[11]

In order to complete the picture it should be added that the hero of the story, by stopping to do a generous act, lost his quarter section of land to a companion of the Run whom he had paused to help. This incident reveals the hard and inhuman quality of the individualistic economy. When the struggle is between man and man, victory goes to the strong, and even to the ruthless. In such a world noble sentiment is a weakness not to be indulged. *Business is business.*

The doctrines of economic individualism were written into the fundamental law of the land by the founding fathers. The federal Constitution reveals a deep distrust of strong government and collective restraints of all kinds. This is clearly shown in the separation of powers and the system of checks and balances contained in its provisions. It is also shown in the first ten amendments to the Constitution, which are supposed to protect the individual against the Congress in his exercise of so-called natural rights, including the right of property. The tenth amendment itself, moreover, declares that "the powers not delegated to the United States by the Constitution, nor prohibted by it to the states, are reserved to the states respectively, or to the people." Numerous decisions of the Supreme Court have further protected the rights of private property; and the state constitutions have added their support to the position taken by the national system. Although contrary tendencies may be observed from time to time, and particularly since the onset of the great depression, the American people have generally endeavored to separate politics from economics.[12]

Economic individualism has also left its stamp on the American school system. In fact the ordinary citizen has re-

[11] Edna Ferber, *Cimarron* (New York, 1930), 25–26.
[12] See above, Part Two, Chapter X, "Government."

garded that system, even though it represents an invasion
by government of a realm once left to private enterprise, much
as he would regard the natural resources of the country, that
is, as a means of personal aggrandizement. But this question
has been treated elsewhere in the present volume.[13]

<h2>THE BREAKDOWN OF INDIVIDUALISM</h2>

That the doctrines of individualism in economy are having
a difficult time in the age of technology is entirely patent. It
should of course be conceded that these doctrines never were
applied fully and completely in the United States or in any
other society. They merely constituted a logical framework
for comprehending an economy that did place individual initiative in wealth accumulation at the center of things. Moreover, as the evidence presented in earlier chapters shows, successful assaults upon economic individualism have been going
on for more than a century. Indeed the household and neighborhood economy of the colonial era was no sooner destroyed
by the release of the individual than tendencies were discernible that pointed toward a new integration. Nevertheless the
present epoch does mark to a peculiar degree the passing of
this time-honored tradition.

The breakdown of individualism in economy is revealed in
many aspects of the contemporary situation already reported
in this volume. It is revealed in the gross inequalities in the
distribution of wealth in normal times, in the prevalence of
poverty, unemployment, slums, and the manifold evidences
of physical privation among great masses of the population; it
is revealed in the phenomenon of unemployment, which is
widespread even in periods of so-called prosperity; it is revealed in the inability of the industrious and willing workman to acquire property; it is revealed in the worthlessness of
property to millions of farmers who can find no market for
their produce; it is revealed in the disaster that overtook

13 See above, Part Two, Chapter V, "Education."

American society in 1929, a disaster Justice Brandeis declared to be worse than war. The fact must be recognized that the anarchy of an individualistic economy brought the country to the very brink of ruin.

A more searching examination of the American economic system shows that the basic institutions and presuppositions of individualism have been either abandoned, destroyed, or profoundly modified by the rise of industrial society. In certain wide areas the institution of private property bears little resemblance to its historical antecedents. "To Adam Smith and to his followers," say Berle and Means, "private property was a unity involving possession. He assumed that ownership and control were combined. Today, in the modern corporation, this unity has been broken. *Passive property,*—specifically, shares of stock or bonds,—gives its possessors an interest in an enterprise but gives them practically no control over it, and involves no responsibility. *Active property,*—plant, good will, organization, and so forth which make up the actual enterprise,—is controlled by individuals who, almost invariably, have only minor ownership interests in it."[14] Adam Smith, sensing this tendency in the corporation and thinking in terms of the psychology of individual enterprise, predicted the general failure of corporate undertakings.

This division of ownership and control also appears in the concept of wealth. "To the holder of passive property, the stockholder," according to these same investigators, "wealth consists, not of tangible goods,—factories, railroad stations, machinery,—but of a bundle of expectations which have a market value and which, if held, may bring him income and, if sold in the market, may give him power to obtain some other form of wealth. To the possessor of active property,— the 'control'—wealth means a great enterprise which he dominates, an enterprise whose value is for the most part composed of the organized relationship of tangible properties, the

[14] *Op. cit.,* 346–347.

existence of a functioning organization of workers and the existence of a functioning body of consumers. . . . The two forms of wealth are not different aspects of the same thing, but are essentially and functionally distinct."[15]

Equally profound changes have been wrought in the other divisions of the traditional economic structure. In the corporation private enterprise is disappearing. Economic undertaking is conducted, not by "an individual or a few partners actively engaged and relying in large part on their own labor or their immediate direction," but by "tens and hundreds of thousands of owners, of workers, and of consumers" combined in great associations.[16] Individual initiative is going the way of private enterprise. Only "at the very pinnacle of the hierarchy of organization in a great corporation . . . can individual initiative have a measure of free play. Yet even there a limit is set by the willingness and ability of subordinates to carry out the will of their superiors. In modern industry, individual liberty is necessarily curbed."[17] With the separation of control from ownership the rôle of the profit motive changes. As a rule, the owners, that is, the stockholders, have comparatively little opportunity for reaping the larger rewards of enterprise; and those in control deal in such huge sums that the old conception of initiative must be modified. "It is probable," wrote Berle and Means, "that more could be learned regarding them (effective motives today) by studying the motives of an Alexander the Great, seeking new worlds to conquer, than by considering the motives of a petty tradesman of the days of Adam Smith."[18] Finally, with the growth of giant enterprise and a corresponding increase in fixed charges of various kinds, competition seems to have lost much of its effectiveness as a regulator of industry. "Today competition in markets dominated by a few great enterprises has come to be more often either cut-throat and destructive or so

15 *Ibid.*, 348.   16 *Ibid.*, 349.
17 *Ibid.*, 349.   18 *Ibid.*, 350.

inactive as to make monopoly or duopoly conditions prevail."[19] Thus, at least in vast areas, the theoretical and practical foundations of individualism in economy have been undermined or destroyed. Even the farmer, the very symbol of this cherished tradition, being dependent on distant markets for the disposition of his produce, is practically helpless, unless he overcomes his ancient prejudices and unites with his fellows in the protection and administration of his interests.

THE COLLECTIVIST TREND

The corporate or collectivist trend in American economy has moved hand in hand with the advance of industrial civilization. This conclusion is suggested by data presented in practically every chapter of the present volume. For a time, as the family surrendered its functions, the burden was often transferred to individual and private enterprise. But eventually the community, through co-operative or government action, reasserted itself in area after area, but on a vastly enlarged scale. Thus in the spheres of communication and education the state early took a hand. And in the realms of health, recreation, science, and art the trend is clearly toward restraint on the profit-seeking motive, toward co-ordination and socialization of services, and toward the growth of public concern. Even in the field of the administration of the law, the most conservative of institutions, the sense of social responsibility is being quickened. In this section, however, no attempt will be made to summarize the findings presented in earlier chapters. Rather will the more fundamental lines of argument be brought together and pointed toward the problem under consideration.

The rôle of technology in this trend of the age can scarcely be over-emphasized. Under its impact the relatively simple society of the early nineteenth century, in which economic individualism flourished, has all but vanished. The compara-

[19] *Ibid.*, 351.

tively self-sufficient family or small community has practically disappeared. The rise of a closely interdependent economy, embracing the entire country and binding together in one comprehensive integration all branches of industry and agriculture, is recorded in the most common facts of daily life and intercourse. It is recorded in 250,000 miles of railroad, in 26,000,000 motor vehicles, in 700,000 miles of surfaced highways, in 46,000 miles of air routes, in 257,000 miles of telegraph lines, in 20,000,000 telephones, in 23,000 motion picture houses, 16,000,000 radio sets, in 3 or 4 great news-gathering agencies, in 600 broadcasting stations, in the concentration of the film industry at Hollywood. It is also recorded in the division of labor among regions, districts, plants, departments, and workmen that has rendered unthinkable the economic independence of individual, family, or neighborhood; in the integration of countless specialties in mass production that makes necessary the nationwide organization of consumption; in the vast and intricate structure of finance and credit that provides the vehicle for the exchange of goods and services; in the conquest of mechanical power that has solved the problem of production, inaugurated an era of potential plenty, and united all men and occupations in a common dependence on the machine. To speak of strictly private enterprise in such a world is to disregard the changes in modes of production and exchange that have occurred during the past one hundred years.

The modern corporation may be regarded as almost symbolic of the decline of the rôle of the individual in economy. The way in which this new instrumentality has undermined the very foundations of traditional economic thought has already been reviewed. In fact, the corporation is a form of collective enterprise, coming upon the scene when individual enterprise proved incapable of marshaling the huge aggregations of capital necessary to launch and sustain the vast undertakings demanded by industrial society. What far-reach-

ing implications this institution may hold for the further evolution of industrial society have been suggested by Berle and
Means in the closing paragraph of their study:

"The rise of the modern corporation has brought a concentration of economic power which can compete on equal terms
with the modern state—economic power versus political power,
each strong in its own field. The state seeks in some aspect to
regulate the corporation, while the corporation, steadily becoming more powerful, makes every effort to avoid such regulation.
Where its own interests are concerned, it even attempts to
dominate the state. The future may see the economic organism,
now typified by the corporation, not only on an equal plane
with the state, but possibly even superseding it as the dominant
form of social organization. The law of corporations, accord-
ingly, might well be considered as a potential constitutional law
for the new economic state, while business practice is increasingly assuming the aspect of economic statesmanship."[20]

Changes taking place in the economy have been attended,
somewhat haltingly, by changes in the sphere of government.[21]
The state has gradually been forced to abandon the principles
of *laissez-faire* and to assume responsibilities formerly left to
private enterprise. It early became interested in banking, in
protective tariffs, in transportation and communication, and
in the administration of schools. More recently it has turned
its attention increasingly to making provision for health, recreation, and poor relief, to extending services to business, agriculture and labor, and to exercising a degree of control over
social and economic forces.[22] One measure of this growth of
governmental activities is the increase in governmental costs.

[20] *Ibid.*, 357.   [21] See above, Part Two, Chapter X, "Government."
[22] See Carroll H. Woody, "The Growth of Governmental Functions," Chapter XXV, and Charles E. Merriam, "Government and Society," Chapter XXIX
in The President's Research Committee on Social Trends, *Recent Social Trends
in the United States* (New York, 1933), II.

According to Charles E. Merriam, "the proportion of estimated national income devoted to governmental purposes rose
from 9.1 per cent in 1915 to 12.8 per cent in 1929. The expenditures of all governments, federal, state and local, rose from three
and one-third billion dollars to nearly eleven and one-half
billion, or, allowing for changing price levels, to six and three-
quarters billion."[23] Of particular significance, from the standpoint of the tendency toward collectivism in economy, is the
growing concern of government with respect to the conduct of
business. "Central control over social and industrial forces,"
says Mr. Merriam, "is an almost inevitable outcome of the economic development of the time, and especially of the rapid rise
of large scale combinations of industrial power, not readily kept
in restraint by the ordinary processes of competition or by the
older procedures of government (as in the case of railways,
utility companies and great trusts) and of new types of commercial fraud and unfair trade practices."[24]

The interest of government in the conduct of the economy
has been greatly accentuated by the depression. Whether this
development is to be regarded as a permanent change in social
policy or merely as an effort to meet a passing emergency is
a question that cannot be answered fully today. But whatever
remains after the Roosevelt administration has passed into
history, it seems clear that profound changes are taking place
in the habits of thought of the American people. Already the
world has been irrevocably altered. Private business, having
proved itself bankrupt, has turned to the government for
both aid and leadership. Consequently, for the moment at any
rate, the theory of *laissez-faire* has been completely repudiated.
The line between politics and economics, between public and
private interests, is becoming more and more difficult to
discern. And the immediate agents of this revolution very fittingly, if paradoxically, speak the language and wear the mantle
of Thomas Jefferson.

[23] *Op. cit.*, 1501.   [24] *Ibid.*, 1502.

The trend toward a socialized economy is also revealed in the growth of social planning. Aside from its rôle in Utopian thought from Plato to H. G. Wells, this idea is to be identified with the spread of technology. The latter, parent and genius of industrial civilization, directly opposes, because of its planful and rational character, the chaos, the secrecy, the irrationality of the principle of competition and the rule of individual caprice. Appearing first in the sphere of scientific management in industry and proclaiming the revolutionary gospel of efficiency, social planning has spread from one area to another. Charles A. Beard, writing more than two years before the advent of the present national administration, thus outlined the prospect:

"Nor can government and society as a whole escape the impact of this planning process. Engineering rationality is the staff of industry, it runs into business, and inevitably into government and social arrangements. These too are founded on an economic base and are involved, by the nature of things, more or less intimately in the operations of productive economy. Thirty years ago, city planning was almost unknown in the United States, at least as an organized science; now that interest is represented by a national association, a magazine, a national conference, university chairs, practising professions, volumes of statutes, and achievements of no mean order. Yet it stands merely at the beginning of its career. Hard upon this development comes regional planning. State planning creeps up over the horizon. The word has scarcely stolen into the regular vocabulary of Washington politics, but national planning is implicit in innumerable works of the federal government, in the effort of the Farm Board to coördinate agricultural production, in the action of President Hoover when he called upon leaders of all branches of national economy to cooperate in holding production to a steady level of performance."[25]

[25] Charles A. Beard, *Toward Civilization* (New York, 1930), 301.

A final observation should be included in the record. In modern society there is a collectivism of disaster. The current depression shows how helpless the individual or family may be in the face of social forces. When a great economic storm sweeps through modern society, none can fully escape its impact. To be sure, the power of the storm will be felt very unevenly by the different economic classes. Yet no one can remain secure. With great enterprises going bankrupt, wages, salaries and profits being lowered, workmen and executives alike joining the ranks of the unemployed, and the total social income being reduced by half, only the stupid can view the situation with indifference or complacency. Even the members of the plutocracy must regard their condition as precarious. Economic values, being a product of the functioning of society, are beyond the control of the individual. Whether men wish it or not, they live today in a world in which they must share increasingly both prosperity and adversity.

CHAPTER II

THE NEW DEMOCRACY

The great trend from household to nation, from individualism to collectivism in economy, from a loosely organized to a closely integrated society, which appears to be reaching its culmination in the epoch now opening, has created chaos, confusion, and bewilderment. It has introduced innumerable conflicts, contradictions, and inconsistencies into American life and culture. It has destroyed the material foundations of inherited modes of living and of moral conceptions which have been cherished for generations. The American people consequently face an enormous task of mental, as well as institutional, reconstruction.

The major difficulty resides in the fact that the march of events has proceeded very unevenly in the several parts of the social structure. Thus science, technology, and invention, with their devastating implications for traditional practice and thought, have moved much more rapidly than government or even economic arrangements. Within the field of economy, moreover, methods of production have changed far more radically than methods of distribution. And the prejudices, the ideas, the thought of the people with respect to many basic social relationships and institutions have remained relatively static for generations. An intellectual equipment suited to the age of the ox-cart, human energy, and handicrafts lingers on in an age of motor cars, mechanical power, and automatic factories.

The central responsibility of public education in this situation is to bring the mentality of the American people into accord with their surroundings, to prepare them for life under profoundly altered circumstances, to encourage them to discard dispositions and maxims derived from the individualistic economy, and to re-furnish their minds with a stock of knowledges, attitudes, and ideas capable of functioning effectively and harmoniously in the new reality. The nature and magnitude of the problem will be illuminated by a review of some of the more pertinent findings of the social sciences as presented in the earlier chapters of this volume. First the wealth of the material and cultural heritage, which the American people have received from nature and the past, will be noted. Then attention will be directed to the conflicts and contradictions marking the administration of this heritage. The chapter will close with an attempt to resolve these conflicts and contradictions in the spirit of the ideal of democracy.

THE MATERIAL AND CULTURAL HERITAGE

From the standpoint of their material and cultural heritage the American people occupy a peculiarly favored position among the nations of the world. They would seem to have everything needful for the building of a great civilization. They have the social ideals, the natural riches, and the technology. In an address on *The Fortune of the Republic,* delivered in 1878, Emerson directed attention to this fact. "Never country had such a fortune," he said, "as men call fortune, as this, in its geography, its history, and in its majestic possibilities."[1] The passage of time has not weakened this estimate of the great philosopher and teacher.

Apart from being the direct heirs of one of the most fertile branches of human culture and besides sharing today in the spiritual riches of the entire human race, the American people have become peculiarly identified with a great ethical ideal. This ideal, derived from a long line of prophets reaching back to antiquity and fostered by conditions of life on the new con-

[1] Ralph Waldo Emerson, *Miscellanies,* Volume XI of Emerson's Complete Works (Boston, 1893), 412.

tinent, lends to their history whatever moral significance it may have for mankind. Moreover, they have regarded their country, and in this they were supported for generations by other peoples of the earth, as the scene of a bold social experiment designed to realize the ideal of democracy. In an age of overt and unabashed class rule and political despotism they proclaimed to the world the principle of the moral equality of all men and their devotion to the welfare of the common man. In imperishable historical documents, in social institutions, in the ordinary human relationships, they have given expression to this faith. In spite of disillusionment and changing circumstances democracy remains today the most authentic expression of the genius of the American people. It is a spiritual legacy of supreme worth and must provide the touchstone of any social or educational program.

The American people possess unusually rich natural resources. Their country has been peculiarly blessed by nature. The favorable combination of climate and soil has given to the United States an unrivaled foundation for agriculture and human habitation. Almost one-fourth of the arable land of the temperate zones of the globe lies within the boundaries of the nation. In their primeval state the forests covered an area of 850,000,000 acres and were the finest to be found anywhere in the world. And for the support of an industrial civilization this land is yet more richly endowed. Originally, according to authoritative estimates, it contained approximately 40 per cent of the mineral resources of the earth. Also it is the only country possessing adequate quantities of all of the principal industrial minerals. Nowhere else, moreover, are these minerals grouped so favorably for human use. Finally, not the least of the riches of this favored region is its natural beauty. The fertility of the soil, the variety of the climate, the luxuriance of the vegetation, the abundance of the lakes and rivers, and the irregularity of the topography, all combine to make it a beautiful land. While the American people exploited these resources shamelessly during the reign of individualism, they still have sufficient, under wise administration, to develop and maintain for centuries a great industrial civilization.

In their technology the American people have participated in the revolutionary advances of the past one hundred years. In fact, because of peculiarly favorable natural and cultural conditions on the new continent, they have pursued farther than any other people the logic of technological development. It is generally known that until well into the nineteenth century the fundamental processes by which men made their living or traveled about were not greatly unlike those in use in the days of the ancient empires. The work of the world was done mainly by human beings, supplemented by domestic animals and to a limited extent by fire and wind and water. Everywhere man cultivated the soil, harvested the crops, built houses and cities, and fabricated tools, weapons, and garments with his own strength. Today all but a relatively small portion of the burden has been shifted to other shoulders; and the feeble instruments which nature placed in the hands of men, such as the ox and the horse, are being rapidly superseded. Out of the mines of the United States have come 1,000,-000,000 iron horses which require neither rest nor sleep. When harnessed to machines these modern engines are capable literally of showering the American people with goods and services of every description. Moreover, with the spread of knowledge and means of birth-control the melancholy formula of Malthus may be laid to rest forever. While in the past man has of necessity lived by the "sweat of his face," in the age he is now entering he need do so no longer.

CONFLICTS AND CONTRADICTIONS

Such a picture of the material and cultural heritage of the American people suggests that they should already have disposed of the economic question and turned their energies to the basic tasks of spiritual development—to the tasks involved in the rational, humane, and æsthetic ordering of life. At least it would seem that the richness of their natural resources, coupled with the power placed at their disposal by technology, should have enabled them to achieve any reasonable standard of physical well-being to which they might subscribe. That no such goal has been attained or even approached is proved by the most ordinary facts of daily life. American society is the scene of deep conflicts and contradictions that lead to a perpetual frustration of hopes and to a profligate dissipation of energy.

Family. A fundamental factor conditioning these conflicts and contradictions is to be found in the dissolution of the self-contained family. In the household of the pre-industrial era, supplemented by the specialties of the rural neighborhood, most of the functions necessary for the maintenance of society were ordered more or less harmoniously and rationally, depending on the application and competence of its members. Today, in the case of the American people, the unit for the performance of these functions is the entire nation, supplemented by the specialties of a great world complex. Tradition, however, continues to place upon the family responsibilities which it is no longer capable of discharging. Certainly it cannot manage and co-ordinate the economy in which its various members must of necessity find employment and gain a livelihood. And the larger social unit has not yet reached that point of integration essential for the efficient conduct and control of the activities now carried on by its various specialized organs and structures. The theory and practice of individualism served to hasten the dissolution of the family integer, but failed to provide that automatic regulation of human affairs which the early advocates of *laissez-faire* optimistically predicted and attributed to the beneficence of an inscrutable providence.

More concretely it may be said that the family has ceased to be the relatively compact social unit that it was in the days of agrarian society, maintaining a high degree of integrity through the generations. Today it tends to break up, re-form itself, and disintegrate again in the lifetime of the individual. Thus the ordinary person has the experience of being born into the family of his parents, of gradually severing these first domestic ties, of founding a family of his own, and finally of seeing his children one by one pass out into the larger social world. The family has been compelled to abandon many forms of productive activity; it has been forced to send its sustaining members into shop and factory; it has lost its one-time self-sufficiency and independence; it has become incapable of providing its members with economic protection and security; it has surrendered numerous educational, recreational, and cultural functions to other agencies; in a word it has been swallowed up in a vast society in which the lines dividing family from family have been so weakened that they are perhaps no stronger than those separating parents and children. At the same time ideas of family and family responsibility, generated in an age when the household partook of the nature of a social microcosm, continue to prevail.

Particularly difficult is the position of woman in the changed order. In the less favored classes of the population she was forced by economic pressure to follow industry out of the home. But here she found herself in a strange world where she was subject to prejudice, discrimination, and exploitation. Even today, after the passage of many decades, she is often looked upon as an intruder in a realm that is presumed to belong to man. Her changed position is by no means accepted; and the idea is still widely held that, at least if she is married, she should not seek a livelihood outside the routine of the household. Partly as a result of this conflict women in the middle and more favored classes find themselves occupying an adventitious position in the economic order. Denied the right, because of the perpetuation of an outworn tradition, to engage in remunerative labor and finding no adequate outlet for her energies within the home, she is offered no alternative, at least during a considerable period of her life, to playing the demoralizing rôle of a social parasite. The situation is aggravated by the productivity of the machine and the failure of private capitalism to achieve a rational organization of the labor forces of the country. In the severe competition for employment married women are placed at a serious disadvantage and society refuses to make full use of a large part of its human resources.

Economy. In the economic sphere the conflicts and contradictions, particularly numerous, vivid, and injurious, may be seen on every hand. In spite of the miraculous conquests of mechanical power and the equally miraculous growth of productive capacity, the great masses of the American people seem to be quite as absorbed in questions of food, clothing, and shelter as ever before in their history. Indeed, as they face the uncertainties of contemporary industrial society, they may feel themselves even less secure than did their pioneering ancestors. While the machine has doubtless banished certain evils, it has brought its own special forms of misery; or at any rate men have not learned to control the machine in the common interest. A mastery over the forces of nature, surpassing the most extravagant dreams of Utopia, is accompanied by extreme material insecurity. After all possible qualifications have been made, this remains a terrible and sustained indictment of the present administration of the economy.

In so-called normal times life is barren and harsh for the majority of the population. The benefits derived from the advance of technology and the exploitation of matchless material resources are very unequally distributed. At the one extreme is a small favored minority, firmly entrenched behind the barriers of law and custom, holding title to the social means of production and pursuing a life of luxury, extravagance and even ostentation; at the other is another minority composed of the handicapped and the unfortunate, who because of hereditary weakness, defective education, or simple adversity fill the ranks of pauperism. The remainder, nurtured on a tradition of material success, live in a mental state evenly compounded of hope and fear—hope of ascending to the world of the privileged and fear of sinking to the realm of the destitute. For all except the most favored or those who have accepted defeat, life is an endless battle either for the bare necessities or for social status founded on the acquisition and display of property.

Even during the so-called period of prosperity ending in 1929, 2,000,000 men were out of work. certain great industries, such as agriculture, coal and textiles, were in a state of chronic depression, and 60 per cent of the population were living below the level of comfort and decency. In the best of times all but a small fraction of the people live in more or less continual dread of the grim spectres of unemployment, sickness, and old age. And if in days of good fortune the individual accumulates certificates of wealth against the hour of adversity, he may see his savings of a lifetime vanish under the impact of forces he can neither understand nor control. Sobriety and industry thus forfeit their claim to be classed among the virtues and life is made to assume the guise of one vast irrationality.

Perhaps the most basic contradiction of all is the theory, bequeathed from a pre-technological age, that the general good in a great society lacking the controls of the neighborhood will best be served if every individual will devote himself single-mindedly to the guarding and advancing of his own economic interests. Under the mandates of this doctrine the natural endowment of the nation is exploited without thought of the future; a high-powered productive mechanism is harnessed to money-making rather than to supplying the population with needed goods and services; human labor is viewed as a commodity to be bought and sold in the market place; government is often converted into a dispenser of special favors and privileges to those who have; the speedy dissipation of a severely limited resource is regarded as an inalienable right of business enterprise; the wages paid to workmen are too meagre to enable them to purchase the things they make; the concentration of income in a small class leads to the export of capital and the building of factories abroad; the productive capacity of industry tends to grow more rapidly than the effective buying power of the consuming public; goods of all kinds accumulate in the rooms of store-houses and on the shelves of retail shops; extravagant consumption is converted into a resounding civic virtue; a philosophy of deliberate waste and improvidence is proclaimed as the highest economic wisdom; parasitism in the form of racketeers, gangsters, and speculators is accepted with polite indifference; the science of psychology is employed to stimulate the wants and overcome the "sales-resistance" of the consumer; credits are granted to distant countries to enable them to absorb both commodity and capital surplus; the struggle for foreign markets leads to bitter competition and ultimately to war; a government commission advises cotton-growers to plow under every third row of cotton; the entire country rejoices at the news that the total wheat crop will be the smallest in a generation; everybody is encouraged to mortgage the future and engage in a wild orgy of spending; finally, as the day of reckoning dawns, the leaders of the nation resort to prayer and incantation, declare that business troubles are psychological, and, employing the language of the stock market, appeal to the people not "to sell America short."

At last, however, the expedients run out. Business refuses to respond to the hypodermic needle. The entire productive and distributive mechanism becomes jammed in its operations. Goods find no purchasers, factory wheels stop turning, locomotives stand idle, ships remain in port, workmen lose their jobs, banks and trust companies fail, the financial structure collapses, money passes out of circulation, barter comes into vogue, business houses go bankrupt, the total social income falls, the tax burden rises, men become dependent on charity, life is narrowed to a struggle for bread, theft and robbery increase, cultural services decline, starvation reaches into many homes, bitterness enters the hearts of men, and the spirit of revolt broods over the land. At the height of the depression, in the spring of 1933, the country contained perhaps thirteen millions unemployed, nine millions working but one or two days a week, other millions on less than full-time in industry, more millions who had never known employment, additional millions who were living in perpetual fear of losing their jobs, and yet more millions on the farms who were wondering how they could sell their produce for sufficient to pay their taxes. And so today men starve in the presence of plenty. Here is the most terrifying of the many contradictions found in contemporary society.

Communication. A major, indeed a crucial and essential, factor in the growth of industrial civilization and in the precipitation of the conflicts already recorded has been the invention and perfection of new forms of transportation and communication—the railroad, the automobile, the steamship, and the airplane; the press, the sound-picture, the telegraph, the telephone, and the radio. Through these agencies the isolation and self-sufficiency of family and neighborhood have been destroyed and modern man has been ushered into a world of wholly unprecedented extent and complexity. In this world the ordinary citizen finds himself confused and bewildered. To be sure, his great-grandfather knew little about what occurred beyond the horizon; but in order to pursue a fairly rational existence he did not need to know. What occurred beyond the horizon affected him but little. Today the scene is entirely changed. Happenings in the most distant parts of the earth may bring prosperity or adversity. How can the human mind span the globe and hold in careful balance all that takes place on the five continents and the islands of the sea? The question answers itself. There would seem to be a deep contradiction between reality and the traditional theory of democratic government. The world in which the individual must live and act and exercise the rights of citizenship transcends his powers of comprehension. In the great society of the twentieth century the omniscient and omnicompetent citizen is a myth rooted in the soil of an earlier and simpler age.

The present confusion, however, is not due altogether to the extent and complexity of contemporary social relations. It is also due in part to the fact that the American people have made no comprehensive and rational effort to organize the new agencies of communication for the simple purpose of spreading enlightenment and understanding. On the contrary, developing under the system of individualism, these agencies have generally been regarded, not as cultural instruments of society as a whole, but rather as tools of special groups and profit-making enterprise. Again and again they have been employed to confuse the public mind and to render issues more obscure. They have been used to spread propaganda inimical to the general welfare. This tendency has been manifested particularly in the practice of advertising, in the campaigns of certain powerful vested interests to win popular favor for their policies and in the reporting of any important event involving conflict, such as strike, revolution, or war. Society today possesses the instrumentalities for creating a relatively informed public opinion, but it does not direct them to that end. It even permits them to be pointed toward a contrary goal. At their best, with rare exceptions, they are administered as business undertakings, purveying to the masses of the people what the masses of the people are thought to want.

Health. In the sphere of health the conflicts and contradictions of the economic order are clearly reflected. Since the physical well-being of a people rests on material foundations, the inequalities and the interruptions in the distribution of income have their counterpart in the realm of bodily vigor and vitality. Here general living conditions are far more important

than the state and agencies of curative medicine—food, clothing, shelter, and physical surroundings are more to be desired
than drugs and hospitals. In ordinary times millions of men,
women, and children in the country and city alike are still
undernourished: multitudes dwell in slums, in highly congested areas, in cramped living quarters, in badly planned
towns and cities, in districts lacking parks and playgrounds
and sunshine. During periods of depression the situation
grows markedly worse. And all of these evils continue even
though the resources are at hand, in the form of materials,
machinery, energy, skilled labor, and trained intelligence, to
build sanitary and beautiful dwellings and cities for the entire population.

The use of the facilities provided by society for the promotion and guarding of health is also marked by contradictions.
In the aggregate the nation is apparently well supplied with
such facilities. The advance of medical knowledge is being
vigorously prosecuted, great institutions for professional training are generously supported, more than 1,000,000 trained persons are engaged in the several branches of the health service,
and clinics, hospitals, and other agencies for disseminating
knowledge, diagnosing disease, and providing medical care are
maintained. Yet preventable illness on a large scale is associated with the unemployment of physicians; while deficiency
of medical facilities in one field or region is linked with surplus in another. Moreover, whereas prevention is far more
efficacious than cure, major emphasis is placed on therapeutics
and the welfare of the physician is made dependent on the
presence of actual illness and defect. Also in the realm of
disease control jurisdiction trespasses upon jurisdiction, authority clashes with authority, and responsibility is divided where
unified direction is essential. The possibilities resident in
medical knowledge are only very imperfectly realized.

Education. The disorganization of the family, accompanied
as it was by the growth of large-scale industry conducted on a

profit-making basis, had a profound effect on the education of the young. Children, like women, followed industry out of the home and into the factory. But it soon became clear that industry, in its impersonal and calculated drive for gain, was an unsafe place for boys and girls. In order to protect them from exploitation under the regime of profits, society felt constrained to pass laws barring them from many kinds of labor and separating them to a degree from life and life's responsibilities. This tended to force them into idleness and into a search for new forms of amusement. Their position consequently assumed an aspect not dissimilar to that of women whose husbands could afford to support them at home. The passing of child labor laws was therefore followed by the enactment of compulsory school laws. There was thus substituted for the genuine tasks of the family the artificial and bookish tasks of the school. Educational leaders, sensing the inadequacy of this substitution, contended with growing vigor that the school should be related to life; but with life dominated in so many of its divisions by private enterprise bent on wealth accumulation, the gulf between school and life has proved largely impassable.

In its purposes, moreover, the school has remained bound to the traditions of a strongly individualistic economy. Except for a more or less perfunctory reference to social and civic obligations, which is largely negative in its emphasis, the school system is organized from top to bottom about the principle of helping the individual to succeed in competition with his fellows—in his struggle to raise himself into the ranks of a privileged social class. It still rests on the eighteenth century assumption that if every individual will only devote himself earnestly to the promotion and guarding of his own selfish interests, then, as the simplest arithmetic will prove, the greatest total good will be achieved. It is one of the ironies of the age that advertising and salesmanship should be taught in the public schools and supported from taxes levied on the general consumer. The people continue to view organized education as a way of escape from manual labor and as a ladder reaching to preferred occupational and social status. The bankruptcy of this idea is revealed in the 5,400,000 adolescents attending the high schools of the country in 1933. If all climb the ladder to the top, or even a considerable proportion of them, the situation becomes incongruous. A social outlook, derived from a selective tradition in secondary education, persists in an age when all principles of selection have been abandoned.

Recreation. Recreation is the scene of a number of deep conflicts. The increased productivity of technology and the associated reduction in the hours of labor have apparently been accompanied, not by a general easing of the tension of living, as might reasonably have been anticipated, but rather by an actual heightening of that tension. More hours away from work have not meant more genuine leisure. Through unregulated competition on the part of business enterprise for his attention, the individual has been subjected to a perpetual bombardment of stimuli and appeals. Thus the strain of life has been intensified. From this bombardment there is practically no escape, unless he loses the use of his sense organs or possesses the means necessary to enable him to retire to some distant and isolated region to which industrial civilization has not penetrated.

Equally disturbing is the form in which the rewards of increased productive power are administered. In a rationally organized society one might expect gains in efficiency in the making of goods to be transmuted quickly and generally into reduced hours of labor and increasing security of income for the working population. That an altogether different condition prevails is entirely obvious. For multitudes of men and women, ranging from perhaps two millions in good times to fifteen or twenty millions in days of depression, the ordering of leisure is utterly chaotic and irrational. For them hours from labor assume the aspect of total unemployment and interruption of income, not for definite and known periods, but for undetermined and unpredictable intervals. Leisure of this kind is of course no leisure at all. Indeed it is far worse than excessive hours of work. Under such conditions the individual of necessity spends his days and nights in a state of fear and deep anxiety. In time his self-respect may depart and his character disintegrate. And this is the fruit of increased efficiency.

Even the recreations provided for the so-called hours of leisure often lack the elements essential to the physical and cultural growth of the participant. They do not serve really to re-create the individual. In spite of the great increase in leisure hours, the American people have been so absorbed in the problems of economic security and wealth accumulation that they have given but little attention to the development of a balanced program of leisure-time activities. Although certain fields have been invaded by public agencies, recreation remains very largely a region to be exploited by commercial enterprise. Moreover, certain great inventions, such as the cinema and the radio, which may be regarded as the miracles of the age, are very generally employed in the promotion of cultural standards of very questionable merit. Indeed, not infrequently they contribute to the debasement of popular taste. As a general rule, commercialized recreation is expensive, primitive in its appeal, and designed to make of the American people a nation of sitters, listeners, and watchers. Recreation thus degenerates into entertainment and amusement.

Science. In science men have a tool of most extraordinary power—a tool that might be employed deliberately and planfully in promoting the welfare of all mankind. While this instrument has no doubt been the author of much good, it has also brought much misery into the world. But the point to be noted here is that organized society has taken almost no steps to harness, control, and utilize this mighty force. As a consequence, though scientific research is the recipient of huge sums and is conducted on a large scale in the United States, it exhibits little co-ordination and much duplication and waste of effort. Yet more important is the fact that it is often directed toward narrow and even anti-social purposes. It emphasizes the immediate and the practical at the expense of the abiding and the fundamental. To a very large extent, moreover, as measured by expenditures, it serves not the general good but profit-making enterprise. Out of this situation arise such strange practices as the guarding of trade secrets, the suppression of knowledge, the exploitation of the consumer, and even the misrepresentation of fact—all in the name of science. Here the competitive economy finds itself in direct and irreconcilable conflict with the essentially collective and rational spirit of science.

Art. In the sphere of art may be found some of the deepest contradictions in American life. Under the reign of private capitalism the state retired into the rôle of a policeman, the community lost its spiritual integrity, and men everywhere became absorbed in the struggle for profits. Grand art, representing public enterprise, practically disappeared; and commodity art, the domain of the craftsman, was reduced to a cheap appeal to the market. The aim of production was neither strength nor beauty, but quick and repeated sales. Goods were fabricated for the moment. Art consequently tended to lose its intimate connection with the practical affairs of life and to be relegated to the hours of leisure or even to a leisure class. It came to be regarded as something apart—to be cultivated for its own sake and preserved from the sordid touch of the world. Its devotees were looked upon as the practitioners of an esoteric cult.

Out of this situation arose cities of unbelievable ugliness, dirty factory towns, dark and filthy slums, rows of cheap houses and flats, congested living quarters, devastated forest regions, mutilated landscapes, and the omnipresent scourge of advertising. In sharp contrast with such conditions, environing the lives of the masses of the people, may be set the luxurious palaces, the magnificent estates, the spacious country clubs of the wealthy classes, where no expense is spared that might be expected to add comfort or beauty. Here, moreover, attention is often focused less on æsthetics than on ostentation. And this contrast between the rich and the poor, which is being relieved now by the growth of social planning, can be matched only by shops whose shelves are loaded with cheap and shoddy goods standing beside museums wherein are collected the art objects of the past. The fact should also be noted that certain new inventions, such as the cinema and the radio, which possess enormous potentialities for promoting the æsthetic and cultural growth of the population, are often prostituted to serve the ends of private gain. That a growing volume of protest on the part of the public has moderated somewhat the grosser evils here reviewed does not weaken the indictment.

Justice. In similar fashion the administration of justice is forced into the molds of economic interest. While inheriting from their Anglo-Saxon forebears the ideal of freedom and equality of justice, the American people enjoy neither free nor equal justice. Because of delays, court fees, and costs of counsel the poor man is often denied even access to the courts. And if he is able to make his voice heard at all, he is put at an overwhelming disadvantage in any contest with a rich adversary. Moreover, he is more subject to arrest and to inhumane treatment than the well-to-do. He is treated simply as a person of inferior moral worth. The same general statement may be made regarding the extension of justice to cultural and racial minorities—to the immigrants, the Indians, and the Negroes. In the case of the Negroes especially is there a flagrant and perpetual denial of justice. Political non-conformists, propagators of new ideas, advocates of fundamental social change also are often refused the full protection of the courts. The passion of the mob, frequently whipped up by a hostile press and the might of powerful vested interests, may reach into the halls of justice and tip the scales of the blindfolded goddess. The position of such dissenters and innovators is commonly made more difficult by the factor of poverty. As a rule their resources are extremely limited.

Government. The conduct of government has been marked by many contradictions. But perhaps the supreme contradiction is the fact that at least throughout a large part of the history of the American democracy the people have not ruled and the state has not served the general welfare. In fact government has not even functioned as the effective police force required by the doctrines of *laissez-faire.* In 1930 James W. Gerard, one-time ambassador to Germany, gave the statement to the press that the nation was ruled by sixty-four men. Among these men, all of whom he named, he included neither the President of the United States nor any government official. Most of those designated were heads of large private enterprises and men of great wealth. Leaders of organized labor were added to the list only as an afterthought. Although the statement aroused a large amount of discussion, few informed persons took serious issue with the underlying argument. In the past economics has been mightier than politics.

As a rule American government, whether local, state, or national, has not been the obedient and enlightened servant of the total population, even when due allowance is made for the pluralistic character of a complex society. On the contrary it has commonly been the tool of powerful groups devoted to the attainment of special ends. While these groups range from the Women's Christian Temperance Union to the United States Chamber of Commerce, the most influential have been the great industrial and financial interests of the nation. Government everywhere is brought into the struggle for economic advantage and privilege. The avowed champions of competition and individualism in economy have gone to the state for tariffs, concessions, and outright financial subsidies. The corruption or perversion of the political life of the country has been the consequence. And the agents of that corruption or perversion are commonly the nation's most aspiring and successful business men—the very persons whom the younger generation is taught to emulate. The ethics of the market place invade and often take possession of legislative halls, executive mansions, and even seats of justice. While Mr. Gerard admitted in the late summer of 1933 that his sixty-four leaders had been dethroned either by the depression, the new president, or acts of God, that the government has at last been brought into the service of all the American people scarcely merits credence. Class control of the state would seem to be securely rooted in the institutions of capitalistic society.

World Relations. The final and most disastrous conflict generated by the inherited social system is *war*. Though as old as human society, this institution has assumed a peculiarly frightful aspect in modern times. Owing to the advance of science and technology it has become far more costly and deadly than ever before. Practically every civilized nation totters under the burden of debt caused by past and prospective wars. Indeed this institution time and again has shattered the financial structure of powerful nations and even of the world. Also all peoples, with few exceptions, live in perpetual fear of a war that might even destroy civilization itself. And yet the very course which each government feels constrained to pursue in order to protect its own interests—participation in the race of armaments—seems destined sooner or later to precipitate international conflict. Preparations undertaken in the name of peace seem inevitably to lead to war. This is the supreme irony and contradiction in contemporary world society.

War today is first of all a product of a condition of world anarchy. Although numerous steps have been taken during the past two generations that point toward some form of international government, the earth and its resources continue to be apportioned among nations that look upon themselves as entirely independent and sovereign. And war remains the instrument by which political boundaries are drawn. To date mankind has found no other method for settling the vexed questions arising out of the uneven distribution of population and natural riches over the earth, and yet inevitably war seems to raise more questions than it settles and to plant the seeds of future conflicts. Moreover, the internal economy of every capitalistic nation contains elements that tend to create war conditions. This economic system seems to require an ever-growing market for manufactured goods and surplus capital, and an ever-growing quantity of raw materials. As a consequence, the private business interests of the more powerful nations engage in a struggle for markets and raw materials and strive to draw their respective governments into the struggle. To private munitions makers war is financially profitable. And newspapers and demagogues often exploit a conflict situation and feed popular passion in order to advance their own immediate interests. Thus, in every country mighty forces, usually economic in character, are tending to disrupt the peace. Probably no nation ever desires war; but practically all nations, as represented by their governments, desire those things that inevitably lead to war.

COLLECTIVE DEMOCRACY

In the resolution of the fundamental conflicts and contradictions in American society the public school will unquestionably have to play an important rôle. The common view among both teachers and laymen, however, that the task can be delegated to some obscurely conceived process called education is scarcely tenable. On the contrary, if the school is to grapple successfully with the problems of the age, such a resolution must first be effected in thought, working within the limits set by the contemporary reality, and then be embodied in educational theory and program.

If the analysis presented in this volume is essentially valid, then the trend from individualism to collectivism in economy must be recognized by educational statesmen as fundamental in the preparation of their policies. It should of course be made entirely clear that there is no desire here to argue the respective merits of the two forms of economy. Such an issue is purely academic in character. It has been decided by the movement of history. The practical man has no choice but to make his peace with the great trend toward an interdependent society. To attempt to restore the economy of a century ago or to erect an individualistic superstructure on socialized foundations would be utterly Utopian. To move in this direction would be to court disaster. The hands of the clock of cultural evolution cannot be turned back. Already men have been irrevocably changed by the new forces.

The point requires emphasis again, however, that the present is an age of transition, that the earlier economy still persists in tradition and institutional arrangement, that the road to the future has many branches. To say that the American people are well into a highly socialized economy does not mean that they are denied all power of decision and are but the pawns of an inscrutable destiny. Truth in fact would seem to lie in precisely the opposite direction. Collectivism is an extremely broad category and may shelter radically different social systems and theories. The present generation therefore faces the task of making a great historic choice.

In this situation, so heavily freighted with consequences for the future, the nation must turn to a critical examination of its condition and inquire into the purposes of national existence and of social institutions. In this inquiry chief guidance may be derived from American history in its world setting. Running through that history, obscured though it may be by ignorance and hostile forces, is the ideal of democracy—the ideal of a society devoted to the welfare, not of a special class, but of the great masses of ordinary working men and women. Though associated with social forms and arrangements that have been outmoded, it has by no means run its course. It remains today the most profound expression of American genius and the most vital tradition in American life. To repudiate it would be tantamount to a repudiation of national existence. The need today is merely that it be applied to the changed and changing circumstances of the age. If it does not hold the key to the resolution of the conflicts and contradictions of contemporary industrial society, then is the nation headed for a condition of yet more profound chaos.

The application of the democratic ideal to the trend towards an integrated society calls for a three-fold course of action: the dissociation of democracy from its historical connections with the individualistic economy of the past; the free and voluntary acceptance of the interdependent economy out of knowledge and understanding; and the organization and administration of the economic mechanism in the interests of the masses of the people. Each of these three points will be briefly developed.

The traditional democracy rested upon small-scale production in both agriculture and industry and a rather general diffusion of the rights of property in capital and natural resources. The driving force at the root of this condition was the frontier and free land. With the closing of the frontier, the exhaustion of free land, the growth of population, and the coming of large-scale production, the old economic foundations of democracy have been destroyed. To repeat the traditional formulæ, therefore, is to confuse the issue. If democracy cannot be transferred to the collective base, then America will be democratic no longer.

In order to remove all chance of misunderstanding, the point should be made that the acceptance of the socialized economy does not involve the rejection of the ideal of the worth of the individual and the encouragement of personal cultivation and growth. Quite the contrary is in fact the case. The rise of collectivist economy has placed unprecedented power in human hands. Consequently, if the complete and uninterrupted functioning of the present productive system could be attained, a condition which depends on a clear recognition of the new reality, the foundations would be laid for a measure of freedom for the many that mankind has never known in the past. Even in the days of free land in the United States the ordinary man led a harsh and narrow existence. Today he may live a life of material security and spiritual abundance. Such a goal, and not cultural regimentation, is entirely compatible with the rational and humane organization of a collectivist economy. In fact it can be attained today by pursuing no other course. The last four years have shown that the coercion of a chaotic and undisciplined economy constitutes one of the most terrible forms of despotism. The people have submitted to it merely because they have been led to believe it to be essentially an act of God or an expression of natural law.

In a society with democratic traditions and aspirations the acceptance on the part of the people of the collective economy should come through the voluntary recognition of the reality, and not through external compulsion. It should take the form of a free adaptation to the necessities of the situation; it should emerge naturally from knowledge, thought, and understanding. The point should be made, however, that the only form of compulsion to be feared is not the dictatorship of some minority group. Equally brutal and terrifying may be the dictatorship of ignorance, incompetent leadership, and the breakdown of economic institutions. From such a dictatorship of confusion the American people have been suffering since the autumn of 1929. It should also be admitted that the ideal of acceptance of the new order through voluntary recognition of the reality is an ideal that can never be fully realized. Every society contains powerful groups with rights vested in the inherited social system. To these groups something more than sweet reasonableness may be necessary, if they are to accept fundamental change. To them physical force may have to be applied from time to time. The conflicts of interests in capitalistic society are deep and abiding; and real conflicts of interests are not reconciled, but clarified and sharpened, by discussion.

This brings the argument to the most crucial issue raised by the transition from individualism to collectivism in economy. In whose interests are the unrivalled productive forces of the nation to be employed? In whose name will the natural riches, the industrial equipment, the science and technology of the country be administered? In a word, who will control the machine? Conceivably it might be controlled either in the interests of some small ruling caste, or in the interests of the masses of the people. It is at this point that the battle of the age is being fought in all of those countries that are moving into the era of collective economy. In the light of the democratic ideal there can of course be but one answer to this question. Whatever institutional arrangements may ultimately prove most satisfactory, the interests of the ordinary man and woman must always be regarded as paramount. No other solution of the problem can be tolerable to the American people. It represents the application of a great historic ideal to the realities of industrial civilization. It represents the union of democracy and some form of collectivism in economy.

This union of the past and the present is supported by the initial report issued and approved by the members of the Commission. In *A Charter for the Social Sciences* they vigorously affirm their faith in the American democratic ideal of "a reasoned equality of opportunity for all men and women."[2] Also they recognize the trend toward collectivism in economy and the end of the reign of *laissez-faire* in government. One of the ten great goals "which must of necessity shape instruction in the social studies," they declare, is "national planning in industry, business, agriculture and government to sustain mass production of goods on a high level of continuity and to assure the most economical and efficient use of our material

[2] Charles A. Beard, *A Charter for the Social Sciences in the Schools* (New York, 1932), 80–81.

resources."[3] Only through such a recognition of the collective nature of industrial economy can the innumerable contradictions of contemporary society, involving the conflict of private and public interest, be resolved. And only by making the welfare of the masses of the people dominant can the democratic tradition of the American people be preserved and fulfilled.

In conclusion a word should be said regarding the emphasis placed on the economy in the present and the preceding chapter. To many this may seem to imply the subordination of spiritual to material values. Such, however, is not the intention. The economy requires attention today, paradoxical as it may appear, in order that men may be liberated from slavery to material things. Under present circumstances the American people are far too much absorbed in questions of food, clothing, and shelter and in the battle for wealth and property. This is in fact one of the tragedies of the epoch. But the situation cannot be altered until the principle of economic competition is removed from the focus of attention and the economy is so ordered that men may achieve a measure of physical security. If the engineers are to be trusted at all, the natural and technical resources are at hand to enable the nation to dispose of the economic problem once for all and to move on to conquests of a more humane order. At last men may enter a world in which they may devote their energies, not to the savage struggle for bread, but to the cultivation of the things of the spirit. This, and this alone, is the object of the emphasis on the economy in these pages.

[3] *Ibid.*, 79.

Chapter III

THE PUBLIC SCHOOL

The task of formulating educational policy in the light of the analysis and interpretation of American life presented in this volume is a task of staggering proportions. Yet it is no more difficult than that faced daily, though often unconsciously, by teacher and school administrator. Moreover, it cannot be escaped. To refuse to attempt the task is not to evade it, but rather to do it badly. Every educational policy, however casually it may have been constructed, rests upon and reflects some analysis and interpretation of the condition and prospects of the society involved. If education were merely a form of abstract contemplation, unrelated to the world of men and things, the social situation might be disregarded altogether. This, however, is clearly not the case. At bottom and particularly in a highly complex and dynamic social order, education, in discharging its function of inducting the child into the life of the group, stands at the focal point in the process of cultural evolution—at the point of contact between the older and the younger generation where values are selected and rejected. In the case of organized education presumably all of this is done rationally and deliberately and in the light of some large conception of welfare. For the educator to seek justification for evasion, inaction, and postponement in a profession of ignorance is to issue a proclamation of incompetence. Such a course is no more seemly for him than it is for the statesman.

EDUCATION AS A FORM OF ACTION

The obligation of the educator to base his policies on as profound an analysis of social life as he is capable of making can best be expounded by first examining the relation of education to social action. About this question there seems to be a good deal of confusion.

The American people have a sublime faith in the school. They have traditionally viewed organized education as the one unfailing remedy for every ill to which man is subject. And when faced with any trouble or difficulty they have commonly set their minds at rest sooner or later by an appeal to the school. Today, as social institutions crumble and society is shaken by deep convulsions that threaten its very existence, many persons are proclaiming that education provides the only true road to safety. They are even saying that it should be brought into the service of building a new social order.

In an earlier generation this faith took the form of a trust in simple literacy. It was confidently assumed that if all men could read, everything would be well. The mass of voters, according to the argument, being able to follow the course of events and being keenly aware of their own interests, would keep the ship of state on an even keel and hold it firmly on its course toward the distant goals of democracy. How insecure were the foundations of this faith is revealed by the confusion which now pervades the public mind in every country whose citizens have been initiated into the mysteries of reading. Apparently the printed page has become an instrument of deception as well as of enlightenment. Powerful interests employ it to mold the public mind and to gain support for their policies. Literacy made possible the age of propaganda.

More recently the faith in education has taken a new form. The assumption now seems to be widely held that the entire process of cultural evolution should begin *de novo* with each generation, that the child should be completely freed from the bias of the past, and that the program of instruction should contain no great decisions with respect to the values and ideals

of living. Such decisions should presumably be left to the
next generation in the firm belief that, if boys and girls could
only once escape the rule of parents and elders, they would
proceed unerringly and with enthusiasm to the correction of
all the mistakes of their ancestors and to the building of a
world founded on truth and beauty and justice. Thus is education converted into a substitute for positive thought and
action on the part of the present adult generation.

There is every reason for believing that this faith also will
prove to be unfounded. It represents in fact an unwitting confession of bewilderment on the part of its proponents. It is
a refuge of ignorance—an escape from reality—a shirking of
responsibility. It is, moreover, quite beyond the limits of
attainment and is certain to bring disillusionment. Inevitably
education *is* a form of action—enlightened or befuddled, depending on the social insight of its author. An educational
program that is a product of bewilderment will itself beget
bewilderment. The more difficult problems of society will not
be resolved by passing on to children facts whose implications
are beyond the comprehension or the courage of adults. In
the selection of facts to be transmitted, moreover, large decisions are made.

If education is to grapple with a given social situation, it
must incorporate a social philosophy adequate to that situation—a social philosophy that has substance as well as form
—a social philosophy that represents great historic choices.
Education, emptied of all social content and conceived solely
as method, points nowhere and can arrive nowhere. It is a
disembodied spirit. When education is thus generically conceived, it is a pure abstraction. Moreover, it is not education.
A practicable educational program or theory cannot be gen-
eric: it must be specific: it must be suited to a particular time
and place in history. If adults assume that, after becoming
mentally confused, they may deposit their confusion on the
doorstep of education and then retire to peaceful slumbers,

they are only deceiving themselves. They are placing their trust in a modern form of sorcery.

Society possesses no such easy road to the future. Education will be called upon to play its part. But it will be an education that is carefully designed, both as method and as content, for the present day and generation. It will be an education that recognizes the impossibility of moving in all directions at once, that chooses deliberately and intelligently one fork of the road rather than another, and that does not hesitate, when occasion warrants, to make fundamental decisions regarding national destiny. Ordinarily, moreover, these grand choices will be made for children by adults. To think otherwise is to chase rainbows. Any concrete school program will contribute to the struggle for survival that is ever going on among institutions, ideas, and values; it cannot remain neutral in any final and complete sense. Partiality is the very essence of education, as it is of life itself. The difference between education and life is that in the former partiality is presumably reasoned and enlightened.

That education involves positive action and decision with respect to many matters is entirely obvious. Those in charge of an educational institution must make innumerable choices before the institution can begin to function. And each choice involves rejection as well as selection. Thus choice has to be made with respect to physical surroundings. Here far-reaching decisions regarding æsthetic values are necessarily involved. The school building will represent, not all styles of architecture, but some particular style. Likewise the wall decorations will reflect some standard of taste. Even the door to a classroom will be given a definite location. If these questions about physical surroundings are viewed as unimportant, then this in itself is an expression of a very fundamental choice. Much the same line of analysis may be applied to the selection of teachers, of subjects or fields of study, of textbooks and equipment, of methods of instruction. Of peculiar

significance is the way in which the life of the school is organized—the relations of pupils to pupils, of pupils to teachers, of teachers to teachers, of teachers to administrators and
supervisors, and of all to the public. Any organization will
express some theory of government and will tend to generate
certain ideas and values. As William T. Harris observed many
years ago, the child "simply gets used to established order and
expects it and obeys it as a habit. He will maintain it as a
sort of instinct in after life, whether he has ever learned the
theory of it or not."[1]

Then every school must make some decision concerning
the motives to which to appeal in stimulating and guiding the
process of learning. At no point can the school assume complete neutrality and at the same time become a concrete, functioning reality. It is concerned with a growing organism; and
growth must have direction. The determination of this direction is by far the most crucial of all educational problems.
Whether this responsibility is to be discharged by parents,
teachers, politicians, statesmen, or various powerful minority
groups is not the question at issue here. But whatever the
agent, the responsibility must be discharged.

A fact never to be forgotten is that education, taken in its
entirety, is by no means an exclusively intellectual matter. It
is not merely, or perhaps even primarily, a process of acquiring facts and becoming familiar with ideas. The major object
of education since the beginning of time has been the induc-
tion of the immature individual into the life of the group.
This involves not only the development of intellectual powers, but also the formation of character, the acquisition of
habits, attitudes, and dispositions suited to a given set of living conditions, a given level of culture, and a given body of
ideals and aspirations. Contemporary American society would
seem to require quite as much emphasis on moral education
as any primitive tribe.

[1] Merle E. Curti, *The Social Ideals of American Educators* (New York,
1934).

The foregoing argument, however, is not intended to convey the impression that education, since it involves a large measure of imposition, requires a severe regimentation of the mind, a rigorous teaching of a body of doctrine as fixed and final. However adequately such a conception of education may have served certain of the relatively static societies of the past, it would be extremely dangerous in the highly dynamic social order of today. A distinctly critical factor must play an important rôle in any educational program designed for the modern world. An education that does not strive to promote the fullest and most thorough understanding of society and social institutions, of which childhood and youth are capable, is not worthy of the name. The child should not only be permitted, he should be encouraged, to question all things. But this does not mean that a particular educational program may not be dominated by certain great social ideals. In fact no social ideal merits support today that does not make generous provision for the free play of intelligence.

The rôle of critical intelligence in the educative process, however, must bear some relation to the maturing of the individual. Immaturity in the human race is a very real and remarkable fact. When the members of the species enter the world, they are in an extremely helpless and undeveloped condition. The process of maturing, moreover, goes forward with exceeding slowness. During the first months of life the infant is entirely dependent on his elders. At this time his every act must be carefully watched lest he suffer serious injury, form wrong habits, or expose himself to unfavorable environmental conditions. Doubtless much of the debate over the amount of freedom to be extended to the learner arises out of failure to delimit the age under consideration. While in a university graduate school of science the educative process may be reduced to its bare intellectual elements and the student practically freed from the restraints of tutelage, the work of the kindergarten, the primary school, or even the secondary school has to be conceived and organized in quite different terms. This of course does not mean that the interests of children should not be utilized at every level of instruction. But it does mean that the extent of guidance provided by the older and more expert members of a group must vary inversely as the degree of maturity.

EDUCATION IN AN INTEGRATED SOCIETY

If education is to be regarded, like statesmanship, as a form of action, involving the making of positive decisions with respect to national destiny, any body of citizens charged with the responsibility of shaping educational policy must relate their recommendations to the great trends of the age. In the case of the American people, the most profound truth here is that they are passing from an individualistic to a collectivist economy. The meaning of this change for education will be considered from the standpoint of its bearing on purpose, curriculum, and teaching personnel. And under curriculum emphasis will be placed on the social sciences. The chapter will be closed with a reference to the relation of the school to other educational agencies and to the total educational task of society.

Purpose. The most fundamental conclusion for education implied in the data presented in this volume is that the present age requires a radical revision of the controlling purpose of the American public school. This is due to the fact that, since the founding of the institution, interdependence has replaced individualism in the sphere of economy. Here is the fundamental reality that cannot be escaped. Here is the great guiding conception of any educational program capable of serving contemporary society. Educators might wish that it were otherwise, but their wishes would be of no avail. From this verdict of history there is no appeal. To resurrect the loosely organized economy of the world that created "the little red schoolhouse" is impossible. That economy has been overwhelmed by the onward sweep of technology. The school of the twentieth century must function in an economy that in its basic structure is becoming thoroughly socialized.

Beyond this point, however, as noted in the preceding chapter, the facts would seem to leave some room, indeed enormous room, for choice. Presumably the collective economy, involving, as it does, the close integration and co-ordination of the productive energies of the entire population, might be organized primarily in the interests of some ruling caste or privileged minority, possibly composed of those holding title to property. To the masses of the people would go a fixed quantity of goods and services, a kind of balanced ration for the human animal, perhaps scientifically determined so as to sustain him at the optimum level of working efficiency and to inoculate him against the harboring of revolutionary ideas. Given the premises of such a society, to do more would be a form of economic waste. The remainder of the social income, increasing with the advance of science and technology, would accrue to the members of the aristocracy and be employed to protect them in the enjoyment of their privileges and to enrich their lives in every way that human ingenuity could contrive—to support a police and military force of sufficient strength to intimidate the populace and to quell occasional uprisings, to convert the more beautiful and pleasant portions of the country into extensive parks and playgrounds for their exclusive use, to maintain vast and numerous estates and menages as forms of display, to transfer to the domain of personal service the surplus labor occasioned by the increased use of automatic machinery, to provide opportunities for luxurious travel over the continent and the world in search of comfort or some new sensation, and generally to maintain a life of leisure and extravagance that would far surpass anything of its kind in history. The fact that membership in this caste might shift gradually from generation to generation through the operation of some sifting process sanctified by the name of individualism, freedom, or democracy would not greatly alter the situation. Indeed such an arrangement would merely increase the stability of the social order and serve as an insurance against popular revolt. It is of course entirely patent that the American people, without being aware of it, have been drifting toward a collectivist society of this kind for several generations.

The purpose of popular education in such a society is easily discernible. The major function of the school would be to inculcate into the minds of the rising generation the idea that the existing institutions, including practices with respect to the distribution of wealth and income, power, privilege and opportunity, were expressions of the immutable laws of human nature. The school might also serve to select out of each generation the more energetic and gifted, those most likely to become actively discontented, and lift them into positions of privilege, if not directly into the ranks of aristocracy. The children of the ruling caste, on the other hand, would be sent to special schools designed to instill into them a feeling of superiority and to teach them the language, the manners, the sports, and the outlook upon the world suited to their class. They would also be made to feel that their privileges rested upon the sanction of nature or divinity.

The social situation, however, undoubtedly contains a second possibility of broad dimensions which is far more in harmony with the deepest loyalties and aspirations of the American people. Conceivably, a closely integrated economy might be managed in the interests of the great masses of the population. Under such an arrangement no class or group would be regarded as a means for the elevation of another, no aristocracy of either birth or property would be allowed, no great concentration of wealth or income in private hands would be permitted, no grinding poverty or degrading slums, placing their indelible stamp on the generations, would be tolerated. On the contrary, the moral equality of all men, as proclaimed in the Declaration of Independence, would be recognized as a controlling ideal and would be accepted as a guiding principle in the reconstruction of social life and institutions. The productive energies of the nation would be devoted first to laying the foundations of material security for all. Thereafter they would be dedicated to raising the cultural level and enriching the lives of the people, to making the entire country a pleasant and beautiful place in which to live. The natural endowment and the resources of technology would be administered in the name of society as a whole. According to evidence advanced elsewhere in this volume, an economy, not only of security, but of abundance lies within the realm of the possible. The American people merely lack the will, the knowledge, and the discipline necessary to achieve it.

That educational leaders, at least if they are speaking for the public school, must make the second choice is fairly obvious. Whatever may be their legal position, they represent the masses of the American people and are therefore under obligation to protect the interests of those masses. The second choice, moreover, as already pointed out, carries on and fulfills the great tradition of democracy. If this ideal of human worth is to survive, it must be transferred to the foundations of a collective economy. Public education in the United States therefore will not only work within the limits of the emerging reality; it will also assume that the evolving order will make paramount the welfare of the great rank and file of the working men and women of the nation.

If the argument up to this point is sound, then the purpose of public education in the present epoch of American history is clear. It is to prepare the younger generation for labor and sacrifice in building a democratic civilization and culture on the foundations of a collective economy. This means in very considerable measure the abandonment of ideals that have dominated the school for generations. In spite of many protestations to the contrary education is still regarded primarily as a road to special privilege and personal aggrandizement. The motive that drives parents to send their children to high school and college and that drives boys and girls through the routine of the curriculum is the allurement of preferred occupational and social status. As a consequence, under the inherited system of arrangements, knowledge and competence acquired in schools maintained at public expense are often turned to the purpose of the exploitation of the handicapped. At a time when the economic struggle was primarily between man and nature, the result was perhaps defensible; today, when the struggle involves increasingly the relationship of man and man, the result is intolerable.

The aim of public education now should be, not to elevate A above B or to lift gifted individuals out of the class into which they were born and to raise them into favored positions where they may exploit their less fortunate fellows, but rather to abolish all artificial social distinctions and to organize the energies of the nation for improving the condition of all. In industrial society men do not and cannot live alone. The school should be permeated, not with the competitive, but with the co-operative, spirit. It should strive to serve society as a whole, to promote the most inclusive interests. This does not mean that it would refuse to give knowledge and competence to the individual, but rather that with knowledge and competence it would give a strong sense of social obligation. It would then be concerned primarily not with the promotion of individual success, but with the fullest utilization of the human resources of the country for the advancement of the general welfare. The result, moreover, would not be to deny the individual the joys attending successful accomplishment. On the contrary, his successes would be as genuine as ever and might even be far more profound and satisfying than they are when recorded in purely personal terms.

Perhaps the most serious charge directed against the traditional education is that it holds out no great ideal capable of enlisting the loyalties and disciplining the energies of child-hood and youth. This of course is the logical result of the attempt to build a school program on the foundations of eco-nomic individualism, which in the very nature of the case can scarcely be regarded as a social ideal. For individualism is a divisive rather than a unifying force, and tends to reduce organized society to the rôle of policeman. In the earlier years of the republic the ethical defects inherent in the economy were softened somewhat by the solidarity of the family, the neighborliness of the small community, the passion for po-litical democracy, and the idealism of Christianity. The ef-forts to correct these defects today are often both pitiful and tragic. On the one hand, children are nourished on moral platitudes that bear little relationship to the current social reality. And on the other, they are taught a brand of pa-triotism that is identified with the glorification of war and of willingness to bear arms. Such a narrow conception of patriotism is the perfectly natural fruit of a society which achieves unity of purpose only when it organizes to repel in-vasion by a foreign foe or to engage in military conquest. In an integrated society definitely committed to the democratic ideal, men would find glory and honor in the struggle with nature and the war on poverty, pestilence, ignorance, injustice, and ugliness. An education intelligently harnessed to such a purpose would merit the fullest support of the entire popula-tion.

The reference to war suggests that the ideal here proposed cannot be identified with a narrow nationalism. Technology has bound the nations together only less tightly than it has united the inhabitants of a single country. The economic foundations are being laid for the integration of the world and the curbing of the forces of competition in the interna-tional no less than in the domestic field. Indeed, in view of the devastation wrought by war conducted with modern weapons, the achievement of the former might seem to be even more urgent than the achievement of the latter. Yet, it should not be forgotten that the two forms of competition are not to be clearly distinguished and that the one may be transmuted into the other. Thus the ideal of interdependence must not be confined within the limits of a narrow patriotism. The great purpose of the public school therefore should be to prepare the coming generation to participate actively and courageously in building a democratic industrial society that will co-operate with other nations in the exchange of goods, in the cultivation of the arts, in the advancement of knowledge and thought, and in maintaining the peace of the world. A less catholic purpose would be certain, sooner or later, to lead the country to disaster.

Curriculum. The primary object of the curriculum, which should be thought of as embracing the entire life of the school, as well as the so-called subjects of study, should be the fulfillment of the great purpose just outlined. Indeed that purpose should permeate every activity of the school and give unity to the entire program. The more significant implications of this position for the curriculum as a whole and particularly for the social sciences will be briefly indicated. But since the present volume is directed primarily toward the teaching of the latter, the reference to the total program will be highly abbreviated.

The reconstruction of the curriculum in the light of the democratic ideal operating in a world marked by economic interdependence would not call for the addition of new subjects. Indeed, to superficial observation, perhaps no important changes would be discernible. The same disciplines would be taught; the same activities would be organized. Children would learn to read and write and figure; they would work and play together. But the spirit, the approach, the orientation would be different. Pupils and teachers might be doing the same things as before, but the motivation would follow unwonted channels. The appeal to the egoistic and possessive tendencies would be strictly subordinated; the emphasis everywhere would be placed on the social and co-operative and creative impulses. From the earliest years the whole life of the school would be organized so as to bring out and strengthen these qualities. No individual would be rewarded merely for overcoming or surpassing another.

This does not mean that high achievement would be frowned upon or that a single standard of mediocrity would be imposed upon all. Indeed, quite the contrary would be the case. In a closely integrated society the fullest development of the varied gifts and abilities resident in the population is demanded by the common welfare. Such would, in fact, be one of the major objects of organized education. To fail here would involve, not merely a dwarfing of the individual concerned, but the impoverishment of the group. To overlook personal talent in any field of social usefulness or cultural worth would not only involve a form of injustice, but would also be tantamount to wasting a valuable natural resource. Such a thing might happen, but it would be the result either of folly or of inefficiency. The springs of achievement, however, would be different. All would be united in the common task of raising the material and cultural level of the total population.

Also the emphasis on social utility, which might be expected in an interdependent society, does not mean necessarily that education would be narrowly practical. The stress would depend no doubt in considerable measure on the richness of the natural resources, the level of technology, and the pressure of population on the means of subsistence. In a land marked by severe struggle for the bare necessities of life, the emphasis might indeed be restricted to "bread and butter" considerations. But in a land like America, where material security and abundance are easily possible, the opposite should be expected. With the removal of competition in the display and conspicuous consumption of goods and services, energies would presumably be released for cultural and spiritual development. Economic concerns might at last be forced into a definitely subordinate rôle in society. And this would of course be reflected in the educational program.

The several divisions of subject matter composing the curriculum would all be given a social meaning. This may be illustrated by reference to geography, science, and art. Geography would be taught and studied, not merely as a body of information useful and interesting to the individual, but as the physical basis for the building of a finer civilization and culture. The natural resources of the nation would actually be regarded as possessions of the nation—as the source of a richer and more abundant common life, rather than as fields for the operation of profit-seeking enterprise and the accumulation of great private fortunes. In similar manner, science and technology would be looked upon neither as a leisure-time activity of a special class nor as an instrument for personal aggrandizement, but rather as the spear-point of man's age-long struggle with nature. And art would be taught primarily, not as a vehicle of individual expression, as important as that is, but as a means of enriching and beautifying the common life. Instead of spending itself in museums and galleries and the private homes of the rich, it would bring beauty of line and form and color to factories, cities, highways, parks, great public buildings, the objects of ordinary use, and the dwellings of the people. All of the subjects of study would be integrated by the mighty and challenging conception of the building of a great industrial civilization conceived in terms of the widest interests of the masses.

Finally, a word should be said about provision for specialized training. A society based on a collective economy would of course require proficiency in the entire range of occupations, except those which are definitely predatory or parasitic in character, such as advertising, speculation, and racketeering. Vocational training, however, would always be given a social purpose. Care would be taken lest the specialist regard his training as a species of private property which he is entitled to exploit at the expense of the general population. Also the program of occupational preparation would be approached and organized from the standpoint of the needs of society rather than in terms of the ambitions of particular institutions, departments, or persons. In other words, an effort would be made to co-ordinate the training facilities of the country and, in the case of each calling, to meet the requirements of the economy. Such of course is the implication of any comprehensive scheme for economic planning.

Much more could be written regarding the reorganization of the curriculum as a whole which is demanded by the emergence of the new economy. The object of the present treatise, however, does not permit the further elaboration of this topic. Attention will therefore be directed to the problem of the teaching of the social sciences.

The point should be made at the outset that there is nothing in the social sciences themselves that compel their inclusion in any educational program. In fact throughout the major part of the history of the school these subjects occupied a distinctly minor, if not a negligible, position in the curriculum. Whether or not and in what measure they are to be included is a question of social and educational philosophy, informed of course by the findings of the social scientist. From the standpoint of the school, however interesting and significant they may be to the investigator or the scholar, they are but means to some desirable end. They must take their chances with Sanskrit, astronomy, and automobile mechanics. Yet, since education itself is a social process and therefore a proper object of study for the social scientist, the relation between education and social science is always extremely intimate.

In the light of the analysis of American life presented in Parts One and Two of this volume—an analysis derived from data furnished by the social sciences—American society is seen to be in transition from a loosely organized to a closely integrated economy. Also that analysis reveals the presence in American history of a great ideal which presumably will continue to give direction to the evolution of American institutions. The selection and the organization of materials in the teaching of the social sciences therefore will be determined by the needs of a society that is moving from individualism into some form of collectivism conceived and administered in terms of the interests of the masses of the people. It is within this framework that the social sciences will have to function in the schools.

This is not to say that the social sciences are to be converted into an instrument of propaganda, that history is to be falsified, or facts suppressed. To pursue such a course would be to court disaster. Any sound program of instruction must rest upon and utilize the findings of science. This is not a debatable question. And yet it is equally obvious that the social sciences themselves possess no inner logic that can be relied upon to furnish positive and adequate guidance in the selection and organization of materials. They merely place at the disposal of the educator a practically inexhaustible body of data and generalizations, bodies of knowledge and systems of thought, regarding the history and functioning of human institutions. As to whether American children should study the life of Australian aborigines, the marriage customs of the ancient Romans, or the rise of parliamentary government among the Anglo-Saxon peoples, they are completely silent. Until some purpose is agreed upon or some set of values injected into the situation, choice among available materials is irrational and without meaning.

The controlling purpose to be employed here has already been outlined. The social science instruction in American schools, according to the argument, is to be organized within the frame of reference provided by the ideal of a democratic collectivism. From the standpoint of such a frame of reference, it is argued here that the social science curriculum should include the following points of emphasis: the history of the life and fortunes of the masses of the people, the evolution of peaceful arts and culture, the development of the ideal of democracy, the rise of industrial civilization and collective economy, the conflicts and contradictions in contemporary society, the critical appraisal of present-day life in terms of the democratic ideal, and the thorough examination of all current proposals, programs, and philosophies designed to meet the needs of the age.

In the first place, the social sciences should be called upon to prepare for the coming generation a fairly accurate and comprehensive account of the lives and fortunes of ordinary men and women throughout the ages and in diverse societies, but focused upon the course of events in the western world and culminating in the modern age in America. An effort would be made to piece together the record of how the masses of the people have lived, worked, played, loved, worshiped, thought, and died; how they have governed and been governed; how they have toiled and struggled to raise themselves above the brute. Certainly, in a society "dedicated to the proposition that all men are created equal" such an emphasis would seem to be far more rational than the traditional stress on the doings of aristocracies, princes, kings, and emperors. And it should be observed, incidentally, that social science itself offers no clue as to whether the one or the other emphasis should be adopted.

In the second place, the social sciences should be asked to tell the story, as fully as time permits, of the evolution of the peaceful arts and culture. While this principle is perhaps subsumed under the first category, since wars have commonly been the concern of ruling classes, it is of so great importance, from the standpoint of the ideal chosen, that it merits separate consideration. The conclusion should not be drawn, however, that war ought to be ignored altogether. This institution has played too tragic and central a rôle in human history to be deleted from the record. The distinction between wars of liberation and wars of conquest would be recognized. Also in general the treatment of military conflict would be altered. The object of the account would not be to prepare the mind of the coming generation for the profession of the soldier, as in the past, but rather to give understanding of war as a social phenomenon that has brought much misery and suffering into the world. Warriors and military leaders would be placed in a minor rôle, and attention would be concentrated on the great creative spirits of the past—the inventors, the explorers, the organizers, the statesmen, the teachers, the scholars, the scientists, the artists, the philosophers, the prophets of mankind. The fact would be stressed throughout that human culture is not the product of any single nation, but the common achievement of the efforts of many races and peoples working and striving through the ages.

In the third place, the social sciences should trace in broad outline the development of the ideal of democracy. And here there should be no disposition to accept a narrow definition of the ideal or to confine attention to its evolution on the North American continent. Rather should it be identified with the emergence of the conception of the worth and dignity of the common man. As such it would lead to certain of the great religions of the past and to various revolutionary and humanitarian movements in the modern world—to the overthrow of chattel slavery, to the liberation of the serf, to innumerable popular revolts against privileged classes, to countless struggles for human liberty, to the emancipation of woman from many ancient disabilities, to the growth of organized labor, to the abandonment of various forms of cruel and inhuman punishment, to the spread of ideas of tolerance and co-operation, and to the rising demand for the abolition of war as an instrument of national policy. Since the program of instruction is being devised for American children, a realistic and unvarnished history of democracy in the United States should be presented. This is peculiarly necessary because of the practical disappearance of the conditions that nourished the ideal for several generations.

In the fourth place, the social sciences should recount in considerable detail the growth of industrial civilization and the emergence of an integrated economy. The drawing of a sharp contrast between the life of today and that of the generation which founded the union would be peculiarly illuminating. The development of science and technology and the growth of man's power over nature would be brought into the center of the picture. Also the repercussions of these new forces in the various departments of life would be observed and studied—in family relations, in economy, in communication, in health control, in education, in recreation, in art, in religion, in government, and in morals, thought, and philosophy. The account might well culminate in a consideration of the passing of *laissez-faire,* the reunion of economics and politics, the rise of social planning, and the movement toward world integration and organization.

In the fifth place, the social sciences should be required to describe the conflicts and contradictions so numerous in contemporary society—prosperity and depression, poverty and riches, privation and extravagance, starvation in the midst of plenty, organized destruction of wealth, preventable illness and unemployed physicians, great inventions converted into instruments for the debasement of culture, scientists engaged in the discovery of "secrets," costly art museums in ugly and congested cities, an avowed democracy ruled by a plutocracy, corruption of government by respectable business men, the widespread subordination of human to property rights, the Church of the carpenter of Nazareth accepting gratuities from entrenched wealth, whole nations rushing to war in the name of peace, the general subordination of the ends to the means of life, and the many other conflicts and contradictions listed in the present volume. The younger generation is entitled to an honest and unprejudiced account of these strange phenomena.

In the sixth place, the social sciences should provide youth with the materials for a critical appraisal of present-day life in terms of the democratic ideal. To transmit this ideal to school children, without at the same time providing the opportunity for applying it rigorously to the criticism of existing institutional arrangements and practices, would be the height of intellectual dishonesty. Yet this is precisely what has been done in the past. As a consequence, when boys and girls, after leaving school or before, learn how the world is actually run, they tend to rate their teachers as either knaves or fools. If the school is to function at all in the betterment of the social order, it must expose pitilessly and clearly the shortcomings in contemporary society. It should never convey the impression that the democratic ideal has been fulfilled in the United States. To do so would be to draw a heavy veil over the eyes of youth.

In the seventh place, the social sciences should be required to introduce the coming generation to all the more pertinent proposals, programs, and philosophies that have been called forth by the needs of the age and that show any signs of strength. Among these should be included such social theories as capitalism, syndicalism, anarchism, socialism, guild socialism, distributism, communism, and fascism. Also wherever any of these theories are being given trial in the world today, opportunity for the careful study and fair appraisal of the results should be systematically provided. No idea should be kept from the minds of youth on the grounds that it is dangerous. Each proposal, however, should be critically examined in the light of American history and the ideal of democracy. Not to permit this free flow of thought will be far more inimical in the long run to the best interests of society than any undesirable consequences that might arise from allowing young persons to become acquainted with a new idea in the classroom and under the tuition of a competent scholar. The present situation demands informed intelligence of the very highest order distributed widely throughout the population. The days of complacency with respect to inherited institutions and conceptions are over. If the people of the United States cannot think their way through the great difficulties that lie ahead, then must they be prepared for the twilight and then the night of democracy.

Questions regarding ways of organizing and methods of presenting the materials of instruction in the social sciences are essentially far less important than questions of content. Regardless of form the fundamental ideas embodied in any program will be grasped by the better minds of the coming generation and thus be incorporated sooner or later into the main body of social thought. And the great need in American society today is for a radical increase in the breadth and the depth of the ideas in general circulation. The first task therefore is to advance the quality of the content of social science teaching in the public schools. If only books dealing competently and thoughtfully with the social situation in its historical and world setting could be made widely accessible to the more able members of the younger generation, the gain in raising the intellectual level of the population would be infinitely superior to that derived from the mere refinement of method, however thoroughly done. It is sheer folly to assume that the world will be much improved by doing mediocre or irrelevant things excellently.

The organization of the content to be taught, however, is a matter that cannot be ignored. If instruction is to proceed, there must be some organization; and there are doubtless better patterns to follow. That any effective plan for the presentation of materials must take into account the experience, the powers, the interests of the learner is entirely obvious. A more fruitful guiding principle, however, may be found in the process whereby the child grows to maturity in social understanding and competence. Beginning with the cradle he gradually pushes back the boundaries of his world along the two dimensions of space and time and in so doing widens his knowledge and deepens his powers of thought and action. Through manipulation, exploration, travel, reading, social intercourse, and converse with his peers and elders, he moves out from the immediate and the present into the ever-widening realm of geography and history.

Social science instruction in the schools should build upon, facilitate, and direct this process. It should take the child in the first year of the elementary school and lead him systematically and steadily out of family, neighborhood, and community into the state, the nation and the world, always following naturally those lines of trade and communication which bind the near to the remote and create a general condition of interdependence. In similar fashion, pursuing the genetic method, it would move from the present into the past and back again and give understanding of customs, institutions, ideas, interests, and conflicts. Also as the child matures and advances in intellectual grasp, the emphasis would shift from the surface to the depths and from data to thought. The point merits great emphasis, moreover, that the isolation of the school should be reduced to the narrowest possible proportions and that "classroom instruction" should be closely bound into the life and labor and aspirations of society. Thus from the kindergarten through the secondary school and on into the college and university there would be one unbroken and integrated social science program which would carry a single process to ever wider and more intense expression. Permeating and vitalizing this program from bottom to top would be the great purpose of organizing the energies and resources of the nation in improving, enriching, and refining the common life of the people.

Such a conception of the task calls first of all for the preparation of an extensive body of printed materials to be used in the home, the school, and the library. Primary reference is made here, not to textbooks, necessary as they may be, but to a children's literature which will illuminate the modern world and express the spirit of the industrial age. Much of the children's literature bequeathed from the past, while worthy of preservation because of its artistic excellence, contributes nothing to social understanding. Also a considerable proportion of the reading matter employed in the lower grades to train children in the habits of literacy possesses neither literary merit nor useful content. The great need is for rich materials written with charm and simplicity and designed to give to children authentic information regarding the human past and the world of today—materials which tell in story form of the evolution of basic social institutions, the achievements of the race, the diversity of peoples and cultures, the rise of American civilization, and the manifold characteristics, tasks, problems and potentialities of industrial society. On such a foundation the more systematic study of the social sciences would be organized.

The Teacher. The present volume, as well as the other reports of the Commission, assumes from first to last that the public school may be expected to make a genuine and positive contribution to the solution of the numerous social problems confronting the American people. It assumes that education, as a function of organized society, can exercise some measure of social leadership, or at least that it can make somewhat easier the difficult road to the future. Whether or not this faith is well founded will depend in the last analysis on the teacher, and particularly on the social science teacher. If the person presiding over the classroom is meanly gifted, if he is inadequately or inappropriately prepared for his post, if he lacks a clear and sufficient conception of his responsibility, and if he is surrounded by unsuitable working conditions, there is no hope. Commissions may come and commissions may go; they may leave voluminous reports behind them; but if the teacher remains substantially unchanged, the schools will be as ineffective as before, even though numerous alterations of school procedures may be introduced. New testing devices, new methods of instruction, new courses of study, unless they impart new knowledge, power, and spirit to the teacher, are but the gyrations of a treadmill. Attention will therefore be directed to the crucial questions involved in the selection, training, and working conditions of teachers.

The question of the selection of teachers is fundamental. Yet it depends in no small measure on the conditions of work which society provides for those who are to have charge of its children. Consequently this question will be answered in part under the other headings. Something, however, may be said here. Unless young men and women of intelligence, spirit, capacity for leadership, and devotion to the popular welfare are drawn into the schools, very little can be expected of public education. Without these qualities teachers may indeed continue to be obedient to their superiors, meticulous with respect to small matters, mindful of the wishes of the most powerful and respectable forces in the community. They may even succeed in holding their jobs, unless a depression cuts severely into the social income. But as a profession they will not rise to the level of educational statesmanship; they will not influence the course of history, except perhaps to do what they can to equip children for a world that is gone and thus add to the difficulties of social adjustment. Leadership in society requires courage and competence.

If it may be assumed that gifted persons in reasonable numbers will be drawn to teaching, the next problem is that of training. Although in a technical sense teachers are far better prepared today than ever before, the ordinary training program is woefully inadequate to the task outlined above. To be sure, the country is well supplied with normal schools, teachers' colleges, departments of education, and universities. Yet nowhere, with very few exceptions, are the issues being squarely and fully met.

The major difficulty seems to lie in partial or erroneous conceptions of the nature of the educative process. In the special training schools the emphasis is too generally placed on the mastery of the methods and techniques of teaching and on what is called the science of education. The inevitable result of pursuing such a program of preparation is a narrowing of the intellectual interests of the student and an absorption in the mechanics rather than the substance of teaching. The concept of the science of education seems to rest on the assumption that an objective study of the processes of learning and of administering education will result in the discovery of certain laws of procedure that are largely independent of and superior to culture. If this assumption is sound, then a systematic study of American history, institutions, and ideals is quite unnecessary. The difficulty is that the essence of any actual educational program is intimately related to the evolution of a particular culture.

If one turns to the various special departments of the university for an enlightened form of teacher training, the situation is found to be equally unsatisfactory. If the teachers' college is lost in the science of education and the cult of pedagogics, the university department, whether it be language, science, or history, is lost quite as completely in its pursuit of highly specialized knowledge. The latter very commonly even prides itself on its devotion to a species of scholarship that has no interest in the practical affairs of men. Then when it accepts the responsibility of training teachers, it assumes that this peculiar academic mentality should be introduced into the secondary and even lower schools. So the prospective teacher is too often compelled to choose between two types of preparation, neither of which represents an adequate conception of the task of teaching. The one would equip him for action divorced from deep understanding; the other would prepare him for understanding matters that can have little or no relation to any desirable or probable form of action.

The need is for a new type of training institution—an institution which would embody the best features of the two types already described. A college for the preparation of teachers should first of all be a center of liberal learning—a center through which would run the main currents of modern thought. It should be a place for the study of American culture in its historic and world connections, but for a type of study that would not be purely academic in character. In the halls of any institution devoted to teacher training, the past and the future should meet; the most profound questions of national policy should be debated and understood. And this should be done, not as an intellectual exercise, but for the purpose of shaping educational programs. Out of such an institution should come persons genuinely qualified to provide American communities with a vigorous, enlightened, and public-spirited type of leadership, ready and competent to challenge the power of selfish interests and to champion the cause of the masses of the people. The attention devoted to purely technical preparation would assume extremely modest proportions. On public education, as on statescraft, the findings and thought of the social sciences should be brought to a focus.

If teachers were given this type of training, they would in all probability immediately demand proper conditions of work. The question, however, is of such importance that it should not be passed over altogether.

That teachers should have adequate compensation, reasonably secure tenure, and a high degree of freedom from annoyance at the hands of educational laymen is axiomatic. Moreover, being products of American institutions for the most part, their loyalty to the deeper ideals of the nation cannot be questioned. Since they are the servants of society as a whole, they may generally be expected to be at least as disinterested in the promotion of the common good as any other body of citizens. Without security and freedom professional competence is impossible. In order to get these conditions, teachers should organize and place their case forcefully, intelligently, and persuasively before the public. Because of the peculiar difficulties of their subject matter, provided of course they attempt the kind of program outlined in this volume, the teachers of social science are under special obligation to make this appeal effective.

Of equal importance is the matter of administrative organization. Under the influence of the mechanistic and atomistic psychology which swept through education during the past generation, a theory of school administration took root that might well prove disastrous to the public schools. According to this theory, it is the duty of the teacher to take orders from the head of the department, of the head of the department to take orders from the principal, and so on from level to level of the supervisory hierarchy. As a result, in many school systems teaching has become largely a matter of following instructions received from some official not immediately responsible for the work with children. The tendency was no doubt accelerated by the ideal of efficiency derived from big business and by the spread of the so-called objective tests. A school system thus took on the aspect of a vast and intricate mechanism designed to pass on to the younger generation certain reading habits, number combinations, and facts about geography, history, and civics. Needless to say, this entire procedure represents a travesty on education, primarily because it tends to destroy the personality and initiative of the teacher. The first object of any policy of school administration should be the growth of the teacher in courage, power, and refinement. Under such a policy, if it should become widespread in the nation, able young men and women would be attracted to the profession in ever-increasing numbers. Education then might grapple with the most profound problems of national policy.

SCHOOL AND SOCIETY

This consideration of the responsibilities and opportunities of the school under the conditions of industrial civilization may well be concluded with a reference to the relation of school and society. Here a word of caution will be uttered regarding the powers of organized education.

Although the school is the focal point of the educative process and the only form of education under the conscious and reasoned direction of society, its power for influencing social change is strictly limited. Various studies undertaken by the Commission, as well as others, make this fact altogether clear. Industrial society is marked by various powerful and competing groups and interests, each of which seeks to impose its will upon the school. The task of steering the course of public education among these conflicting forces requires the highest qualities of leadership.

The primary aim here, however, is to direct attention, not to the play of social forces upon the school, but rather to the number and strength of the non-scholastic educational agencies. Thus, the family, in spite of its loss of functions during the past century, remains by far the mightiest single formative influence in the life of the individual. There are also the time-honored agencies of church and community association which, though weakened, continue to mold the minds of the young. Then there are those relatively new instrumentalities that have either appeared or waxed powerful since the rise of industrial civilization—the press, the library, the cinema, the radio, and various other forms of communication. While the school has grown with great rapidity during the past two generations and may now be regarded as a major social institution, it is clearly but one among many educational agencies. Consequently, if it is to become a positive factor of any great strength in American society, its programs and policies will have to be intelligently conceived and efficiently executed. Teachers in particular are inclined to exaggerate its influence, partly because of the widespread tendency in America to identify education with the work of the school. It is well therefore that they be asked from time to time to view this institution in proper perspective.

Moreover, as organized and administered in American society, the school is greatly weakened by the artificiality of its activities. In a word, the school tends to be definitely separated from life. For generations educators have lamented this fact and have argued most cogently for a more intimate relationship between organized education and the community. But their laments and arguments have seemingly fallen on deaf ears. The school continues in its tradition of isolation; and teachers as a rule have relatively little contact with the real world. Francis W. Parker once said that "the best-taught school in a densely populated city can never equal in educative value the life upon a good farm, intelligently managed." Although he was perhaps speaking under the romantic spell of the farming tradition in America, his statement contains a large element of truth.

The fault, however, would seem not to rest primarily with the schools or the teachers. The fact cannot be stressed too strongly that in capitalistic society, where large areas of life are reserved to the operation of business enterprise, a sharp line divides public from private interest. It is this line that educators have been unable to pass. As a consequence, the school is forced into an artificial world and organized education is pushed out upon the periphery of existence. In order to meet this situation, which is a product of very recent development, educational philosophers have evolved the doctrine that children have interests quite unlike those of adults and should therefore organize a society of their own. According to this doctrine, the school should become a second society in which boys and girls would be permitted to live a full and rich life. The idea has had many and able advocates. Yet it would seem to be a totally inadequate conception. A genuine society is composed of neither children nor adults, but of persons of all ages living together in close interdependence. It is in such a setting that life goes on. And until such a setting is provided for the school, organized education will be lacking in genuineness.

Any completely satisfactory solution of the problem of education therefore would seem to involve fairly radical social reconstruction. The fact is that for the most part contemporary society is not organized primarily for the education of its children or for the achievement of any other humane purpose. Such matters are largely subordinated to the processes of wealth production and accumulation. Even the recreational, cultural and æsthetic interests of the population are exploited for material gain. Nothing is permitted to "injure business." This is axiomatic in the inherited social order. Yet it clearly means an unnatural and irrational transposition of values.

This condition can be corrected, as the argument of the entire volume proves, only by the clear and frank recognition of the collectivist character of industrial economy. The productive energies of the country will then be directed squarely toward the laying of the material foundations of a great civilization and society will be organized to foster the cultural and spiritual development of the masses of the people. In the achievement of the second purpose all the educational resources of the community will be co-ordinated and utilized to the fullest. The press, the cinema, and the radio will no longer be devoted to profit-making. Travel will doubtless take the place of textbooks in many instances. Even industry will again become an educational enterprise. It may also be discovered that many of the burdens placed upon the school during the past century can best be borne by other agencies. The scope of operations of the school may consequently be greatly reduced and children may again be inducted into the life of the group through actual participation in the activities of society. But in the meantime the school, whatever its strength or weakness, is under obligation to devote its energies to the task of bringing such a society into being.

INDEX

Abbott, Grace, on women's mental equality with men, 115

Abrams, Jacob (The Abrams case), 415–417

Adamic, Louis, on labor leader turned racketeer, 171–172

Adams, Henry, on rise of industrialism, 361

Adams, James Truslow, on colonial life at close of 17th century, 80

Adams, John, excerpt from a letter to his wife, 349

Adams, John Quincy, on rapacity of early settlers, 495

Adler, Herman C., on race prejudice in courts, 411

Agricultural Marketing Act, 434

Agricultural Relief Act, 452

Agriculture, the sorry plight of, 152–153; co-operation in, 179–182

Ahern, George P., on forest despoliation, 161–162

America, lure of, to immigrants, 10

American Federation of Labor, 184

American frontier, levelling tendency of, 13; influence of economics of, on politics, 14–16

American Medical Association, 248

American people, devotion to democracy by, 9–10

Anderson, William, his summary of the charter granted to Albany in 1686, 488–489

Andrews, Israel D., on high cost of early transportation, 129

Annalist, on index of business, 149

Aristotle, on the human worth, 11; anticipated technology, 68

Art, concern of ordinary men and women, 347–348; America long considered hostile to, 348–349; influence of the frontier on, 349–350; gradual attainment of maturity in, 350–351; effect of settlers on, 451–453; spread of democracy and its influence on, 353–354; interruption in the evolution of institutions disastrous to, 355–356; growth of an artistic tradition, 356–361; scarcity of skilled artisans, 357; artistic development of dwellings and objects of ordinary life, 359–360; colonial art also served community, 359, 360–361; machine forcing out the craftsman, 361; the Homestead Act, 362; its effect on arts, 362; the appearance of "hardheaded" and "hard-hearted" breed of men, 362–363; sacrifice of the æsthetic for "business," 364 ff.; monstrosities in art as result of time-saving devices, 366–367; attempts to revive the handicrafts, 366–367; shifting environment unfavorable to the flourishing of, 367; importing art from Europe, 367–368; first attempts at art in keeping with modern life, 368; reaction to blighting effects of industrialism on, 369–370; architecture, the coming of age of, 370–374; painting, 369; trend toward its alliance with architecture, 374–375; sculpture allied with architecture, 375; music, 369; improving taste in, 376; æsthetic enhancement of life through planning, 376–378; new forces released by industrial civilization, 378; automobile as a work of art, 378–380; its influence on beautifying scenery, 380; also places natural beauties at service of population, 380; the æsthetic evolution of the airplane, 379; cinema, originally conceived as a business enterprise, 380–381; see Cinema; reasons for its low cultural level, 382–383; influence of radio on æsthetic life of nation, 383–384; see Radio; sport, æsthetic element in, 384–385; division of fine and practical arts, 385–387; the closing of gap between Beauty and Use, 387; contradiction of American life in art, 523

Dongan, Governor, his charter of 1686, 488

Douglas, William O., and Clark, Chas. E., on increase of litigations, 393

Eastman Kodak Company, research laboratories of, 327–328

Eberlein, Harold D., on quality of early architecture, 359

Eberlein, Harold D., and McClure, Abbot, on work of the settlers, 358; on early crafts, 360

Economy, union of agriculture and manufacture in pre-industrial, 121–124; absence of market in, 124–125; human labor, main source of power in, 125; relative security in, 125–126; separation of manufacture from agriculture, 126–127; specialization of labor and market, 126–135; new traits of character, a product of change in, 133; advance in productive power and efficiency as result of specialization, 134; producing for *sale* rather than for *use*, 134–135; *laissez-faire* theory, 135–140; *see* Government; results of *laissez-faire*, 140 ff.; national wealth and income, 140–146; unequal distribution of wealth, 141–142, 150–151, 157; of income, 142–143, 150–151; depression, unequal burden of, 144–146; six forms of inefficiency, 146; interruption of production, 146–149; inco-ordination of production and consumption, 149–155; depressions, 150–151; chronic condition of, under-consumption, 154; forcing goods on consumer, 149, 150, 156; irrational use of energy and materials, 155–157; disregard of long-run interests of society, 157, 165; *see* Natural resources; waste of, 157–167; disregard of moral and æsthetic interests in, 167–172; failure to utilize science and technology, 172–177; *see* Science; consolidation of enterprise, 175; co-operation in agriculture, 179–182; organization of labor, 182–185; government intervention in business, 185–187; uncertainties in, 188; transition from individu-

alistic to collective economy, 486–487; individualistic tradition not old, 487–489; two factors responsible for overthrow of collective tradition, 489–493; westward movement, individual enterprise, 489–491; rise of middle class, 491–492; difference between early and predatory business individualism, 492–493; power of individualistic tradition over American people, 493–498; in economic theory, 494; in conquest of continent, 494–495; harsher features in this struggle, 495–497; doctrine of individualism written in fundamental law, 497; influence of, on American school, 397–398; *see* Education, also Public School; breakdown of individualism in, 498–501; collectivist trend in American economy, 501–506; rôle of technology in this trend, 501–502; modern corporation a collective enterprise, 502–503; government's interest in, 503–505; *see* Government; social planning, 505; collectivism of disaster, 506; conflicts in economy, 513–516; union of democracy and collectivism in, 530–531

Education, as statesmanship, 1–6; as expression of society, 1–2; contribution of social sciences to, 2–6; as a form of social action, 2; equal opportunities of, 27–28; in earlier times, 252–253; in pre-industrial society, 254–256; four major changes of, 256; weakening of old agencies of, 256–258; increased magnitude of, 258–259; new agencies of, 259; growth of school, 259 ff.; popular faith in, 260–261; *see* Public School; school plant, 261–264; educational opportunity, 262–267; number of students in all schools in 1930, 262–263; class discrimination, 263; poverty, a factor of elimination, 264; racial discrimination, 264–265; inequality of opportunity, 265–266, 268; curtailing opportunities of poor during depression, 266–267; administration of, 267–270; tradition of local

Parker, Francis W., on value of farm life as educative agency, 561

Parry, Edward A., on partiality in administering justice, 397–398

Pasteur, Louis, 238

Pastoral Letter of General Ass'n of Massachusetts, extracts from, on attitude of orthodox clergy on woman's rights movement, 108–109

Peek, George N., hailed destruction of cotton crop, 155, 182

Permanent Court of Arbitration, 478

Permanent Court of International Justice, 479

Petroleum, reserves of in U. S., 46

Phipps Institute for Tuberculosis, 218

Phipps Psychiatric Clinic, 218

Pikagon, a converted Pottawattamie chieftain, on destruction of pigeons, 160

Planning, elements of in pre-industrial family, 83; cost of city, 170; in industry, 186, 448; on a world-wide scale, 481–482

Plato, on teacher as ruler, 169, 505

Polakov, Walter, on perspectives to mankind through technology, 68

Population, distribution of in America in 1790, 127

Pound, Dean Roscoe, on trials as amusements in rural America, 390; on legal institutions, 390–391; on provincialism in law, 394–395; on issues involved in denial of justice to the poor, 399; on activities of U. S. Department of Justice, 419–420

Preemption Act of 1841, 490

President's Research Committee on Social Trends, on changing American society, 2; on social planning, 186–187; on growth of government functions, 425

Press, growth of, 196, 198; commercial motive in, 200–203; propaganda in, 206–210, 211; see Communication

Pruette, Lorine, on women, 118

Public opinion, molding of, 206–209; see Communication

Public School, 532–563; see Education; rôle of, in resolution of Fundamental conflicts in American Society, 526; relation of, to social situation, 532–533; America's faith in, 533–534; in earlier generation, 533; new forms of faith in recent times, 533–534; new forms also unfounded, 534; needs adequate social philosophy, 534–535; cannot remain neutral, 535; involves action, 535–537; must make choice with respect to physical surrounding, 535–536; with respect to motives, 536; major object of, 536; rôle of critical intelligence in, 537–538; responsibilities and opportunities of in industrial civilization, 538–560; transition to collectivist economy, its bearing on purpose of 538–544; might be managed in interests of ruling caste, 540; or in interests of great masses, 540–541; purpose of in present epoch, 541; must abandon ideal of personal advancement as purpose of, 541–542; instead advancement of general welfare, 542; holds no great ideal, 542–544; curriculum, reorganization of demanded by new economy, 544–547; no new subjects, but emphasis on social and co-operative and creative impulses, 544–545; personal talents not overlooked, 545; emphasis on social utility no narrow practical education, 545–546; social meaning given to subject matter, 546; specialized training, planning of, 546–547; social-sciences curriculum, 547–549; 7 points of emphasis in, 549; social sciences should relate lives and fortunes of ordinary men and women, 549; should relate evolution of peaceful arts and culture, 549–550; should trace ideal of democracy, 550–551; should recount industrial civilization, 551; should describe conflicts and contradictions in contemporary society, 551–552; should provide critical appraisal of present-day life, 552; should introduce the coming generation to all proposals, programs, and philosophies, 552–553; emphasis on quality of content of, 553; need for integrated social-science program, 553–554;